Making Mexican Chicago

HISTORICAL STUDIES OF URBAN AMERICA

Edited by Lilia Fernández, Timothy J. Gilfoyle, and Amanda I. Seligman
James R. Grossman, Editor Emeritus

Recent titles in the series

MAKING MEXICAN CHICAGO

From Postwar Settlement
to the Age of Gentrification

MIKE AMEZCUA

The University of Chicago Press
Chicago and London

The University of Chicago Press, Chicago 60637
The University of Chicago Press, Ltd., London
© 2022 by The University of Chicago
All rights reserved. No part of this book may be used or reproduced in any manner
whatsoever without written permission, except in the case of brief quotations in critical
articles and reviews. For more information, contact the University of Chicago Press,
1427 E. 60th St., Chicago, IL 60637.
Published 2022
Paperback edition 2023
Printed in the United States of America

32 31 30 29 28 27 26 25 24 23   1 2 3 4 5

ISBN-13: 978-0-226-81582-4 (cloth)
ISBN-13: 978-0-226-82640-0 (paper)
ISBN-13: 978-0-226-81583-1 (e-book)
DOI: https://doi.org/10.7208/chicago/9780226815831.001.0001

Library of Congress Cataloging-in-Publication Data

Names: Amezcua, Mike, author.
Title: Making Mexican Chicago : from postwar settlement to the age of gentrification /
    Mike Amezcua.
Other titles: Historical studies of urban America.
Description: Chicago : The University of Chicago Press, 2022. | Series: Historical studies
    of urban America | Includes bibliographical references and index.
Identifiers: LCCN 2021050846 | ISBN 9780226815824 (cloth) | ISBN 9780226815831
    (ebook)
Subjects: LCSH: Mexicans—Illinois—Chicago—History—20th century. | Mexican
    Americans—Illinois—Chicago—History—20th century. | Mexican American
    neighborhoods—Illinois—Chicago—History—20th century. | Mexican Americans—
    Housing—Illinois—Chicago. | Urban renewal—Illinois—Chicago—History—20th
    century. | Segregation—Illinois—Chicago—History—20th century.
Classification: LCC F548.9.M5 A64 2022 | DDC 977.3/110046872—dc23/eng/20211025
LC record available at https://lccn.loc.gov/2021050846

♾ This paper meets the requirements of ANSI/NISO Z39.48-1992
(Permanence of Paper).

To the memory of my parents,
Lourdes y Manuel,
for their hustle and struggles in the city

CONTENTS

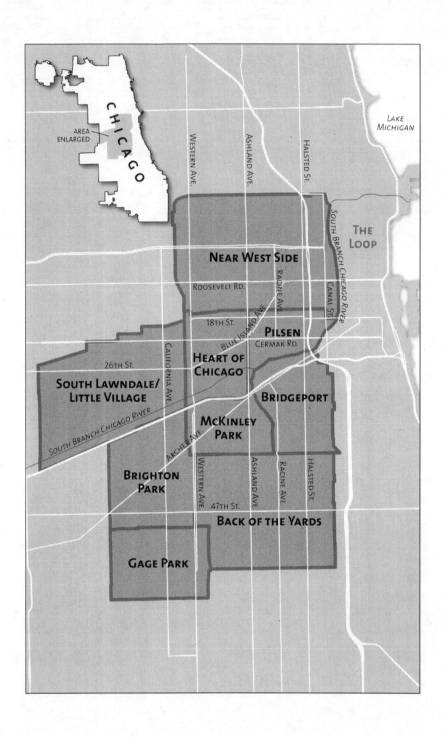

1 :: Crafting Capital

In 1957, Anita Villarreal was arrested by federal agents and charged with conspiracy to violate US immigration law.[1] A midwestern Mexicana, born in Kansas and reared in Chicago, Villarreal opened her first real estate office in the city in 1946.[2] By the time of her arrest a decade later, she had helped secure housing for thousands of Mexican migrants—part of an estimated seventy-five thousand Mexican immigrants and Mexican Americans who, by the late 1950s, called Chicago home.[3] Fearing that many of these immigrants would become public charges, federal investigators interrogated Villarreal on how and where these "outsiders" had found shelter and sanctuary in the city. Claiming that she had helped immigrants secure fraudulent visas, the court found Villarreal guilty (though the judge suspended her sentence and gave her five years' probation).[4] The case was a flashpoint in the Cold War era's criminalization of undocumented migrants and those who aided them.

By renting and selling homes to these newcomers, Villarreal was doing more than building her own upstart real estate business. She was also participating in one of the largest recruitment drives of Mexican immigration to an American city in the twentieth century, a drive that linked hope from the South to the promise of economic opportunity in the North. All too often that promise was thwarted by exclusion. Every time Villarreal secured housing for a Mexican or Mexican American in Chicago, she was pushing back against a relentless and punishing immigration-control apparatus—a racialized system that consigned Mexicans, US and non-US citizens alike, to a perpetual state of alienage. Villarreal was not alone. After World War II, a loose network of intermediaries and stakeholders participated in a clandestine enterprise that shuffled tens of thousands of undocumented (and illicitly documented) immigrants to Chicago's factories, railyards, packing-houses, and fields to fuel the engines of US capitalism. While postwar Chicago was built on this labor, Mexican settlement was unwanted, undesirable, and contentious in the eyes of the city's white majority. Nonetheless, by the end of the twentieth century, this wave of immigration and settlement would transform Chicago into the third-largest Mexican metropolis in the United States, with profound implications for the city's survival and renaissance.[5]

Making Mexican Chicago explores how the Windy City became a Mexican metropolis in the second half of the twentieth century. In the decades after World War II, Chicago's working-class neighborhoods became sites of struggle as Mexican immigrants and Mexican Americans attempted to build new communities in the face of white resistance and exclusionary regimes of citizenship that cast them as perpetual aliens. The book charts the diverse strategies that Brown Chicagoans devised as they fought back against the forces of residential segregation, economic predation, and gentrification. In the process, *Making Mexican Chicago* offers a powerful multi-racial history of the city, shedding new light on the origins and endurance of urban inequality. It recounts not only the stories of Mexican and Mexican American Chicagoans but also those of the varied and diverse brokers who facilitated the transformation. For her part, Anita Villarreal belonged to the class of real estate merchants with immigration expertise who functioned as stewards of the city's Mexicanization. These stewards found shelter and sanctuary for Mexican immigrants and Mexican Americans in white ethnic working-class neighborhoods that were racially exclusive and often hostile. They persistently championed Mexicans as reliable renters and homebuyers, hoping to convince anxious propertied whites to suspend their biases against Mexicans (and Latinos, more generally) and to convince them that renting or selling their homes to them was a sound investment.

One building at a time, Villarreal pushed the residential boundaries of Mexican settlement into all-white neighborhoods. Her motives were complex and even contradictory. On the one hand, when she encouraged Mexican Americans or Mexican immigrants to buy a home, she was demanding their inclusion in the postwar American dream of homeownership. At the same time, Villarreal coveted the properties of whites because these properties maintained their value in volatile, racially restrictive markets. She sought to provide migrants with a sense of belonging while simultaneously facilitating their conscription into the profoundly exploitative, racial capitalist labor regime that fueled Chicago's postwar growth.

Figure 1.1. Anita Villarreal, real estate broker and property manager, finds shelter for recently arrived Mexican immigrant workers in her apartment building, 1949. (Image courtesy of the Villarreal Family.)

Chicago has always been a city of insiders and outsiders, inclusion and exclusion. Its founding as a settler-colonial trading post had been built on the violent removal and extermination of Native Americans. In the early 1800s, Chicago's white settlers initiated a project of proprietary belonging and protective localism at the gates of US western expansion. Over the nineteenth century, successive groups were cast as outsiders who ostensibly threatened the local power structure: indigenous tribes who were displaced in the 1830s and 1840s, African Americans from the South who came to Chicago after the Civil War, and the Southern and Eastern European immigrants who arrived between 1880 and 1920. By the 1920s, anxieties among locals instigated a backlash in the form of restrictive immigration quotas designed to slow the influx of Europe's "undesirables." At the same time,

Chicago was emerging as a crucial epicenter of progressive reform efforts to assimilate European immigrants into American whiteness.[6]

Over time, these new European immigrants established a political machine that reinvigorated a defensive neighborhood localism that appealed to established European ethnics by constructing Chicago as "a white man's town." African Americans making their way to the Windy City during the Great Migration on the promise of freedom from Jim Crow encountered a deeply entrenched localism and a white populace ready to preserve a hierarchical racial order. Whites and their locally rooted identities were perched on top of a segregated Black metropolis. Historians of Chicago have tended to focus on this confrontation between Black and white communities, and with good reason: the city was the site of extraordinary structural and interpersonal violence against African Americans. But this book places Mexican immigrants at the center of the city's modern history. Between the First and Second World Wars, the city's steel, meatpacking, and manufacturing companies recruited workers from across the US South and the Americas. Untethered by quota laws, Mexican immigrants became the ideal expendable labor force. They were presumed to be docile, transient, perpetually deportable, and permanently controllable. Imperialist and colonialist hegemony over the Americas, along with US capitalism's thirst for unregulated labor, impelled state bureaucrats and influential lobbyists to turn Mexico and Puerto Rico into distribution centers for migratory labor. This created diasporic nodes of workers in Chicago and the greater Midwest. By the 1940s and 1950s, the presence of Latinos in the Windy City unsettled the city's racial order, provoking locals to redraw boundaries yet again.[7]

Of course, Chicago was not the only place where the flow of Mexican immigration alarmed locals who feared that the borders around their neighborhoods were dissolving. Mexican enclaves, *colonias* (colonies) or "little Mexicos," proliferated across the midwestern industrial landscape in the 1910s and 1920s.[8] These communities were created independent of the US Southwest's legacy of conquest that had supplied Anglo settlers with a socio-racial lexicon in which to locate Mexicans. In the urban North, making sense of Mexicans, their place, and their race had to be invented in the twentieth century.[9] This project of "making sense" of these newcomers was spearheaded not only by the city's influential elite and policymakers but also by Chicago's white ethnic residents. In particular, Irish, Polish, Italian, Slavic, Czech, and Lithuanian residents were, over time, assimilated into whiteness via their European heritage, an emergent mass culture, and industrial unionism.[10] While these various ethnic groups became "white," people of Mexican descent and/or nationality were reconstituted as "Mexicans," a nonwhite, ethno-racial category that proved remarkably effective as a tool of exclusion precisely because it was so broad. The term made little distinction over immigrant status, naturalization, American birthright citizenship, or government categorization. By eliding such distinctions, "Mexican" became a marker for nationality, ethnicity, and race all at once.[11] The vagueness of the term allowed white locals to weaponize it by portraying all Mexicans as racially inferior and unassimilable outsiders, unfit for the benefits of modern urbanity. As the twentieth century unfolded, Mexicans were cast in a perpetual alienage that followed them into the neighborhoods where they tried to create new homes and start new lives.

Making Mexican Chicago places the Mexican experience at the center of the modern history of the central city and its everyday contests over neighborhoods, segregation, and the white defense of property rights. The successive waves of Mexican immigration to Chicago from the 1940s to the 2000s make clear that those contests can only be understood in a multiracial context. White ethnics in Chicago not only mobilized against Black settlement, they also vigorously defended their communities against Latino settlement. White propertied mobilizations against Black Americans have received considerable attention in chronicles of the postwar urban crisis, and rightfully so, as they helped to shape Black apartheid and suburban entitlements.[12] But the city's Latinos were also segregated, disenfranchised, under-resourced, and scapegoated. Simultaneously, like their African American counterparts, they helped turn the central city into a staging ground for equity-seeking, opportunity, resistance, and rebellion.[13]

Yet the Mexican story diverges from the African American story in that it has centered so heavily on immigration status. The white ethnic mobilization against the Mexican "threat" in places like Chicago can only be understood in light of the covert dimensions of living and being Mexican in the United States. People who have been cast in varying states of alienage have, by design, tried to evade documentation, have been severely under-documented, or more strikingly, fraudulently documented. For this reason, patterns of migration and settlement defy the kinds of data urban historians hold indispensable: property deeds, maps, demographic reports, zoning and municipal codes, fair-housing laws, and community-organization records. In fact, the act of migrating, securing shelter, and simply *being* in the United States while Mexican have often constituted, through structures of immigration control and enforcement, acts of crime or conspiracy. Therefore, the history of Mexican settlement in US metropolitan areas is also a history of fraudulence and concealment, involving clandestine networks of recruitment, smuggling, illegal border crossing, blockbusting, tenement busting, fake documentation, and the obscuring and hiding of these acts. For instance, Latino building managers who operated white-owned apartments in transitioning Chicago neighborhoods were often incentivized to conceal both the number of renters and their ethnicities in order to hide an overcrowded tenement of Spanish-speaking migrants from would-be "adversaries" like building inspectors, tax collectors, insurance appraisers, immigration agents, and anxious neighbors worried about their property value. These stories require interrogating the noninstitutionalized archive as much as any other.

If these stories shed new light on modern urban history, they also help to explain the realignment of US politics in the late twentieth century as New Deal liberalism was displaced by conservative hegemony. The constitutive role of racial antagonism in the urban North in that realignment is well known: urban whites in places like Chicago sold their properties, gave up their parishes, and headed to the suburbs, where many abandoned their longstanding commitment to the Democratic Party, which they had come to associate with redistributive policies that favored minorities at the expense of the white working class. But this book argues that the transformation was not driven solely by a strict backlash against the Black civil rights movement or Great Society redistributive programs.[14] The transformation also played out in Chicago neighborhoods, where white residents attempted to exclude Mexican settlement and where Mexican immigrants and Mexican Americans sometimes competed and sometimes collaborated with various stakeholders over access to neighborhoods, property ownership, commercial opportunities, and political power. The conservative revolution was felt and experienced at a micro level in neighborhoods where white city dwellers watched from their windowsills and front stoops as an emergent Mexican immigrant-built environment took shape.

This book thus poses the question: What does the rise of modern conservatism look like when Mexicans and Mexican Americans are placed at the center of the story?[15] Despite the city's longstanding reputation as a Democratic stronghold, in the 1950s and 1960s Chicago's blue-collar neighborhoods became seedbeds of white backlash rooted in antigovernment, antidiversity, and white-entitlement politics.[16] From their windows, those in the Southwest Side of the city seethed as their neighborhoods changed from white to Mexican, block by block. Decades before the call for Mexican immigration restrictions became a pillar of contemporary nativist conservatism, white-rights proponents innovated micro-policies in their own neighborhoods and local communities that generated Mexican spatial segregation, containment, and market exclusions.[17] By inventing anti-Mexican exclusions in housing and business, propertied whites scripted segregation when the law was not enough. This book explores the spatial and racial politics that emerged from white-fight/white-flight mobilizations as European American ethnics considered whether to leave the central city or stay and protect their neighborhoods from the mass arrival of migrants from the Global South.[18] While these white ethnics thought a lot about African Americans—and historians have examined the various manifestations of that thinking—they also thought a lot about Mexicans and Brown people as they confronted them in apartment halls, on doorsteps, and on city streets.

This book also explores the complex structures of feeling for all stakeholders as Mexicans and Mexican Americans gradually transformed the cityscape.[19] For would-be immigrants and the Mexican diaspora in Chicago, this structure encompassed individual and collective ambition, equity seeking, and dreams of opportunity, however circumscribed by the exigencies and exploitation embedded within US capitalism. For white ethnics, the feelings were often those of loss and a sense of being under siege from hostile external sources. Mexican settlement engendered white resentment over the scarcity of resources, the perceived unassimilability of outsiders, and the fear that neighborhoods would degrade and property values would decline. These fears and resentments were exacerbated by housing policies and speculative markets directly tied to race. Propertied whites came to understand that statist penalties could be levied against them if their neighborhoods became ethnically and racially heterogeneous. That logic was articulated as early as 1933, when a University of Chicago–trained economist and former real estate agent, Homer Hoyt, published his influential study *One Hundred Years of Land Values in Chicago*. Hoyt ranked ethnic and racial groups according to their detrimental impact on property and land values. On a scale of one to ten (with ten being the worst), Hoyt ranked African Americans ninth and Mexicans tenth. These two groups were at the bottom of the scale not only for their negative correlation to property value but also because that correlation was supposedly immutable. Improving these groups' economic situation, Hoyt predicted, would *not* improve their negative impact on land and property. Hoyt qualified his scale as being "scientifically wrong from the standpoint of inherent racial characteristics" and presented it as a reflection of the undeniable realities of the marketplace.

For his data, he surveyed contemporary real estate agents who relied on this scale in their own daily operations in the 1930s.[20]

Hoyt's studies powerfully shaped New Deal–era federal housing policies and mortgage-lending programs. Through the government-sponsored Home Owners' Loan Corporation (HOLC) and the Federal Housing Administration (FHA), federal bureaucrats and insurers created what they called "security maps" for most of the nation between 1935 and 1940. These maps drew from Hoyt's work and assigned grades to help the government analyze where to grant (or deny) mortgage financing and homeownership. On an A–D grade scale, racial and ethnic diversity would usually guarantee a neighborhood a D—colored red on the map and thus referred to as *redlined*. Mexicans in Chicago were rarely named in the security map descriptions, but they were always accounted for. Their presence in any neighborhood almost certainly guaranteed a shading of red. Homer Hoyt's study filtered down to New Deal mortgage appraisers and eventually to Chicago's white blue-collar homeowners. Along the way, they collectively constructed a racial identity for Mexicans that deeply embedded them in degraded land and property.[21]

Propertied whites in Chicago may not have known about Hoyt's scale, but the racialized logic embedded within that scale compelled them to seriously consider the stakes of Mexican settlement at their doorsteps. Feeling subjected to property devaluation and unwanted diversity, white ethnics marshaled local community networks to prevent the Mexicanization of their neighborhoods. As they did so, they often clashed with the capitalist and liberal imperatives of the city's power brokers and corporate bosses who recruited Mexican workers as providers of cheap labor but who left it up to others to decide where these workers ought to live. Again, the contrast with the African American story is illuminating. As real estate speculators and statist instruments propped up Northern Jim Crow through various designs of containment of Black people, holding the line against Latinos required a more ad hoc approach.[22] Through nonstatist policies and practices, white ethnic blue-collar homeowners innovated their own homegrown *restrictionist populism* to fortify themselves against the twinned perils of property devaluation and unwanted diversity. It was *restrictionist* in that it aimed to restrict outsiders from buying and renting in specific areas and to police any potential violation of that restriction. It was *populist* in that it aimed to put the reins of control in the hands of ordinary white ethnic residents and community groups. In Chicago, this restrictionist populism was expressed through neighborhood-improvement associations, political clubs, church-property alliance groups, insurance appraisers, real estate agents, propertied whites, and landlords. Restrictionist populism was fueled by two entwined threats: Mexican immigration and Mexican residential settlement. After 1950, restrictionist populism prevented, slowed, or contained Mexicanization across various Southwest Side neighborhoods from Pilsen to South Lawndale to Back of the Yards to Gage Park and beyond.

Although restrictionist populism played out at the neighborhood level, it sometimes snowballed into larger demands for municipal and federal restrictions. One of the most successful mobilizations of white paranoia aimed at Mexicans (documented and undocumented immigrants and Mexican American US citizens) came in 1954 when immigration authorities sought more control over the presence of unauthorized migrants. At this time, when the Immigration and Naturalization Service (INS) shifted the focus of Operation Wetback, a domestic military campaign to deport over one million Mexicans, from the US Southwest to Chicago, many white blue-collar Chicagoans who felt their ethnic enclaves had been invaded by Spanish-speaking foreigners expressed glee. INS Commissioner Joseph M. Swing promised to comb through the city's Little Italy to purge it of its Mexicans no matter the cost.[23] In the ensuing decades, immigration agents grabbed Brown people off the street and broke down tenement doors to purge and banish Mexican residents through detention and deportation, thereby creating an air of ongoing hypersurveillance in Latino communities.[24] This local violence was key to the postwar construct of the "illegal alien" and its frequent conflation with the category of the "Mexican."[25] By casting the city's Mexican population as eternal foreigners, protective neighborhood groups delegitimized their claims to good housing, property and business ownership, and other commercial aspects of urban life. This ideology contrasted sharply with an earlier vision of Chicago as an urban sanctuary that afforded relief to vulnerable European immigrants. Chicago's restrictive populism was an amalgam of several features: central city blue-collar discontent and frustration, the national imperatives of immigration control, and a nascent law-and-order politics that criminalized the figure of the illegal alien. As the northern frontier for illegal immigration from Mexico, Chicago became a site of contestation as some stakeholders worked to restrict this population while others offered them sanctuary.

But ordinary, propertied, working-class whites could only wield so much power. Municipal and federal authorities enacted the most enduring exclusionary designs for racialized migrant communities. The city's power brokers used both statist and federal policies and incentive structures for private and public housing development, urban renewal, slum clearance, highway construction, and other instruments to shape the urban infrastructure in ways that perpetuated racial apartheid.[26] Within an inequitable and segregated metropolis, city leaders attempted to manage ethnic-racial strife within the contexts of federal divestment; economic restructuring; deindustrialization and an expanding service sector; and redevelopment projects designed to expand the tax base and generate corporate wealth.[27] Racialized migrants and minorities were displaced by urban renewal and slum clearance. While many poor African Americans were shunted into the concrete cages of public housing, Mexican residents were steered into substandard housing on the edges of white ethnic neighborhoods and adjacent to isolated Black enclaves, municipally starved of city services. Most Mexican families resided in substandard tenements and overcrowded dwellings with high rents in transitional areas.[28] While the drive for profit among landlords and property owners was able to reinforce white spatial entitlement, it would also sometimes undermine it. That fact was not lost on white ethnics, who began to blame the city for the perceived breakdown of their neighborhoods. Many left the city altogether, while others stayed and fought for their properties.[29] Meanwhile, municipal leaders, ever fearful of white flight, redoubled the maintenance of metropolitan segregation through tax expenditures designed to placate white fears of demographic change and depreciating property values and to compete against the federally subsidized incentives that awaited whites in the suburbs, if and when racial apartheid in the central city came undone.[30]

Making Mexican Chicago takes a fine-grained look at the landlords, building managers, and real estate brokers who saw in white flight not loss but opportunity, not an end but a beginning, as they sought to monetize white-held properties. Historians and housing activists have provided valuable insights on the pernicious devices of slumlords, blockbusters, and contract sellers who profiteered at the expense of the most market-restricted of Chicagoans—Black Americans—by unleashing a market of previously restricted neighborhoods.[31] And there is no doubt that predation was very real. But repeating this tale of unscrupulous actors and hapless victims can obscure the more complicated and nuanced power relations and social exchanges that occurred inside neighborhoods, homes, storefronts, community centers, and churches. As we saw in the case of Anita Villarreal, the landlords, rental-property owners, and community real estate agents who

Figure 1.2. Spot clearance. Children play on top of rubble left behind from a torn-down tenement in a section of the Back of the Yards that housed many Mexican families, 1950. (Image source: box 3, folder 2, Mildred Mead Photographs, Hanna Holborn Gray Special Collections Research Center, University of Chicago Library.)

facilitated the Mexicanization of Chicago were not all white. They came from diverse racial, ethnic, and class backgrounds, and their motives were complex.[32] This was a propertied class of people that sought to generate their own private wealth. But some of them were also invested in racial and ethnic empowerment via property ownership and endowing Brown Chicagoans with a sense of belonging, even if this form of investment was implicated in larger structures of racial confinement and inequality. This book proceeds from the premise that the making of the multiracial and multiethnic postwar metropolis requires provisionally decentering narratives of white–Black relations to broaden the cast of stakeholders that monetized white-held properties for profit, power, and opportunity.

This book thus opens up new vistas for understanding the delicate negotiations and intricacies that accompany neighborhood change. This is a story that involves whites but is not white-centered. Figures like Villarreal helped initiate the opening of white neighborhoods to Mexican settlement, block by block, arranging sensitive property transactions with white ethnics by attending to their racial, financial, and emotional attachments and investments. This process often required buy-in from white homeowners who might have felt a sense of precarity about the future of their neighborhoods but who were also tempted by the prospect of turning a breakup with their native city into a lucrative financial transaction. Anita shrewdly sold what we might call a "white-flight script" to these anxious white homeowners, evoking a sobering appraisal of the dire financial state of their neighborhood. She might reference, for instance, the shuttered storefronts along South Lawndale's once bustling, Bohemian commercial corridor, Twenty-Sixth Street. She would then turn around and sell an alternative script to arriving Mexicans, promising them a bright future of neighbors, businesses, and clients who would eventually look like them. In the beginning, her acquisition of white-owned properties was interpreted as a violation of the silent covenants that protected white residents from the invasion of Brown "foreigners." The response was white retribution through intimidation and violence: the torching of Mexican-owned properties, protests outside Villarreal's office, the gunning down of Mexican workers walking through the "wrong" neighborhood, surveillance and arrest by federal authorities, and more.[33] But over time, her market inclusion of Mexicans became, simply, good business. Soon enough, other property merchants were adopting her business model and making handsome profits off of Brown property-hood. White and Latino real estate brokers, ethnic community leaders, and even blockbusters and slumlords promised white property owners an orderly and nonthreatening transition as their neighborhoods became Mexicanized. In short, Mexicans were not passive victims: they made white neighborhoods Mexican, often through creativity, smarts, shrewd business dealings, and a keen agility when it came to managing (and placating) white racial fears.

So successful were these strategies that they contributed to a major shift by the early 1960s, as white Chicagoans largely suspended their earlier restrictionist populism. The recognition that the "Browning" of Chicago could be a source of profit facilitated the growth of the city's Mexican population. Likewise, the passage of the Hart-Celler Act in 1965 had the effect of shaping and augmenting undocumented immigration because it applied a quota for immigration from Latin America, including Mexico, for the first time. These new limits compelled many to circumvent the quota and enter the United States as undocumented migrants, providing property merchants in cities like Chicago with an ever-expanding pool of Mexican renters and homebuyers. As the bald restrictionist populism of an earlier era receded, white ethnic community leaders across the Southwest Side managed the arrival of Mexicans to their respective areas in different ways. Leaders in the deindustrializing Back of the Yards neighborhood employed strategic containment through a variety of zoning and spot-clearance techniques, being careful not to ignite a sudden exodus of long-established Polish and Lithuanian Americans from the neighborhood. Meanwhile, leaders in the mostly Czech neighborhood of South Lawndale, desperate to revitalize their district, rebranded their single-family bungalows into a welcoming Little Village. This provisional transformation of the "Mexican" from property menace to property asset was inextricably tethered to anti-Black sentiments, softening the line for Mexicans while hardening it for African Americans. The Black urban rebellions and unrest of the late 1960s, which included the torching of storefronts and commercial properties, reaffirmed white ethnic community leaders' preferential outreach.[34]

But white ethnics and their Brown counterparts were not the only ones engaged in a struggle over the future of the Southwest Side. The city's power brokers and planning regime coveted the same area, particularly the wards along the south branch of the Chicago River.[35] That regime was led by members of the Chicago Real Estate Research Corporation, a corporate-interest group with a pro-growth agenda that advised the mayor. Armed with speculative studies of land use and projections of high tax revenue, they primed the area for major redevelopment and land-expropriation schemes to bring the federal bulldozer and the private developer to the Mexicanizing wards.[36] Later chapters of *Making Mexican Chicago* explore what happened when neighborhood propertied whites and Mexican renters and home-buyers confronted urban gentrification efforts in the 1970s and 1980s. In different ways, white and Brown denizens resisted the city's redevelopment plans for the river wards, which included high-rise condominiums with boat garages and riverfront walkways.[37] In corporate boardrooms and in city hall, bureaucrats who hoped to attract a professional class of residents with expendable income played a long game for the gentrification of the central city. That game drew on long-standing racist assumptions and policies and would entail the displacement and dispossession of Latino, Black, and white working families. At the same time, city planners formed contingent alliances and interacted with local decision makers who were rooted in the neighborhoods themselves.

By reconstructing the history of the postwar Mexicanization of Chicago, this book puts forth two key interventions. The first is to restore Mexican immigrant and Mexican American agency to community development in the postwar era. To be sure, in the following pages, I look at how restrictionist neighbors, community merchants, and statist forces shaped Mexican containment. But I also show how Mexican immigrants and Mexican Americans marshaled their own efforts to inscribe opportunity and empowerment onto the spatial landscape and in the unstable vacancies created by white flight. This book returns to the central city as a key site to interrogate the spatial designs for a multitiered and multiracial segregation of people, economies, and markets inextricably linked to the broader metropolitan, national, and global transformations shaping US life. In the throes of economic restructuring, postindustrialization, racial exclusion, and eventual gentrification, Mexican immigrants and Mexican Americans were placemakers and community builders who shaped their neighborhoods and instilled in each other a sense of belonging, despite the odds.

The second intervention is to revise our understanding of modern US conservatism in two distinct senses. First, I argue that anti-Brown racism was shaping conservatism several decades before 2016, when Donald Trump campaigned for the presidency on his nativist chant, "Build the wall." In cities like Chicago, white ethnic blue-collar neighborhoods became incubators of anti-immigration and anti-Latino sensibilities that grew out of the drastic demographic changes that residents were witnessing—quite literally—outside their front doors. The conservative backlash in places like Chicago did not play out solely along racial lines of Black and white. It also developed alongside and throughout Mexicanizing neighborhoods as Latinos struggled for inclusion.

Second, Mexicans and Mexican Americans were not only targets of the conservative revolution. I argue here that they also helped to shape it. *Making Mexican Chicago* thus contributes to a growing recognition that as a group, Latinos in the United States defy easy political categorization. Long before activists of the Windy City's Chicano movement in the late 1960s would lead school walkouts, occupy community centers, and emblazon buildings with colorful murals, Mexican Americans and Mexican immigrants had grown disillusioned with the New Deal political order's ability to uplift the barrio. After providing steady loyalty to the Democratic Party of Roosevelt and Kennedy, many Mexican Chicagoans by the 1960s lamented the party's failures to alleviate their economic plight and recognize their political voice. Their growing disillusionment emerged in part out of the issue of homeownership. Federal policy on race and housing insecurity from the New Deal to the Great Society touted the same land-expropriation agenda over any real commitment of resources to expand minority private homeownership, stoking frustration in the barrio.[38] No less important to Mexican Chicagoans was access to commercial property ownership, operation permits, and business investment in neighborhoods where an entrenched white political power structure acted as a gatekeeper to Latino commercial activity in the wards. Richard J. Daley's Democratic political machine exercised a systemic repression of Mexican Americans and denied their civic incorporation, a process that created Chicago's fullest realization of a *colonia*, one of the most enduring sociological concepts used to describe the city's Mexican enclaves.[39]

The growing disillusionment with midcentury liberalism propelled many Mexican American youth toward Chicano activism. This book, however, focuses on how moderates and conservatives within the community responded to the changing political landscape. Recognizing how power was concentrated at the municipal level, Mexican Americans and Mexican immigrants engaged the local structures of a colonial-style, one-party rule and navigated the power relations that regulated its subjects' economic and political ambitions. From the 1960s to the mid-1980s, moderate and conservative Mexican Americans helped maintain and reinforce white political control in Latino wards. This reinforcement helped them to unlock the commercial ventures and entrepreneurial desires of Mexican Chicagoans as they embarked on small-merchant capitalism. As white-flight-depressed commercial districts in emergent Latino barrios were successfully revitalized, conservative Mexican Chicagoans pivoted away from the Great Society and positioned themselves locally between moderate Daley Democrats and chamber-of-commerce Republicans.[40] They embraced certain constitutive features of the rightward turn, including antitax sentiment, law-and-order politics, and do-it-yourself bootstrapism. One conservative barrio publisher, Tony Hernandez, captured this political trajectory when he wrote in 1975, "We Mexican Americans have never received anything on a 'freebee,' and have been proud enough to pay for our own way."[41] He notes his disdain for the "utterings of lightheaded radicals and liberals who urge that 'we have funds coming and we should get our share,'" signaling the conservative politics of those who identified as "Americans of Mexican descent [who] have always given instead of stood in line as helpless indigents waiting for hand-outs."[42]

The political divide within the community often played out along generational lines. Whereas conservative, business-minded Mexican Americans and immigrants sought to remake the barrio through homeownership and commercial power, younger Chicanos turned it into a staging ground in the struggle for decolonization. Inspired by calls for self-determination, Third

Figure 1.3. Chicana/o movement protesters march through the streets of downtown Chicago, calling attention to the city and federal government's hoarding that kept Mexican American barrios bereft of vital resources, circa 1971. (Image courtesy of Lucia Moyado Barba.)

World revolution, and "Brown Power," a younger generation of activists, students, and community members mobilized direct-action campaigns, boycotts, marches, and protests against the establishment machine. They also launched multiscalar critiques against city, state, and federal governments for their complicity in the resource hoarding that kept Latino barrios locked out of services, goods, protection, wealth, and power. Regardless of whether someone was propertied or landless, Chicano activists proclaimed that *la raza* (the people) deserved both political rights and a redistribution of economic resources at all levels of government.[43]

This youth revolt fueled an urban renaissance. Beautification projects coupled with antipoverty dollars led to the creation of community centers, free clinics, day care facilities, and job-training programs. Many old buildings were adorned with colorful murals that celebrated the vitality of Mexican identity. The Southwest Side neighborhood of Pilsen became the political and cultural mecca of the midwestern Mexican American civil rights struggle. A new wave of cultural placemaking—shaped by revolutionary and pre-Columbian aesthetic iconography and architectural customization—transformed drab buildings, storefronts, parks, and viaducts into a vibrant Chicano-Mexicano–built environment. But while critical resources and ethnic pride did reach areas like Pilsen, Little Village, and Back of the Yards,

Mexican neighborhoods continued to face widespread inequities well into the 1980s and 1990s. Predatory speculators primed Pilsen for the return of white suburbanites and professionals, who now hoped to return to the city in search of an "authentic" urban lifestyle in which ethnic diversity was newly chic. Eager to cash in on the yuppie phenomenon, speculators and rehabbers stormed the barrio, installing a beachhead of gentrification and building their fortunes on the very sweat equity generated by the successive waves of Mexican migrants and Mexican Americans whose labor had revitalized those communities in the first place.

Near the end of the twentieth century, from the purview of her real estate office on bustling Twenty-Sixth Street in La Villita (Little Village), Anita Villarreal took in the changes that had remade her city into the Mexican metropolis of the North. She was one of the countless nonwhite merchants who had shaped the Latino experience in Chicago, not by demanding resource redistribution and political rights, but instead by fighting for the market inclusion of Mexican American and Mexican migrant workers in property ownership and commercial power. The city showcased her pioneering role when she appeared annually as a guest of honor during La Villita's celebration of Mexican Independence Day. Meanwhile, conservatives, liberals, business owners, and community organizers in the barrio continued to debate how to best stabilize Mexican communities in the face of ongoing gentrification, exploitation, dispossession, poverty, and racialization. These forces remained in play, even as restrictive populists were replaced by an ostensibly color-blind gentrifying class. From the era of urban renewal to the age of gentrification, Mexicanization was a political and economic project wielded by various stakeholders, but most passionately by Mexican Americans and Mexican immigrants themselves. The conditions within which they did so were not—and had never been—of their making. As wealth and capital were redistributed upward, spatially confined Mexican Americans set out to control the terms of their incorporation within the central city. Villarreal and others like her pinned their highest hopes on homeownership and private property as the conduits to full inclusion in American society. Government programs, in her view, could not achieve this kind of incorporation. In 1980, when she feared that the liberal excesses of the Democratic Party had gone too far, Villarreal cast her vote for Ronald Reagan on his promise of anti-government measures and the rollback of federal programs. She had grown wary of the political mobilization of what she called "our rebellious youth."[44] She came to interpret Mexican immigration as one of the bravest free-market acts an individual could make and as the purest expression of capitalist mobility.[45] From the purview of her office window, the world outside looked very different: on storefronts and buildings and in the streets, Mexican culture was now celebrated rather than stigmatized. But at the start of the twenty-first century, the same condition of Mexican spatial precarity remained.

2 :: Deportation and Demolition

In 1953, Mexican residents of the Near West Side were invited to a neighborhood meeting at the historic social settlement Hull House hosted by the Mexican American Council of Chicago. Two items on the agenda were timely. The first was to notify residents that the city had selected their area for slum clearance and redevelopment, part of a larger plan to rid the city of blighted areas and replace them with modern residential and commercial development. Attendees were encouraged to participate in a resident planning board that would represent the community's voice on the proposals and help shape the area's future during urban renewal. The second item was an immigration law, the McCarran-Walter Act passed in 1952, which greatly limited most immigrant residents' right to live in the United States. By the time of the meeting, many Mexican residents had already witnessed or experienced arrests and deportations prompted by the new law. Both issues, the prospect of demolition and the risk of deportation, threatened their livelihoods and their beloved Halsted Street, the economic anchor and center of public life for Mexicans in Chicago. While impossible to know at the time, by 1963 city and federal bulldozers would come to demolish sections of Halsted Street, Hull House, and the Mexican Near West Side to make way for an urban campus of the University of Illinois.[1]

At the time of the meeting, few residents considered displacement, whether by way of demolition or deportation, to be inevitable. Yet these issues became interlocking circumstances for Mexican Near West Siders throughout the decade, as the federal government unleashed forms of state power that would drastically impact their lives. The immigration-control regime rendered Mexicans a powerless subclass outside the bounds of rights, positioning them as unassimilable "aliens," "illegals," and "wetbacks" (a pejorative that denoted crossing the Rio Grande illegally). In contrast, re-development and civic planning could potentially engage Mexicans as residents, neighbors, homeowners, and storekeepers, otherwise empowering them with a sense of belonging. By participating in the reform efforts, Near West Side residents were hopeful that they could counteract the stigma of illegal alienage and demonstrate their compatibility with the liberal democratic project of building and improving their community. Mexican Near West Siders wanted not only a say in the future of their homes, businesses, and community institutions, but also to legitimize their claims to civic inclusion.

Confronting them, however, was a redevelopment regime initiated during World War II that wanted to monetize and profit from slum clearance. While liberal New Deal housing policies privileged cultural pluralism in theory and rhetoric, in practice the federal government reinforced racial segregation to exert order onto the demographic changes of urban America. In Chicago, those changes were pivotal as an influx of Black migrants from the South along with a decrease in the white population reconstituted the way elites viewed city policymaking. Northern segregationist tools—zoning, restrictive covenants, residential steering, credit blacklisting, and others— were devised to contain Black communities. Some of these strategies were also applied to multiethnic/multiracial neighborhoods like the Near West Side and other central areas of the city that were redlined and locked into cycles of disinvestment. Downtown leaders pioneered innovative slum-clearance and redevelopment legislation and secured unprecedented municipal power, exploiting public policy to revitalize areas for private profit and to redirect the increasing flow of capital that was streaming out to the suburbs in the postwar years. These initiatives resulted in legislation such as the Blighted Areas Redevelopment Act of 1947 and its accompanying Relocation Act of 1947, which created the Chicago Land Clearance Commission to appropriate land through eminent domain without having to abide by federal antidiscrimination provisions. It also helped secure the Urban Community Conservation Act of 1953, preparing a bureaucratic landscape that privileged total city control over urban-renewal federal dollars when released through the Housing Act of 1954. City officials and downtown elites used urban renewal to shape urban space in an attempt to achieve a desired racial and class demographic and activate tax-producing real estate.[2]

But where downtown elites saw slum, others saw sanctuary. Mexican newcomers carved a space for themselves out of the multiethnic Near West Side, once an entry-point neighborhood for waves of European immigrants prior to 1924. By 1953, more than thirty thousand Mexicans were living on the Near West Side and were helping to revitalize it economically through small-scale neighborhood capitalism.[3] They lived spread out across the boundaries of the Near West Side but were more concentrated on its eastern end around Halsted Street. Mexican Near West Siders transformed abandoned spaces of white flight, segregation, and disinvestment through sweat equity and bottom-up revitalization. Beginning with a small cluster of businesses in the 1920s, the Mexicanization of Halsted Street bloomed in the 1940s and 1950s, becoming a symbol of economic strength and community perseverance for the growing Latino Midwest. By 1954, immigrant merchants had organized a Mexican chamber of commerce to protect their interests and streetside businesses. That year was also a turning point in the escalation of immigration control as people on Halsted Street and in the Mexican Near West Side became targets of an intense campaign to deport thousands of unsanctioned immigrants through Operation Wetback, a military-style deportation offensive of the Immigration and Naturalization Service (INS). Arrests of Latinos on Halsted Street by immigration agents became commonplace.[4]

The campaign to extract "illegal aliens" from urban neighborhoods like the Near West Side had consequences beyond the removal of undesirable immigrants. The INS's 1954 Operation Wetback and its ideological apparatus diminished the political power of area residents, civic agencies, and organizations that fought against the deportations. These campaigns helped reinforce a link between illegal aliens and city slums, elements seen as mutually dependent that then needed to be eradicated. INS agents exploited and weaponized the spatial segregation of Mexicans. Mexican enclaves were under siege as the campaigns harmed local businesses, suppressed Latino public life, and criminalized people living in buildings and areas that were deemed "slums." Adding insult to injury, municipal leaders and city planners placed in their crosshairs these same buildings and areas, targeting the densest pockets of Mexican settlement and seizing on a politically disenfranchised base that, in the logic of Operation Wetback, had no right to live there. By 1956, the Chicago Land Clearance Commission designated this area the "Harrison-Halsted" project, slated for bulldozing and urban renewal.[5]

In this context, Mexican residents insisted on staking a claim to their neighborhoods' future by participating in resident committees to plan for urban renewal. Whereas the deportation regime dispossessed residents of political rights, urban renewal as a federal policy stipulated that community input from affected groups be included, creating an opportunity for the civic inclusion of Mexican Near West Siders. Here, they could speak back to planners and try to exert influence over their community's redevelopment. In fact, initially, residents felt hopeful that urban renewal would provide access to improved, low-cost housing, complete with a Mexican shopping center that would modernize Halsted Street and signal the city's valuing of Latino placemaking and commercial vitality. But that vision ended abruptly in 1960, when they discovered the mayor had given the Harrison-Halsted site to the trustees of the University of Illinois to build a Chicago campus. Residents felt betrayed and mobilized to try to stop the mayor's decision, albeit unsuccessfully. By 1963, the Chicago Land Clearance Commission razed most of the Mexican Near West Side. In its place, a new, modernist university campus emerged, and Mexicans were sent scrambling to rebuild in other white-flight neighborhoods. The mayor's decision achieved what downtown business elites had desired all along: a large institutional anchor in the central area that would raise property values and replace the population with higher-income residents.[6]

At the time of the 1953 meeting in Hull House, the significance of congregating in a space with a history of providing sanctuary for immigrants was not lost on visitors, but few could have predicted that urban renewal and mass-deportation campaigns would lead to their removal from the neighborhood and, for many, from the country. What was clear was that a more punitive immigration-enforcement system was deployed to hunt "wetbacks" far beyond the US-Mexico border, inside the American neighborhoods that housed them.

The *Wetback Suite*

Anchored in colonias like the Mexican Near West Side, the *wetback suite* was an improvisation that became a routine centered on the recruitment, sheltering, and redistribution of unsanctioned workers to help satisfy the region's marketplace for Mexican labor. This system grew as a counterpart to the US-Mexico guest-worker agreement known as the Bracero Program, begun during World War II, that brought tens of thousands of Mexicans through legal contracts to work in the agricultural fields and railroads of the United States, including the Midwest.[7] But as historian Mae M. Ngai has demonstrated, what was "supposed to be a solution to illegal immigration" in fact "generated more illegal immigration."[8] Many workers who were unable to secure bracero contracts were prompted to cross illegally, drawn in by economic incentives to the industrial and manufacturing economies of

Chicago.[9] The rising presence of unsanctioned immigrants in the city added to the changing social landscape of illegality, which grew harsher and more racialized with time. In lieu of harsher enforcements that could be seen as threatening to employers, immigration authorities only lightly dangled the threat of deportation, the occasional dragnet, and other methods to contain and control the surplus of Mexican workers. The work of recruiting, housing, and redistributing unsanctioned laborers fell to civic groups, neighborhood agencies, and local businesses.

The *wetback suite* could not operate without the intricate network of recruiters, smugglers, rooming house owners, and employers that fueled it. Dramatic episodes of deportation enforcement occasionally brought this system out into the open. In June 1948, Chicagoans learned of a staged immigration sting in the city. It began when law enforcement kicked down the door of a tenement in the Mexican Near West Side after receiving a tip that forty smuggled immigrants were hiding inside.[10] The police raid stood apart from others when the public discovered that the immigrants endured a "rugged voyage" from Mexico to Chicago by riding inside a truck's hidden compartment underneath a large cargo of cantaloupes.[11] Arrested alongside the immigrants were two couples and their small children, all American citizens who were accused of coordinating the operation. All were immediately arrested, and their children were placed in the custody of a local orphanage. While questioned by police and immigration agents, the driver Reynaldo Sanchez told authorities in his defense, "This was my first trip in the business."[12] Newspapers reported that the smuggling was funded by a local Mexican Chicagoan who "escaped through a window during the raid" and who investigators believed was working for local employment companies in the business of importing illegal Mexicans "to be poured into industry and railroad work."[13] The "cantaloupe raid" was one of many that took place across the nation that summer, as regional immigration offices (cooperating with local law enforcement) engineered routine purges of "illegal" Mexicans when their numbers were deemed too high, or as critics noted, when the harvesting season was over.[14] In July 1948, the US Immigration Department reported 207,000 Mexicans deported at the close of the fiscal year, a significant increase.[15] The cantaloupe raid revealed the performative nature of exercising control and consent over unsanctioned immigration.

Like the smugglers and the police, defenders of the undocumented also formed part of this network of role players, implicated in the system even as they condemned it. Journalist John Bartlow Martin learned of the community's involvement in the *wetback suite* while on assignment in the Mexican

Near West Side, just a few years after the cantaloupe raid. He met with Director Martin Ortiz of the Mexican American Council of Chicago (MAC), who described a thriving local economy of recruiters, notary publics, legal aid professionals, and interpreters all working to satisfy America's market for undocumented labor. Martin jotted down Ortiz's description of how farmers routinely hired agents to recruit in Chicago.[16] Ortiz was trained as a sociologist and applied an academic lens to his community work. But on the weekends, he enjoyed jazz drumming, which gave him further insight into the give and take of various players in a coordinated suite.[17] From inside the Hull House settlement where MAC operated, Ortiz told Martin that just "down [the] street, two blocks [away]" are "Mexican labor agencies," out in the open, that collected hefty fees for their services. Ortiz told Martin that one agent, a "Greek man," collected "$5 for info re: jobs" from potential recruits.[18] Ortiz also did not shy away from exposing Mexican American–owned businesses that "send whole families" to employers.[19] One report exposed their complicity, noting that the "situation with notary publics in the community is alarming," citing that "some agencies are known to import wetbacks and then exploit them[,] then turn them into Immigration."[20]

Remarkably, this orchestration, as the journalist would come to learn, became a kind of default liability insurance for the government and the employers: neighborhood agencies and local Mexican organizations assumed all the risk in the trafficking of wetback labor. Mexican civic agencies lent logistical aid to immigrants, authorities, and employers alike. In doing so, they hoped to be a resource to Mexican workers, offering shelter and cultural belonging. Employers frequently called on the groups to handle their disputes with Mexican workers. If workers were laid off or had their contracts terminated, local Mexican organizations stepped in to redistribute the workers to another employer.[21] Smuggled immigrants were steered into tenements, assigned to employers, and added to the tempo of Mexican urban life in Chicago. "Their lives are not easy ones," explained Ortiz in a report, "Thousands have been apprehended and returned to Mexico but the illegal migration from Mexico continues."[22] Even the most upstanding of civic agencies were implicated. MAC, for instance, offered a menu of free services to undocumented workers in this system, including interpreting, job referrals, and legal advice. "The Council is also concerned over the treatment received by 'wetbacks,'" MAC reported to its members.[23] Another civic agency that had its fair share of supporters and detractors was the Mexican Civic Committee of the West Side (MCCWS), an ardent defender of Latino immigrants that fought for improved housing and education.[24] But some residents accused MCCWS of defending "illegal" immigrants to the point of violating the law, helping them elude federal authorities—especially during mass raids.[25] Critics of the group believed the MCCWS directly cooperated with the INS as an informal outsourcing agency that housed, fed, and found work for undocumented workers whenever the INS required it.[26]

The Mexican Near West Side's complicity in the trafficking of "wetback" labor was not nearly as revelatory as three other key observations John Bartlow Martin made. First was the circuity of the *wetback suite*: "Wetbacks, [as] they are called, . . . follow the fruit and sugar beet harvests eastward from California up through Minnesota and Wisconsin and Michigan, packed into cattle trucks, paid almost nothing, preyed upon by farmers and labor agents alike, and at the end of the harvest season they are dumped out in Chicago to shift for themselves, speaking no English, hunted by immigration authorities, homeless, facing the cold Chicago winter. . . . Almost every Saturday the immigration authorities make a sweep down Halsted Street, like hunters driving pheasants."[27] His second observation was the segregation the *wetback suite* relied on to function, evoking the familiarity the agents needed in this enclosed urban landscape: "They flush the wetbacks from the crannies of the falling-down buildings, load them into airplanes, and send them back to Mexico."[28] Martin's third observation was how Mexican immigration transformed the former Jewish and Italian colonies: "The largest settlement is around Hull House. . . . Here they have virtually taken over the old ghetto and Little Sicily. They are crammed into hovels, they are sleeping in shacks."[29]

During his visit, Martin developed a better understanding of the link between deportation and Mexican segregation. He took note of the "ancient apartments" Mexicans lived in while on a slum tour of the Hull House colonia. Their concentration in dilapidated tenements reinforced for the journalist the spatial segregation that aided and perpetuated the *wetback suite*. The dense living conditions made Mexicans easier to recruit and even easier to apprehend.[30] Ortiz and his staff of Latino social workers, translators, and service providers supplied the journalist with their own collected data on Mexican segregation and containment. The Mexican Near West Side was not the logical result of classic ethnic and racial succession that Chicago sociologists usually wrote about, where social and economic advancement moved a group outward into the next concentric circle. The Mexican Near West Side was locked in place; this once point-of-first-arrival neighborhood was a containment zone for waves of Mexican immigrants. As such, MAC described the conditions in very real terms, calling attention to the poor "standards of living," even at risk of airing disparaging representations of the colonia. John Bartlow Martin adopted this tone: "Doors, garbage, and naked children spilling down the steps, probably a thousand people dwell [in one building, . . .] nobody knows really how many," he wrote in his description.[31] While the staff at MAC were university-trained social workers, not radical leftists by any means, they believed that ascribing poor living conditions to a temporary economic station in life erased the real power dynamics that existed underneath. As long as there was a demand for alien Brown bodies to provide cheap, flexible, and improvised labor, the *wetback suite* would play on.

Although initially born out of necessity, profit, and convenience, the *wetback suite* also helped reproduce the criminalization and delegitimization of Mexican settlements by furthering a system that perpetuated this group's racialized foreignness.[32] Between the end of the Second World War and the early 1950s, overenforcement worsened in Mexican colonias like the Near West Side, as the state increasingly targeted and terrorized them for the role they were forced to play as havens for unsanctioned immigrants and as a marketplace for cheap labor. This occurred as these colonias struggled to realize ambitious civic visions for their communities. In turn, their neighborhoods were seen solely through the prism of illegality. Staged sting operations in old tenement buildings evolved into mass sweeps of entire neighborhoods. The constant threat of deportation materialized into actual deportation and the erosion of due process. The *wetback suite* prompted President Harry S. Truman to commission a federal investigation into the "illegal entry of Mexican migrants," leading to the formation of the Truman Commission on Migrant Labor.[33] Congress and the president signaled to the nation that Mexico's "good neighbors" had not only outstayed their welcome but were now a subversive element living within the nation's borders. Meanwhile, Truman's administration continued to appease employers seeking Mexican labor through the renewal of guest-worker contracts. Journalist I. F. Stone noted, "The community is kept steadily 'churned up' to maintain it as a source of cheap labor in constant flux."[34] Congress continued to make concessions for the powerful grower lobby, while introducing laws to establish enforcement mechanisms that would not disrupt employer prerogatives.

In March 1952, members of Congress in the Democrat-controlled House of Representatives authored and passed legislation that proposed severe penalties for those who harbored illegal immigrants. What newspapers called the "anti-wetback law" was a congressional attempt to moderately curb the rise in Mexican immigrants in cities like Chicago and elsewhere. It gave immigration officials the "authority to search private properties" for undocumented immigrants without a warrant, a practice already in place in Chicago, as evidenced by the "cantaloupe raid" and countless others. It also approved fines and jail time for "anyone who recruits, transports, or conceals or harbors any illegal alien" with a proviso: employers were exempt.[35] In clamping down on the *wetback suite*, immigration control could now be tightened to make the city's Mexican colonias inhospitable.

Making an Inhospitable Landscape

Along the US-Mexico border, the federal government pursued more militarized enforcement and stringent control of unsanctioned border-crossing. The INS collaborated with Mexico's government and immigration officials to prevent emigration from one side of the border and immigration into the other. This cross-border policing, as historian Kelly Lytle Hernández explains, was gradually built up over ten years (1943–1954) when they began developing innovative techniques in raids, apprehensions, and mass deportations.[36] While subject to severe episodes of mass detention and deportation, undocumented Mexicans in Chicago did not initially experience the same high level of surveillance as those closer to the US-Mexico border. This changed with time, however, as the INS more aggressively pursued unsanctioned border-crossers no matter where they were found.[37] By mapping its enforcement jurisdiction onto the bodies of mobile migrants in the far north, the INS greatly expanded its reach and presence in the industrial Midwest and in cities like Chicago. With federal priorities shifting toward security and border controls, INS did not have to consider the economic impact on employers as it expanded and consolidated its enforcement practices.[38]

By the early 1950s, the city's *wetback suite* was out of harmony with the INS's objectives for a total and sustained militarism against unsanctioned immigrants during the escalating Cold War. Mexican undocumented immigration as a casual arrangement of convenience and compromise was no longer an acceptable optic.[39] Armed with the Internal Security Act of 1950 and the McCarran-Walter Act of 1952, the Department of Justice and the INS seized on the security and anticommunism prerogatives newly enshrined in law to hunt undesirable immigrants.[40] During this period, Mexican Chicago was subjected to escalated overenforcement against not only unsanctioned immigrants but legal immigrants and American-born citizens as well. The high volume of unsanctioned immigrants into the US, as many as 1.5 million in 1953, provoked public fears of a "Mexican invasion" that reinforced the rationale for heightened enforcement.[41]

In Chicago, deportation enforcement campaigns established a siege-like environment in the Mexican colonias. In the spring of 1952, Sarah Sayad Paz, a Chicagoan of Assyrian descent and longtime defender of immigrant rights with the Mexican American Council, noted the timbre of this terroristic siege on Mexican Chicago in a letter to the *Chicago Sun-Times*: "In front of steel plants, packinghouse plants, churches, etc. these trucks are parked waiting for these pitiful human beings, who are then forced into these trucks on the first lap of the journey to the border where they are dumped."[42] Disturbed by the lack of uproar, she added, "Not having seen a word of protest against the tactics used by our immigration officials in rounding up thousands of human beings right here in Chicago and herding them into trucks like animals, I hereby register my protest against such indignities."[43] Sayad Paz witnessed agents roving about the colonias "without search warrants and using tactics similar to those used in totalitarian countries, homes of American citizens of Mexican descent are searched for these men, who are then arrested and not even given a chance to get their clothes or money together, and taken to a terribly overcrowded jail."[44] That same year, the packinghouse workers' union passed a resolution denouncing the raids in Mexican communities that "resulted in wholesale arrests of Mexican workers, invasion of private homes and other forms of intimidation."[45]

Community members noted an increasing perception of foreignness about Mexican colonias as anti-Mexican and anti-immigrant mobilizations ramped up. Colonias that were once seen as exemplary sites of wartime inclusion through calls for Good Neighbor-ism were now deemed harbors of illegal *wetbackism*. Sarah Sayad Paz responded sardonically, "On Pan-American Day in April, we will stand in public places and proclaim the good relationship we have with our Good Neighbor to the south of us."[46] She discerned the apparent unmaking of the Rockefeller barrio, the Mexican urban colonias in Chicago (and elsewhere) once ascribed geopolitical importance in expanding US imperial and economic objectives across the Americas.[47] In the heightened anticommunism of the Cold War, exploitable Mexican workers and the communities that housed them were no longer of strategic value to the state and became one of the greatest threats to domestic security.[48] The passage of the McCarran-Walter Act in June 1952 held significant consequences for Mexican immigrants in Chicago as it expanded federal powers to punish immigrants suspected of being communists or "subversives" with imprisonment and deportation. As long as migrants continued

Figure 2.1. A group of apprehended Mexican immigrants are on board an Illinois Central deportation train leaving Chicago for the US-Mexico border under guard of immigration officers, September 3, 1953. (Image source: United Press Telephoto.)

to extend the borderlands of life, work, and opportunity northward into Chicago, the INS now had the policy apparatus to punish illegality, which included unauthorized entry and the aiding and transporting of unauthorized aliens, and make Mexican colonias inhospitable. Cold War immigration law gave written license to the INS to constitute immigrants as threats to the nation's security and the legal tools to apprehend, incarcerate, denaturalize, and deport.[49] This prompted the Mexican American Council to hold information sessions at Hull House so "all Chicagoans of Mexican descent [could] know the good and evil effects of the bill."[50] In the years following passage of the McCarran-Walter Act, the INS flooded Chicago district courts with captured Mexicans accused of being in the country unlawfully. Hundreds were prosecuted and convicted for violation of the United States Code, Title 8, Section 1324—which outlines the bringing in and harboring of aliens—thus leading to prison time, fines, and eventual deportation.[51]

The Department of Justice, the INS, and other government agencies increasingly took steps to target and capture individual immigrants—especially those linked to radical organizations—considered to be enemies of the state.[52] In Mexican Chicago, no one was deemed more of a threat to the state, big business, and Cold Warriors than the immigrant labor leader Refugio Roman Martinez. His long persecution by the Justice Department signaled an escalating deportation regime designed—through the use of state terror and violence—to disenfranchise and dislodge Mexican Chicago.

Martinez, a field representative for the United Packinghouse Workers of America (UPWA), became a symbol of injustice that underscored the precarity of Mexican colonias in Chicago and across the United States. When Martinez first crossed the border in 1924 at the age of nineteen, he, like thousands of Mexican immigrants during the 1920s, journeyed north for employment. But also like many young Mexicans, Martinez was fleeing his native country and home state of Tamaulipas, where he had been steeped in a tradition of Mexican radicalism that found expression in the Mexican Revolution (1910–1920) but that also put his life in danger.[53] Martinez headed north and settled in the rail, steel, and meatpacking hub of Chicago, keenly aware of the injustices of capitalism and the exploitation of workers. In 1932, in the depths of the Great Depression, Martinez witnessed the miserable living standards of thousands of Mexican families in Chicago who were unable to work and ineligible for state relief benefits.[54] Making matters worse, the US government under President Herbert Hoover propagandized and scapegoated Mexicans and their American-born children as the cause for the nation's economic woes. This led to a nationwide effort to deport and repatriate thousands of Mexicans, either through voluntary, forced, or coerced means.[55]

The campaign seized on the racialized foreignness of Mexicans by not distinguishing between legal immigrants, illegal immigrants, or American citizens.[56] In Illinois, 5.3 percent or nearly 5,500 people were repatriated from a total of 29,000 Mexicans in the state in 1930, along with a nationwide total of 345,839 between 1930 and 1935.[57] Martinez and his comrades organized unemployed councils, secured provisions, staged strikes, and raised money for food and burials, often in the face of police repression. Martinez joined the Communist Party, and many of his Mexicano peers joined various leftist groups.[58] Alfredo DeAvila, one of Martinez's comrades in the Unemployed Workers Council No. 10, recalled that while they were raising money for destitute families, "police attacked us all the time," in part because the authorities saw their acts as a threat.[59] Their council grew as the indignities of hunger, poverty, and police harassment radicalized people. DeAvila recalled, "The club lasted a few years and [became] the training ground for some Mexicans who later distinguished themselves in organizing the CIO unions, mainly in steel and packinghouses."[60]

Refugio Martinez, Alfredo DeAvila, and hundreds more formed a local chapter of El Frente Popular Mexicano, a radical antifascist and anticapitalist Mexican organization in Chicago that combined a fervent mix of activists, communists, socialists, and anarchists.[61] From this group emerged the cultural architects that would successfully recruit Mexicanos by the thousands into the fold of the Congress of Industrial Organizations (CIO) unions from 1937 to 1943.[62] They energized workers with powerful speeches that fused Mexican nationalism with a radical internationalism in the service of workers' rights and cultural pride. Charismatic and talented, Martinez organized dozens of locals soon after, on behalf of the CIO across various cities including Los Angeles, St. Paul, Omaha, and Kansas City. He became a founding member of the Packinghouse Workers Organizing Committee (PWOC), where he led the fight against the Armour, Swift, Wilson, and Cudahy packing companies, citing wage theft as these companies' profits soared. Other former Frentistas such as Rodolfo Lozoya and DeAvila did the same for electrical workers and steelworkers.[63] The PWOC levied attacks against the packers' deployment of a pernicious and violent white nativism designed to instill fear and keep workers of color from organizing. In October 1943, the PWOC succeeded in winning recognition for the UPWA, a historic victory in the representation of workers of color, immigrants, and racial minorities against the giant and powerful meatpacking industry and a major boost for the wartime labor movement, with the union reaching 150,000 members nationwide.[64]

As a member of the UPWA's Anti-Discrimination Department, Martinez underscored the importance of taking a firm stance in favor of protections against systemic racism within and beyond the slaughterhouse. "I think it is important that this Conference go on record with a strong resolution, condemning the practice of discrimination against Negroes and Mexican workers and other national minorities," he told his union brothers in 1943.[65] Martinez and other members made unprecedented advances in grassroots interracialist politics by getting the union leadership to see beyond its Black and white membership and to consider what the packing companies well understood: it had Spanish-speaking workers among its ranks. Instead of using Latinos as a wedge group against other workers, Martinez spearheaded efforts to mobilize a united front on issues that affected Black and Brown workers not just inside the plants but across the city as well. Both groups were corralled and segregated, faced severe housing discrimination, and constantly endured acts of racial violence. Martinez and Jose T. Ramirez from District 1 joined with their Black union brothers to fight Northern Jim

and Juan Crow.[66] The UPWA picketed discriminatory theaters, lunch coun-
ters, and public housing projects. Later, they would dispatch committees to
investigate racial disturbances and threats against Black residents, such as
during the Cicero race riots in 1951 and the Trumbull Park riots in 1953.[67]
The UPWA became the backbone of a postwar, New Deal, working-class
consciousness that would lead on progressive race and class politics in the
1940s and 1950s. Martinez and his comrades ensured a space for Mexicanos
within this political culture. His talent for organizing and his appeals for
linking ethnicity and race with social justice resonated with workers across
those very lines. This made him an asset in the UPWA and a threat to the
big packing companies, who pursued every avenue imaginable to undermine his influence and make his adoptive home of Chicago inhospitable.

Refugio Martinez faced nearly two decades of harassment by law enforcement and immigration authorities; between 1934 and 1953, he was
subjected to a constant torment of jailings, interrogations, beatings by police, and orders of deportation. Although immigrants in the labor movement would be frequent targets of red-baiting throughout the McCarthy
era, the persecution of Martinez (a legal Mexican immigrant) predated the
McCarthyite witch hunts. Almost immediately upon first being jailed in the
1930s for distributing union leaflets, his immigration status as a permanent
resident (i.e., non-US citizen) was weaponized against him. By April 1941,
he received the first warrant for his arrest and deportation. Over the course
of that decade, government officials deployed the entire onslaught of the
emerging Cold War legal apparatus to turn Martinez into an "illegal" immigrant, a category that, as historian Mae Ngai points out, "gave a powerful sway to the notion that Mexicans had no rightful presence on United
States territory, no rightful claim of belonging."[68] By 1947, his supporters
established a nationwide defense committee to raise awareness of his un-
just persecution and collect money for his legal expenses.[69] Martinez was
tried for violation of the Smith Act of 1940, the Internal Security Act of
1950, and finally, the McCarran-Walter Act of 1952. In October 1951, INS
agents entered his home and dragged Martinez out in front of his family
to arrest him and begin deportation proceedings. By then, Martinez was
in terrible health, having suffered a stroke that paralyzed half of his body.
As supporters monitored his case, the Comité Patriótico Mexicano (CPM)
noted, "Just before Martinez was arrested, some 200 of our people were being rounded up in midnight raids and deported," underscoring the parallel
"terrorization" of Martinez and the Mexican community at large.[70] This
number increased substantially—as INS District Director Marcus T. Neely

admitted, "Almost 300 wetbacks are deported here every month."[71] By then, Martinez's deportation case had made its way to the Seventh Circuit Court of Appeals and would eventually reach the Supreme Court, where on January 12, 1953, the Court upheld his deportation on the basis of the McCarran-Walter Act, which "provides for the deportation of an alien who at the time of his entering the United States or thereafter is affiliated with the Communist Party."[72]

While Martinez was considered a threat due to his labor organizing, his influence within Chicago's Mexican colonias was just as threatening to authorities. Martinez spent years counteracting the forces of displacement by deportation and building civic and civil-rights organizations to make the city more hospitable to Mexicanos. Although little attention has been paid to this dimension of his life, Martinez focused just as much on building an equitable civic infrastructure anchored in opportunities for fair housing, employment, and business ownership for Mexicans—and people of color and immigrants more generally—as he did on unionizing packinghouse workers. He joined with hundreds of other Mexican immigrant *comerciantes* in the city when he embarked on a little neighborhood capitalism of his own.

The labor leader turned from communist to capitalist as a small-business owner of a modest restaurant in the bustling Mexican business corridor in the Near West Side. There, on 901 South Halsted Street, in a restaurant known as the Acapulco, Refugio Martinez and his wife Andrea turned their culinary skills into a few hard-earned dollars while working for social justice throughout the 1940s and early 1950s.[73] These were the same years that the INS's deportation regime ratcheted up in Mexican Near West Side and other colonias and Martinez faced tremendous legal obstacles in his defense against deportation. Yet even as Refugio and Andrea were confronted with the siege of their colonia, they continued to dish out resistance in their restaurant. There, Mexican trade unionists planned strikes, and civic agencies shared resources and information with patrons about raids. Meetings were convened by various organizations such as the CPM, the MCCWS, and the Lázaro Cárdenas Club—all groups that Refugio Martinez had been a founding member of, dating back to the 1930s, and whose leadership they still depended on.[74] The Acapulco became a space of momentary relief from the daily indignities of life, labor, and state violence for many Mexicanos. In her work on Mexican restaurants in the 1940s and 1950s, historian Natalia Molina describes how these spaces "offered a ready-made social network for immigrants new to a dauntingly large, foreign city," and where "the language, food, and atmosphere were reassuringly familiar."[75] The Acapulco shared these qualities and became a place in which to imagine exercising the full privileges that a metropolis could offer despite one's own social position. Here, patrons, friends, and groups imagined—and then realized—demands for better housing, protests against police brutality, and demonstrations against deportations.[76]

One of the most notable events in the Acapulco restaurant's brief history, however, came in April 1950 when two young Mexican Americans—Alfonso Najera and Fred Varela—received the death penalty on a murder conviction for killing a white cab driver. Feeling strongly that Najera and Varela had been wrongfully convicted and that police had planted evidence to frame them, Mexican Chicagoans rose up and pled for clemency and mercy on behalf of the young men and their families.[77] The State of Illinois denied their request and upheld the sentence; the warden granted the two men one last meal.[78] The men and their families requested that Martinez prepare their final meal in the Cook County Jail's kitchen.[79] A deliberate and symbolic form of protest, Martinez agreed and used the occasion to turn jailed Mexican immigrants awaiting deportation into his kitchen assistants, exposing and juxtaposing the social death of immigrants slated for deportation with the actual death of criminalized Mexican Americans. They "lovingly cooked up" enchiladas, chile con carne, and frijoles with "large helpings of tortillas," noted one observer.[80]

Although the meal by Martinez and the jailed immigrants left a hidden transcript of resistance and protest of state violence committed against Mexicans and their communities, it also underscored the calamity that constituent organizations faced during the escalating deportation regime. In many instances, the INS asked Mexican groups to cooperate by reporting illegal immigrants to the agency, an appeal to an earlier time of collaboration between immigration agencies and Mexican civic organizations. In other instances, they were surveilled by an array of local law enforcement agencies, including the Chicago Police Department's secret "Red Squad," private investigators, agents from the Department of Justice, and the American Security Council of Chicago. The escalation of apprehensions and deportations from 1950 to 1953 forced Mexican organizations into an agonizing dilemma about whether to openly resist the INS and DOJ or to comply and avoid any undue attention. Organizations closely affiliated with Martinez (or any other targeted Mexican) risked the possibility of red-baiting, subpoenas, and investigations, and placed members' livelihoods at risk. However, even at great risk, Mexican organizations like the CPM and MCCWS came to Martinez's defense. "We recognize that our entire community will be further endangered unless we join in fighting through on the Martinez case," declared the CPM in 1952.[81]

The terrorization and siege of Mexican colonias forced groups to protest the deportations and the McCarran-Walter Act, not only on behalf of Martinez but of all Mexican immigrants who were now rendered undesirable laborers while criminalized as subversives. In 1952, the Lázaro Cárdenas Club hosted a "Refugio Martinez Defense Benefit Dance" in collaboration with District 1 of the UPWA, the Midwest Committee for Protection of the Foreign Born, and the Labor Committee in Defense of Mexican-Americans. The press release for the benefit dance called for these groups to unite to "strike a blow to the oppressive mass-scale deportation of over 500,000 Mexican people from the United States annually."[82] But for Mexican organizations, being outspoken also went against the anticommunist liberal and conservative consensus of the decade, and sometimes came with consequences. For instance, in 1951 the Chicago Area Project threatened to withhold state funds from the MCCWS and dissolve the organization by removing its director, an outspoken Martinez supporter. As a board member, Martinez came to the director's defense: "It violates our autonomy and our basic rights to be apprized and consulted with, as to when and under what circumstances our director can be asked to resign."[83] Martinez and the MCCWS considered this an affront to their right to "free expression, as individuals and as members of an autonomous body."[84] Nonetheless, the retribution against Chicago's Mexican organizations during the Cold War weakened their ability to defend their constituents during the most dire of times.

The mass mobilizations of Mexicans to protect their colonias from persecution were dealt a major blow when Refugio Martinez, having lost his Supreme Court case, suffered a stroke that killed him on a deportation train to Tampico in May 1953.[85] News of his death traveled quickly. "12 Years of Justice Dep't Torment Ends in Death for Refugio Martinez," read one headline in the *Daily Worker*.[86] "You might say the packers killed him," added of one of Martinez's coworkers.[87] Chicago's Mexican organizations saw it as murder at the hands of the American government and a dark turn in the unrelenting repression and banishment of Mexicans in the United States. Refugio Martinez's years-long persecution and death illustrated the great lengths to which the INS and DOJ went to purge Mexican immigrants from the country while also shedding light on the mass-scale deportations. The Mexican community pointed to his death as evidence of the Cold War assault on their neighborhoods. Perhaps not everyone in the colonias could see themselves reflected in Martinez's radical labor organizing, but many could identify with other dimensions of his life as an immigrant, a small-business owner, and a father and husband. Through mobilizations to defend Martinez and other targets of deportation, Mexican Chicago tried to come to terms with the precarity of their colonias. It was but one chapter of a longer Cold War assault on their communities.[88]

Operation Wetback Comes to Chicago

The military-styled, mass-deportation campaign named Operation Wetback was unleashed across the US Southwest during the summer months of 1954, purging an estimated five hundred thousand undocumented Mexicans from the country.[89] That venture almost left the INS coffers empty, but they were soon replenished to target Chicago, which INS Commissioner Joseph Swing believed had "probably the largest" concentration of "illegals."[90] Operation Wetback's campaign in Chicago was not simply a replication of its operations in the US Southwest, but an opportunity to dislodge the communities that Mexicans had built in the industrial North. The INS exploited the racialized foreignness that turned Mexican settlements into potential footholds for communism, seizing on the inhospitable landscape it had helped create since the late 1940s.[91] Chicago's Operation Wetback began on September 16, 1954, Mexican Independence Day—intentionally chosen to coincide with a major cultural event in the Mexican Near West Side as residents prepared for a week of celebration, including an annual parade with floats, marching bands, performers, and a dance at a nearby ballroom. On this day of jubilant celebration, when people were more likely to be outside of their homes, agents began rounding up busloads of people, detaining them in Cook County Jail, and deporting them two days later.[92]

The INS sweeps continued for the next several months, pulling people from their domiciles, worksites, and leisure spaces on a relentless pursuit to extract between twenty thousand and forty thousand Mexicans from the city.[93] The very name of this federally funded military offensive was borrowed from a decades-old disparaging epithet. The INS took the word as part of its official name for its operation campaign to arrest and remove those who had entered the country without legal authorization or a work contract.[94] But for Americans of Mexican descent, their citizenship could not protect them from suspicion or from being caught in an immigration dragnet. As historian Louise Año Nuevo Kerr explains, "Their claims of permanence and longevity no longer sufficed to distinguish them from newly arrived in-migrants."[95] In newspapers, "wetback" was widely used indistinguishably from "Mexican immigrant." In immigrant Chicago, and particularly for other ethnic groups, the word "wetback" gave them license to recast and racialize Mexicans as perpetual foreigners, illegals, criminals, and fundamentally unassimilable people. Any person visibly read as Latino was potentially in the country illegally, and thus could be a "wetback." The ideological power behind this word made it easier to rationalize their expulsion from the neighborhood and the nation.

INS Commissioner General Joseph Swing had set his sights on Chicago as a significant problem area and astutely understood the embedded landscape of Latinos living within a long-settled Italian community.[96] In the months leading up to Operation Wetback, the *Chicago Sun-Times* portrayed the Mexican Near West Side as a hotbed of filth, criminal activity, illiteracy, and "wetbacks."[97] Swing and his local District Director for Chicago, Walter A. Sahli, arrived prepared to initiate their urban campaign. "First, we're going to get them all out, then we're going to keep them out," Sahli brashly told reporters.[98] To achieve this goal, the INS had to bring in agents from all over the country, underscoring the wide scale and aim of this operation.[99] "A small army of immigration officers searched throughout the city for offenders," reported the *Chicago Daily News*.[100] The Operation demonstrated a massive military expanse of manpower, vehicles, technical warcraft, and detention powers. The campaigns in the US Southwest had been urban-warfare rehearsals that could now be perfected in a denser city.[101] Indeed, Chicago's industrial urban topography provided a different *feel* than other Operation Wetback sites in California, Arizona, and Texas with their sprawled-out, low-density landscapes. In contrast, the highly dense living quarters of Chicago's central-city neighborhoods eased INS agents' search-and-arrest task.

During Chicago's Operation Wetback, Sahli publicly encouraged an orderly "voluntary" deportation process, promoted by the city's newspapers. The INS urged undocumented Mexican nationals to turn themselves in by signing an INS registry at the district office and voluntarily leaving the country. Newspaper headlines such as "Wetbacks Get Help In Returning" and "Here 33 Years, Wetback Gives Up" helped promote the INS's narratives and suggest that a humane deportation process was being carried out.[102] To incentivize undocumented Mexicans to turn themselves in, a discounted $40 passenger fee on an army plane was offered to those who wanted to return to Mexico by air. At the start of the campaign, the INS pointed out that Mexican aliens were indeed "surrendering," and that in one single day 172 people voluntarily turned themselves in.[103] Still, it was a far cry from the tens of thousands the INS hoped to deport. And while the INS was promoting this method, it had already begun a series of aggressive, military-style mass raids throughout various Chicago neighborhoods.[104]

INS agents entered and combed through the Mexican enclaves of the Near West Side and other neighborhoods. They used what the INS called "general searches" to enter multi-unit tenement buildings full of residents, sometimes breaking down doors. These were large-volume dragnets that did not necessarily target one specific person, but took a kind of detain-first, ask-questions-later approach. Agents rounded up Mexicans and Mexican Americans and hauled them off for further processing. "Officers, normally without specific leads, search places where illegal aliens may be found, seeking their apprehension," an INS report explained, "these operations produced excellent results."[105] Agents turned up at apartments, storefronts, movie theaters, bars, places of work, and other businesses. They did so unannounced using "special mobile force units," essentially an urban infantry of armed agents who employed surprise to maximize apprehensions. General Swing referred to this as going "in depth."[106] INS reports showed a campaign style tailor made for "urban areas and . . . to apprehend newly arrived illegal aliens whose presence would otherwise be undetected."[107] This required the INS apprehend people in a social context, either in association with or proximity to other Mexicans. In short, those targeted were guilty by association, and the burden of proof rested on them to prove residency or citizenship on the spot. Moreover, since INS agents followed workers from the factories to their communities, Mexican boulevards, stores, and leisure spaces became targets. Operation Wetback primarily focused on working-class laborers in factories, but it also arrested shop keepers and business owners, whose stores were seized and closed after their deportation. Property seizure of vehicles, homes, and businesses were handled during detainee processing. Any financial debts or charge accounts were to be settled, if not at least recorded, for future repayment, likely a difficult burden to meet while incarcerated.[108]

Arrests of family members and spouses at home were terrifying and incited panic. In one case, the arrest of a Mexican packinghouse worker in early October 1954 caused his American-born wife of Mexican descent— who was pregnant and had a small child—to flee and disappear.[109] When the first four Mexican female deportees of Operation Wetback were reported, the idea that women (mothers and wives) would be caught in the raids was so novel that it made headlines.[110] But soon it was so commonplace that it hardly registered as news, as Mexican women and children were just as fiercely targeted as men.[111] Many Latinos felt vulnerable and unsafe. INS agents entered Spanish-language movie theaters to check people for their "papers," inciting chaos as people ran in all directions searching for the exits. Agents boarded city buses to check for undocumented immigrants among the passengers. INS also entered churches, but priests, protective of their parishioners, turned them away. During one such occasion, Father Thomas Matin of St. Francis Church in the Near West Side told the INS agents, "This is the House of God and such immoral behavior will not be tolerated."[112] Here agents discovered one of the few domains they were unable to pass through, where priests and nuns exercised complete authority over their spiritual real estate.

Feeling particularly vulnerable, some Mexican Americans, Puerto Ricans, and legal immigrants avoided being out in public, if not for fear of deportation then to avoid constant harassment. Operation Wetback cast a wide net of suspicion and criminalized Latino citizens. "The [INS] is making mass arrests and deportations of Mexicans in disregard of whether they were born in this country, are naturalized or entered legally," charged Latino packinghouse workers from District 1 of the UPWA.[113] Public apprehensions quickly devolved into spectacles as onlookers, community members, and families watched in fear and terror as their neighbors, coworkers, and family members were yanked away in front of them. This created terror and trauma among the witnesses, who felt helpless to stop the expulsions. Newspapers reported that as many as fifty to seventy-five Mexicans were being detained daily in the month of September and into October. While they did not all lead to deportation, the public roundups, apprehensions, and detentions created an unprecedented police state in Mexican Chicago.[114] Dr. Jorge Prieto had a small medical practice in the Mexican Near West Side and witnessed Operation Wetback unfold from his doorstep. He recalled that many of his patients lived under constant fear of deportation. One of his patients, Hilario, who had arrived in the city nine years earlier as a much-needed worker during World War II, was caught in a dragnet and quickly deported to Mexico, leaving his wife and children without a husband and father. Dr. Prieto underscored how Hilario, once considered an essential worker for the "Arsenal of Democracy" had now become expendable due to the country's "economic distress."[115]

Dr. Prieto's disillusionment underscored how the industrial landscape that the wartime economy had once bolstered had become an arsenal of deportation. Chicago's Operation Wetback did not let up for the remainder of the year and, in fact, was a momentary boon to the sagging local economy as the INS repurposed a deindustrializing landscape for the business of detention and deportation. It removed immigrant laborers from factories amid labor strikes, relieving employers' obligation to pay wages, expanded the number of federal immigration officers in the region, and deputized local law enforcement officers to help in the dragnets.

A Deindustrialized Deportation Regime

Operation Wetback not only required manpower and lawbreakers (i.e., "illegals") to function, it also needed space and material resources. The federal government thus repurposed out-of-use assets like formerly decommissioned planes, trains, buses, factories, and warehouses for the state's hypercontrol of Mexican immigration. Operation Wetback brought deportation and deindustrialization together through necessity, as well as by the economic reconfigurations of capitalism, labor, and production.[116] The recession in the mid-1950s greatly affected northern industries such as steel, meatpacking, and manufacturing.[117] Deindustrialization set in as midwestern industries searched elsewhere for cheaper labor, closing plants and shutting down production in cities like Chicago, Detroit, and St. Louis.[118] Throughout the 1950s, dozens of factories in the once bustling South and Southwest Sides of Chicago closed and laid off thousands of workers as capital flowed to other regions of the country.[119] As manufacturing and the postwar economy suburbanized, Mexicans and racialized minorities were barred from following capital into the suburbs. Now, Mexicans' proximity to deindustrialized urban space made their incongruity with the shifting metropolitan economy even more apparent to those who deemed them expendable and excludable. Operation Wetback transformed this landscape of shuttered factories and decommissioned technologies into a deindustrialized deportation regime.

With the spike in apprehensions, authorities needed a space to detain and process immigrants before prosecution and deportation. The Cook County Jail, one of the few carceral facilities within city limits, was already overcrowded due to the criminalization of Black and Latino males during the 1940s and 1950s.[120] Although the INS contracted the Cook County Jail, it was not considered ideal since it could not hold the high volume of suspected immigration violators that federal authorities planned to apprehend.[121] Former manufacturing and industrial plants, however, could. One such facility was the former Studebaker Corporation Plant situated in the Southwest Side of the city (5555 South Archer Avenue) on fifty-five acres of urban land. After the war, and due mainly to a drawdown of defense mobilization, the Studebaker Company experienced financial troubles that slowed down their production and shuttered many of its plants around the country, including Chicago's.[122] The federal government was the lessor to the Studebaker Company and seized back control of the property as "surplus" space, renamed it Air Force Plant No. 52, and immediately placed it on the market for purchase by potential government contractors. It was advertised as a "truly top-notch facility adaptable to manufacturing or warehousing."[123]

"Warehousing" Mexicans was precisely the INS's goal when it decided to lease and repurpose the building as a detention facility. For the INS, detaining aliens in so-called "contractual jails" was not uncommon; it already relied on over three hundred city and county jails across the country.[124] However, according to the INS, "the detention of aliens in contractual jails poses an administrative problem where the inadequacy of detention space frequently determines or limits enforcement activities."[125] The massive Studebaker plant held no such limitations; the INS could exert absolute control over every square foot of the building.[126] In addition to the deindustrialized Studebaker facility, the INS repurposed a building in the South Loop on 1245 South State Street into a "new 150-cot processing center."[127] It was ideally situated one block away from the Illinois Central Train Station, which became important for returning deportees by rail to Mexico.

The INS's repurposing of the Studebaker plant for alien detention and deportation did not contradict the government's vision for Air Force Plant No. 52. In government plans detailing the site's benefits, diagrams highlighted cargo shipping by land, air, and sea.[128] It was designed for the rationalization and mobility of surplus commodities, including potentially alien labor. From this perspective, commodities no longer of value to metropolitan Chicago could be reassigned and streamlined out of the local market with ease and efficiency. The INS's leasing of Air Force Plant No. 52 aligned with the broader ideologies of the military industrial complex, a defense-minded rationalization that, in this case, re-envisioned an American city as a staging site for a cold war on immigration, US Attorney General Brownell's stated goal.[129] Repurposing the plant for Mexican detention and deportation brought these broader ideologies to fruition not only to control illegal immigration but also, they explained in their 1954 annual report to Brownell, to prioritize the apprehension of "aliens here illegally who may be subversives or criminals."[130] This was an influential set of criteria for the Attorney General, who asserted, "It is the aim of this Administration to utterly destroy the Communist Party, U.S.A. and its activities."[131]

Beyond the ongoing rationalization for deploying a police state in Mexican Chicago, the INS was also proactive in demonstrating how the Studebaker plant's architecture could meet the goal of apprehending twenty-five thousand to forty thousand undocumented immigrants. This was intentionally promoted not just to strike fear in the Mexican community but to justify using such a large site.[132] "The huge Studebaker plant at Archer and Cicero aves [*sic*], will become a temporary Ellis Island for detention of the aliens awaiting transportation back home," reported one newspaper. "Overtaxing the county jail will be avoided with installation of cots and other facilities at the automobile plant."[133] The comparison to New York City's Ellis Island was certainly a misplaced analogy. The Studebaker plant was not a gateway for the arrival and processing of immigrants, but an unmistakable detention center deliberately used to streamline the deportation process. The comparisons severely masked the terror and brutality of Operation Wetback. The INS harnessed local newspapers to report on the Studebaker facility's usage and portray a positive picture of hospitality; they even went so far as to report that a chef from the border region was brought in to prepare Mexican meals for the detainees.[134]

The architecture of the industrial factory turned deindustrialized cage allowed for the full exertion of hypernation and control. Building No. 1 was referred to as the "Manufacturing Building," and was the largest, with approximately 699,840 square feet of space controlled and surveilled by armed INS agents.[135] Agents were temporarily brought in from around the country to contribute manpower.[136] Mexicans caught in the mass raids were caged there. "They're using this factory as a concentration camp to cage Mexicans like animals," wrote the Latino packinghouse workers of District 1 of the UPWA who circulated news about the detention center since many of those detained were stockyards employees.[137] Detainees were held without bail and often their families were left to wonder where they were.[138] Conveniently situated next to railroad tracks and Midway Airport—the busiest in the United States during the 1950s—the building's proximity to transportation hubs was perhaps its most appealing feature.[139] This carceral landscape allowed the INS to use deindustrialized technologies to speed up deportations, even if it meant violating due process and suspending civil liberties. In the first couple of weeks of Chicago's Operation Wetback, it did just that when plane loads of Mexicans were flown out of Midway with very little administrative processing.[140] The INS boasted of its twenty-four-hour turnaround time for apprehension, investigation, and deportation.[141]

The INS deported Mexicans by land, air, and sea. Overland deportations were often by rail, via the Illinois Central Railroad, the very train that had brought waves of migrants from the Global South to the Windy City since African Americans came during the Great Migration. Mexicans who were deported through the Illinois Central were often transferred onto ships in the Louisiana harbor, and then by sea through the Gulf of Mexico to Veracruz. The INS also deployed an airlift process for deportation and greatly expedited the removal process with a squadron of demilitarized C-46 army planes.[142] Ironically, the army's C-46 planes were rebranded at the conclusion of the war as "caravans of commerce," for their capacity to transport large amounts of products quickly to markets. With Operation Wetback, these "caravans of commerce" were rebranded once more as part of the "Border Patrol Air Transport Arm."[143] Opponents to the mass deportations incorrectly credited Commissioner Swing with establishing this "Chicago-to-Mexico airlift."[144] In fact, these deportation flights were not new to Chicago; they were used in the aftermath of the "cantaloupe raid" of 1948, and with greater frequency ever since. Again, deindustrialized materials were repurposed to reverse Mexican immigration and undo their settlement in the city.

The zealous use of the Studebaker plant, Midway Airport, and C-46 planes expedited deportation. Every C-46 flown out of Midway carried a "plane load of 50 Mexicans" to points along the US-Mexico border such as Brownsville and McAllen, Texas, at least once and sometimes twice a week.[145] This spatial formation evidenced a high-alert security environment that justified the use of demilitarized and deindustrialized architecture, transportation, and technology as instruments for Mexican deportation. While the INS's shoddy recordkeeping makes it difficult to tell if the agency met its goal of deporting twenty thousand to forty thousand illegal aliens from Chicago, the INS did report that through airlift alone it deported "11,459 aliens" during the fiscal year of September 1954 to June 1955, but this number did not include those banished by rail or bus.[146]

As terrifying as this carceral cage hidden in plain sight was to Mexicans and Mexican Americans alike, an even bigger threat remained. The deportation campaign was stripping people from their emotional and material investments in their communities. Moreover, the unrestrained power of the state, through the INS, reinforced the notion that the neighborhoods Mexicans lived in were of no consequence; this group was seen as "illegals," not homeowners, residents, and neighbors. Longtime Mexican immigrants who had lived in the city since the 1920s and crossed the border when laws were less stern were just as susceptible to arrest and deportation as those who arrived as "illegals" in the 1950s.[147] Operation Wetback continued to reinforce the stereotype of Mexicans as transients—an enduring economic, political, and social form of justification to remove, racialize, and criminalize them.

Civil liberties and civil-rights groups in the city fully condemned Operation Wetback, but only after being caught off guard initially. Local chapters of the Midwest Committee for Protection of Foreign Born (MCPFB) and the Illinois Division of the American Civil Liberties Union (IL-ACLU) were unprepared to face Operation Wetback's Midwest campaign. This was partly a failure to recognize the years-long deportation regime that had formed around Mexican communities since the end of World War II. The two groups, rather than collaborate against the roundups, viewed each other as "competition," even in their pursuit of similar civil-liberties objectives.[148] The IL-ACLU pursued what it believed was a more reasoned legal approach. They met with District Director Sahli to seek assurances that due process would be followed and that immigrants' civil liberties would not be violated. Legal protections were but one remedy for the more progressive and outspoken MCPFB, which highlighted the capitalist underpinnings of Mexican removal as a solution to the overabundance of cheap labor during troubled economic times. Nathan Caldwell Jr., the Executive Secretary of the MCPFB, asserted that the Mexican deportation crisis required an "understanding ideologically of the economic base of oppression of Mexican people residing in this country—certainly the role which deportation plays in this oppression."[149] The MCPFB sought an injunction against District Director Sahli to stop the raids, with little success.[150]

Unprepared for the use of makeshift detention centers, the MCPFB turned to its Southern California chapter for help. "We're in the midst of a deportation dragnet similar to the one carried out in L.A. several months ago," wrote Caldwell to the Los Angeles chapter, "The attorneys here have had no previous experience before the Service [INS] or in the Courts around a drive of such mass character."[151] Lawyers and activists scrambled to aid immigrant detainees awaiting deportation without a trial or legal representation. During Los Angeles's "Operation Round-up," the INS turned Elysian Park, a large public space located in the heart of a predominantly Mexican American community, into a makeshift detention center.[152] While the similarities between Elysian Park and Chicago's Studebaker plant were not exact, the use of both sites as cages by the government beckoned comparisons to "concentration camps," "estilo Hitler," as one Mexican group remarked.[153]

But even with the INS's use of the built environment for strategic detention, the state showed no compunction for the new heights of Chicago's

Mexican expulsion and banishment campaign. Operation Wetback punished countless unsanctioned immigrants with swift deportation, dispossessing them of their lives in Chicago. "Deportation is worse than prison," argued Harriet Barron, an immigrant rights defender, "it means the destruction of homes and families."[154] Operation Wetback also violated the rights of US citizens who were as likely to get caught in the raids as non-citizens. Many of those detained, the *Illinois Worker* asserted, were "native born U.S. Citizens, Puerto Ricans, and others," all targets of "over-zealous Immigration officers, who consider Spanish speech and a dark complexion to be 'de facto' evidence of being a 'wetback.'"[155] As historian Lilia Fernández has shown, "Although Puerto Ricans were citizens, most Americans could not distinguish them from Mexicans."[156] Most consequential, however, was how Operation Wetback neutralized local Mexican organizations through political repression, censorship, and defunding their civic and social-welfare projects, greatly mitigating their influence in neighborhood decision-making.[157] Groups such as the MCCWS and CPM, led by outspoken and progressive immigrant labor leaders, were frequently embroiled in deportation proceedings. Members of these groups evoked past community trauma when they wrote, "The blood is still dripping from the hands of those who murdered Refugio Roman Martinez . . . when now those same murderers intend to repeat their work," as notable Mexican trade unionists Rodolfo Lozoya, Jose T. Ramirez, and dozens of others faced deportation and state persecution following Martinez's death.[158]

Chicago's progressive and leftist organizations rallied a mass defense against the deportations, as they had in the past, but beyond challenging each case in court they had few other remedies.[159] Captured Mexicanos resisted deportation by their own means, some refusing to pay the required transportation fee back to Mexico, as did Jesus Olaniz Campos, a bus boy at the Hilton's Palmer House Hotel who was later prosecuted.[160] Operation Wetback eventually came to a grinding halt, not due to protest and resistance, but because of the Chicago winter, budget limitations, and more conveniently, the end of the harvest season. INS Commissioner Swing proudly touted the fact that 266,788 Mexicans had been deported since the start of Operation Wetback.[161] Abner Green of the American Committee for Protection of the Foreign Born (ACPFB) reported that more than one million Mexicans were deported during the entire year of 1954.[162] The ACPFB brought international attention to the long history of state-sanctioned racial violence against Mexicans. In April 1959, a group of citizens, civil-liberties activists, and scholars presented *A Petition to the United Nations on the Treat-*

ment of the Mexican Immigrant, in which they declared that this "shock-ing record of inhumanity" was in "clear violation of the provisions of the Universal Declaration of Human Rights adopted by the United Nations in 1948."[163] It is a powerful transcript of the systematic removal of Mexicans, both nationals and US citizens, from the United States.

Chicago's Operation Wetback left an enduring collective trauma on Mexican Chicago for the dehumanization and racial terror it unleashed. It also unfolded during a time of immense Latino spatial instability due to pending land clearance and urban renewal. At the same time the immigration-control regime was dislodging a settled residential community, postwar civic planning was underway to remake the central city and rid it of slums, including Mexican colonias. The immigration-control regime tar-geted Mexicans, while the urban-renewal movement—led by city leaders, business interests, and urban planners—targeted the blighted infrastruc-ture and built environment that Mexicans occupied. These two projects, separate but overlapping, did not go unnoticed by Mexican civic groups or observers like journalist John Bartlow Martin, who noted that "the falling-down buildings" in the Mexican Near West Side only reinforced the target Mexicans already carried on their backs.[164]

Planning for Whom? Building Latino Civic Authority in the Shadow of Deportation

Even before public policy could remake the Near West Side, the policies of the deportation regime and banishment campaigns had already shaped Mexican urban space and civic politics of inclusion and exclusion. As civil liberties groups, community leaders, and labor activists fought against the mass deportations, local Mexican civic organizations received notification that parts of the Near West Side were slated for land clearance and urban renewal. The Chicago Land Clearance Commission (CLCC), a city agency with the power to procure properties, bulldoze them, and sell the land to private developers, initiated its planning phase to demolish parts of the Near West Side.[165] In 1954, CLCC surveyors conducted studies of build-ings in preparation for the massive slum-clearance program. They handed out leaflets notifying tenants and homeowners, "The house in which you live stands in an area which the Chicago Land Clearance Commission will acquire for redevelopment by private enterprise. This building, like other structures in this area, will be demolished to make way for a new neigh-borhood."[166] The Mexican Near West Side was particularly vulnerable; the housing, businesses, and cultural spaces that anchored their community life were at stake. Residents of the Mexican Near West Side questioned whether the "new neighborhood" the CLCC spoke of included them.

The city's ambitious slum-clearance and redevelopment program created during the Second World War came to fruition in the 1950s.[167] Ongoing land clearance and demolition of blighted buildings persisted throughout the decade in the blue-collar, multiethnic Near West Side to make way for the city's new expressways. The Congress Street Expressway, begun in the 1940s and not completed until 1957, displaced as many as sixteen thousand families. These massive civic projects strained the limited housing stock as displaced residents moved to other tenements.[168] As the city planners' focus shifted from expressways to slum clearance, local residents joined the Near West Side Planning Board's (NWSPB) efforts to engage in a broader national discourse over postwar planning and housing redevelopment from a local grassroots perspective. Established in 1949, the NWSPB argued that "those who live here and those who work here, can be the first to demonstrate in this field that democracy can function practically, economically and intelligently in remaking the world they live in."[169] The NWSPB leadership— mostly white liberal professionals associated with Hull House—articulated high-minded principles for the local residents, promoting the idea that even in a so-called "slum" democracy could be put into action. The ad hoc group tried to be inclusive of the multiethnic makeup of the area and, as historian Lilia Fernández has demonstrated, "it truly distinguished itself as a model of community-controlled development long before such approaches gained wider popularity."[170]

But the area's working-class ethnics, immigrants, and racial minorities quickly grew frustrated with the NWSPB's ineffectiveness in representing the diverse community's interests. Some of the loudest criticisms came from Italian American residents who viewed the professionals as "outsiders" whose "inactivity" was jeopardizing the future of their homes and properties.[171] They believed the NWSPB was acceding too much power to the city administrators in identifying which buildings were blighted and needed tearing down. Only a year after the NWSPB was founded, Italian American neighborhood activists from the western end of the Near West Side quit the board in protest.[172] Protecting their self-interest, they mobilized support from local machine bosses (to the dismay of the NWSPB), to lobby the City Council to pass an ordinance that would protect their properties from land clearance, arguing that "in the area west of Racine there is very little blight and rehabilitation is feasible."[173] If these west-of-Racine homeowners agreed to invest in some home improvement, held the city officials, they would save their homes from the wrecking ball. With that same ordinance, they stopped the Chicago Housing Authority from building additional public housing in their community, which the Italian Americans saw as a "threat" that would guarantee a Black "invasion" into their area, as they felt the Jane Addams Homes had done in years past.[174]

The City Council passed the Italian Americans' ordinance, which moved the crosshairs of demolition onto less influential residents. The Chicago Plan Commission wanted more from the concession with the Italian Americans, including a fifty-five acre area that the CLCC wanted to demolish, bounded by Morgan Street to the west, Roosevelt Road to the south, the Congress expressway as the northern boundary, and the future South Expressway as the eastern boundary.[175] The ordinance shifted the target of demolition to the densest pockets of the Near West Side: the eastern end, which by no coincidence was also the area with the densest concentrations of Mexicans, along with Puerto Ricans, African Americans, and less well-off Italians. This area had also been heavily targeted during Operation Wetback. The Mexican American Council surveyed the area in 1949 and found that it contained an estimated twelve thousand Mexicans, the densest concentration in the entire city.[176] Second- and third-generation Italian Americans utilized political channels through their alderman to stave off destruction of their community along Taylor Street, an area with a strong Italian identity but that had recently experienced white flight and increased settlement of Latinos and Blacks. In later years, the alderman promised that "there would be no Negroes and no Mexicans living in the new community."[177] Passage of the ordinance changed the designation of the western end from a "slum" in need of demolition to a "conservation and rehabilitation area" that could be remedied without land clearance, a significant victory for the Italian ethnic bloc. Mindful that the city preferred demolition over conservation—and that city and federal agencies would insist on land clearance—the white ethnics gave up the eastern end of the area to the CLCC in exchange for saving their side of the community.[178]

Mexican residents living within the proposed demolition areas were shut out of the closed-door negotiations, a sign that they not only lacked political influence but were also deemed expendable, transient, and undesirable to the area's future. City officials made no effort to reach out to Mexican civic groups. As the future of the new community was being debated, disenfranchised Mexican residents excluded from the debate were faced with the prospect of demolition and permanent displacement from their homes, businesses, and community institutions. Their exclusion from these negotiations was rooted in the idea that Mexicans are "aliens" devoid of the right to exercise the channels of city government, underscoring how the immigration-control regime continued to shape the politics of Mexican urban space.

However, Mexican Near West Siders repeatedly challenged this premise by insisting that they be included in the planning for urban renewal. One such resident, Anita Villarreal, whose efforts were mentioned in chapter 1, was deeply devoted to the ideals of Roosevelt's industrial democracy, immigrant workers' rights, and fair housing as an anchor for the American dream. She believed Mexicans needed to organize as an ethnic bloc to exercise their right to belong and have a say in urban-renewal affairs. But even as a US-born Latina, she too was stigmatized and criminalized by the deportation campaigns of the 1950s for speaking out against the expulsion of Mexicanos and immigrant labor leaders. She had even been arrested by federal agents and tried in federal court on charges that she conspired to violate immigration laws when she assisted Mexicans with immigration paperwork. Earlier, she had taken guardianship of the daughters of her martyred friend Refugio Martinez and raised them with her own six children.[179] Her personal and political aid to persecuted immigrant workers marked her as a radical and communist, affecting her credibility and reputation (including that of the MCCWS) when the Mexican Near West Side needed credible defenders.[180] Nevertheless, she continued to be a voice for residents facing demolition, just as she had been for those facing deportation. Both issues crossed her desk daily throughout the 1950s as she handled immigration and housing cases with the MCCWS, and with her own business, Agencia Villarreal. She became one of the first Latinas in the city to earn a real estate license and used her expertise in federal housing policy to buy and sell homes, especially to Latino servicemen returning from World War II and the Korean War, as well as to Mexican immigrants. This latter role had earned Villarreal a seat at the initial meetings of the NWSPB as they planned for the area's redevelopment to improve housing, which dissolved with the Italian residents' protest. Villarreal worked to recast Mexicans as stabilizers and revitalizers of the community. But with an eye on the fallout from the deportation campaigns, this would mean supporting, not opposing, urban renewal, so long as it made space for them.[181]

Meanwhile, the Hull House leaders of the former NWSPB reorganized into a new group that focused their advocacy on residents living within the boundaries of the demolition zone, now referred to by its busy street intersection as Harrison-Halsted. The Hull House leaders saw this advocacy as necessary because, according to one observer, "The Harrison-Halsted area was the more ethnically diverse and poverty stricken," and did not have "the same protected legal status, or representation by local councils, to work for them."[182] They wanted to make sure residents in the demolition area were not *planned out* but *planned with*. They witnessed firsthand how the Italian ethnic bloc exercised political muscle to save their homes from the bulldozer but left entire acres of the community without any defenders. Perry J. Miranda, a youth-delinquency researcher who closely observed the social dynamics in the demolition area, also noted the uneven power relations between the two groups: "The Mexican has never had any political power in the community, while the Italians have retained political power for years."[183]

These realities only exacerbated these groups' different access to political power as they carved out turf in the Near West Side. Italians' long presence in the Windy City afforded them a place within the political machine, which in theory guaranteed them representation in governance and matters of the state along ethnic lines, in typical machine fashion. More fundamental were the social transformations that allowed Italian Americans to enter American mainstream life and access the material and economic privileges of whiteness.[184] These dynamics did not extend to Latinos who were racialized and whose immigration was criminalized. Latinos had no representation in political affairs, and during the 1950s, many Mexicans became increasingly distrustful of the state given the mass-deportation campaigns and the McCarthyism that had eroded their civil and labor rights. Unfortunately, the Hull House leaders, whose treatment of the community displayed a WASP-y paternalism, understood little of this historical context. They regularly dismissed Mexican-Italian conflict as the daily quarreling of working-class ethnics fighting over the same slum.[185] Others, however, felt strongly that the ordinance, whether by coincidence or design, held the color line and placed the crosshairs of demolition on an area of Brown poor people.[186] Still, the Hull House leaders remained hopeful that not all was lost for those residents of the demolition neighborhoods; despite their lack of political clout, they could have a voice in planning their communities.

In October 1954, settlement house leaders initiated the Hull House Citizen Participation Project to mobilize residents in the demolition neighborhoods. Since passage of the Housing Act of 1954 placed clearer guidelines on the categories of federal government involvement, the project would provide Hull House neighbors with "information about conservation, land clearance, and urban renewal developments."[187] With a grant from the Emil Schwarzhaupt Foundation, a private New York institution focused on citizen education ("citizens" defined loosely to include everyday working people), this project would teach ethnic slum residents the language of housing and urban planning.[188] Alvin H. Eichholz, director of the Citizen Participation Project, focused on leadership training, education, and fostering cooperative action among neighborhood residents. They referred to the residents as the "Hull House neighbors," signaling the bond between the settlement house and those living in the demolition area, whose survival was actually linked. In fact, it was in Hull House's interest to recognize the preponderance of Latinos living within the demolition area, since permanent displacement of their clientele (people who relied on Hull House services such as childcare, afterschool programs, and citizenship, language, and vocational instruction) would render the historic social settlement useless, a relic of the past. They expressed concern that replacing current residents with white-collar professionals who did not need Hull House's services was undesirable and that the measures they were taking would "result in retaining the area for the ethnic groups now living and working in it."[189]

As the Citizen Participation Project gained momentum, residents became hopeful that urban renewal would lead to low-cost, improved housing. One staff member captured this spirit in 1956: "The Land Clearance Commission made its proposed survey, expressway acquisition has neared completion, the conservation program has been officially designated and undergirded. The community is cleaner, more hopeful, and the experience of working together has strengthened its morale."[190] Moreover, as he told a colleague, Eichholz hoped to "create a better understanding of the needs of the Mexicans in the area."[191] Between 1956 and 1958, Eichholz reached out to the League of United Latin American Citizens (Chicago chapter), the Mexican American Council, and other Latino civic and religious groups to help coordinate neighborhood surveys and door-to-door visits to mobilize support for the project.[192] To Eichholz's credit, the Citizens Participation Project was effective in bringing the heads of city agencies like the CLCC and CPC face-to-face with resident, civic, and religious groups who "could communicate with city authorities" and "influence" the planning.[193] The proposed demolition zone included, as Lilia Fernández has shown, 835 dwelling units and approximately 3,500 people, or an estimated 700 families.[194] When the city created the Department of Urban Renewal in 1957, residents felt somewhat assured in the "workable program" outlined for the Near West Side. The details were released in the 1958 *Development Plan*

A Social Settlement

in Times

of Neighborhood Change

How Chicago's Hull-House

Serves Its Young People

in

Reporting the Year 1957   These "Years Between"

Figure 2.2. The 1957 cover of this Hull House brochure promoted the settlement's important role in the lives of the area's youngsters, specifically Latinos, during a time of "neighborhood change" brought on by urban renewal. (Image source: box 61, folder 17, National Federation of Settlements, Social Welfare History Archives, University of Minnesota.)

for the Central Area of Chicago, confirming for demolition-area residents what the CLCC had promised all along: it would "include new multifamily residential development and a limited amount of new commercial development."[195] More remarkable was how leaders from the Citizen Participation Project linked urban renewal with democracy, a pitch that projected white middle-class values onto nonwhite residents, even when housing experts were criticizing urban renewal nationally as a form of minority removal. Engaging in the postwar planning of America's neighborhoods, the Hull House leaders contended, was fundamentally a democratic project. Thus, they created a conduit for nonwhite residents to embrace these values and feel ownership over the changes underway.

But for all their lofty idealism, the Hull House Citizen Participation Project staff also held deeply condescending views of Latinos, Blacks, and other migrant groups. The mass deportations and Operation Wetback had stigmatized Mexican residents as "illegals" and colored the way Hull House leaders viewed its Mexican clientele.[196] They frequently reinforced the stereotype of Mexicans as a "transient" population, drawing from popular representations of the neighborhood as a bastion of "illegals."[197] As such, the Hull House staff neglected to engage thousands of Mexican Near West Siders because outreach hinged on these narrow misconceptions. Raquel Marquez, director of the Mexican American Council (MAC), helped counter these assumptions by informing the project leaders that despite the recent mass deportations, there were "many 'wetbacks' who have returned to Chicago legally because of legitimate marriages [to American citizens]," and that "as they become citizens, [they] will become very vocal."[198] But, Marquez warned, regardless of citizenship, if "the Mexicans have a feeling that conservation and land clearance program is a means of pushing them around . . . they will organize against this."[199]

Since the early days of the backroom ordinance that first proposed the land-clearance area in the early 1950s, to its official designation in 1956, and to the release of the 1958 central-areas plan detailing the fifty-five acres that would be cleared, Mexican Near West Siders had exercised their right to participate in the area negotiations.[200] In addition, they were fighting against their association not just with wetbackism but also with blight—often perpetuated by the press, social workers, and most consequentially, city officials who proclaimed, "This was one of the worst areas in the city."[201] Mexican residents wrote to newspaper editors, attended meetings with representatives of city agencies, and issued statements to challenge negative stereotyping or call attention to the external forces behind their poor housing. Black Chicagoans had challenged these very kinds of stereotypes for years, as municipal and state authorities along with the real estate industry allowed associations between Blackness and blight to shape policy that further contained and concentrated Black life in the city for generations.[202] To be sure, the threat of Mexicans did not have the same influence on residential and housing policy, but it was beyond evident that these associations with blight had real, material consequences that could lead to their displacement. Their roles in community-based planning allowed them to exercise freedoms in ways that underscored their stake in their investments as residents, workers, and consumers.

Mexican residents attended Hull House meetings, even when city officials and other powerful actors tried to exclude them. It was one thing for city officials to disregard Mexican residents as transients; their neglect was a matter of convenience to push forward with the demolition plans. It was quite another for the Citizen Participation Project, which was intended to help groups like Mexicans, to cast them as disinterested renters living in slums. Their own report disproved this presumption in June 1958: "The data on housing needs indicate that there are fewer transients in the area than was suspected. . . . [M]uch of the area is made up of families and individuals who either own their buildings or have rented in the area for many years and want to remain."[203] That same year, a housing report commissioned by the federal government indicated that Mexicans, African Americans, Puerto Ricans, and Chinese Americans were systemically barred from buying in suburbs while simultaneously displaced by land clearance in the central-city areas, with nowhere to reside in between. The report, aptly entitled *Where Shall We Live?*, outlined the challenges racial groups faced because the housing industry and federal home loan programs rendered them detrimental to property values and restricted them to living in blighted central-city areas. While the report advocated for more antidiscriminatory measures, it also showed how liberal housing policies were rarely enforced.[204]

But both of these reports failed to capture the cultural investments and placemaking efforts of Mexican American and Mexican immigrant tenants and homeowners who persevered over the structural decay and shifting racial and economic changes to forge bonds of belonging. For example, the Guerreros, proud owners of a brick two-flat on 1113 South Morgan Street, the borderline of the demolition zone, typified working-class community placemakers in the Mexican Near West Side. The head of the family, Joaquin Guerrero, was a packinghouse worker and a veteran of the Mexican Revolution; his wife Soledad was a homemaker; and together they raised a large family. Their sons Delfino and Peter were veterans of the Second World War, and their younger son Richard, a veteran of the Korean War. Throughout the 1940s and 1950s, their humble two-flat bulged with extended family that included the Sotos, the Hernandezes, the Mendozas, and the Gonzalezes. As the families grew they expanded to other properties along Morgan Street, complimenting their labor and war service by founding and contributing to neighborhood civic, religious, and cultural institutions. They became instrumental in groups like the St. Francis Wildcats, Manuel Perez Legion Post, Cordi-Marian's Women's Auxiliary, and the Comité Patriótico Mexicano, groups indispensable to Mexican Chicagoans' sense of permanence in the city.[205]

The Guerreros' home, along with hundreds of other buildings, fell squarely within the demolition zone.[206] In response, the Guerreros and many Mexican Near West Siders took issue with city agencies' character-

Figures 2.3a–b. The Guerreros' brick two-flat on 1113 South Morgan Street. Several families lived here. A site of pride, celebrations, and family gatherings, the Chicago Land Clearance Commission designated the Guerreros' building as blighted and proceeded with its demolition. (Image courtesy of Cynthia Guerrero.)

ization of their area as a "slum" and as "blighted." More than words, these were official designations that allowed agencies to release federal urban-renewal money for land clearance, which the city greatly desired.[207] The Guerreros were proud of their building, which they kept in pristine condition. Their Italianate-styled two-flat, with brick exterior, decorative flat roof, and elegant window moldings, was built in the Chicago style typical of workingmen's homes constructed between the 1860s and 1880s. By the 1950s, the combination of these buildings and racial minorities frequently made them targets for city clearance projects. Next door was a vacant dirt lot, which Marcella Guerrero fondly remembered as an important gathering space: "In the winter this was the site of many snowball fights which sometimes involved aunts, uncles, and cousins and we would be pulled on sleds by our older family members."[208] To city officials, however, it was an eyesore and an underexploited parcel of taxable land, adding to the rationale for demolition. But for hundreds of Mexican children with few parks in

Figure 2.4. Mexican residents of the Near West Side host a meeting with Mayor Richard J. Daley to discuss the city's redevelopment plans of their residential and commercial spaces, circa 1958. (Image courtesy of Arthur R. Velasquez.)

their environs, the vacant lot was a much-needed playlot. These were only some of the factors residents evoked as they questioned why the scheduled demolition targeted predominantly Mexican-occupied buildings when their homes were no worse off than the Italian-owned properties. In 1959, Angeline Guerrero, a Greek American who grew up in the area and married into the Guerrero family, grew frustrated that the Hull House meetings were not reaching a solution to save these homes. She attempted to organize a neighborhood coalition with the more influential Italian residents against the CLCC but found few allies at the time.[209]

Not all Mexican Near West Siders lived in the demolition zone. Jesus and Anita Faz were former migrant farmworkers who now lived with their children outside the land-clearance area. The Fazes spent years crisscrossing fields in Iowa, Kansas, and Michigan, picking sugar beets, onions, and tomatoes, before moving to the Near West Side. In the 1940s and 1950s, they lived convivially among Italians, sharing space, schools, and parks in the areas that Italian American activists fought to conserve. From their six-flat on Aberdeen Street and Vernon Park Place, they could see the bulldozers and land clearance taking place just to the north of them.[210] This was a familiar experience for many Near West Siders, who were surrounded by the swirl of redevelopment but were not directly displaced by it. As such, the political stakes figured little into the texture of their daily lives.

As the Harrison-Halsted Redevelopment Project got underway, it remained unclear how the Mexican commercial corridor would fare. Hull House leaders encouraged participation from merchants, particularly business owners from the Mexican Chamber of Commerce who operated storefronts along South Halsted Street. Although the CLCC's proposal for the Harrison-Halsted site indicated that buildings in the Mexican commercial strip would be purchased and bulldozed, the merchants shared in the optimism of Hull House leaders, who noted, "There is distinct awareness [among the Mexican merchants] that the physical changes in the area are on the way and that in the long run they are for the best interests of all."[211] For these small-business owners, supporting community planning in the shadow of deportation was a way of aligning with the mainstream consensus of the 1950s, which supported the Housing Act of 1954 and believed in the federal government's role in improving American cities without impinging on the freedom of private enterprise. In meetings they demonstrated a "co-operative spirit" and "acceptance of the Land Clearance plan."[212] By 1958, the merchants had formed the Illinois Federation of Mexican Americans (IFOMA), a political vehicle to unify the various civic, social, and religious groups and try to build clout with city hall.[213] They hosted a community town hall with the new mayor, Richard J. Daley, who in his first term inherited many of the urban-renewal projects still in progress, including Harrison-Halsted. During the meeting, IFOMA leaders discussed the city's role in Mexican immigrants' well-being and the relocation challenges brought on by urban renewal.[214] In turn, Daley assured the attendees of the city's support, but made no firm commitments on housing, relocation, or business support, except for a few paltry gestures of recognition about the cultural contributions the Mexican community made to the city.

The Mexican Chamber of Commerce and IFOMA continued to cooperate with urban renewal, motivated to steward what they saw as a great and valuable economic asset: the commercial and consumer center of Mexican Chicago and the greater Latino Midwest. Up to this point, the Citizen Participation Project leaders—despite encouraging residents to "practice the art of democracy" and to "influence the planning for physical change"— had not recognized the contribution Latinos had already made to the area's spatial and economic revitalization.[215] Through years of sweat equity and bottom-up beautification, Latinos had taken aging buildings and storefronts and filled them with civic and cultural institutions, churches, and businesses to make redlined areas into bustling ones.[216] Even the planning board understood that the epicenter of Mexican consumerism, "the Halsted-Roosevelt shopping district," produced "the third largest volume of business of any such district in the city."[217] Evicting the merchants wholesale, they explained to the project leaders, would obliterate the Mexican Near West Side. Project leaders eventually concurred, and since part of the redevelopment plan included new housing for those displaced, it only made sense that their commercial stores would also be restored.

By late 1959, while partial demolition was underway, city officials denied most bids from private developers for new housing and commercial construction yet were still pressuring people to sell their properties, frustrating residents and small-business owners alike. Additionally, city officials were dishonest brokers in their meetings with Harrison-Halsted residents. While promising new housing to neighborhood residents as formalized in their own 1958 plan, behind closed doors they pushed the mayor to use the site for something else.[218] In September 1960, the mayor offered the Harrison-Halsted area as the site for the Chicago campus of the University of Illinois.[219] In selecting the Harrison-Halsted site, the mayor looked to seize an opportunity to bring a university institution close to the Loop and win over the support of powerful downtown interests who stood to gain from the revitalization it would produce. By rezoning the area for university use, the city could get millions of dollars in federal money for its urban-revitalization plans, making slum clearance even more profitable for the city.[220] Opponents immediately launched a neighborhood resistance movement of the area's multiethnic and multiracial cohabitants to prevent the city and university from taking the land, which not only included the fifty-five acres of Harrison-Halsted but portions of the conservation area as well. Italian American resident Florence Scala, who lived in the conservation area but saw the land grab as a betrayal of the community's trust, mobilized hundreds of women and their families to protest, including members of the Guerrero family. But they were swiftly defeated. By May 1961, the City Council voted to build the university on the Harrison-Halsted site, over the jeers and boos of the area's residents. Monsignor John J. Egan, director of the Catholic Archdiocese's Conservation Council, declared the city was making the Near West Side "extinct." With "the district's commercial heart cored out of it, pitted with dubious and perilous parking lots," he asked, "what future is left for the survivors?"[221]

Between 1959 and 1964, the city forced people to sell by order of ordinance, pushing them out of their homes and businesses and offering little in relocation resources. Approximately 4,800 Mexicans were displaced during this period, including the Guerreros, who were forced out of their two-flat on Morgan Street.[222] Those numbers grew as more university-related clearance occurred. According to Carolyn Eastwood, "Approximately 45 percent of families and 33 percent of single residents displaced by the university were Mexican."[223] Renters were given thirty to sixty days to vacate. Halsted Street businesses such as *tiendas* (shops), *carnicerías* (butcher shops), eateries, and *panaderías* (bakeries) were scheduled to be torn down. Bulldozers quickly followed, leveling buildings and turning them into mounds of rubble, dirt, and debris. Hull House was razed, and with it, its hopes that "the people can self-determine the kind of community it should be."[224] In its place arose a concrete campus with masonry walls that insulated it from the neighborhood that remained. Students arrived in the spring of 1965, many of them the commuting suburbanites the city had long desired. Magazine features were quick to revise the university's controversial history. *Architectural Forum* devoted an entire issue to its modernist design in September 1965 but noted that the campus "is content to sit behind its brick and concrete walls, uninvolved in plans for urban renewal in the surrounding areas."[225]

: :

Despite Mexican Near West Siders' efforts to engage in the Harrison-Halsted Redevelopment Project and legitimize their claims to the neighborhood as residents and merchants, the legacy of immigration-control enforcement and its deportation regime plagued their efforts and hastened their dispossession. They were expendable in the eyes of city officials. Just as an immigration-control regime had made them deportable, city decree made them removable. The demolition lines drawn around the heart of the Mexican Near West Side and of people who were deemed "slum" dwellers and transients spatially converged with a deportation regime that targeted the area for being filled with "wetbacks," "illegals," and "birds of passage."

While historians have shown how the nation's midcentury urban-renewal and land-clearance programs frequently uprooted poor and working-class immigrants and people of color, the removal of Mexicans was compounded by the exploitation of their perceived racial alienage. For Mexicans, urban renewal and immigration policy were enjoined forms of material dispossession and urban erasure. In cities like Chicago, Detroit, Los Angeles, and other metropolitan centers, federal banishment campaigns like Operation Wetback destabilized community enclaves that were then condemned materially and symbolically and primed for intrusive urban-renewal projects in the name of modern progress. In Chicago, the manufactured impermanence around the Mexican Near West Side that residents had fought so hard to counteract helped city leaders devalue the neighborhood and displace its inhabitants.[226] Both projects created the material dispossession that would come to shape their politics, which became anchored in the struggle for visibility, dignity, space, and opportunity.

Amid the relocation and steering of embattled Mexican residents into the Lower West Side, the mayor took steps to engage them as important constituents, although not always substantively. He signaled their visibility more often than not through the prism of symbolic acts of Cold War liberalism. In 1959, during a visit to the Mexican Near West Side by the President of Mexico Adolfo López Mateos, Daley paraded the leader through cheering crowds on Halsted Street and spoke of the long friendship between the US and Mexico, paying lip service to liberalized immigration politics when he requested that "no sentries patrol their 2,000 mile common border."[227] The mayor subsequently incorporated Mexican Chicagoans as goodwill ambassadors when the city hosted the 1959 Pan American Games, and in the years that followed he became a regular guest of honor at Mexican Independence Day celebrations, relocated to downtown.[228] But in areas of substance, the mayor withheld many of the legacy programs of the New Deal era (i.e., public housing, neighborhood infrastructure, job training, and loan programs) and instead banked on Mexican Chicagoans' ad hoc disposition to entrepreneurialism, bootstrapism, and trepidation in dealing with the state, characteristics that he conveniently read as the Mexican ethos instead of spatial survival. No sooner had the city successfully forced the dispersal of Mexicans from one area, then six miles to the south in the stockyards neighborhood, white ethnics worked to successfully contain them in another.

3 :: From the Jungle to Las Yardas

When Mayor Richard J. Daley visited the stockyards district in the summer of 1955, the Back of the Yards neighborhood was undergoing drastic changes. The slaughterhouses and meatpacking plants that had defined the community were closing and leaving the city. Racial change along with economic restructuring and diminishing sources of employment were causing longtime white residents to gradually relocate to nearby suburbs. The neighborhood, famously immortalized in Upton Sinclair's 1906 novel *The Jungle*, a melodrama about the hardships of Eastern European immigrants and the unsanitary industry of animal slaughter, was at a crossroads in 1955. Now, amid deindustrialization, not all seemed bad. During a ribbon-cutting ceremony to commemorate the opening of a new suburban-style subdivision built right in the Back of the Yards, Mayor Daley noted the neighborhood's hopefulness. The Jungle was modernizing. Destiny Manor, as the residential subdivision was called, reflected a turning point in the neighborhood's rebirth and the resilience associated with the people of the stockyards. The slaughterhouses may have closed, but the packinghouse worker ethos lived on in residents who were determined to stay and improve the neighborhood. This was the message that all parties present that day hoped to reinforce. The mayor, aldermen, neighborhood leaders, real estate agents, business owners, clergy, and residents were there to celebrate the Back of the Yards' achievement in self-help. Destiny Manor represented the manifestation of their resolve to find their own solutions through local financing of conservation projects and new home construction without municipal, state, or federal government involvement and without the heavy hand of urban renewal or land clearance.[1]

But the neighborhood's rescue strategy went beyond Destiny Manor's stylish slanted rooftops, colored-brick facades, and single-family homes on twenty-five-foot lots. Destiny Manor represented one feature of a multipronged effort designed to preserve a white neighborhood and contain racial minorities at its edges. Long before the ribbon-cutting ceremony, white community leaders, South Side politicians, and propertied interests considered the single biggest threat to be the arrival of African Americans. Black families who dared move into the working-class Southwest Side were confronted with racial violence by angry mobs of whites who created a dangerous climate of violent enforcement from the 1940s to the 1960s. Under pressure from civil rights groups and the public, white Southwest Side leaders took care to avoid endorsing their constituents' violent acts without succumbing to calls for *open occupancy*, the push to end discriminatory practices in housing in their wards. Ever resistant to racial integration, these white leaders maintained a posture of Northern liberalism while distancing themselves from Southern-style white racism. Southwest Side leaders turned to what historian Arnold Hirsch called "private means" (as opposed to government means) to reinforce segregationist goals and oppose any notion of "integration" for fear of upsetting their cottage and bungalow dwellers who stood firmly against it.[2]

The term "integration"—along with the vernacular of Cold War civil rights—fails here as a useful concept to describe the on-the-ground racial dynamics of Chicago's Southwest Side and the uniquely situated district of the Back of the Yards where the presence of Mexicans, their racialization, spatial placement, and segregation defied frameworks designed to understand Black-white conflict and to signal the aspirational politics of the Black freedom struggle. In the Back of the Yards, white anxieties around Black encroachment had at times been tempered by more animated calls for working-class and racial unity in the packinghouses, a direct result of the strength, message, and victories of the United Packinghouse Workers of America (CIO) founded in the district. But that message hardly extended beyond the slaughterhouses, despite the UPWA's extensive efforts to build an interracial housing project in the district. Moreover, with the postwar industrial collapse of the meatpacking industry, the weakening of the unions that promoted a progressive racial consciousness and countered white supremacy, and the continuous in-migration of Black and Brown persons, Chicago's segregation deepened, producing more structural inequality in employment, housing, and economic opportunity. Unemployment, deindustrialization, and the rise of minority populations rekindled long-held racial anxieties and raised alarm over the precarity of material resources.

US financial institutions and government-backed loan programs taught city whites that the fruits of postwar abundance were no longer found in the central-city neighborhoods but in the metropolitan suburbs and outlying townships, where many relocated. For those who remained, continuing to live in the central-city of a postindustrial America required innovation.[3]

All That Is Solid Melts into Innovation

Southwest Side leaders innovated and engineered a racialized "Juan and Jim Crow" landscape in the Back of the Yards to mitigate what they saw as a constant threat of Black home seekers from the South Side attempting to move westward into their district. They invested in innovative segregationist techniques that reinforced the color line by Browning it with Mexican enclaves, creating a solid zone that separated white Back of the Yards from Black Bronzeville. Leaders used race, racism, and the idea of differentiated racialized spaces to build their blockade and achieve two results: the restriction of Mexican settlement and the all-out exclusion of Black Americans. This innovative segregation technique rested on material and symbolic measures. The former were often procedural, political, and economic efforts to steer Mexicans and reshuffle white ethnics in separate residential directions. The symbolic measure was a series of decades-long cultural campaigns to promote the Back of the Yards as a hardscrabble, "all-white" district and engender a natives-versus-transients stance among locals that would instill a sense of "cultural ownership" in the district. Another innovation was to push against postwar convention that all blight would eventually lead to blockbusting and subsequently to Black settlement. Instead, white leaders, civic associations, and real estate groups contended that *some* blight, if managed carefully, could fortify neighborhood boundaries by propping up one moderately undesirable group to keep another unwanted group from moving in. It was no secret that white district leaders were reinforcing Black residential exclusion by predicating it on Mexican containment and segregation. Settlement workers, critical of these practices, described it as "a community with sharply defined boundaries beyond which Mexicans cannot move and in which the entire community is out-of-bounds to Negroes." Since Mexicans already inhabited pockets of blighted buildings on the east and west sides of the Union Stock Yards, efforts were made to limit their mobility to those restricted boundary zones while encouraging and promoting their purchase of homes in those areas. Also used throughout the 1950s and 1960s were more classically and conventionally segregationist techniques such as exercising political control of zoning; monopolizing the real estate market; and instilling among homeowners a strict discipline of holding the line—all of which created what one observer would come to call a "white little island."[4]

Mexicans, however, formed part of a heterogeneous, although contentious, ethno-racial community consisting of mixed settlement from the moment they first began to arrive in the area in 1915. By the 1920s, there were several thousand in the stockyards district. During the interwar years, Polish, Lithuanian, and Mexican families predominated, contentiously living side by side even as they moved in different social and economic directions. Eastern European immigrants and their US-born offspring clamored to escape to better areas further south and west, while Mexicans were crammed into every unit that Poles and Lithuanians vacated. These groups swelled the dilapidated cottages and tenements that land developer and homebuilder Samuel Eberly Gross had proudly sold as "the working man's reward" in 1891. The rows of sturdy cottage homes across from the yards had declined ever since their first purchasers—Germans and the Irish—began moving out in the early twentieth century. Surveying the neighborhood in 1940, Eunice Felter, a graduate student from the University of Chicago, noted the area of small two-story wooden structures as "very badly deteriorated." Those restricted to this area behind the stockyards occupied the lowest position in the slaughterhouse pecking order, in contrast to workers who had skilled positions, higher pay, and better housing away from the stockyards.[5]

Yet their shared class position did little to stymy the regular, violent clashes between Poles and Mexicans over occupancy, employment, and social relations. Economist Paul S. Taylor documented this history of violence, writing in 1932 that "methods [whites undertook] of making their hostility effective included physical assaults, and even killings, smashing of windows or similar attacks upon property," making a "common practice" out of fending off Mexicans. When Mexicans did manage to find housing, it was often in the most dilapidated and overcrowded buildings, where even then "they faced considerable violence from local neighbors," as historian Paul Street documented. As conditions grew more cramped during and after World War II, neighbors engaged in acts of arson such as *burnouts* (torching buildings) to terrorize Mexicans—a practice that had, until then, been reserved for African Americans. Along with violence, organized protests were also utilized. In 1943, when Alfonso and Mercedes Moyado and their three children tried to purchase a home in the district after years of renting, they encountered a terrifying resistance. Hundreds of organized white residents drew up a petition of signatures and walked it over to the local savings and loan institution that was to underwrite the Moyados' purchase. Residents threatened to withdraw their money from the bank if the Mexican family received the loan. Fearing this customer backlash, the bank capitulated. Two years later, in 1945, congressional hearings in Chicago for the Fair Employment Practice Commission gave UPWA's research director, Lyle Cooper, an opportunity to testify about the local racial animosity and organized resistance that, as he expressed, caused Black packinghouse workers to admit that for Mexicans, "housing restrictions [were] even more severe" than those imposed on them on the South Side.[6]

These episodes of anti-Mexican violence and inter-ethnic tension from the 1910s to the 1940s were ultimately unsuccessful in securing an all-white enclave. Moreover, much to the chagrin of locals, Southwest Side leaders and property interests began openly helping—or at least not obstructing—Mexicans to establish a firmer foundation in the district. Real estate agents, hoping to squeeze mortgages out of dilapidated and sagging buildings, began courting Mexican buyers. "This past year or two, two or three families have bought homes," reported a settlement staff member in 1944, "real estate companies are urging them to buy. One company came to the settlement and asked us to tell [Mexicans] there were houses for sale. It must mean our other national groups are or will be buying houses farther south and west." Southwest Side leaders and those with vested interests discretely took control of Mexican settlement and anchored it in place. While facing considerable backlash from Poles and Lithuanians, Southwest Side leaders operated under the reasonable premise that all desirable "ethnic succession" headed in a southwesterly direction. Leaders took the initiative to drive Eastern European families out of the slum and into better housing, but not out of the Back of the Yards, which local leaders continued to fear for decades.[7]

Mexicans were steered into a four-to-five-block perimeter directly behind the stockyards. In the 1930s and early 1940s, they attempted to establish a church of their own after local Irish, Polish, and Lithuanian Catholic churches repeatedly refused to "bury, marry, or baptize Mexicans." Hopeful parishioners rented storefronts within the strict boundaries prescribed to Mexicans, an area filled with so many taverns and saloons that the Claretian fathers were initially reluctant to support it. One hundred Mexican families met in a butcher's storefront to discuss securing a parcel of land large enough to build a church comparable to the other Catholic churches in the district. The first catechism class was taught inside a small flat where packinghouse worker Encarnación Chico and his wife, Juana, lived. So many Mexican children were spotted in the backyard that the landlords were called in to break it apart. The families soon discovered their options were limited financially to small storefronts and by a strict unwritten policy of informal racial covenants. Moreover, the sweat equity poured into every storefront they rented to practice their faith came at their own expense. "We'd rent a place that was in such bad repair no one else would have it. We'd fix it up and then we'd lose the lease. We've been doing that for seven years," one parishioner told a reporter in 1941. Finally, in November 1945 they realized their dream when they celebrated the opening of the Immaculate Heart of Mary Vicariate ("La Capilla") on 4515 South Ashland Avenue. The opening of La Capilla was seen as a major victory and source of great pride for the hundreds of stockyards families that collected funds, helped with materials and labor, and cooked and sold food for the church effort.[8]

If forging bonds of belonging was one explanation for the establishment of important community institutions, then the segregationist politics embedded in the church's placement disguised other motivations. The church's location helped reinforce the colonia's boundaries, marking the spatial restriction/segregation of Mexicans in the Back of the Yards. Like a signpost for visitors and a reminder to locals, the church's placement appeared "natural" while cloaking the white leadership's deliberate boundary-making and boundary-shaping efforts by endorsing its location and supplying it with financial donations. Ashland Avenue, the main thoroughfare that bordered the perimeter of the Mexican colonia, became increasingly useful to local interests, politicians, and leaders as a site of innovation—a place to design a differentiated racial space that was neither white nor Black. Ashland Avenue would come to signal a battleground, a buffer, a border, and a wall. While the once solid components of an industrial community—industry, immigration, labor, housing, and religion—melted in transformation or were reconstituted in an era of economic restructuring, an all-consuming effort was waged to innovate the practice of segregation and assure the protection of the Back of the Yards' "white little island."[9]

The Global South Stockyards and Localist Democracy

As local leaders tinkered with their racial and spatial barricade, in the foreground stood the historical site of American capitalism that brought these workers to Chicago to begin with: the Union Stock Yards, with over four hundred acres of cattle and pig pens, slaughterhouses, boiling vats, and packing and canning plants, all mobilized to supply meat and other animal by-products to the world. Inside its gates, between 1936 and 1943, packinghouse workers led relentless organizing drives against the "Big Four" meat-packing firms: Armour, Swift, Wilson, and Cudahy. The labor militancy and radicalism of the CIO, bolstered by Franklin D. Roosevelt's New Deal, engineered these drives to address social and economic barriers that workers, including workers of color, faced. As the previous chapter recounted, the labor successes in the slaughterhouse rested not only on the CIO's militancy but also on the radical imagination of Global South workers, Black and Brown migrant laborers in the stockyards who helped raise the stakes by pushing the union to address its nonwhite rank-and-file workforce's needs. As these workers moved across the Americas, they were economically displaced and repositioned by global capitalism and found themselves subjugated by white supremacy in the industrial north. Together, the CIO and the New Deal promoted cultural pluralism to challenge the white nativism ingrained in older labor unions and to unite workers across race, ethnicity, and nationality. These efforts were met with varying degrees of success and, at times, failure. To Black and Brown labor migrants, their identities as racialized workers from faraway regions such as Alabama, Mississippi, Michoacán, Jalisco, and the Caribbean became central to their struggle for recognition and for their fight for critical antidiscriminatory measures in the workplace and housing. This struggle resonated in the violent and segregated neighborhoods adjacent to the stockyards—particularly in the "legendary, racist, white-ethnic Back of the Yards," as historian Paul Street points out, where workers who aligned with the CIO waged a campaign "to abolish racial terror and discrimination." Here, the local adage from the 1919 race riots, "No Negro better show his face west of Ashland Avenue," remained true.[10]

African Americans and Mexicans who held the most menial jobs, often in unsanitary conditions, were the last hired and first fired, a common practice employers used during the Depression to prevent workers of color from accumulating seniority. As Jesse Perez, a CIO steward and one of a few butchers of Mexican descent in the Armour plant, told an interviewer, "I found myself one of the first to get laid off along with other Mexicans and Negroes." Black and Brown Global South migrants were also more attuned to recognizing the divide between the interracial mobilization of union members in the slaughterhouse and persistent racist attitudes in the neighborhoods. Perez saw it both as an injustice that he and his family were one of the "few Mexicans living in my immediate neighborhood," an area of "mostly Poles and Lithuanians," he explained. "The majority of my people are in quite the same social and economic position as the Negro,"

Perez said, underscoring Black and Brown workers' shared struggles. As important as it was to advance racial, class, and workplace issues, the question remained whether the union battle could link the struggle to reform capitalism with the fight for antiracist policies and practices while achieving mass support. To the dismay of Black and Brown packinghouse workers and their supporters, their vision of Global South radicalism—an anti-imperial, multiracial, working-class struggle against capitalism—failed to destroy the structures of segregation that upheld Juan and Jim Crow in wartime and postwar Chicago. The cultural pluralism the CIO and the New Deal promoted had limited impact in the domestic sphere of white workers' lives, thus calling into question the unity of worker culture when it came to race in the neighborhoods.[11]

Nevertheless, another kind of "movement" did emerge, one that substituted the visions of Global South radicals for a localist fervor in the service of community action. The architects behind this movement were a University of Chicago–trained criminologist and delinquency expert with the Institute for Juvenile Research, Saul D. Alinsky, and a park director with blue-collar roots in the stockyard neighborhoods, Joseph B. Meegan. In 1938, sensing that the district was on edge because of the union drive and the accompanying antilabor violence that threatened to culminate in open warfare on the streets of an already derelict, depression-ravaged area, the two men set out to build alliances that would bolster the aims of the packinghouse workers. Alinsky had been attracted to the David-and-Goliath struggle in the Yards and was motivated to help channel its enthusiasm and harness the spirit and rhetoric of the CIO and the New Deal, two institutions he cared about deeply. Alinsky also hoped to realize an ambitious agenda of his own: to organize everyday working people living in what he termed "industrial areas." He had grown frustrated with the narrowness of the sociological study of crime and delinquency and considered it flawed if not taken as symptoms of deeper, more collective political, economic, and social realities. In the storied Back of the Yards, Alinsky found the perfect setting of a downtrodden, poor, immigrant district, one that, as he would later write, had come to symbolize "in the eyes of the American people a byword for disease, delinquency, deterioration, dirt, and dependency." It was in this community, he would argue, that the need and challenge to enliven a spirit of grassroots democracy was at its greatest.[12]

With the help of the "homegrown" Meegan, Alinsky launched the Back of the Yards Neighborhood Council (BYNC) in 1939. In a paper published two years later, "Community Analysis and Organization," Alinsky outlined

his theories for a community organization built on uniting "organized labor" and "organized religion," two major constituencies already within
the fold of the CIO and the New Deal. The BYNC quickly became noteworthy for its ability to get priests and parishioners from different national
parishes—Polish, Slavic, Lithuanian, and Irish churches, for instance, that
had been dismissive of or outright hostile to each other—to work with trade
unionists and local merchants to address common community problems.
Meegan became the "executive secretary" and Alinsky the "technical consultant"; and in a move to solidify its legitimacy in the predominantly Catholic neighborhood, they appointed the auxiliary bishop of Chicago, Rev.
Bernard J. Sheil, as honorary chairman. This was paramount to shoring up
community support for the union and for the BYNC, since, by selecting a
Catholic bishop as BYNC chairman, it assured the Catholic residents that
the group would not tolerate the influence of communism. Within months
the BYNC mobilized over 185 neighborhood groups to become dues-paying
members. They summoned delegates from the various groups to an annual
meeting, or "community congress," where they voted on an agenda and
various committees to begin attacking local matters of juvenile delinquency,
public health, and recreation, and to create free lunch programs for school-
children. This formed the basis of the BYNC and the vehicle for their brand
of localist democracy that Alinsky and Meegan helped stoke. At its most
basic level, it was a civics education for a blue-collar district on ways to access state-sponsored resources to help solve social and material problems
and wield local control.[13]

But mere organizing was not enough. To achieve their goals, Alinsky and
Meegan used high-pressure tactics, including demonstrations, boycotts,
the press, and public shaming of powerful adversaries and elected officials.
Their notoriety (and influence) multiplied when they warred with the Chicago political machine and the professional social-service establishment—
two early battles the BYNC won. Alinsky proved masterful at propagan-
dizing and manipulating the press to get favorable coverage and cast his
enemies in a negative light. With each victory, the BYNC and its motto,
"We the people will work out our destiny," ignited an urban do-it-yourself
movement across industrial cities that gained the attention of the national
press, which amplified the narrative that in the Back of the Yards, democracy was in the hands of the average citizen, not powerful companies or
political parties. Before long, Alinsky spread his "Back of the Yards movement" to other meatpacking cities under the umbrella of his new group, the
Industrial Areas Foundation (IAF).[14]

In Chicago, the BYNC borrowed from the progressive rhetoric of cultural pluralism to promote the district as a polyglot world of different groups finding common ground to improve their communities in the name of localist democracy. "The impossible is happening [in] Back of the Yards in Chicago," wrote *Survey Graphic* in 1940, "representatives from the local Chamber of Commerce, the American Legion Post, the AFL, the CIO, the Catholic Church—Protestants, Jews, Irish, Slovaks, Mexicans, Poles—are gathering together in a new kind of attempt to solve the problems of a community." Although the BYNC presented the district as a site of cultural, religious, and racial tolerance (their printed literature often used the phrase "regardless of race, color, or creed"), to those who actually lived in or were familiar with the district, that was far from reality. Real estate agents openly practiced racial discrimination through restrictive covenants, and white mobs could be mobilized at a moment's notice to terrorize any Black family attempting to move in. On different occasions, Saul Alinsky himself admitted that the Back of the Yards was a "powder keg" on the verge of a race riot. Economically, the district wrestled with unemployment and petty crime connected to poverty, two issues that fueled anxieties around the threat of racial minorities. Yet confident narratives about overcoming local bigotries remained important to Alinsky, no matter how far from the truth they were.[15]

Since most of the area consisted of an Eastern European white ethnic population that was fiercely anti-Black and, to a lesser extent, anti-Mexican, Alinsky made some attempts to quell racial anxieties toward the latter group and, in the process, lend credibility to his "melting pot" image of the BYNC. Alinsky presented those of the Mexican colonia as rightful members of the Back of the Yards community and the Council: During BYNC assemblies, prominently hung CIO posters featured Mexican American girls dressed in ethnic *china poblana* outfits with the PWOC and SWOC logos printed underneath; Mexican packinghouse workers and active trade unionists were seated as delegates right next to Alinsky during BYNC functions; and the BYNC gave financial support to La Capilla. "Mexicans are a minority group and poor," the BYNC repeated to reporters, "so the whole community chipped in to buy them a church." These were small but symbolic gestures designed to convey to the BYNC's white constituents (the majority of the district) that, like them, Mexicans had sacrificed on behalf of labor and were devout Roman Catholics and members of the community. Joseph Meegan helped with this messaging. He grew up in Fuller Park, a subsection of the larger Back of the Yards district that had been Irish but by the 1940s contained an enclave of Mexicans clustered around Wentworth Avenue and 46th Street, a racial borderline. He knew many of the Mexican families there personally. Meegan also knew that Mexicans were the most poorly sheltered in the district, occupying most of the dilapidated housing adjacent to the stockyards.[16]

The BYNC photographed Mexicans' living conditions inside their homes and sleeping quarters, focusing on the children's environment. This visual documentation complemented the BYNC's descriptions of the daily lives of the people they organized. Since homes in other parts of the district were in better condition, Mexican life in the Yards provided the authenticity that the BYNC needed to tell their story of uplift for "the welfare of all residents of that community, regardless of their race, color, creed, so that they may all have the opportunity to find health, happiness, and security through the democratic way of life."[17] In short, the BYNC movement needed Mexican Back of the Yarders to authenticate Alinsky and Meegan's message of realizing New Deal social democracy in the neighborhoods. They also

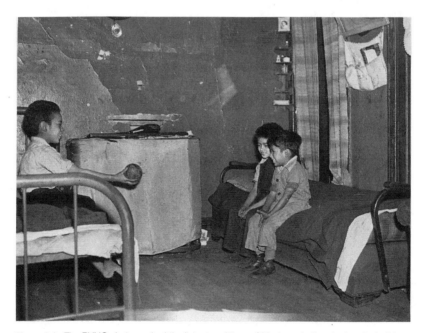

Figure 3.1. The BYNC photographed the living conditions of Mexicans in the stockyards. In this photo, smiling children are juxtaposed with the meager furnishings of their sleeping quarters and the cracking paint on the wall, described by staff as "Back of the Yards children at their home—typical of this section." (Image source: box 171, folder 1738, Industrial Areas Foundation Records, Special Collections and University Archives, University of Illinois at Chicago.)

hoped their embrace of the Mexican colonia would engender acceptance among the predominantly white ethnic district. While this "acceptance" would remain nominal and precarious throughout the twentieth century, the effort allowed Alinsky and Meegan to project the ambiguously progressive rhetoric of the New Deal without violating the homogeneity that white Back of the Yarders desired.[18]

The BYNC's borrowed rhetoric of cultural pluralism carried little significance in the everyday lives of Mexicans compared to the more transformational dynamics the Second World War created. During the war, President Roosevelt called upon industrial cities like Chicago to help produce the "Arsenal of Democracy" to support the Allies in the war effort. Overnight, meatpacking plants became national-defense facilities with provisions to only employ American citizens. This wartime policy immediately forced Mexican packinghouse workers to become naturalized or lose the jobs they had held for many years. Before long, they were sending their sons off to the battlefields of Europe to fight on behalf of the Allies and Western democracy. Hundreds of Mexican Americans from the stockyards were conscripted into the armed services. Enrique and Valeria Venegas of 1417 West 47th Street, both packinghouse workers and parents to thirteen children, sent their four eldest sons off to war. Lorenzo Lopez of 4530 South Laflin Street, an immigrant packinghouse worker, joined the service along with his son Eloy. Beatrice Gonzalez of Justine Street joined the war effort through the Women's Army Corps. But while war service gave Mexican Back of the Yarders a sense of pride and belonging, it did little to mitigate segregation, inequality, and racial violence on the home front. For instance, when Pvt. Monico C. Amador of Fuller Park returned home as a decorated soldier for his bravery during the Normandy landings, he discovered that his father had been gunned down on 47th Street by a white man who hated Mexicans.[19]

Returning war veterans raised families and contributed to building new ethnic, social, and civic organizations and clubs to serve their postwar lives. In 1946, Monico Amador, the Venegas brothers (Henry, Aurelius, Alfonso, and Daniel), and more than seventy-five Mexican American veterans from the Back of the Yards formed the Incas SAC (social-athletic club) to "interest local Mexican youth in organized political, social and athletic movements." The Incas used La Capilla's social hall for meetings and events, as did other groups. La Capilla furthered its role in the colonia following the war. In 1947, Rev. Raymond Sunye wrote, "We have strongly encouraged the various parish societies to sponsor socials that the Mexican youth of the neighborhood will not have to frequent public dance halls and the local taverns for their amusement." Hoping to fulfill the leisure and recreational needs of the colonia, Sunye reported, "The parish sponsors a boxing team as well as two basketball and baseball teams." La Capilla's social hall was also used as a shelter: "We have given both room and board gratis to the 'Brazeros' (workers) recently immigrated from Mexico. All are presently employed in the stock yards and are under our supervision."[20]

The ambitions of the postwar generation of Mexican Back of the Yarders often clashed with the residential restrictions they faced throughout the 1940s. Before 1940, no more than a dozen Mexican families lived west of Ashland Avenue in the district. The majority lived east of Ashland and north of 47th Street. One *Chicago Tribune* article displayed a fascination with the dozens of Mexican children concentrated on the corner of Laflin and 45th Streets, with a positive headline, "Big Families Fill Small Neighborhood Area." This reality frustrated the growing aspirations of Mexican Back of the Yarders who desired access to better living opportunities. The Southwest Side real estate firms, full-fledged members of the BYNC, continued to enforce residential steering even as the BYNC pushed a progressive message on housing and cultural pluralism. The combined factors of residential restrictions and enclave overcrowding further strained housing conditions. Moreover, the slaughterhouses and packinghouses became more dependent on Mexican labor to replace white workers who were moving on to better jobs, creating a dire need for more housing. Yet the undesirability of the overcrowded homes forced many arriving migrants to settle outside of the stockyards district including Pilsen and the Near West Side. As Mexican immigration increased in Chicago during the 1940s and 1950s, residential population growth in the Back of the Yards was disproportionately low, consisting of an estimated 11,000 people of Mexican descent (a conservative estimate) in a district of 125,000 people by 1953.[21]

Although Black and Brown packinghouse workers forged a militant culture to break down racial and gender barriers within the stockyards, out in the neighborhoods, breaking down housing segregation was more challenging. Still, Alinsky and Meegan thought the message of cultural pluralism undergirding the packinghouse struggle could be repurposed to empower a working-class white ethnic localism. The BYNC established itself through an effective campaign drawing on the language of cultural pluralism, do-it-yourself democracy, and local control, but they avoided using it against housing segregation. "The Council's call for unity was not meant to disturb the racial housing patterns," one Alinsky biographer described years later. Shaming white Back of the Yarders for their bigotry was not in Alinsky's best interest. In the eyes of the BYNC, pursuing a localist democracy did not depend on attacking segregation; thus, a movement of ordinary residents organizing on behalf of their own self-interest remained a noble mission. The press, academics, and community organizers lauded the BYNC's organized localism, particularly its ability to challenge powerful adversaries and empower ordinary citizens. But in the years that followed, the BYNC distanced itself from its progressive and radical roots and came to define its organization as a mostly white ethnic and Catholic group looking to protect its neighborhood from change and outsiders.[22]

Industrial Restructuring and the Scripts of Condemnation

No sooner had the blue-collar residents of the Back of the Yards forced a momentary realignment of the power relations in their district and reinvigorated a spirit of dignity rooted in industrial culture than the economic rug was pulled out from underneath them. In 1952, Swift and Company shuttered its hog-slaughtering operations after showing a significant decrease in profits. Soon, more meatpacking plants closed and relocated their operations to Missouri, Kansas, Nebraska, and Iowa. Smaller midwestern towns and southern cities lured packing companies away from Chicago with the promises of nonexistent unions, cheaper labor, lower taxes, and higher profitability. Trucks and the new Interstate Highway System made it easier to transport cattle and hogs to and from smaller packing plants to the distributor. Armour, Swift, Wilson, and Cudahy were no longer beholden to the aging one-stop-shop system in the Union Stock Yards. This galvanized the BYNC to defend its people from a devastating economic blow. Its leading spokesperson, Joseph Meegan, gave congressional testimony on the implications of economic restructuring for the people of the Back of the Yards. "It's a disaster," he told members of the US House of Representatives. Small businesses were facing "financial ruin and near bankruptcy." "The exodus of the packinghouse industry," he told the committee, "has brought about the beginning of the end." The outlook was bleak. Meegan pursued government resources, even asking Congress to create an aid package to support small businesses in declining industrial communities like theirs. More importantly, the BYNC and business leaders hoped to get the government to pressure city officials to condemn the Union Stock Yards and rebuild, with grave implications for those who stood in their crosshairs.[23]

Industrial flight from Packingtown cast most of the Mexican enclave as condemned land that, if razed and improved, could be used to attract new industry. In the ensuing years since the first plant closures, policy debates centered on what to do with the Union Stock Yards' 136 acres of buildings and infrastructure, particularly the packing and slaughtering plants. Mexicans occupied the area adjacent to the stockyards in the 45th Street and Ashland Avenue vicinity (hereafter referred to as Las Yardas). Back of the Yards district leaders began seeing Las Yardas not as a residential area but as a valuable appendage to be added to the rest of the former stockyards and pitched to new companies. Many, including Joseph Meegan, saw this as part of a larger, potentially valuable area if the "building monstrosities [that] were left abandoned" could be condemned and razed. Throughout the 1950s and 1960s, the BYNC lobbied local and federal government to address their economic plight. Leaders from the Back of the Yards carefully navigated their congressional lobbying as they sought reasonable but restrained federal intervention and resources to remake Packingtown. In this new vision of Packingtown, light industries such as clothing, candy, plastics, and electronics-manufacturing firms would relocate there and operate in an improved, sleek, sanitary setting. New firms would benefit from the nearby expressways and Midway Airport to transport their goods around the world. With convenient transportation provisions already in place, new firms could draw from the available labor supply of Back of the Yards residents.[24]

The ensuing discussions placed Mexican Back of the Yarders on the receiving end of two condemning logics. On one end, most white Back of the Yarders considered Las Yardas an eyesore, and sacrificing it was justified to modernize Packingtown. On the other end, that Mexicans occupied the oldest and most dilapidated section in the district, which most other immigrant groups were able to escape, generated negative connotations about them. After two generations, Mexicans were unable to live in nicer sections of the Back of the Yards, and whites saw this as a result of the group's own shortcomings, not structural racism, residential steering, or systems of segregation and containment. These condemnations would have lingering material and cultural implications. Despite the BYNC's earlier attempts to include Mexicans in their "culture of unity," many longtime Eastern European residents did not consider Mexicans a permanent part of the district. They saw Mexicans as undesirable and temporary, almost as seasonal workers, perpetuating the age-old anti-Mexican racial trope of "birds of passage." They lived next to "a vacant wasteland" and did not represent the workforce that new corporations would want. To local whites, Las Yardas stood outside the bounds of the BYNC's bootstrap moral philosophy of self-uplift; they perceived Mexicans as the opposite of self-reliant and considered their impoverishment to be a roadblock to modernization.[25]

The spatial restructuring depreciated the district's once-mighty economic value. However, the employment loss affected whites and Mexicans differently. Historian Dominic Pacyga has shown that before 1939, around 80 percent of white ethnic families "depended directly on the packing industry for their livelihoods." By contrast, during the 1950s, many white workers had aged out of the strenuous packinghouse jobs or found better employment in cleaner industries. Young whites of Polish, Slavic, and Lithuanian ancestry depended less on the packinghouse jobs and sought better employment opportunities in the suburbs and downtown. Many attained college educations and moved out of the city entirely. By 1950, white population growth in Chicago had stalled and decreased steadily throughout the century. But not every neighborhood experienced a sudden exodus of whites. Many older whites kept their properties, bucking the trend of white flight or at least delaying it by moving further south and west of the district, even amidst rising property taxes and dwindling city services. Proximity to their parishes, structural rootedness, limited finances, and age were some of the main factors.[26]

African Americans and Mexicans were the majority of the workforce in the twilight years (1950s and 1960s) of the Union Stock Yards, as historian Dominic Pacyga has shown, and bore the brunt of the hardships that spatial restructuring caused. Although the population of Mexican residents living in the Back of the Yards remained comparatively small, the number of Mexican workers in the stockyards remained high. This meant that Mexicans from other wards worked in the stockyards until its final days, while those in the district were transitioning away from stockyards work. Mexican Back of the Yarders survived the plant closures by finding employment in other industries such as food processing, textiles, and electronics manufacturing. Nevertheless, their adaptability to the decentralization of industrial production combined with their racialized residential restriction made them highly exploitable. This manifested in several ways, including low wages, lack of education and vocational training, and little to no opportunities for wealth accumulation or savings.

In 1953, the Mexican American Council of Chicago (MAC) noted this underemployment and was pleased to discover that the packinghouse union locals were offering Mexican workers "welfare and financial assistance." While MAC sometimes relied on tired explanations of language and culture as reasons for Mexicans' limited social and economic mobility, the council also pointed to structural discrimination that exacerbated their underemployment: "His income is low, his employment security uncertain, and his acceptance by other ethnic groups in doubt. . . . [J]udged by even the minimum American standards of health and decency, he is in general 'ill-housed, ill-clothed and ill-fed.'" These descriptions echoed the stigmas that Alinsky had captured in 1940, but now they rang doubly true for Mexicans. In an era of American suburbanization and growing earning power, Mexican Back of the Yarders were inheriting poverty rather than wealth. These conditions overlapped with larger Cold War era narratives that casually associated Mexicans with "wetbacks" and "criminals." This ascribed identity left an enduring portrait for white Back of the Yarders to justify doubling down on the racial border they made of Ashland Avenue, no longer to prevent Blacks from moving in, but out of fear that their neighborhoods would be run down not by capital flight or economic restructuring but by poor Mexicans. This economic, spatial, and cultural condemnation was the longest-lasting outcome of meatpacking's spatial restructuring on Mexican Back of the Yarders. The spatial hardening of class, race, and immigrant distinctions in the postwar years mapped two prominent scripts of condemnation onto the geography of the district: the white Back of the Yards west of Ashland Avenue was American and hardworking; the Mexican colonia east of Ashland and north of 47th Street was immigrant, illegal, foreign, and relief dependent.[27]

"They Want the Mexican of the Back of the Yards to Become Something"

Although Mexican Back of the Yarders faced condemnation that often materialized into underemployment, housing, and educational inequality, residents were not deterred from making place in "the jungle." The four-to-five city streets adjacent to the stockyards—El Barrio de las Empacadoras, as they were known—although never fully homogenously Mexican, were much more Mexicanized in the 1950s than in previous decades. Here, a transgenerational community of families created a world of their own. It consisted of people (peasants, proletariats, journalists, radicals, conservatives, and the religiously devout) who fled the Mexican Revolution of 1910; immigrants who arrived on the heels of the 1919 Chicago Race Riot and the 1924 Johnson-Reed Act as recruited strikebreakers and later CIO pioneers; and children of these immigrants, Chicagoans whose young lives were shaped by the transgenerational traumas of migration, repatriation/ deportation, and capitalist-racist exploitation. Perhaps the longest-lasting influences on this community were war and peacetime. Families' participation through military service in World War II and the Korean War helped frame their worldview through a lens of belonging-through-militarism and acceptance of American values of meritocracy, capitalism, and anticommunism. This was a shift away from the labor radicalism and transnational sentiments of Global South workers in the slaughterhouses during the 1930s. The erosion of neighborhood support for the UPWA's District 1, particularly its civil rights and immigrant rights advocacy, further illustrated this shift. Nevertheless, even as the Mexican Back of the Yards embraced its newfound US patriotism, the neighborhood was suffering more immediate conditions of poverty, delinquency, and youth gangs.

Alleviation from these pressing urban conditions was the primary mission of the University of Chicago Settlement House, a large, four-story brick building where local residents could enjoy respite from the outside world of crowded homes, barren recreational resources, and volatile ethnic boundaries. Mary E. McDowell, the progressive social reformer and suffragette, founded the settlement house in 1894 to help Irish and German immigrants with employment, Americanization, alleviation of unsanitary conditions, and the promotion of public health. Since then, waves of immigrant groups—including Poles, Lithuanians, Slovaks, and Mexicans—drawn to the promise of packinghouse jobs had been the basis of its growing clientele. The free services and programs the University of Chicago Settlement provided were supported by the philanthropy and fundraising efforts of Hyde Park's university elite, including faculty, administrators, and socially conscientious spouses.[28]

Throughout the first half of the twentieth century, the settlement house's approach evolved from Victorian compassion and welfare into professional, dispassionate social work. A live-in staff of social workers, volunteers, and a head resident served toddlers, the elderly, and everyone in between. The progressive reformers' legacy and preconceptions of American democracy were instilled into the clientele and its programs and activities. "The overall goal is the teaching of democratic principles," the settlement house reports explained, "and the development of leadership." Behind the settlement's doors, poor Catholic immigrants and their offspring were exposed to the sensibilities of New England Protestant privilege exemplified in the decorative living room with cherrywood paneling and a glass chandelier, fireplace, reading chairs, a library, and a piano. There were also girls' and boys' gymnasiums, showers, and multiple recreation rooms. It was here that Mexicans organized during the 1930s over matters of labor unionism, anti-imperialism, and Mexican nationalism—sometimes at the displeasure of settlement house staff, whose job it was to assimilate immigrants. One such immigrant, Enrique Venegas, a young packinghouse worker from Zacatecas, attended meetings of the radical Frente Popular Mexicano inside the settlement, as did his wife, Valeria Venegas from Guanajuato, who worked the nightshift as a sausage trimmer and also served as secretary of her own group, the Club de Damas Mexicanas. Their political agendas contrasted with the staff's Americanization goals; nevertheless, the settlement's recreation rooms, childcare, job referrals, and other resources were critical to families like the Venegases and many others. By World War II, the settlement house had established more direct programming with immigrants' offspring through its sponsorship of social and athletic clubs, camping trips, and other programs that instilled the values of American citizenship, helped curb juvenile delinquency, and reduced interethnic strife.[29]

In 1945, the BYNC took aim at the University of Chicago Settlement in a series of public attacks that challenged its jurisdiction and effectiveness in addressing the problem of youth gangs and juvenile delinquency and questioned its legitimacy in the district. In this turf war, Alinsky criticized the entire settlement-house movement as a cadre of professional social workers who were content "adjusting people to difficult situations" but not to developing tools to change those situations. "They come to get these people 'adjusted,'" he wrote, "so they will live in hell and like it too. It would be difficult to conceive of a higher form of social treason." By contrast, Alinsky, the criminologist, promoted himself as the street intellectual from the slums with modern ideas to empower young people, not serve a clientele of dependency, as he believed the settlement was doing. Alinsky, the BYNC, and by extension, his Industrial Areas Foundation sought to control the arena of youth delinquency and the windfall of federal and state funding that would increase in the postwar era. The BYNC also went after the settlement house's four-story building, demanding that the University of Chicago sell it to the council for one dollar, which it refused to do.

Alinsky utilized his press connections to criticize the social-work establishment and dislodge it from the neighborhood while crafting the BYNC's image as champions of independence and self-sufficiency. One favorable article in *Women's Home Companion* explained: "So who redeemed Packingtown, they asked. Not college professors, helpful as they can be, not lady bountifuls and, good as they are, not social workers, but themselves!

Packingtown's workers. Sons and daughters of older workers." Agnes E. Meyer, writing for the *Washington Post*, amplified the BYNC's criticism of the settlement when she editorialized: "The Chicago University Settlement Trustees remain in an obstinate, righteous isolation, indifferent to the creative activity and the dynamic democracy swirling about their disintegrating institution. Seen through the eyes of the surrounding population, who are struggling for dignity, self-respect and self-expression, the Chicago University Settlement makes social work look like the meaningless plaything or the hypocritical subterfuge of a morally bankrupt civilization." In their campaign to discredit the settlement, BYNC leaders Joseph Meegan and Bishop Sheil delivered perhaps the most damning charge, accusing the settlement of being outsiders who violated the moral codes of a Catholic community with every distribution of contraceptives to women and girls.[30]

Although these attacks on the "disintegrating institution" raised doubts among its funders about its future, the University of Chicago Settlement was hardly ready to close its doors. The settlement remained surrounded by a dense Mexican enclave containing hundreds of youths who enjoyed its programs, resources, and amenities. Eighty percent of the participants lived within four blocks of the settlement house. This reality helped demonstrate the institution's legitimate need as its new leaders, Bert H. Boerner (head resident) and Daniel De Falco (assistant head resident), enhanced its delinquency-prevention efforts through programming for Mexican and Polish youth. They offered alternatives to joining street gangs by organizing recreational and social activities, such as dances, baseball games, bowling leagues, and other events. While their programming centered on nurturing the democratic values of liberal white Protestant culture and stripping away the vestiges of "immigrantism," it also expanded activities to prevent juvenile delinquency. By contrast, while Alinsky focused on the criminalization of youth of color to organize against police brutality, exemplified in his work with African Americans in Kenwood and Mexican Americans in California, he neglected to do so in the Back of the Yards. Thus, the settlement house filled a void for local youth that the BYNC, despite its grandstanding in the press, could not. Indeed, the settlement's programs were not designed to counteract the scripts of condemnation that Mexican youth faced, but they did offer resources not available anywhere else. Moreover, the settlement staff were much more familiar with the problems of Mexican youth and the criminal justice system since they lived in the community.[31]

During the 1950s, Boerner and De Falco helped mend relations with the BYNC, becoming dues-paying members of the council while continuing to make the University of Chicago Settlement a transformational space for neighborhood youth. They ushered in the postwar years with a commitment to stem nativism, bigotry, and intra-Catholic divisions among the children of immigrants and to socialize them through competitive sports, recreation, writing, and art. What emerged was a Latino generation that forged their own bonds to Chicago's progressive traditions while rooted in working-class culture punctuated by family gatherings, church activities, dances, and sports. Dozens of ethnically mixed social clubs were formed under Boerner's and De Falco's directorships to curb ethnic hostilities and to build organizational and leadership skills. Clubs such as the Ospreys, Unicorns, Feds, and many others became avenues into adulthood and civic life. Annual camping trips to Camp Farr in rural Chesterton, Indiana, were organized to escape the congested urban neighborhood, to teach kids how to work with farm animals, and to breathe the open air in an atmosphere of inter-ethnic teamwork. Back at the settlement house, popular dances were held in the girls' gymnasium with live rhythm-and-blues, boogie-woogie, and rock-and-roll bands, often performed by Black artists from nearby Bronzeville, such as Jump Jackson and His Band. The settlement house sparked many inter-ethnic teenage romances that led to marriages between white ethnics and Mexican Americans. These wedding ceremonies often took place in La Capilla, since many of the priests in the Eastern European churches sternly disapproved of these unions and considered them akin to racial miscegenation. While the settlement remained as invested in Americanization as in erasing ethnic tensions, there was little doubt that the institution was being influenced by its immediate cultural environs too. One of its best basketball teams, the Guadalupes, featured white and Mexican American players; tamale fundraisers were organized to help the settlement pay bills, and citizenship parties were celebrated with piñatas.[32]

While the trustees of the University of Chicago Settlement maintained a country-club-like culture and were hostile to having neighborhood representation on the board of directors, Boerner and De Falco remained committed to the settlement's users. Neighborhood youth that grew up as settlement-goers, like Adel Martinez and Ray Alcala, eventually became staff members and oversaw many of the social clubs. Boerner and De Falco hired some of the first African American and Asian American graduate student workers. These staffing decisions were also intended to develop high expectations among settlement-goers to do well in high school and to promote academic achievement, producing some of the first college-educated

THE UNICORN COEDS

Back Row: R. Lopez, R. Alba, F. Venegas, R. Kucinski, L. Maestra, D. Cortez,
    D. Ramirez, E. Castenada, T. Doyle, J. Lopez.
Middle Row: J. Smercak, J. Spinner, R. Garcilaso, R. Jacobczyk, C. Lindsay,
    T. Palenik, S. Miller, I. Lopez.
Front Row: R. Spinner, J. Gallardo, L. Alba, F. Maestra, J. Cortez, R. Cedano.

— 5 —

Figure 3.2. Dozens of social and athletic clubs were formed with the help of the University of Chicago (Mary McDowell) Settlement House, drawn from the Back of the Yards' ethnic mix of Mexican American and Eastern European American youth and young adults. Pictured here are the Unicorn Coeds, 1950s. (Image courtesy of John and Lucia Sanchez's personal collection.)

Mexican American professionals from the Back of the Yards. Some would even become social workers and educators at the settlement house, including Lucia Gallardo Sanchez, John C. Sanchez, Adel Martinez, and Bertha Venegas.[33]

Despite these successes, Mexican Back of the Yarders still faced condemnation outside the settlement's walls. While whites could safely traverse multiple ethnic neighborhood boundaries to attend the settlement, Mexicans could not. Grammar schools, high schools, and places of employment were located outside their enclave, and the daily commute to work and school often came with an indignity or harassment by passersby or patrolmen for being Mexican in the wrong neighborhood. These ethnic and spatial boundaries and the potential for conflict further compelled settlement staff to encourage mixed clubs. This aligned with the settlement's philosophy of valuing ethnic pluralism so long as it did not impede their underlying mission of Americanization. Consequently, some community members called on the institution to do more to address their material conditions beyond the settlement. "The main reason for a Settlement House to exist in a neighborhood should be because of its concern and interest in the welfare of the people of that neighborhood," wrote Adel Martinez, a youth worker who grew up in the Mexican Back of the Yards. She added: "We should be concerned about the types of schools our people attend; about the kind of jobs our people hold; about the conditions of the homes in which our people live. These things should be as important to us as their mode of behavior in our House."[34]

While many neighborhood residents considered the University of Chicago Settlement a critical resource that satisfied their social and recreational needs, some wanted to form all-Mexican social clubs to mitigate the condemnation and discrimination they faced collectively as a group. In 1949, a dozen young Mexican American men in their early twenties, mostly military service members, formed the Ospreys SAC. Like the Incas before them, the Ospreys fielded sports teams and organized dances while also aspiring to influence political and neighborhood matters. The Ospreys' expressions of self-determination were not couched in a language of militancy; rather they were intended to show that their lived experience was vastly different from that of their white peers. Clubs like theirs, they argued, were important to challenge the negative stigmas and patterns of discrimination they suffered as Mexicans from the Back of the Yards. The following year, a group of young women in their late teens and early twenties named the Halo Girls echoed this sentiment. In 1950, after listening to a presentation by the Ospreys, the young women, convinced of the need for all-Mexican clubs, voted to change their club name to the Osprey Girls. Fran Dungan, the clubs' advisor, recorded the sentiments of the young Latinas in the group: "They want the Mexican of the Back of the Yards to become something. The girls seem a little more determined to make this a strong club; they want to give at Christmas time to the needy children of the neighborhood." Soon thereafter, the Osprey Girls wrote a new constitution to reflect their goals: "to provide good recreation for all members" and "to make the community a better place for all people to live."[35]

But the Osprey Girls' constitution soon ignited controversy among some settlement staff who took issue with its requirement that "the majority of the members" be Mexican. The Halo Girls had been an ethnically mixed group until then, and now the Mexican Americans were telling the whites they had to leave. Settlement social clubs organized by nationality and ethnicity were common in the 1920s and early 1930s but had fallen out of favor with social workers after the New Deal and World War II. Dungan was not moved by their appeals to form an all-Mexican group for the purpose of ethnic uplift. She discouraged it, calling the Osprey Girls' membership requirement a "policy of discrimination" and noting that expelling the white women violated the settlement's multiethnic values. To young Brown women, many who worked in factories and spent time searching for better employment, the idea of coming together after a long shift to play sports, be convivial, and share in common struggles was reason enough for the existence of the Osprey Girls. Despite the advisor's protests, the Latinas proceeded with their policy, telling Dungan: "The Ospreys want their name and membership to really mean something in the neighborhood. They want their club to get to the place where they have political influence." To achieve the latter goal, the former needed to be built on ethno-racial pride and a new public confidence.[36]

Throughout the 1950s, the Ospreys became influential in the Back of the Yards and across the city thanks to the club's athletic prowess on football fields (men's) and volleyball courts (women's) and the popularity of their dance socials, which drew hundreds of people. Each event helped push the boundaries of social and spatial exclusion while raising expectations and a new resolve for the postwar generation of Mexican Back of the Yarders. Locals attributed the acceptance of the Ospreys by white Back of the Yarders with helping to normalize Mexican conviviality in white sections of the district where they were previously unwelcomed. Those who were likely to attend an Ospreys function or be a club member were also more likely to witness the loosening restrictions of the racial border of Ashland Avenue. Conquests in football coincided with conquests over property restrictions, as dozens of Mexican families moved west of Ashland Avenue into homes along Marshfield Avenue between 43rd and 47th Streets in a slow trickle in the late 1940s that turned into a wave in the 1950s. This confluence of recreation did not overcome all racial restrictions, but it helped move the racial line west by one city street to Marshfield Avenue, a short distance on the map but a significant shift in the Back of the Yards. Relaxing residential restrictions even by one street opened better housing to the large Mexican families living in overcrowded conditions. Longtime families like the Chicos, the Maestres, the Perezes, the Magallanes, and many others purchased sturdy two- and three-story cottage homes from Eastern Europeans who were ready to sell their properties to the highest bidders, much to the disapproval of the local realty industry. The Ospreys established their clubhouse on the first floor of a two-story building on Marshfield Avenue.[37]

As important as social clubs, fraternal organizations, football games, and dances were to traversing racial and neighborhood boundaries, agencies like the Mexican American Council of Chicago (MAC) believed there was no substitute for a community-organizing program with a Latino civil rights agenda. The agency, located in the Near West Side, took this message to the heart of the Mexican Back of the Yards, holding meetings at the settlement house repeatedly throughout the early to mid-1950s. MAC was influenced by University of Texas scholar and professor George I. Sánchez, whose advocacy for Latino citizens' rights through research gathering, legal strategy, and a focus on the Fourteenth Amendment gained him wide recognition with civil rights and civil liberties groups. Sánchez had recently invited MAC along with Saul Alinsky's Community Service Organization, League of United Latin American Citizens, and the Colorado Latin American Conference to help launch a national operation for Latino civil rights advocacy. This operation would follow a Black civil rights model of test cases and court filings on various issues, including housing segregation, educational discrimination, voter disenfranchisement, and police brutality. Building on this momentum, MAC met with groups at the University of Chicago Settlement with "the aims of establishing a neighborhood committee" not only to expose conditions in America's "jungle" but to help those who were "unable to vocalize or channel his complaints against the patterns of injustice and discrimination."[38]

These discussions, however, failed to mobilize Mexican Back of the Yarders. MAC made earnest efforts between 1952 and 1954—in conjunction with representatives from the settlement as well as the Lázaro Cárdenas School and the UPWA-District 1—but failed to produce community action. The two latter groups consisted of veterans from the CIO and Frente Popular Mexicano who, in the 1930s and 1940s, were in the vanguard of an intersectional civil rights movement led by Global South Black and Brown packinghouse workers. But in the 1950s, the Lázaro Cárdenas School and UPWA-District 1 were weakened by the packinghouse closures and the red-baiting brought on by the Cold War. Postwar Mexican Back of the Yarders were moving away from labor-based politics. Another challenge in organizing residents was the narrow civil rights discourse in 1950s Chicago that defined rights mobilization in terms of the African American struggle. Despite UPWA-District 1's best attempts to push a progressive, multiracial consciousness, the narrower discourse was constantly reinforced by other liberal organizations, reportage on racial struggle in the north, and the Southwest Side communities of Chicago. Even Saul Alinsky chose to organize Mexican Americans two thousand miles away in California.[39]

Although the Incas and the Ospreys may have seen themselves as ambassadors of the Mexican race, they did not necessarily view themselves as civil rights crusaders in the ways MAC or even George I. Sánchez envisioned. This disconnect between ethno-racial struggle and political activism contributed to the absence of calls for Latino civil rights in the Back of the Yards during the postwar years. The post–*Brown v. Board of Education* landscape raised the racial antennae of northern white ethnics who were resentful of the new federal mandate that threatened to place Black children in their schools, making the Black freedom struggle in the urban north a fulcrum for white ethnic mobilization. These racial resentments bellowed through the all-white Bungalow Belt communities of Gage Park, Marquette Park, and Garfield Ridge—nicer, more exclusive districts to the southwest of the Back of the Yards—that would eventually explode into violent acts of white grievance in the summer of 1966. But long before this moment, in the 1940s and 1950s, Mexican children from the Back of the Yards crossed these racial boundaries every day as they were forced to attend schools in neighboring Gage Park out of necessity, since few public high schools existed in the stockyards district. The lack of violent reaction or organized resistance to the enrollment of Mexican students in Gage Park High School underscored the anti-Black focus that dominated white rights mobilizers. It also underscored the indifference of white parents and school administrators to Mexicans in the context of the Black freedom struggle. Many of the Incas and Ospreys were products of Gage Park High School, and while some endured casual racism and racist epithets from teachers and classmates, these experiences paled in comparison to the organized white mobs that mobilized at the presence of Black children in Gage Park.[40]

The Incas and the Ospreys, aware of the stigmatization of Mexicans, nevertheless were unlikely to participate in civil disobedience campaigns, sit-ins, or other forms of nonviolent protest. Instead, these clubs defined their political activism as influence building among the white ethnic power structure through sociable displays of respectability. The Incas' president, Catarino G. Diaz, a decorated World War II veteran who grew up attending the settlement, became an influential business owner along Ashland Avenue's row of storefronts. The Incas and the Ospreys engaged the Irish American–controlled political power structure in the district. The Incas brokered friendly relations with the 14th Ward Regular Democratic Organization; at one point the Democrats paid for Incas baseball uniforms in exchange for having Alderman Clarence Wagner's name stitched across the jerseys. On Election Day, La Capilla's social hall was used as a polling station, and Catarino Diaz was there to take parishioners to cast their votes.

The Ospreys' dances were significant influence builders as well, as they presented opportunities to invite machine politicians from the 11th Ward and 14th Ward Regular Democratic Organizations to enjoy dancing rhumbas and mambo to live orchestras over cocktails, favors, and votes. The 14th Ward organization elected Matt Rodriguez, its first-ever Mexican American precinct captain in the early 1950s, to tend to the municipal needs of Mexican Back of the Yarders living in the second precinct. Rodriguez was considered a perfect fit for the job since he was well known in the neighborhood for running the bingo games at La Capilla and delivering groceries as an employee for La Tienda Colorada. Attempts to enlist Mexican Back of the Yarders in a national Latino civil rights movement to potentially launch litigious action against housing, employment, or education discrimination fell by the wayside. Nevertheless, clubs like the Incas and Ospreys made significant inroads in challenging the condemnation of their communities and improving, even if only slightly, Mexican Back of the Yarders' social and economic opportunities.[41]

Meanwhile, settlement houses across the country, including the University of Chicago Settlement, shifted into more direct advocacy in community development while aligning their goals to the politics of the Cold War. Initiatives like community development and the production of poverty knowledge gained strategic significance during the Cold War, especially in their application to nonaligned nations, funded by the US State Department's war chest. Social workers who once jockeyed for professional positions in big-city settlement houses were lured away by community-development projects in distant places like Africa, Asia, Latin America, and other parts of the nonwhite world to advance ideological projects of US democracy among decolonizing peoples. But many remaining in the settlement house proposed democracy projects in the Back of the Yards, drawing on these Cold War frameworks to approach their clientele (in this case mostly Mexicans) in the same way as impoverished populations in developing nations. "For a number of years, we have been building a foundation of good relationships with the families and groups in our community," wrote Boerner in a grant request to the Field Foundation of New York, "we want to use this foundation to develop a program for bringing immigrants into American life in a way that will make for their full participation and from which they can derive real satisfaction." In 1953, they launched their pilot program called "Democratic Participation Among the Foreign-Born," with the objectives of "integrating the foreign-born and their offspring into community life" and instilling "more active participation in neighborhood activities and in civic and national life," describing the stakes of this project to be high since "their experiences under other systems of government make the foreign-born an excellent target for bigots and those who seek to play one group against another."[42]

Cold War imperatives alone did not drive the new focus on their clientele; another motivating factor was the primacy of the BYNC, whose monopoly over community development in the district worried settlement professionals. Internal reports by administrators associated with the settlement charged that the BYNC's community-development efforts were a pretense for Black residential exclusion. Among the settlement staff, some felt that Mexicans' crossing of Ashland Avenue had also thrown the district into a panic, with residents seeing it as a harbinger of declining property values, the arrival of Black homebuyers, and a threat to their way of life. Internal memos did not hold back in declaring that Jim Crow segregation and anti-Black racism were very much alive in the Back of the Yards. Conversely, this frankness about the differentiated racial borders in the district and the need for a solution came at a weak point in the settlement's influence. In 1955, the president of the University of Chicago, Lawrence A. Kimpton, pulled the university's financial support, ending the institution's sixty-year sponsorship of the settlement, urging "the university community to keep its charitable efforts closer to home" in Hyde Park. When the university denied the settlement use of its prestigious name, it renamed itself after Mary McDowell, its founder. Defunded and underresourced, the settlement pursued community-development dollars and sought a role in possible urban renewal. A 1955 confidential report on the BYNC commissioned by the National Federation of Settlements laid out various internal crises endemic to the BYNC's oversized influence over urban policy and community development in the district, namely its role in maintaining white homogeneity by effectively opposing public housing and using extralegal methods to control real estate in a years-long effort to keep Black and Brown people out.[43]

Conservation, Counter–White Flight, and Racial Fortification in the Jungle

In 1953, the BYNC embarked on a conservation campaign, spurred in part after Joseph Meegan made an alarming discovery that his district's white population had shrunk from 102,000 people just a few years earlier to 85,000 by that year. Meegan convened an emergency meeting of all financial institutions, businesses, and realtors in the neighborhood to warn them

Figure 3.3. The Back of the Yards Neighborhood Council's conservation program during the 1950s was heralded by observers and policymakers alike for modernizing old properties, building new homes, and restoring pride in the district, all designed to reverse white flight to the suburbs. (Image source: June Blythe, "Back of the Yards Reverses the Flight to Suburbia," *Commerce*, January 1956, 20–25.)

that without a serious, well-organized effort to modernize the Back of the Yards, more whites would be lured away to the suburbs. The Back of the Yards had been redlined since the 1940s, blacklisting it from mortgage lending and improvement loans, and no new construction had taken place since the 1920s. More alarming to the BYNC member delegates were the imaginable implications of a white-less Back of the Yards: abandoned and unkempt properties, blight and decay, the arrival of racial minorities, a rise in crime and delinquency, and the closure of businesses and Catholic churches. In response, all of the district's twenty-two savings and loans institutions immediately opened up lending to fund what became an aggressive conservation program in home rehabilitation, vacant-lot procurement, and new home construction, all with the goal of keeping whites in the district. A street billboard was posted at the edge of the district asking would-be white flighters: "Why move away?" It was dubbed "Operation Destiny," named after the BYNC's moral moniker of bootstrapism: "We the people will work out our own destiny." A new suburban-styled subdivision of homes went up, christened "Destiny Manor," with rows of three-bedroom brick homes designed for young families who otherwise would be suburb-bound.[44]

Conservation was a "more moderate form of property rehabilitation," as historian Amanda Seligman has described, whereby "conservation projects generally funded the repair of existing properties without requiring residents to depart." This form of redevelopment was distinct from the large-scale land clearance and residential displacement typically associated with urban renewal. The BYNC seized onto this tool of urban policy to enact a counter-white-flight campaign. They anticipated the state's passage of the Urban Community Conservation Act of 1953, which gave extraordinary municipal powers to city administrators to seize urban land for conservation on the basis of slum prevention, even in areas that were not yet blighted. It also established mayor-appointed Community Conservation Councils, where local community organizations were empowered to represent the interests of their conservation areas. Amid this swirl of city-renewal policy, the well-organized BYNC informally appointed itself as the local decision-maker and controlled all aspects of conservation in the district. The BYNC convinced the city to allow it to build new homes, as historian Dominic Pacyga has illustrated, "on lots smaller than the traditional twenty-five-foot Chicago lot." What made the Back of the Yards unique was the immense political clout the BYNC held, mainly due to its reputation for defeating rivals, political or otherwise, in the public arena. The BYNC used this clout to kill any unwanted policies like proposed land clearance, public housing, or unfavorable tax assessments. In one instance, the BYNC forced the Chicago Housing Authority to sell back land it had purchased for a public-housing site in the district. What came to be known throughout urban America as NIMBY-ism (not in my backyard) drove the BYNC's decision-making.[45]

BYNC's Operation Destiny flourished not only as a conservation program but also as a vehicle for political and economic mobilization to address white Back of the Yarders' racial anxieties. Although newspapers rarely covered the racial exclusion rooted in the conservation effort, it was a well-known open secret that most white Back of the Yarders were "determined to keep Negroes out," as one resident said in the mid-1950s. Stricter segregation of Mexicans was also a goal. The Mexican population had reached over 10 percent in 1957, a moderate increase relative to other areas but one that still required reinforcing their confinement to the northeastern end of the district. In 1963, the new director of the McDowell Settlement, Guido J.

Tardi, quickly learned that "the Mexican still cannot live anywhere he may choose in our community." The BYNC controlled real estate by making sure homebuyers, sellers, and realtors honored and respected the preservation of ethnic homogeneity and that they pledged to maintain their homes to certain standards. The BYNC also participated in a real estate buying operation for the sole purpose of "keeping it from going to Negroes" and other racial minorities. According to IAF organizer Nicholas Von Hoffman: "People are organized district by district and block-by-block, what is more all the banks are organized, all the savings and loan associations are organized, all the contractors are organized, all the real estate firms and real estate agents are organized. . . . To top it off the [BYNC] uses the *Back of the Yards Journal* as a powerful medium of both persuasion and public coercion." Meegan wielded the financial assets of its lending institutions to renovate and purchase properties. The BYNC quickly absorbed hundreds of vacant lots and tax-delinquent homes. Frances Mazurk, a local realtor and member of the BYNC who also sat on the Chicago Real Estate Board, spoke of the "social pressure and fierce pride" that motivated people to fix and remodel their homes. Another important institution in the racial-fortification effort was the Archdiocese of Chicago, which had a vested interest in keeping the district all white since it owned a considerable amount of real estate in the form of Catholic churches, schools, and other parish buildings. The district's strong Catholic identity made the BYNC leadership feel justified in their exclusion of African Americans on the basis of religion, as illustrated by Alinsky's comments when he told an author: "When a community changes from white to Negro, the Catholic church is in a different position from the Protestant and Jewish churches. It has a bigger real estate investment [and cannot sell] as easily as other sects can." Attempting to square this position with his progressive reputation, he claimed the BYNC was not so much "anti-Negro" as it was "pro-nationality Church." But Meegan was blunter when he stated, "Negroes don't have anything in common with the people who live here."[46]

While conservation efforts helped appease white homeowners in the district, some civil liberties and civil rights groups expressed concern over the BYNC's goals and position on race and integration. Lucy P. Carner, a progressive liberal with the Council of Social Agencies, told her colleagues that although the BYNC-inspired local-control movement was notable for empowering everyday citizens to protect their neighborhoods from abusive adversaries, it could also be weaponized to restrict people of color from buy-

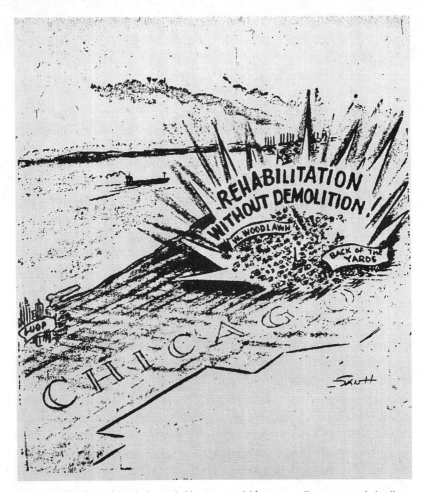

Figure 3.4. The Back of the Yards was held up as a model for conservation programs during the 1950s, a better alternative to the dislocation and land clearance associated with urban renewal. (Image source: W. F. Graney, "Rehabilitation Without Demolition," *The New World*, April 25, 1958, 3.)

ing and renting homes in all-white areas. Liberal and progressive leaders worried that the proliferation of neighborhood councils throughout Chicago in the 1950s, and their varied race politics, could perpetuate hostile territorialism veiled as "grassroots democracy."[47]

While some neighborhood councils were racially progressive, embraced civil rights, and aided the transition of ethnic and racial succession in their communities, others were as virulently segregationist as white citizens' councils in the Jim Crow South. In June 1958, an openly white supremacist neighborhood council, the South Deering Improvement Association (South Chicago), infamous for its violent role in the Trumbull Park Homes Race Riots of 1953–1954, found enough common cause with the BYNC to warn them about the threat the McDowell Settlement House posed. In their weekly bulletin, published under the heading "White People Must Control Their Own Communities," they condemned the settlement's Camp Farr program and "certain teachings" in the center's club programs for promoting "racial mixing and blanket fraternizations," in which they charged that "little children are used as the innocent tools of the vicious attack against the white man." "Men and women of all races, and we presume all creeds, including atheists and communists, were rolling around on blankets and in the area petting together, eating together and playing together," the newsletter decried. It would not be the only time the BYNC was presumed to share common goals with white segregationist neighborhood organizations.[48]

But city agencies and civil rights groups' concerns over the BYNC conservation campaign's racial fortifications were eclipsed by the chorus of approval from residents, civic groups, and newspapers that heralded the people's effort to beautify "the jungle." Throughout the start of the conservation campaign in 1953 and well into the 1960s, the council also earned adoring praise from academicians, urbanists, and community organizers who assigned their own liberal and progressive attributes to the council. The BYNC was lionized as a champion of the local-control movement. Hundreds of journalists descended on the district to write features and learn firsthand of the "Back of the Yards miracle"—before-and-after stories of how hundreds of rehabilitated buildings were saved from dilapidation and demolition. Meegan and Alinsky led writers on walking tours of the neighborhood, demonstrating the various components of the conservation operation from the material improvements, political maneuvering, economics, and spirit of self-determination it engendered among white Back of the Yarders. Operation Destiny became important source material for books such as Agnes E. Meyer's *Out of These Roots* (1953); Martin Millspaugh and Gurney Breckenfeld's *The Human Side of Urban Renewal* (1960); and Jane Jacobs's landmark *The Death and Life of Great American Cities* (1961)—the nuclei of an emergent literature criticizing urban renewal and city planning. These authors elevated conservation as a promising alternative to the demolition and clearance otherwise favored by downtown business elites and city planners. To Jacobs, the Back of the Yards was "a classic example of the sort of locality which it is conveniently believed must be bulldozed away entire." She placed the district in the context of other former slums in Boston's North End, San Francisco's North Beach, and New York's Greenwich Village, which she held up as models of sweat-equity regeneration. In her examination of the Back of the Yards, Jacobs even coined a verb, *unslumming*, to describe the movement. "Unslumming hinges, paradoxically, on the retention of a very considerable part of a slum population within a slum," she wrote, "it hinges on whether a considerable number of the residents and businessmen of a slum find it both desirable and practical to make and carry out their own plans right there, or whether they must virtually all move elsewhere."[49]

Jane Jacobs's support for Operation Destiny was rooted in her own analysis but also what she learned through Saul Alinsky and Joseph Meegan's accounts to her. She praised the conservation effort, partly because she found it to be an excellent example of her ideas of urban regeneration, a process that had to come from below and not from a planning department or city hall. "To overcome slums we must regard slum dwellers as people capable of understanding and acting upon their own self-interests," she explained. Alinsky and Meegan were deeply invested in protecting BYNC's story as a champion of localist democracy, and they supplied Jacobs with a self-serving narrative of how a tough-minded, multiethnic district overcame its own divisions to fight blight. But this narrative was devoid of the anti-Black and anti-Mexican mobilizations underlying the conservation effort. Although Jacobs did make note of the anxieties residents felt toward outsiders (the "fear of strangers who look too alien"), she fell short of admitting that it was rooted in racism or that it was a primary motivator for Operation Destiny. Enamored of the grassroots spirit of the conservation program, Jacobs regurgitated Alinsky's and Meegan's optimistic narrative and assigned the Back of the Yards a dimension of "diversity" that no longer existed. "Its backbone population is mainly Central European," she wrote, "but all kinds of Central European," emphasizing the "diversity" within Central European groups. But Operation Destiny was not built on diversity; on the contrary, it was a coalescing of whiteness that residents of European ancestry had long embraced. Jacobs, the liberal crusader against oppressive regimes of urban development, failed to criticize or even note the racial fortifications against Mexicans and African Americans in the Back of the Yards.[50]

Jacobs's analysis accurately reflected the racial-conflict-free version of Operation Destiny that Alinsky and Meegan promoted. Although Alinsky only reluctantly admitted in the late 1950s that the BYNC's conservation program doubled as a project of racial exclusion, he believed that a successful community-organizing campaign needed to operate along one of two tracks: gradual racial integration or community control to maintain ethnic/ racial homogeneity. The BYNC was on the latter track. Still, he framed Operation Destiny not as the preservation of a white community but as an "extraordinary self-financing program" that "has become a model for other self-help" groups. Alinsky touted its growing influence in a 1958 report: "Its program of physical conservation . . . has captured the imagination of many organizations and Foundations in the country. Here is the only extensive community re-development program carried through without the benefit of one penny of public funds, either Federal, State or local." Operation Destiny had indeed renovated over four thousand older homes, erected two hundred new homes, attracted some industry to the vacated stockyards, rescued dipping property values, and successfully kept African Americans out and Latinos segregated around La Capilla. The BYNC's discipline and vigilance also kept speculators and blockbusters from penetrating the district, even as neighboring areas like Englewood were swiftly turning over from white to Black. The public perception of success made Alinsky and his Industrial Areas Foundation even more useful to Chicago's all-white Bungalow Belt, which, in the context of Black residential dispersal, desired similar results to those the BYNC achieved. Members of the Organization for the Southwest Community (OSC), an all-white group, captured this sentiment in a letter by its president, Donald O'Toole, to another South Side leader, making his case that, "We are against nobody and nothing except blight. Ours is a 'pro' organization—we are 'for' the present people in the neighborhood staying," speaking in a coded language designed to exonerate him from charges of racism. The OSC expressed their appreciation of Alinsky and his organizers, who came in to help. "We have watched them carefully," O'Toole wrote, "and, I must say, they have never violated our stipulation that they are not to use our community in any way shape or form as an experiment in racial integration."[51]

Operation Destiny—enshrined in Jacobs's *The Death and Life of Great American Cities* and promoted across the country by Alinsky's IAF—rested heavily on the erasure of the Mexican Back of the Yards. Because the conservation program's success was defined as the preservation of the white community, the stubborn presence of a Mexican enclave, albeit largely segregated, presented a problem to local leaders. When a visitor from the Emil Schwarzhaupt Foundation, a New York–based IAF funder, asked Alinsky to tell him more about the Mexicans he saw living in the district, Alinsky's secretary replied: "I do not, as yet, have the answers to your questions on the number of immigrants in the Back of the Yards." Replies like this about the unfamiliarity of the Mexican population foreshadowed the BYNC leaders' repeated attempts to whitewash the district. The BYNC knew that its white constituents did not want Latinos as neighbors and acted upon that mandate in various ways throughout the 1950s and 1960s. Operation Destiny helped racially fortify and segregate Mexicans to the edges of the district. Through tight control over real estate throughout the duration of the conservation campaign, Mexicans were effectively barred from buying and renting any of the four thousand renovated homes or in the new residential subdivision of Destiny Manor. When the BYNC could not "erase" the Mexican colonia through undercounting or by simply not acknowledging it, it tried to make the enclave even smaller.

Shrinking Las Yardas

White Back of the Yarders entrusted the BYNC to safeguard their neighborhoods from the encroachment of Mexicans as it had from Blacks. Meegan knew the racial anxieties whites felt around Latinos and understood he was not simply managing a crisis in Black and white. Animus between white neighbors toward those who sold and rented homes to Mexicans west of Ashland Avenue intensified in the late 1950s and early 1960s. Opening the real estate market to Mexican residents would cause the same white flight as the presence of Blacks would. An instructive lesson for Meegan was the fallout from urban-renewal displacement just two miles north in the Near West Side. There, land clearance sent thousands of Mexicans to nearby Pilsen, provoking an exodus of Central and Eastern European white ethnics to the suburbs. Meegan was determined not to let the Back of the Yards become another Pilsen. Coming off a very successful conservation campaign that maintained property values and kept whites in place, the BYNC leveraged its political influence in city hall to enact urban policy through zoning—an effective way to control neighborhood growth and residential and business patterns. In the postwar era, zoning often mobilized community leaders and their constituents against unwanted ordinances that jeopardized the residential nature of communities or to protect against industry encroachment. In the Back of the Yards, district leaders tried to strike a balance that could please two powerful constituent groups with different aims: the Southwest Side Realty Board that opposed zoning for industry and the Back of the Yards Businessmen's Association that hoped to attract new industry and manufacturing to bolster the economy.[52]

The BYNC pushed for a zoning change in the Mexican Back of the

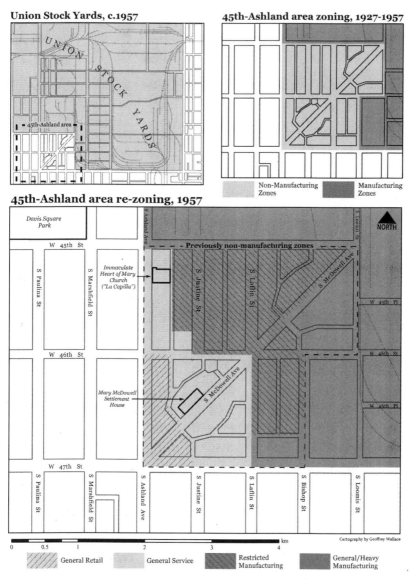

Figure 3.5. Map of re-zoning of 45th-Ashland Area.

Yards (from Ashland Avenue eastward to the Union Stock Yards, and from 47th Street northward to 43rd Street), converting it from residential to business and manufacturing. In the 1950s, the Building and Zoning Committee was largely dominated by white ethnic South Side aldermen inclined to protect white communities from the threat of racial minorities and who used racial zoning for segregation and density control. Issued in the 1957 Chicago Zoning Ordinance, the BYNC rezoned Las Yardas, partly for its convenient location adjacent to the Union Stock Yards, while keeping it far away from most white homeowning sections that desired a suburb-like environment. The rezoning effectively shrunk Las Yardas as a residential community by slowly phasing out homes as they deteriorated or were sold and restricting any new construction to manufacturing plants or wholesale retail usage. This new designation (M-1) eliminated the residential zoning that had existed since Samuel Eberly Gross built his workingmen's cottages there in the late nineteenth century. Rezoning Las Yardas reduced the housing stock and forced Mexicans and Mexican Americans to search for better housing outside the district.[53]

Joseph Meegan set out to shrink the land his Mexican constituents lived on. Rezoning Las Yardas made it materially and numerically smaller, as it reduced housing availability and discouraged Mexicans from the district. With this policy, Meegan and the BYNC upheld Ashland Avenue as a "wall" and restricted Mexican dispersal. Still, the BYNC did not have to admit to its intentions when nobler reasons could be cited, like attracting new industry and regulating manufacturers to meet higher environmental standards, which new zoning enabled. Benefits aside, the new zoning ordinance partially dispossessed Mexicans of an area they had called home since 1916. Every time a resident from Las Yardas tried to renovate or fix up his property, the Building Department denied him permits due to its M-1 designation. In 1959, homeowner Guadalupe Diaz wanted to make some repairs to improve his building, much like his white counterparts were doing during Operation Destiny. The Building Department told him that his property on 4520 South Justine Street sat on land that did not allow residential use, even though he had lived there all his life. Diaz told a reporter, "I didn't know I couldn't improve my property." When he appealed the decision, the zoning board chairman, Samuel T. Lawton, examined the ordinance and noted that "there isn't a factory in the whole block altho [sic] the whole thing is zoned for manufacturing." Denying Latino homeowners the right to fix their own properties accelerated dilapidation and dispossession. Mexican-owned homes in and outside of Las Yardas became subject to over inspection by building officials. In one case, officials found the Osprey's SAC clubhouse on Marshfield Avenue and 43rd Street to be in violation of the zoning ordinance and asked the group to close its clubhouse. Still, Mexican Back of the Yarders continued their appeals to city hall to challenge the zoning ordinance.[54]

The racialized weaponization of zoning was not only apparent to residents of Las Yardas who had sacrificed their entire lives to make a home in the district but also to outside observers. In 1960, Frances H. Brueckner, a consultant with the Welfare Council of Metropolitan Chicago, assessed the needs in the area surrounding the McDowell Settlement and noted the implications of the 1957 Chicago Zoning Ordinance: "Zoned for general manufacturing, junk yards, sand and gravel, garbage disposal and factories of a non-toxic nature . . . this does not produce a picture of the best possible location for a neighborhood house." In consulting with local agencies, she learned of the tension between Las Yardas and the BYNC. "The Mexicans resent the methods of work of the Council," Brueckner wrote, as she was informed of the various ways they were "excluded by the Back of the Yards Neighborhood Council." "Those who are now not led or welcomed into the [BYNC's] activities have the right to such help," underscoring the role the council had taken against its abandoned Mexican constituents. This contrasted sharply with the 1940s, when the BYNC displayed public support for Mexicans, as their donations to the building of La Capilla and recognition of their role in the packinghouse workers union evidenced. The BYNC also came to Mexicans' aid during tribulations with abusive patrolmen. But in the 1960s, neither a common Catholicism nor a shared labor history could transcend the ethno-racial boundaries or prevent the diminution of Las Yardas. Mexicans understood that they were considered second-class Catholics, a distinction rooted in racial difference from Chicago's ethnic Catholics. Leaders from La Capilla worried about the future of their parish community. In 1960, Father Severino Lopez wrote, "Large neighborhoods disappear over night in the city's efforts to blot out blight. The great Stock Yards, in the past the pride of Chicago, are now being decentralized. Enormous buildings are being torn down, leaving a sight of apparent desolation about our little chapel. We don't know what might be in the offing." His words revealed concern about the precarious future of Las Yardas, as pressure mounted from white residents to hold the line against the demographic revolution that threatened the district.[55]

Life in Las Yardas consisted of navigating an inequitable system of urban development and residential apartheid. Its industrial-usage zoning turned it into a de facto mixed-use, residential-manufacturing landscape where Latino residents had to make do. Residents continued living in dense quarters where wood-frame homes sat next to abandoned industrial buildings; vacant lots laid bare awaiting the manufacturing renaissance that came in spurts and stops. Still, Las Yardas residents maximized their use of space where they could. Neighborhood capitalism and consumption operated at a small scale, with first-floor storefronts and domestic kitchens that sourced an informal economy of Mexican foodways such as tortillas, tamales, dried chiles, and other goods. Recreational opportunities were makeshift as well, as neighborhood children played on the streets, in vacant lots, and around the industrial waste. This mixed-use cityscape—decades from being a trendy form of urban development—was the scourge of Middle America in the 1950s and 1960s. Moreover, local civic groups and white homeowners believed "mixed-use cityscapes," as historian Suleiman Osman has shown, "led to polluted industries sitting near homes, insufferable automobile traffic, and blight." The white Back of the Yards, through its own sweat equity, home renovations, and new subdivisions, had been recast into a blue-collar "suburb in the city" but remained threatened by the presence of racial minorities it had allowed in and now desired to confine. Making Las Yardas smaller through rezoning was, by design, intended to squeeze out undesirable elements and bring in new industries and businesses that other parts of the district did not want, all through Latino dispossession. Nevertheless, making place and maximizing the use of limited space had characterized Mexican life in Las Yardas since the first arrivals in the 1910s. Now standing at the crossroads between white neighborhood resistance and the rising tide of civil rights, Mexican Back of the Yarders found their political voice in staying put and claiming home in the district.[56]

Politics and Placemaking in Las Yardas

As white homeowners battled civil rights throughout the 1960s, Mexican Back of the Yarders sharpened their political voices to challenge their confinement. Despite whites' resolve to hold the line against non-Black racial minorities by any means possible, Mexican Back of the Yarders were determined to recast the terms of their racial, social, political, and economic barriers and claim their right to decent housing, employment, and education. Las Yardas residents used sweat equity to fix up their buildings and instill pride in their small corner of the district. They capitalized on the real estate they called their own, opening more brick-and-mortar businesses along the white-abandoned Ashland Avenue. Mexican-owned corner stores and first-floor storefronts provided not only daily provisions but also a sense of dignity, endurance, and belonging. Along with generating vibrant neighborhood capitalism, residents of Las Yardas maintained their strong Catholic ties and packinghouse-worker roots, two areas that failed to fortify common ground with whites but that nevertheless inspired Mexican cultural place-making in Las Yardas.

Although these changes might not have seemed as drastic compared to the wider-scale transformations of Pilsen, Heart of Chicago, and South Lawndale after Mexican displacement from the Near West Side in the early 1960s, the residents of Las Yardas were on the cusp of a political transformation. They turned their spatial confinement into a source of economic and political power, founding new organizations and reviving old ones to represent their political interests. As white Southwest Siders mobilized a counter-offensive against the civil rights movement (and even against Democrats), Mexican Back of the Yarders became stakeholders in the turmoil of the 1960s by gradually, quietly, becoming machine Democrats. They achieved this with help from groups that organized Latino workers through religiosity, culture, ethnicity, and urban opportunity. One such group was the Cardinal's Committee for the Spanish-Speaking (CCSS) that organized Latino Catholics around social, religious, and political issues during the 1950s and early 1960s. While this transformation did not negate other forms of political mobilization on a national and transnational scale, it was civic, residential, and commercial matters that raised their level of engagement with the machine. The radical and progressive politics of labor unions that had called for an interracial coalition to defeat Jim Crow in the district in the 1940s and 50s were no longer influential. At the dawn of the 1960s, the CCSS encouraged Latino political participation through mainstream parties (and chiefly through the Democratic Party). CCSS clergy and volunteers addressed Latinos in their parishes and provided job placement, financial planning, and voter-registration drives. Organized by Cardinal Samuel Stritch in 1955 to help Puerto Ricans, the CCSS eventually expanded services to Mexicans and Cubans. In the context of the Cold War, the CCSS's focus on American capitalism and opportunity was an antidote to communism and anxieties about decolonization movements around the world. The CCSS promoted religious middle-class aspirations and participation in the US project of Cold War civil rights for a Brown citizenry and migrant constituency, and it encouraged using the political system to attain those rights.[57]

Although the CCSS was motivated to shore up the spiritual allegiance of the growing Latino Chicago population, it also aimed to stamp out the influence of communism, militant labor organizing, and the potential for radicalization in Latino enclaves. Mexican Back of the Yarders who attended

CCSS gatherings had strong religious ties, were often military veterans or came from veteran families, and held Cold Warrior politics. These residents formed Los Botantes Latinos Americanos del Barrio de las Empacadoras (Back of the Yards Latin American Voters) in 1960, ahead of the local and general elections that year. Mexican immigrants and Mexican Americans from Los Botantes organized voter-registration drives, hosted political speeches and fundraisers for candidates, and created a structure of Latino support for elected officials, mostly white and Black (machine-aligned) office seekers. The group had around five hundred members in its first year and was led by Catarino G. Diaz (director) and Eriberto Campos (president) to mobilize Latino voters to become an influential bloc with a voice in the Cook County Democratic Party. Diaz, longtime leader of the Incas SAC, was an important member of the business community in Las Yardas and vice president of the Mexican Chamber of Commerce, a group that promoted the interests of Mexican-owned businesses and transnational commerce between Mexico and Chicago. In the 1950s and 1960s, Diaz became a powerbroker in civic and business affairs through his skilled maneuvering of city hall connections. His access to business permits and banking loans aided the postwar Mexicanization of Ashland Avenue as a site of growing consumer and business power. This momentum carried over to the ballot box as Los Botantes organized rallies, registered voters, and mobilized Latino support for John F. Kennedy and local machine candidates. Throughout the 1960s, Los Botantes and the Mexican Chamber of Commerce developed relations with the machine's Southwest Side wards for mutual support and to help expand their business-owning opportunities beyond Ashland Avenue. Campos took up the cause of restoring the residential zoning designation of Las Yardas and led a petition drive to save a children's play lot from becoming a parking lot.[58]

Other sources of political mobilization emerged that reinforced Mexican Back of the Yarders' placemaking efforts. "The [Mexican] group seems to have a good degree of organization in its Club Osprey and in the societies of the Immaculate Heart of Mary Church," noted a social worker from the Welfare Council in 1961, "they are said to be very active in registration and election activities." The uptick in political activity placed La Capilla as the indispensable community center. The Ospreys used the hall to organize political rallies for local Democratic candidates, hold fundraisers for the parish, and host foreign dignitaries from Mexico. Members were invited to serve on the Mayor's Committee on New Residents and the Chicago Commission on Human Relations, which provided Latinos direct links to city hall services. An active Holy Name Society consisting of veteran packinghouse workers and young residents became important for promoting social leadership in the neighborhood. La Capilla became the public signifier of Las Yardas, especially during its annual summer carnival and street festival, which brought visitors from across the entire district to "a land of pageantry," as one visitor put it. It included a Mexican parade that ran westward down 47th Street through the white Back of the Yards, crossing the racial borders that segregated them. Although these efforts turned placemaking into a generative political and cultural act for Mexican Back of the Yarders, in the early to mid-1960s they fractured ties with earlier, more confrontational aspects of race, labor, and immigration-rights organizing.[59]

Las Yardas' newly energized political and cultural placemaking worked to mitigate the structural forces of confinement and dispossession. Residents secured some political and civic representation, challenged persistent discriminatory real estate restrictions aimed at them, and exposed the blight created by exploitative zoning. But these results mostly impacted the district and rarely transcended to Latino citywide battles with urban renewal, restrictive improvement associations, or city hall. Moreover, this all occurred in the shadow of the civil rights movement and the struggle to desegregate Chicago, which captured the attention of the local mainstream press and the national spotlight. Disturbances over racial succession in nearby Englewood in 1963 animated the conflict between the civil rights movement and the resistance of white Southwest Siders. Englewood's sudden demographic change also set the stage for comparisons to its neighbor, the Back of the Yards, which vehemently resisted integration as it got closer to home. Civil rights groups and liberal clergy working to integrate neighborhoods avoided violent districts like the Back of the Yards altogether by leapfrogging or parachuting families of color into softer landing spots and better housing stock further south and west.

The momentum that the civil rights movement gained nationally provoked a growing backlash of white ethnic angst in urban neighborhoods. Along with launching their own countermovement, dismayed white ethnics aimed their frustrations mostly at Democrats they considered responsible for giving unearned benefits to racial minorities and forcibly opening their neighborhoods and schools. Federal measures enacted by the Civil Rights Act of 1964 to integrate schools and neighborhoods angered Chicago's working-class whites, who began defecting from the Democratic Party and found a new home in the modern Republican Party. The shifting allegiance sent a wave of panic through the city's Democratic political machine and its boss, Mayor Richard J. Daley, who had long enjoyed the loyalty of two of the city's essential constituencies: white ethnic homeowners and Black Chicagoans. Although Daley instituted some minor economic and housing relief for his Black Belt constituents, federal mandates became a nuisance for the mayor and began to jeopardize his hold over white ethnics. To appease racially anxious whites, Daley opposed proposals for stricter open-occupancy legislation, leading to its defeat on local and state ballots.

A key site of organized resistance against open occupancy came from working-class whites living in South Lawndale who were active in a group called the Property Owners Coordinating Committee. Its members learned much from the Back of the Yards and felt threatened by racial succession not only from Blacks but Mexicans too. By the summer of 1966, the intensity of the counter-civil rights backlash on the Southwest Side and the enduring structures of segregation drew Martin Luther King Jr. to call attention to Chicago's color line. King and the Chicago Freedom Movement led peaceful marches through white working-class neighborhoods on the Southwest Side to highlight the stark inequality that existed between white and Black Chicago. In Gage Park, Marquette Park, and Chicago Lawn—filled with many middle-class families with roots in the Back of the Yards—marchers were met with violent confrontations. The limits of civil rights gains were captured in the hostile resistance to King as white onlookers hurled racist slurs, carried white power signs, torched cars, and flung rocks at marchers, one hitting King in the head. "The citizens acted not unlike the people of Birmingham and Selma, Ala.," noted one witness. King's visit revealed the city's deeply entrenched structural and social racism. The violent backlash and city hall's political stagnation signaled a key defeat for the Chicago Freedom Movement and civil rights in the north.[60]

Mexican immigrants and Mexican Americans were caught in a political realignment over neighborhood integration that positioned them between white ethnics and the Black freedom struggle. These middle-ground dynamics played out frequently for Latinos across the city. In Woodlawn, for instance, Puerto Ricans were preferred as tenants over African Americans after Julian H. Levi, a prominent white liberal, reportedly saw them as less objectionable than Blacks.[61] Although Mexicans continued to be racialized by language, color, class, and residence, their invisibility within this racial culture war was all the more challenging as they sought to counteract their own economic and residential confinement. Resources to alleviate racial inequality eluded them in the mid-1960s, as did community control over local institutions that remained in the hands of groups like the BYNC. In the 1960s, the BYNC's racist reputation preceded it nationwide as the little neighborhood group that stopped the "relentless march of the color line," keeping the city's demographic revolution from engulfing their district. In the process, the district coalesced into the great silent majority. Alinsky, who for years in the 1950s and early 1960s would neither disassociate himself nor repudiate the group for fear of tarnishing his own legacy, finally severed his ties to it. From 1963 onward, he publicly disavowed the group. "Now, Alinsky considers the neighborhood segregationist," according to a journalist profiling him in 1969. Quoting Alinsky in *Business Week*, the journalist wrote, "'They don't dare say they try to keep Negroes out—just to keep their people in,' he says. When he visited the area last fall, he was dismayed to see George Wallace-for-President stickers plastered on cars in front of the neat little row houses."[62]

The silent-majority conversion of the Back of the Yards, while offensive to Alinsky and liberal newsrooms, was not all negative for Joseph Meegan. His advocacy on behalf of white homeowners through conservation programs, staving off integration threats, and promoting self-help bootstrapism won him municipal recognition. City hall rewarded him with a seat on the board of the Chicago Dwellings Association (CDA) and its parent agency, the Chicago Housing Authority (CHA). The CDA was tasked with building new single-family homes for middle-income Chicagoans, mostly whites. Meegan's unique skillset of lobbying for resources from the federal government while maintaining an antigovernment posture among constituents who were wary of federal and state "handouts" made him valuable in the white-flight era. Still, on the CDA board, prominent African American leaders like Theophilus Mann chastised Meegan for the CDA's complicity in segregation, telling him in 1964, "Come on Joe . . . are we going to sell them [homes] with discrimination or without?" Moreover, Alinsky's reluctance to disassociate with Meegan and the BYNC (until it was politically detrimental) came under intense scrutiny from younger Black activists who were frustrated with the community organizer. "Containment for Negroes has been the aftermath of every Alinsky appearance," wrote Brenetta Howell, a Black housing activist in 1965, referring to him as "the lion-tamer who only succeeded in making the lions there more vicious." In the mid- to late 1960s, as young liberal activists were discovering Alinsky for the first time, racial minority groups had soured on Alinsky and Meegan as two sides of the same coin. Alternately, the BYNC settled into its newfound place in the silent majority even as journalists and authors attempted to reconcile the groups' CIO and New Deal roots with its history of racial exclusion. What few outsiders understood, however, was the differentiated racial designs that Meegan had engineered throughout the group's postwar history; designs that at once prevented Black settlement and also contained Mexican settlement. "The area is already integrated," Meegan insisted throughout the 1960s. "We have Mexicans," he told journalists as he countered charges that the Back of the Yards was not racially diverse while denying the groups' anti-Black racism. Although Meegan recognized the persistence and place-making of Las Yardas, he was also the chief architect of this uniquely small enclave that, amid significant Mexican immigration to the city, utilized policy tools and political influence to steer this group away from the Back of the Yards and into other wards.[63]

: :

The BYNC made one final attempt to tame Las Yardas when it asked the Department of Urban Renewal to consider it for possible land clearance to introduce private capital. "From the survey data obtained by two private consultants, it is clear that the 45th-Ashland area is a slum and blighted area and is eligible for redevelopment," wrote the city agency in its report. Confronted with another round of abusive targeting by the city, Mexican Back of the Yarders turned to the McDowell Settlement for help, which also faced demolition and financial insolvency. Though the land clearance never materialized, the threat mobilized Las Yardas residents to challenge the city's debilitating zoning restrictions and its pretense of reindustrialization. Yet, despite facing similar exclusionary residential barriers as African Americans did, the aims of Las Yardas residents did not immediately coalesce with the broader civil rights movement. One reason was that forms of Latino segregation and containment remained largely unaddressed by government measures to alleviate Black inequality, as the government did not *see* Latinos in the ways the BYNC, the Chicago Real Estate Board, or white Southwest Side residents so readily *saw* them: as harbingers of unwanted diversity. Another reason was that Mexican Back of the Yarders had largely, to that point, opted for nonconfrontational forms of political engagement. Having survived cycles of industrial flight, economic restructuring, and discriminatory barriers, residents of Las Yardas developed a quiet politics of perseverance and piety, working through informal, nongovernmental means to secure resources and opportunities. These "quiet politics" by no means meant they accepted being pushed around and/or displaced, but it underscored a patience that was unacceptable in other corners of the fight for social and economic justice. As it became clearer to the BYNC that the suburbs remained a powerful economic and cultural incentive for working whites, the neighborhood group braced itself for massive white flight in the 1960s. The BYNC and the local real estate agencies began opening vacated housing to new waves of Mexican homebuyers. Taking a cue from Latino newcomers' militant takeover of community-control institutions in nearby Pilsen and Little Village, by 1969, the BYNC appointed its first Mexican American president, John Sanchez, signaling a new chapter in the old jungle.[64]

4 :: Making a Brown Bungalow Belt

From the early to mid-1960s, as the national spotlight framed Chicago's battles over integration, open housing, schools, and property taxes as white over Black, a less perceptible neighborhood transformation was occurring in Chicago's Lower West and Southwest Side. Urban renewal had dispersed Latinos across the central city, but Mexican immigrants and Mexican Americans were steered into a space rife with racial tension and hostility from working-class white ethnics, aimed then mostly at African Americans. Although the sudden arrival of thousands of Mexicans into Polish, Slavic, and Bohemian neighborhoods in the 1960s did not provoke outbreaks of racial violence, it did raise the alarm of neighborhood councils and conservationists. Some city leaders and race-relations experts went as far as to portray the settlement of Mexicans into white areas as relatively easy, even harmonious, ignoring the simmering hostilities Mexicanization provoked and missing deeper racial, spatial, and capital reconfigurations. Mexican immigration and Mexican American resettlement after displacement became another feature of a larger *incentive apparatus* (along with redlining, credit blacklisting, segregation, and inner-city disinvestment) that pulled whites to the suburbs. In short, Mexican immigration helped incentivize white suburbanization. Urban conflict and white spatial entitlement eventually gave way to profitable transactions that depended on white flight and fueled a housing market for new Mexican renters and homebuyers, linking race and capitalism in uniquely layered ways.

The displacement of Mexicans from the Halsted-Roosevelt area created a bonanza of profiteering from white real estate agents (and eventually Mexican American real estate agents) who deliberately steered Mexicans into Pilsen and South Lawndale, reinfusing value into a collapsing real estate market. The racialized dimensions could not be ignored, as property transactions and rental contracts were loaded with racial implications. For whites, selling and renting properties was predicated on a paradox of Mexican purchasing power and anti-Mexican sentiment and fear. Even as it was becoming advantageous for whites to abandon their neighborhoods for greener pastures, their emotional, cultural, religious, and political ties to these spaces were difficult to relinquish and would figure into neighborhood tensions for years to come.

Throughout the 1960s, white ethnic anxieties over open occupancy, integration, declining property values, and anti-Black and anti-Latino sentiment permeated the social and political landscape of the Southwest Side and Bungalow Belt. In response, a small, elite group of Mexican American civic and business leaders abandoned the politics of protest in favor of a *conservative colonia*, conveying a Mexican immigrant/ethnic group that was hard-working, entrepreneurial, loyal to the Democratic Party, and cooperative as they navigated entry into racially tense neighborhoods. This group sought to take stewardship of the resettlement of Mexicans. Their politics were shaped by their recent past with displacement and an ever-evolving search for community stability. In their quest to secure clout within city hall, these leaders allied with Mayor Richard J. Daley throughout the 1960s and 1970s, giving them small but incremental influence in their communities, meanwhile racial conflict, social movements, tax revolts, white flight, and local, national, and international events threatened the machine's hold on the city. These leaders incorporated themselves into the Democratic Party machine and doubled down on their loyalty to Daley, even in the aftermath of contentious moments like the summer unrest of 1966 and the police violence at the Democratic National Convention of 1968.

These episodes coincided with an explosive wave of Mexican immigration to the city, setting the stage for these leaders to give meaning and contour to this settlement. As a civic leader, real estate agent, and former public-housing activist, Anita Villarreal established herself in the Bohemian neighborhood of South Lawndale, southwest of Pilsen. Her pathbreaking aims led to more Mexican settlement. Throughout the 1960s and 1970s, Villarreal turned unstable vacancies left by white flight into a new base for political and economic power. During this phase, Mexican Americans and Mexican immigrants shaped their own *bungalow suburbanism* by making do and customizing their adopted built environment. Although this process was hardly free from conflict with white ethnics, this settlement engendered a politics of Mexican social conservatism predicated on neighborhood stability, business opportunity, and access to patronage services and jobs. In a few short years, Mexican Americans and Mexican immigrants carved their own path further into the Bungalow Belt. The majority of Mexicans in Chicago, however, remained corralled in disinvested and dilapidated parts of Pilsen and the Near West Side. By 1976, when Mayor Daley died, the urban crisis and economic recession had already begun to unravel the Mexican conservative consensus that had been loyal to Daley's machine for over a decade. This loyalty resulted in some short-term gains for Latinos and some long-term losses. Mexican American civic and business leaders participated in a system of complicity that undermined Latino political power and furthered white machine control of majority-Latino neighborhoods.

Out of the Rubble

By late 1963, as Las Yardas continued to face zoning changes that threatened its survival, and the Near West Side was being torn down for the University of Illinois at Chicago Circle, many Mexican residents were dispersed to the Lower West Side neighborhoods. "We fought the city on some issues, particularly, at the time the site was chosen," explained Mario Dovalina, referring to the Near West Side, "My restaurants would be torn down. Many of my people lived there." The forced displacement engendered a lingering resentment in some Mexican American civic leaders and merchants. Some members of the IFOMA, such as Dovalina, squarely blamed Daley and the political machine for their lack of transparency in giving the land to the university. As the publisher of *Prensa Libre* (*Free Press*), a Spanish-language weekly, Dovalina made his opposition well known. "If you start writing editorials against the machine, especially against Mayor Daley . . . I don't know if I should tell you these things, you know, inspectors and things like that," Dovalina cautiously told an interviewer, evoking the retribution he started receiving from the machine for his outspokenness, "I came to the conclusion I could not stay in the restaurant businesses and in the newspaper business at the same time. [Inspectors] would come and they would be more strict. . . . Like when I opened my place near Maxwell Street. I did everything according to the books. But I couldn't get license approval." He described how city inspectors would find small technical violations of any kind: "Every little thing was wrong. It was obvious that they weren't going to co-operate with me if I wasn't going to co-operate with them."[1]

Members of IFOMA remained clear-eyed about what happened to them in the Near West Side in the 1940s and 1950s: municipal disinvestment gave way to deterioration, eventually serving as justification for bulldozing their homes and business enclave. Having lost the ground on South Halsted Street they had fought so hard for, they were determined to find inroads to political power to guarantee commercial longevity and community stability. In the late 1950s, members of IFOMA formed a voting bloc under the name 1st Ward Independent Mexican American Voters and emphasized their independence from machine influence. But urban renewal had significantly weakened their voting-bloc power by dispersing them. Therefore, members reorganized and began reaching out to the mayor to build a more collaborative relationship. This is how they navigated the murky waters undergirding the demolition of the South Halsted Street commercial base of Mexican American merchants and the rest of the Near West Side in the early to mid-1960s.[2]

But IFOMA members were still caught in the middle, between attempting to build new bridges with city hall or continuing to fight the mayor—who could easily punish them through denial of permits or contracts—or harassment by precinct workers. This paradox was brought into sharp relief when one of the leaders of the opposition to the university, Italian American activist Florence Scala, launched her candidacy for alderman of the 1st Ward to challenge the Democratic machine candidate. She, along with the Harrison-Halsted Community Group, an interethnic and interracial organization of displaced Italian, Mexican, African American, and Greek residents, filed a lawsuit against the city and the university. IFOMA endorsed Scala and financially supported the lawsuit. Although Scala ran as an independent, she and the Harrison-Halsted Community Group sought support from the local GOP in securing sponsorships and endorsements to mobilize resources against the machine.[3]

Scala lost that election, and worse, arsonists firebombed her home in an act of intimidation believed to be connected to the 1st Ward crime syndicate. The Mexican American merchants of IFOMA and their brief flirtation with the Chicago Republican Party demonstrated their willingness to look out for their best interests, even if it meant challenging the Democratic machine. Still, the retribution against Scala, Dovalina, and others prompted some of the merchants to keep quiet about their politics as they attempted to rebuild their businesses in Pilsen, also part of the Italian-controlled ward. Others, however, were uneasy with the GOP alliance. IFOMA member and president of the Mexican Chamber of Commerce Arturo Velasquez was not averse to the Democratic machine per se but to city hall's bullying and overreach of authority toward the small businessperson. He understood the IFOMA members, who were simply small merchants trying to relocate their families, keep their businesses intact, and survive, and he cautioned their outspoken positions against the machine, which could make their lives more difficult.[4]

Nevertheless, Velasquez fundamentally believed Mayor Daley would listen to reason when approached with a noncombative disposition and the premise that the city must be a healthy place for business, no matter how big or small. Back in 1960, Velasquez campaigned enthusiastically for presidential candidate John F. Kennedy, prompting him to start a group called the Mexican American Democratic Organization (MADO) along with other merchants. His political mobilization was directly connected to his business aspirations. Velasquez disagreed with IFOMA colleague Mario Dovalina's antimachine opinions and did not blame Daley for their misfortune during the "Harrison-Halsted controversy." On the contrary, Velasquez asked his colleagues to rise above 1st Ward politics and see the bigger stakes at hand: "If the Mexican Chamber of Commerce has faced moments of crisis in the past, it is due to the apathy of its merchants that do not take interest, nor do they see the importance that an organization of this nature deserves."[5] Velasquez encouraged his colleagues to hold greater metropolitan ambitions for commerce and civic mindedness. As a group now seeking business licenses, permits, and other city accommodations to make inroads in machine-controlled, white ethnic neighborhoods, it was in their best interest to build a friendly relationship with city hall during this relocation crisis.[6]

Amigos for Daley

Mexican Americans' route into the Democratic machine came through their civic and community groups, which took on new roles. In the early 1960s, the Mexican American political class sought inroads to metropolitan power through finessing relations and dealmaking rather than outright protest and demonstration. Like many Latino communities throughout the country in 1960, Chicago's Latinos, accompanied by their civic and political organizations, mobilized a broad base of support for John F. Kennedy's presidential campaign. "Nothing existed for what was about to capture the imagination and political spirit of the Mexicano community," recalled Velasquez, crediting the Kennedy campaign as a major turning point in the community's political mobilization. Through strategic coordination between national campaign representatives and local Latino organizations, in September of 1960, Viva Kennedy Clubs were organized throughout the various Mexican

Figure 4.1. A parade float featuring the Mexican American Democratic Organization (MADO) during the Mexican Independence Day Parade on Michigan Avenue, September 1961. (Image courtesy of Cynthia Guerrero.)

communities in Chicago. Frank and Jovita Duran organized a club in Pilsen. After being displaced from the Near West Side, Anita Villarreal and her family relocated to South Lawndale, where she turned her newly opened real estate office on 26th Street and St. Louis Avenue into a "Viva Kennedy" campaign center. Carmen Mendoza, Vice Chairwoman of IFOMA, also opened a campaign center in her community in South Chicago, while Catarino Diaz opened one in the Back of the Yards. Essie Rodriguez and her husband, Andrew, did the same in McKinley Park. Although nationally the Viva Kennedy Clubs represented a major expansion of Latino political action and voter mobilization—from Mexican Americans in California and Texas to Puerto Ricans in New York and Philadelphia—in Chicago, this moment overlapped with a stingy Democratic machine that was unwilling to share political influence with Latinos, even during national Democratic Party courting. This moment demonstrated the nimbleness and restraint of the Viva Kennedy organizers, who shared in the campaign's larger aim to register Spanish-speaking voters and reverse years of disenfranchisement but who as members of the local MADO also sought access to Daley's machine. That access would not be granted by increasing voting rolls but by signaling symbolic gestures of support. MADO did both, supporting Kennedy and the promise of a future Latino vote and showing fealty to Daley for patronage. On the day of the election, most of downstate Illinois voted for Richard Nixon, as predicted, but Chicago delivered the winning vote for Kennedy, allowing him to carry the state. This was preceded by speculation over unproven but highly suspected Chicago Democratic machine tampering with the election results. But beyond that, one thing was clear: Chicago's Viva Kennedy Clubs were well-organized, neighborhood-based political networks that demonstrated the potential power of the Latino vote.[7]

At these events, Mayor Daley's staff came to know Paul Gasca, who, with Velasquez, helped organize the local Viva Kennedy rallies. Gasca, a war veteran with a gregarious personality, spent part of his childhood in Yuriria, Guanajuato, and his adolescent years in Chicago's Near West Side. After returning from the service during World War II, he became a major booster for his neighborhood's social, faith-based, and civic institutions. His propensity for civic work and youth mentorship led him to become a social worker with the Chicago Area Project—a major milestone for any Latino at the time—and to work under the renowned sociologist Clifford R. Shaw, a youth-delinquency specialist. As a social worker, he assisted in improving his old neighborhood's deteriorated physical landscape. With teams of volunteers, he spruced up abandoned storefronts and tenement buildings. And like Velasquez, Gasca engaged top officials in city hall to leverage resources for his community.[8]

MADO, as discussed earlier, was formed to support the Kennedy campaign. Intent on being incorporated into the Democratic Party, a small cluster of civic and business leaders carefully cultivated a new relationship with the mayor through this group. "Foremost on our agenda," wrote cofounder Arturo Velasquez, "[are] jobs, building permits, licenses for grocery stores, bars, restaurants, and other businesses, zoning, standard municipal services like streets and sanitation, and better access to elected officials."[9] Their push for access to patronage in a city that was run by patronage was reasonable. But because city jobs, licenses, and permits flowed downward from ward organizations sliced along ethnic and racial lines, Mexican Americans had no representative they could turn to. MADO strategically forged an alliance with Daley using contacts inside city hall. The group invited him to the opening of their new headquarters in the recently Mexicanized Pilsen neighborhood for cocktails and refreshments, reiterating to the mayor in a 1962 letter: "The purpose of this organization is to (1) foster and promote the political aims and ideals of the Mexican-American citizen; (2) to foster and promote the political aims and ideals of the Democratic Political Party in and among Mexican-American citizens; (3) to foster and promote civic, social, and patriotic and political activity in the Mexican-American community of Chicago."[10]

One of those contacts inside city hall was Paul Gasca. At the close of the 1950s, Gasca accepted a position in the Office of Inquiry and Information, located on the first floor of city hall. Colonel Jack Reilly, the mayor's director of special events and Daley's close political advisor, helped arrange the appointment. Reilly came to know many of the Mexican American leaders, including Gasca, while officiating or attending community events, even a few times as a beauty-pageant judge. Reilly felt that Latinos would become as reliable a Democratic vote as African Americans were, although there were no data to support that premise. Reilly assured the mayor he could find the right representatives to reinforce the machine's interests, and he brought in Gasca to serve as the liaison between the mayor and Chicago's Latinos. People went to him to translate letters from the city, interpret a court summons, get parade and park-use permits, deal with slumlords, and for help with an array of urban problems. Gasca and Reilly felt that with the mayor's important forthcoming reelection in 1963, organizing Spanish-speaking groups in this way would be wise. Gasca and Reilly called this mutually beneficial apparatus the "Amigos for Daley."[11]

Amigos for Daley became the campaign arm of MADO, doing for Daley in 1963 what they did for Kennedy in 1960: door knocking, voter registration, campaign-message translation, and ultimately ensuring that Latinos would pull the "Democrat" lever on election day. The Amigos for Daley canvassers listed the points that would resonate with Spanish-speaking voters: Daley was a family man, a devout Catholic, and a labor-union supporter. To his credit, Daley understood how to connect with working-class voters of all ethnicities. "When I see my neighborhood," Daley would say, "I see all the neighborhoods of Chicago. When I see our home and family, I see everyone's home and family and that's what counts in this city." In exchange for their support, the mayor made sure Mexican Americans were incorporated into their local wards' democratic organizations that were otherwise run by Irish, Italians, Poles, and Czechs. Mexican American precinct captains entered the ranks of Lower West Side and Southwest Side wards in Pilsen, South Lawndale, and Back of the Yards. None of these positions involved participation in the party's decision-making structure, and some Mexican and Mexican American critics of the mayor saw this as no reward at all, but MADO was satisfied with the small concessions and had an ally in Daley.[12]

The Amigos made their way to the upper floors of city hall. "I explained to [the mayor] that in order for me to continue facilitating Mexicano access to City Hall," said Velasquez, "I was going to need an office in the building." Daley provided the Amigos with a small office right next to his own on the fifth floor, where all fifty city council members had their offices. Council members joked that the small closet-sized office belonged to the mysterious alderman of the "51st Ward." Although no such ward existed, it was telling that Daley would rather give away a small corner of city hall real estate than an entire city ward to the Mexicans. Velasquez and Diaz's ties to Daley gave them clout back in their own neighborhoods, and, as businessmen, this went a long way. "Any courtesies shown Mr. Velasquez will be appreciated by Mayor Daley," explained a letter of introduction Daley had Reilly prepare for Velasquez. Daily contact between the mayor and the Amigos allowed for a greater understanding to develop, even if it was that the Amigos had to learn to accommodate the machine's fear of change. Daley was not only mayor but also the chairman of the Cook County Democratic Party, and, as such, he controlled the slating of all candidates for all elected positions. The Amigos learned quickly that slating any Mexican Americans for Democratic positions was out of the question. The Amigos did not blame this on the machine but on what they saw as the internal "disunity" of Latinos in the city. The office became the daily workspace of MADO and Amigo members Arturo Velasquez and Catarino Diaz. From their vantage point on the fifth floor of city hall, the Amigos could more fully grasp the precarious position of Mexicans across the metropolis, a picture that would become clearer during Daley's 1963 reelection campaign.[13]

Mayor Daley's challenger was Benjamin Adamowski, a Democrat-turned-Republican of Polish descent who came from the Bungalow Belt neighborhoods of the Southwest Side. The Bungalow Belt was made up of predominantly second- and third-generation Polish, Slovak, and Lithuanian homeowners with working-class roots in the grittier immigrant neighborhoods of the Back of the Yards. In the 1960s, residents of Polish ancestry were the largest white ethnic group remaining in the city, and Adamowski saw this potential electoral strength as his opportunity to unseat Daley. The

Irish Catholic mayor from working-class Bridgeport had always received overwhelming support from the Bungalow Belt, but he saw that Adamowski was now cutting into his traditional support base.[14]

During the campaign, Adamowski took advantage of white resentment over racial integration in the Bungalow Belt. He also accused Daley of looking out only for bankers and the powerful downtown elites on State Street and presented himself as the candidate of the working-class Bungalow Belt, declaring, "I'll take Western Avenue, Nagle Avenue, Ashland Avenue, and Milwaukee Avenue, where the little people reside." In calling out the old "Polish corridors" of the city, he reinforced the notion that these areas belonged to whites only—an affront to Mexicans who had been making slow but gradual inroads as residents and merchants on these very streets, albeit with great difficulty, for years. The Mexican Chamber of Commerce, which Velasquez and Diaz belonged to, coveted these commercial streets as the lifeblood of their future prosperity and fought tooth and nail to establish businesses there. Both Velasquez's and Diaz's businesses were on Ashland Avenue, and they understood the difficulty in getting Polish property owners to rent or sell to Mexicans. The Amigos doubled their campaign efforts for Daley, who won wards on the Southwest Side that contained large percentages of Latinos and lost wards where Polish Americans were the dominant group. The mayor's skillful tightrope walking on the issue of civil rights not only saved him from losing his reelection bid, as the votes of Black Chicagoans and liberal whites narrowly carried him to victory, but for Mexicans, the Bungalow Belt's support of the Republican candidate helped fasten them to the Democratic machine for a little longer.[15]

The Cook County Democratic Organization wanted to avoid creating a Latino submachine, as it had done with African Americans in the 1940s. By the early 1960s, there were enough Latinos in the city that they could potentially be organized to support or undermine the machine. This momentarily piqued the interest of Saul Alinsky, who was always looking for leverage against the machine. Alinsky had neglected Latinos in Chicago for years to organize them in California. While focused on his Southwest Side organizing campaign, he shot off a memo to his key lieutenant, Nicholas Von Hoffman, to inquire about Mexican Americans' voting situation. Von Hoffman responded with the IAF's routine position: the Mexican population in Chicago remained negligible, which had guided Alinsky's inaction regarding Mexicans in the Back of the Yards in earlier years.[16]

What Von Hoffman dismissed as insignificant the machine saw as opportune. In the meantime, coming off Daley's close victory, the Amigos pressed the mayor for more face time. The Amigos used their favorite Gold Coast haunt, Café La Margarita (co-owned by Cesar Dovalina and Velasquez), to hold meetings over dinner and cocktails. They hosted parties for visiting Mexican radio and film stars, foreign dignitaries, and men of commerce. And they brokered deals with machine politicians, often Col. Reilly or even Daley himself. They secured favors and small amounts of patronage; on occasion, they delicately pressed the machine about the plight of Latinos in the city: discrimination in housing, insufficient civil service jobs, negligent city services with respect to regular trash pickup, clean parks, affordable coal during winter, public libraries, and overcrowded and underfunded schools. Echoing the delicate nature of these requests, in 1965, while visiting with the Amigos, former Mexican President Adolfo López Mateos told a local reporter, "The problems of the Mexican-American community, if any, should be solved by local officials," deferring, as the Amigos did, to the machine's authority.[17]

Amigos for Daley achieved integration into the city's political apparatus, even if only through ceremonial appointments and backroom deals. The Amigos were the conduits between Mayor Daley and the community. With Daley's tax base eroding, the Amigos and Daley calculated what the political future of Latinos would bring. Still, for Daley and his lieutenants, the question remained: Could Mexicans be reliable Democrats, and if so, when would they start voting in large enough numbers to make an impact? Because there was no clear answer to this question, the Amigos for Daley continued to leverage this potential in city hall. Mayor Daley, in turn, continued to make humble concessions. Only now the Amigos wanted more than mere permits or ceremonial roles; they desired a middle-class suburbia of their own, even if it needed to be invented within the city limits.

"Suburbanidad" in the City

The sudden relocation of tens of thousands of Mexicans to white ethnic Pilsen during the late 1950s and early 1960s would have registered a panic of "racial invasion" were it not dwarfed by the simultaneous movement of hundreds of thousands of Southern Black Americans to the West Side in North Lawndale. Still, the making of what Arnold Hirsh terms the "second ghetto" and its expansion into North Lawndale sent fear throughout the heavily Bohemian, Slavic, and Polish Southwest Side. "It is reaching a period now when the next few years will tell the effect of city-wide upheaval," wrote one white real estate broker in Pilsen, "Outside factors which will determine the future are the completion within two years of the Harrison-Halsted campus of the University of Illinois which is bound to bring in a market for homes and apartments. . . . Add to this the business and commercial establishments that are seeking new construction in the area." But not all who stood to profit were hopeful. These seismic racial shifts provoked tremendous anxiety among white ethnic communities that stood in the pathway of Black and Brown demographic explosions.[18]

For the newcomers, beyond the racial steering and contract selling that were common when they relocated to Eastern European neighborhoods, something less emphasized but profoundly alluring "pulled" them in. Mexican immigrants and Mexican Americans who bought and rented single-family bungalows were drawn to the suburban-like characteristics previously unavailable to the Near West Siders and others who were leaving cramped tenements.[19] They arrived hoping to subvert the trauma of displacement that fed directly into their desire for homeownership, homemaking, and stability. Historian Louise Año Nuevo Kerr called these new residents, who now lived on the western edge of the Lower West Side in areas like Heart of Chicago, "West End" Mexicans. New residents dubbed it the "Mexican Suburb" because it had better-quality buildings than the east end, where "at present the Pilsen neighborhood is becoming predominantly Mexican."[20] Fred Garza, a new Heart of Chicago homeowner, said in 1960, "We just bought this house, and to my wife and I, it's the first one we've owned . . . I opened my little business and I'm satisfied—the customers keep me busy day and night."[21]

While historians have drawn sharp lines between urban and suburban space, communities facing spatial segregation often defined their own unique spatial subjectivities, defying these categorical divides. Just a few blocks further southwest from Heart of Chicago was South Lawndale, whose built environment, although perhaps not as magnificent as North Lawndale's rows of beautiful greystones, grand boulevards, and public architecture, still elicited an attractive landscape of single-family brick bungalows and two-flat brick cottages. The design and layout of the bungalow neighborhoods, with an orderly grid and rows of brick homes, fueled the newcomers' imagination as a landscape of good living and bungalow pastoralism. In the early 1960s, Mexican Americans started arriving to the first mile of streets with names like Drake, Avers, St. Louis, and Ridgeway. They populated the east-west throughways of 23rd and 24th Streets, where Mexican and Black families lived close to one another but were divided by a viaduct. Nearby manufacturing plants that were within walking distance or a quick bus ride away were employing Mexicans to replace the whites that were leaving. A Lutheran planning study in 1965 determined that what was once known as the Czech "California" settlement "is [now] somewhat less solidly Czech than it was fifty years ago," hinting at the arrival of Brown and Black families.[22]

Making their own suburbia had less to do with escaping the city than with forming a new relationship to it. The single-family structures with their crabgrass lawns, the opportunity to customize to one's wishes, and home-improvement skills fueled the demand for these homes. The interior layouts of the two- and three-floor brick flats allowed bigger families to extend the extra space to family members or renters. Basements could be converted into extra living space. Such was the advice that Anita Villarreal, the local Mexican American real estate businesswoman, gave to her clients looking for homes in South Lawndale. Villarreal sold the bungalow suburbanism, giving buyers and new homeowners advice as if out of the pages of *House & Home*. Having been displaced herself from the Near West Side, she knew many of the families personally. Villarreal had been a longtime New Deal Democrat, but she emerged from the 1950s critical of the state and its interference in people's lives. Like the outspoken urban activists of her generation, Villarreal was an experienced community crusader who fought against urban renewal. Less privileged and less socially positioned than those engaged in full-time urban critique—and with a large family to support—she abandoned the fight over city planning upon her arrival to South Lawndale, opened her office on 26th Street, and undertook her new crusade as a businesswoman in a landscape ripe for entrepreneurship.[23]

Still, Mexican families could bypass the real estate agents and purchase directly from panicky Czech and Slavic homeowners looking to move out. Apolinar and Fernanda Guerrero moved from a crowded apartment on Morgan Street, where their kids all slept in one room, into a single-family brick bungalow on 2317 South Lawndale, where each could have their own bedroom. The Guerreros paid $12,000 for their home, purchased directly from a Bohemian woman who was ready to leave the neighborhood for the suburbs. One of the Guerrero daughters, Marcella, remembered, "People didn't come out of their houses. They stayed inside." Remaining whites peered out their windows to observe the block-by-block changes sweeping through their neighborhood. Anita Villarreal's youngest daughter Lori recounted, "It was a whole different world for me. Trees lined the boulevard." However, "the ethnic people all kept to themselves. . . . When we moved,

everything was dark, no street lights." Marcella Guerrero noted the difference from the Near West Side neighborhood, "On Morgan Street, everyone sat on the porch and was outside in the evenings, kids played on the
streets and in the empty lots." Similarly, the Barco family also came from
an apartment building on May Street in the Near West Side, where "it was
all asphalt and concrete, not that much grass, it was mostly dirty and a lot
of debris," recalled Dan Barco. The Barcos moved to 24th and Lawndale,
not far from the Guerreros, where "it was real nice, clean, well-kept area, it
was very new to us. Very clean, very fresh. Everybody kept their lawns."[24]

South Lawndale's civic leaders tried to stop residents from selling their
properties to Mexicans, which was not legally prohibited but was nonetheless seen as a violation of unspoken agreements between local homeowners
and real estate agents. "As recently as 1962, the only language you'd have
heard here was Czech," noted a local writer exploring the neighborhood,
"but with the incoming of Mexicans and a kind of hysterical concern over
the nearness of Negroes in Lawndale proper, as much as 40 percent of the
community has moved to Berwyn and Cicero." Alderman George J. Tourek
of the neighboring 23rd Ward, which included parts of South Lawndale,
expressed concern for the decline of 26th Street, the area's commercial corridor. "Something has to be done," he told a group of concerned residents
about the fleeing merchants, "if something is done, the rest of the area will
take care of itself."[25]

A series of race riots and street violence also sent local whites into
heightened panic. A. J. Monaco, a journalist and owner of the local *Community Reporter*, charged that outsiders with "vicious tongues" had accused
them of "acting racial" for wanting to "protect" their neighborhood. On
the heels of residential change, outbreaks of youth violence occurred more
regularly. Most notable was a race riot in July of 1961 that began when a
Black teenager was shot in the head by a member of the Latin Counts, a
Latino street gang, while passing through South Lawndale. The violence
sparked three days of revenge attacks over a two-mile stretch between
Harrison High and Farragut High, an area of overlapping neighborhoods
between South and North Lawndale and the Heart of Chicago. Hundreds
of police squads came to enforce emergency curfews. Although the riot
included white, Mexican, and Black street gangs, news reports sensation-
alized portrayals of "Negro teenage gangs beating up white persons" and
"mass gatherings" of "marauding" and "roving Negro youths," stirring
South Lawndale's segregationist impulse.[26]

Reports by the *Chicago Daily News* that "Negroes, Mexicans and Southern whites in search of a place to live have been jamming their way into the neighborhood for the past several years" mobilized South Lawndale's residents of Czech, Slavic, and Polish descent to deter racial minorities and to stop "panic peddlers" from moving them in. They sent angry letters to their elected representatives and civic leaders, threatening to oust them if they did not more forcefully denounce open housing. Their local group, the South Lawndale Conservation Commission, opposed the proposal of two civil rights ordinances introduced in August 1963. South Lawndale-Crawfordite homeowners organized busloads of neighbors to travel to Springfield to protest the open-occupancy bill being proposed to outlaw racial discrimination in homeseller-to-homebuyer transactions. The NAACP argued for open occupancy, but the homeowners claimed it took away "their right to private ownership" and was "a step leading us down the road to socialism and communism." Daley half-heartedly endorsed the open-housing bill, but it was very unpopular throughout the Southwest Side of Chicago, which was increasingly hostile to civil rights. In South Lawndale, the housing ordinance fight made State Rep. Lillian Piotrowski a local hero for her dramatic "no" vote on the statehouse floor. Piotrowski was a lifelong South Lawndale resident, and even though her constituents included not only whites but also Blacks in North Lawndale and supporters of the bill, she joined with the Eastern European insurgency that Benjamin Adamowski had roused earlier during his mayoral campaign.[27]

Piotrowski's own political antennae drove her to resist not only Blacks but also Mexicans relocating to her ward. In her view, white flight was irresponsible, and people had to be persuaded to stay. Her feelings were echoed in the neighboring 25th Ward in Pilsen, where the group United Property Owners called a meeting to take deliberate action "against open occupancy" in light of the proposed legislation and panic over the recent influx of displaced Mexicans from the Near West Side. "We must keep undesirables out," decried Alderman Vito Marzullo, the keynote speaker, to the 150 residents crowded inside Wozniak Hall at the western edge of Pilsen. In attendance were local property owners, clergy, politicians, policemen, firemen, the publisher of the *Lawndale News* and *West Side Times*, and concerned civic leaders from neighboring South Lawndale-Crawford. "The people really acclaimed their new Alderman," noted an observer, as Marzullo told attendees, "We're against open occupancy" and "private ownership of land is guaranteed." Marzullo galvanized them to express their opposition against restrictions on their rights as property owners, saying, "We can withstand any threat." He also endorsed political candidates for office who opposed fair housing: "We, the people, must pledge our support and remember these men on election day." Whether it was coming from Lillian Piotrowski of the South Lawndale or Vito Marzullo of Pilsen, what became more apparent in these Southwest Side communities was that property owners were fundamentally anti-Black in their opposition, but in the abstract, since African Americans had already bypassed the ward entirely for North Lawndale. Nevertheless, open-housing ordinances became their rallying cry to fight the perceived "imposition" of state and federal law. An external report of Pilsen written a few years earlier noted the "overcrowding and influx of minority groups which are causing additional problems in housing and race relations." Marzullo's ward was receiving the greatest numbers of Mexicans, and both he and groups like the United Property Owners sought to put a stop to it.[28]

Around this same time, Carmen Mendoza, the vice chairwoman of IFOMA, wrote a letter to Monsignor John Egan to inform him of how her group was helping the relocation effort: "Our Federation has been assisting the Mexican residents of the Harrison-Halsted area in our own limited way. Our concern here, of course, is for the Mexican; the one who can speak only Spanish; the one with the low-income; the newcomer who is not necessarily an alien; the new immigrant; the one with the large family who would have a 3 year wait for public housing; the one who if put into public housing won't stay there because he can't adapt to it."[29] As Mendoza painted a more complicated portrait of "the Mexican people who reside in the controversial Harrison-Halsted area," she tried to get across the powerlessness of those being displaced and that they were going to need to go somewhere: "One thing does stand out; and that is the apparent need here for the Mexican's own and established community." Egan was sympathetic but not entirely sure how he could help, confiding to his colleague the Rev. Leo Mahon, "From what [Mendoza] says some real help in relocation is needed. However, this will be a complex matter."[30]

IFOMA and other Latino housing advocates had grown frustrated with the "conservation" talk by community leaders and city officials. Some of the more outspoken members of IFOMA had not forgotten their good-faith attempts to engage with the Land Clearance Commission during the 1950s, only to be told their businesses and homes would not be "conserved" after all. They were now convinced "conservation" was political speak for "planning out" Mexicans. IFOMA urged Egan to get involved, as he was the chairman of the archdiocese's conservation council tasked with overseeing its parishes' real estate, and the Catholic archdiocese had been silent on city planners' destruction of its churches. Mendoza pointedly asked Egan, "Will it then become necessary for the Archdiocese to help us?—and will it help us?—and how?" Leaders like Mendoza and others carried their skepticism about conservation into the Southwest Side neighborhoods, which were now fully engulfed in anti-fair-housing politics and pro-conservation tactics.[31]

White conservationist groups hinged their segregationist desires on things decidedly not associated with race, like modern design and home improvement. But home improvement, modernization, and conservation were loaded with implicit racism. Because the real estate and lending industries incentivized racially homogenous communities, conservation became consistent with segregationist impulses. Therefore, homeowners bound by their properties and investments mobilized to protect their neighborhoods' whiteness. As one critic of the racialism embedded in planning and design put it in 1963: "Overtly or covertly, race is the predominant issue of urban renewal and urban life. Racial design dictates just about all city planning. No auditorium, no downtown apartment house, rarely a supermarket is built in any American city today whose site was not determined by where Negroes live and where they are likely to move." As described in chapter 3, conservation strategies were used in the Back of the Yards in the 1950s to prevent two interrelated trends: African Americans entering the community and the expansion of the Mexican settlement west of Ashland Avenue, "Chicago's Mason-Dixon line." But by the 1960s, almost all of Chicago was engaged in some kind of conservation work in anticipation and prevention of Black and Brown settlement. In South Lawndale, Lillian Piotrowski and her like-minded neighborhoods supported the Real Estate Board's position when its representative, Arthur F. Mohl, stated, "Sub-standard people live in sub-standard housing." This was not simply a value-laden statement but a political call that emboldened white groups to get rid of "sub-standard" people by getting rid of "sub-standard housing."[32]

Latino families purchasing homes in the Southwest Side entered this milieu of panic-turned-conservation activism, driven by their desire to partake in the democratic promise of homeownership with all its underpinnings of postwar domesticity and mass consumption, including homemaking, recreation, and entrepreneurship. Aspiring to become members of the homeowning middle class, they looked past their neighbors' racist stares and tactics. A newspaper profile on IFOMA member Fortino Mendez and his family helped cast a positive light on their displacement and subsequent upward mobility. Mendez "is now in his third Chicago tailor shop," the journalist wrote. "He was forced to close the first two because they were in urban renewal areas. [However,] The Mendez family is in many ways typical. With an income close to the average for Chicago families, they are able to lead a neat, orderly existence." The Mendezes "bought [a] three-story apartment building [in Pilsen] which is their present home, for $14,000 in 1958. Its value is now listed as $19,000, reflecting the economic rebirth of the neighborhood." This was a drastic departure from the viewpoint of Marzullo and the United Property Owners group, who saw their neighborhood in alarming decline.[33]

Localized politics aside, the arriving, upwardly mobile Mexican Americans were "enriching the cosmopolitan cauldron" as supporters of the Democratic Party. In a 1963 speech to the Chicago chapter of the American GI Forum and Women's Auxiliary, Bobby Kennedy reassured Mexican Americans of their rightful place in the Democrats' principles of inclusion. Even with the racial turmoil in the city, systematic racial discrimination, and their own relegation to the least desirable parts of these neighborhoods, Kennedy assured them that they formed a crucial part of the American path of modern progress: "And so it is the current generation of Spanish-speaking Americans that concerns us today, the people who, collectively, have only in modern times begun to rise and free themselves from the status of an underprivileged minority within the mainstream of American life." Kennedy also struck at the heart of their entrepreneurial ambitions: "The 'Latino' could no longer be regarded solely as a man to be employed: in many cases he had become the employer." At the city level, alliances between city hall and groups such as IFOMA, Mexican American Democratic Organization, Mexican Chamber of Commerce, and Amigos for Daley were coming to fruition as well. In seeking influence, they leveraged consumer-based and voter-bloc-based arguments for their inclusion and incorporation into the city hall agenda. The "Democratic Party apparatus" led by Mayor Daley and his lieutenants (primarily Col. Jack Reilly) capitulated by creating new offices or staffing existing offices that Latinos could turn to for assistance: the Mayor's Commission on New Residents, the Mayor's Office of Inquiry and Information, and the City's Human Relations Commission, which by 1964 was recognized as alleviating real estate market discrimination.[34]

This was low-hanging fruit that the mayor could deliver to civic and business leaders without disrupting the party's local power structure. But Latinos still had no policy voice at the city or state level, no appointments in any social agencies, no influence in the city council, and certainly no sway through the aldermanic offices or state representatives, which were

especially hostile to Latinos in their wards and districts. Still, during a tu-
multuous set of years for Daley between 1963 and 1965, when he was frequently booed in public for his weakness on civil rights, Latino relations
with Daley seemed peculiarly calm. Whether the ad hoc nature of Daley's
special Latino liaisons were effective in their advocacy role during this time
of tremendous Latino poverty, overcrowding, continued displacement, and
unemployment was up to interpretation. But what was perhaps clearer to
city hall was that there was no large adversarial Latino civil rights organization to worry about as there was for African Americans. Local chapters
of the League of United Latin American Citizens (LULAC) and American
GI Forum were disengaged from the national agenda for civil rights and
essentially fragmented into the local pro-Daley Mexican American groups.
Still, Latinos were entering increasingly hostile white ethnic strongholds in
the Lower West Side and Southwest Side areas, and Daley's Latino liaisons
were hoping they could countervail any hint of Latino militancy.

Local neighborhood councils doubled their efforts to "preserve" their
way of life through conservation activism. In the 1950s, no matter how noble the intentions of conservation work—home improvement, beautification, new siding, and better yards—in the larger context of Chicago's racial
problems and housing segregation, they could not be extricated from their
racist logics. In his 1964 sociological study of race and cities, *Crisis in Black
and White*, Chares E. Silberman affirmed the dubious intentions of conservation groups when he cited a high-level University of Chicago administra-
tor stating, "Whether one liked it or not, neighborhood conservation and
renewal meant the preservation [of] a primarily white middle-class residential neighborhood."[35] Black housing activists knew these intentions all too
well. While Silberman went to great lengths to praise Alinsky's racial integration work, Black journalists and housing advocates in the mid-1960s such
as Brenetta Howell had grown tired of liberals praising Alinsky's measured
approach, charging that the "lion-tamer" only succeeds in "making the lions there more vicious." "Containment for Negroes has been the aftermath
of every Alinsky appearance," wrote Howell.[36]

For white conservationist groups, there weren't enough Alinskys to
ease their panic or prevent their sinking property values, which remained
correlated with Black expansion. "Americans have itchy feet," wrote Nicholas von Hoffman in 1964 as he profiled white Chicagoans on the precipice
of their changing communities. "I won't be the first to sell, but ya can bet I
won't be the last," stated one of his interviewees. "They can't get in, if ya
don't sell to 'em, so let's everybody stick [together]." This attitude on the

part of blue-collar Catholic whites did not surprise anyone in a city that had seen a rapid decline in whites since 1950. The City of Chicago—attacked both by liberals and the civil rights movement for not doing enough to open up housing and by white communities who felt the mayor was not protecting their property values—commissioned a report on housing in 1964 through its Community Renewal Program and the Real Estate Research Corp (RERC). It found that "members of specific groups in the rapidly growing lower-income and lower-middle-income population, for example, Mexicans, Puerto Ricans, rural white Southerners and some Negroes wish to live together with other people like themselves," downplaying the structural segregation and racial steering rampant in the city. Reading into the irony of these findings and the notion that rang truer for white ethnics than it did for racial minorities (i.e., that people preferred living next to others like themselves), members of the South Lawndale neighborhood got an idea to reinvent their community.[37]

Inventing a "Little Village"

In March of 1964, a thirty-something-year-old real estate agent of Bohemian heritage, Richard A. Dolejs, started promoting a rebranding campaign for South Lawndale. In his earlier role as vice president of the South Lawndale Conservation Commission, Dolejs had learned of the difficulties other nearby councils encountered with do-it-yourself home rehabs. He decided that any local effort needed to go beyond simply shaming or intimidating neighbors to fix up their homes, as other conservation groups had done, and should openly conjure pride and promote the "local heritage" of the area instead. Dolejs proposed renaming the community "Little Village" to evoke the small Czech and Slavic villages "from which his forebears came." Promoting a white, even if immigrant, identity could also sever any association with Black Lawndale. "The undesirable reputation, of Lawndale, be it North or South, has already permeated the citizenry," Dolejs wrote to members of the council, "and our community bears undeservedly the shame of conditions that exist primarily to the North. We must sever any connections with Lawndale if we are to attract responsible home seekers." Dolejs grew up in North Lawndale when it was predominantly Jewish. After returning from the Korean War, he and his father started Andrew M. Dolejs & Sons Real Estate and Insurance Inc. Through his experience in the real estate business, he learned just how lucrative panic peddling and blockbusting could be and used his insider knowledge to prevent it from happening in South Lawndale. Dolejs hoped rebranding South Lawndale as a "Little Village" with a strong Czech and Slavic identity would deter white ethnics from selling, putting ethnic pride before profit.[38]

If the community lacked morale due to their "sense of siege" by North Lawndale, they certainly did not lack financial capital for their rebranding projects. Monsignor John Egan, upon receiving a report on the area's conservation activities, was surprised to learn that, unlike other Chicago neighborhoods experiencing white flight, the numerous savings and loan associations (S&Ls) along 26th Street had assets totaling over one hundred million dollars. Dolejs soon became the most important member of its renamed institutions: The Little Village-26th Street Area Chamber of Commerce, Little Village Community Council (LVCC), Home Owners Preservation Enterprise, and the Little Village Council of Financial Institutions. With money in hand, these groups turned their "Little Village" philosophy into a material reality. Dolejs set out to update the architecture of the commercial storefronts along 26th Street to give it a "flavor of the Old World," hiring a local Bohemian-American architect to produce plans for both commercial and home remodeling to Dolejs's Little Village standards.[39]

Richard Dolejs dispensed with the angular rooftops and midcentury modern siding trendy with conservationist councils during the 1950s and instead employed a playful 1960s-era Disney-pop aesthetic with colorful pastels, evoking a pastoral Eastern European village. "A renaissance is now at hand!" declared the accompanying promotional literature for Dolejs's rebranding campaign. "The up-dating and modernization of many buildings in the area is just the start, and one phase, of the many progressive plans for the community." Renaming the community was not just about keeping certain people in (and others out); it was also about selling the area and letting "prospective homeowners know the community is stable, clean and safe, where a family can be reared." The local financial institutions donated money and offered credit to kick-start the sagging economy of the commercial artery of 26th Street, now promoted as the "miracle mile of values" that would put shoppers back on the once famed Bohemian Boulevard. To set the example for other merchants, the Dolejs real estate office building was given the "unique treatment" of "La Boheme Electrique," what they called their aesthetic remake effort, giving it a gingerbread-house look. "The residents, business and professional men, and their local organizations, are determined that the heritage of those hardy pioneers and the many who followed them, shall be preserved for the present and future generations," promised the modernization literature. Dolejs had designers

$1⁵⁰
per copy

Little Village Album

Figure 4.2. Promotional booklet detailing the modernization plan for South Lawndale's home and commercial properties in the newly renamed Little Village community. (Image courtesy of Richard A. Dolejs's personal collection.)

draw up a new logo that would capture a tranquil Bohemian village at the end of a winding path with mushrooms, foliage, and the words "Little Village" in Old English lettering. He printed up the signs on circular discs to hang on street poles throughout the district. Mexican families arriving at the edge of the neighborhood in the early to mid-1960s, distrustful of their history with "conservation" displacement, wondered if they were on the inside or outside of this "Little Village."⁴⁰

Gestures of Convenience

From his humble, brick storefront office on 3305 West Cermak Road, which also served as his home, alderman Otto F. Janousek of the 22nd Ward could see the rapid demographic changes to that northern end of his district. During a community meeting on conservation, he lamented the white flight: "We can see what happened in areas to the north (N. Lawndale) and the east (Pilsen). They were built by people like us." But he warned the members of the council that conservation enforcement should be compassionate, not a burden to "many of the older people in the community [who] would be unable to comply and would be forced to leave the community." As alderman, he was consulted on all matters the LVCC took up and was supportive of their beautification programs, block clubs, and small home-improvement loans. News of the Little Village "renaissance" was making the papers and earning Richard Dolejs accolades and recognition from Mayor Daley and other city agencies. Nevertheless, the attention was a far cry from the national coverage the BYNC had received a decade earlier during *its* conservation campaign. The difference perhaps underscored that the changing social climate of the mid-1960s made it more difficult to rally around conservation without fully considering its racial dimensions. Even well-meaning social- and racial-justice crusaders, such as Saul Alinsky, Jane Jacobs, and John Egan, were being criticized for their moderate stances on racial integration. Still, Black and Brown minority home seekers continued to be restricted, steered, and held at bay, partly by conservation campaigns. This did not phase local 22nd Ward politicians like Lilian Piotrowski and Otto Janousek, who remained committed to keeping Little Village as white as possible. In 1964, Piotrowski amassed even more influence when she was overwhelmingly elected as the new Cook County Commissioner, riding a wave of support for her defense of "white rights" a year earlier in Springfield, confirming to her and her supporters a renewed mandate for the pursuit of racial fortification.[41]

Mandate or not, a surge of Mexican American homebuyers were afoot, alarming the staunchest segregationists, who flooded Piotrowski with complaints. The 22nd Ward did not just have a "Negro problem," the local shorthand for racial matters. It had a "Mexican problem" too, and the three influential leaders of the 22nd Ward—Piotrowski, Janousek, and Dolejs—were divided on the solution. Piotrowski's political career depended on preserving the whiteness of her district. Piotrowski spent most of the decade fighting neighbors who sold homes to Mexicans. Otto Janousek, the oldest of the leaders and alderman since 1943, knew just about all the first Mexican American "pioneers" in the neighborhood by name and address. Most of these first arrivals settled on the northeastern end of the district. According to Larry Villarreal, who became Janousek's trusted confidant, the alderman grew tired of taking phone calls from angry residents complaining about Mexican street-corner gangs, blockbusting attempts, and loud music. Janousek took to "deputizing" Mexican Americans already living in the area, such as Larry Villarreal, to serve as his eyes and ears and handle his "Mexican problem," much to the chagrin of his white precinct captains.

By the late 1950s, Janousek also appointed his first Mexican American precinct captain, homeowner Salvador Ceja, to handle any problems that arose and, most importantly, to deliver his precinct's votes on election day. But appointing Ceja as precinct captain had more to do with simply finding a native handler for his "Mexican problem." To Janousek, Ceja's precinct, which was roughly half Black and half Mexican, was a microcosm of the ward's future. While appointing Ceja would certainly unburden white precinct captains from having to deal with that area, it became a means for Janousek to build the necessary alliances to stay in power.[42]

Richard Dolejs was the youngest of the three leaders and stood apart by his drive for civic activism, boosterism, and success at running a family real estate company. Dolejs was also not an elected politician but considered a visionary businessman. While he relied on symbols of a utopian Bohemian village to inspire community pride, it was his language of capitalism and opportunity that resonated with residents. These were the ideas that drove people to him and that he used to motivate his employees, colleagues, and customers. As part of his Little Village renaissance, he created a home-and-business exterior remodeling contest called "Operation Facelift." It was an effort to set an example throughout the ward and encourage all property owners to initiate improvements; residents and business owners won prizes for improving and beautifying their properties. The $100 and $50 first- and second-place prizes were symbolic gestures that nevertheless caught the attention of the community and that, as Dolejs noted, exemplified "a highpoint in rebirth of community spirit." In the first contest, Dolejs awarded second place in "home decorating" to a young Latino couple with two kids for the improvements they made on their two-flat brick-cottage home. Dolejs handed out oversized checks to the winners as they assembled for a photo shoot, while one Latino youngster held the new mushroom street sign promoting "Little Village."

What may have been a deliberate attempt to mitigate white anxieties by showcasing a Latino family as respectable homeowners, less panicked observers might have simply shrugged off the demographic changes as what the ward now looked like. Nevertheless, what became clear were the new gestures of convenience from the area's civic, business, and political leaders. Dolejs, for different reasons than Janousek, developed alliances with Mexicans and other Latinos and promoted their arrival to Little Village, welcoming them as business owners and homebuyers. Neither Dolejs nor Janousek were hostile to the presence of Mexicans in the way Piotrowski was, but at the same time, if Little Village had a gate, their willingness to open it came with a price. For Janousek, it meant paying absolute fidelity to his local machine, the 22nd Ward Regular Democratic Organization, a mighty institution of Bohemian political power since the days of Anton Cermak, Chicago's first and only Bohemian-born mayor in an Irish-dominated city. Dolejs wanted to be the first to sell homes to the surge of Mexicans entering the neighborhood.[43]

These transactional desires mattered little in view of the larger, structural undercurrents in 1960s South Lawndale. The 26th Street rebranding was a noble effort that helped stabilize property values momentarily but could not prevent the larger forces of economic decline already underway. The white ethnic population, defensive about racial change, was also decreasing. The residents of the 22nd Ward tended to be older, many aging out of the community, while the younger offspring of those older residents desired suburbs over their immigrant, inner-city roots. They were financially and culturally incentivized to suburbanize and drawn to the new jobs and economies outside of Chicago. Exacerbating the decline was South Lawndale's large-scale deindustrialization, which further evacuated the area of its once strong, middle-class-producing jobs. And as younger whites left, so went the financial holdings of its longtime Bohemian and Slavic S&L institutions, bedrocks of its former economic and entrepreneurial strength. One by one, closures of Eastern European businesses gave the emptied storefronts an abandoned feel. The area struggled to retain its ethnic character. "One fine small restaurant with all the flavor of 'Old Czech' remains," wrote a visitor looking for the final vestiges of the area's old-world character, "[here] you can order Pecená Kachna, Knedlik, a Zeli, or roast duck, dumpling, and sauerkraut." Although many observers assumed the westward move of Mexican settlement was as natural as the seasons changing, following the flow of Eastern European settlement of an earlier era, it was not. Of all the Bungalow Belt neighborhoods, this was the only one in play. Not out of the goodness of forward-thinking Eastern Europeans or enterprising white ethnic civic and political leaders. The gates to Little Village would soon be pried open by those determined to get in.[44]

Poder y Habitación

A threat to the new order Janousek and Dolejs created arrived in the small-statured, brown-skinned personage of Anita Villarreal. She relocated her real estate business from 18th Street in Pilsen to 26th Street in South Lawndale long before any other Mexican merchants had arrived and well before

Richard Dolejs had rebranded the area "Little Village." As described in chapter 2, Villarreal had been a fierce advocate of public housing for communities of color and especially for returning veterans and their families after World War II. Then during the late 1940s and early 1950s, with the oncoming urban renewal, she joined the neighborhood-conservancy effort as a member of the NWSPB, advocating for community participation in planning. But like so many Mexican Americans who initially supported plans to rehabilitate and improve the Near West Side but were soon devastated by the wreckage of displacement and demolition, she became a strong critic of the heavy price communities of color had to pay for "conservation." This was also the overwhelming sentiment of Black communities throughout the South Side and West Side who revolted against the hidden price of conservation. But unlike Black Chicagoans, displaced Mexicans, mainly those affiliated with IFOMA and the Mexican Chamber of Commerce (both former conservation advocates), were now tapering their outrage and open criticism of the mayor. In their quest for habitation and community clout, they strengthened their relationship with city hall. Villarreal, along with other civic and business leaders in the Mexican Patriotic Committee of Chicago, frequently feted Daley as their guest of honor during parades and patriotic gatherings. They took advantage of opportunities to show their appreciation to the mayor, in "recognition of his valuable service and cooperation to the Mexican Community and to this organization," as was engraved on one award he received in 1964. While Villarreal did her due diligence in the citywide Latino groups and parade committees, building power in her new habitat became her focus.[45]

In the early to mid-1960s, the exclusionary white neighborhood councils that had adopted a "keep them [Mexicans] out" policy prompted Mexican American homeowners to start holding meetings of their own to show unified strength and have a voice in community affairs. White neighborhood councils used a variety of tactics to restrict Latino access to housing and commercial properties, challenge business-license applicants, and curtail use of public space. Additionally, white councils encouraged neighbors who were selling their homes to use intermediaries as watchdogs, or "go-betweens," to match sellers and buyers, often using churches as "clearing-houses." This was an illegal method to oversee and approve who could buy and move to a certain neighborhood. White councils emphasized property-owner resistance through zoning activism, neighbor intimidation, and marshaling the police and city inspectors to harass suspected building-code offenders.

While these councils frequently used inclusive language in their litera-ture ("all nationalities welcomed"), their actual activities carried a subtext of anti-Mexican containment. It is important to note, however, that these councils were also messy and complicated, with internal contradictions that reflected the diverse self-serving agendas of the people in them: real estate agents, bankers, social workers, priests, homeowners, and shopkeepers. For instance, white homeowners who would not tolerate Mexican neighbors sat in meetings next to real estate brokers who were fully engaged in contract selling (whereby the seller would finance the buyer's purchase) to Mexi-cans. For some, Mexicans were another white ethnic group that would, in time, "melt" into the white neighborhood. But others who had a more on-the-ground perspective understood the racial scripts of language, culture, color, and colonization that racialized Mexicans. One social worker noted in 1965 that white ethnics believe "there are too many Mexicans" and "the 'whites' want out. The Mexicans resent being thought of as undesirable."[46] Sympathetic priests like Rev. Joseph Peplansky noted "the general feeling among Mexican-Americans that the ring of their names and the color of their skin remain factors that bar total acceptance in a white non-Mexican neighborhood," and "equal housing opportunities are still unresolved is-sues in the minds of the Mexican-Americans."[47]

In Pilsen, the Latin American Organizations' Co-ordinating Commit-tee came together in response to their exclusion from the mostly all-white Pilsen Neighbors Community Council (PNCC). First, in a telegram to a neighboring white council, the Heart of Chicago Community Council (HCCC) declared it an outrage that people with city-agency-funded salaries controlled the PNCC and requested, "Please sirs, do not permit them to use the city agencies to bully the Latin residents." The telegram, sent by the emboldened Latino homeowners, who were often thought of as outsiders by local whites, accused some of the white staff of PNCC of being outsid-ers themselves. They underscored their majority numbers ("90 percent") in their rapidly changing area, demographic realities white councils often denied or underemphasized. Finally, they exposed and questioned whether PNCC was truly a "community group," since some leaders were profes-sionalized by city salaries, a discovery they knew would absolutely perturb the all-volunteer HCCC, who were suspicious of taxpayer funds being used in decision-making over conservation matters. Latino groups helped erode the local authority of the white councils by accusing them of being carpet-baggers and alleging abuse of taxpayer funds and also by building unlikely alliances with groups the PNCC had conflicting interests with.[48]

Also, in the mid-1960s, another group of Latino homeowners came together to unite against discrimination in housing and business opportunities
in Little Village. Behind this push was Anita Villarreal, who was adamant
about empowering her own bloc of Mexican American homeowners and voters, independent of the local white council and, in part, in response to their
exclusion from it. The neighborhood's white institutions frequently challenged her presence as a businesswoman, and early on she was denied membership in the Little Village-26th Street Area Chamber of Commerce and
the Little Village Real Estate Board. Even in her exclusion, the local power
brokers had noted her presence. The moment the Villarreal family arrived,
they were already on Alderman Janousek's radar as a possible threat or asset to his ward. Their first move into a building on Avers Avenue created a
controversy when a Bohemian real estate agent on 26th Street warned their
landlord, a Serbian immigrant man, that his building would be bombed if he
allowed the Mexican family to move in. The landlord obeyed and told the
Villarreals they had to move out. Anita Villarreal demanded that the landlord tell her who had told him this, and when he did, she marched over to
the real estate office on 26th Street, Citizen Realty, and threatened to file a
complaint with the Chicago Real Estate Board for racial discrimination. No
formal complaint was filed, but the Villarreals soon moved, not because of
a bomb threat but because Anita found the right home for her large family:
a sturdy, two-story brick bungalow on 2416 South Ridgeway Avenue. She
recounted these stories to the Mexican Americans she sold homes to, pointing out that homeownership was a stronghold of democracy. To her flock,
this message rang true even in her name—"Villarreal" literally translates to
"true land"—a name she transformed into a powerful local brand.[49]

With her family settled, she focused on her realty business and began
flexing her political muscles inside the ward. First on her agenda was to
organize a big meeting of the homeowners, a group simply known as the
"Mexican-Americans of Little Village," where she would talk about issues
pertaining to home upkeep and finance. The gathering would also be an opportunity to invite candidates from the Cook County Democratic Party to
speak to the new voting bloc so they could see for themselves that Latinos
were an asset to Daley's party. Hoping she could get the mayor to come, but
not wanting to go past Alderman Janousek, she asked the six-foot, five-inch-
tall white man if *he* could ask Mayor Daley to attend the meeting. Janousek
laughed at her, telling Villarreal the mayor was too busy for this kind of stuff,
and even if Daley were to attend, he would have to go to every other small
neighborhood gathering throughout the city. But Villarreal did not need

Janousek to get to Daley; it was simply her gesture of deference. She put in a call with the mayor's office using her own connections with city hall, and the mayor agreed to attend. Afterward, Villarreal called Janousek to recommend that he show up since the mayor was coming. Fear of embarrassment and other political considerations forced Janousek to go. The gathering was held inside a large banquet hall. Daley mingled with residents but focused much of his attention on Villarreal, who conducted the whole meeting and personally introduced him to everyone. The gathering was a strong rally for Daley among Mexican Americans. In a machine-controlled city, proximity to the mayor always connoted power by association. In organizing this event, the alderman learned of the powerhouse that had taken residence in his ward. Villarreal expressed her willingness to cooperate with the ward's power structure, with the understanding that Janousek would recognize her group as hardworking people, homeowners, and now constituents of the 22nd Ward.[50]

Besides earning Villarreal some clout inside the ward, the gathering was significant for other reasons. Otto Janousek took a liking to Villarreal's eldest son, Larry, who had recently been discharged from the army and was now attending law school. Janousek still needed handlers for his ever-growing "Mexican problem," a position that continued to require fielding white ethnics' complaints about their Mexican neighbors, as well as sending somebody out to calm the waters of demographic and racial change. Janousek told Larry, "I want you to be my eyes and ears in the whole ward," as he did with Ceja years earlier. Larry was assigned as an assistant precinct captain to an elderly Bohemian man who could no longer get around to work his precinct. Part of his duties included passing out printed circulars promoting the services of Janousek's 22nd Ward Regular Democratic Organization. Soon he was entrusted with bigger responsibilities, from handling building-permit requests with the deputy commissioner in city hall to being sent downtown on Election Day when the voter counts came in to be tallied from all the wards throughout the city, a role reserved only for precinct captains.[51]

Her son's work with the alderman reflected favorably on Anita Villarreal as she continued to make inroads with the Democratic machine. The 22nd Ward now had several Mexican American assistant precinct captains handpicked by Janousek. In 1965, when a judgeship became vacant, Mayor Daley turned to his most trusted Latino liaisons—Villarreal, Arturo Velasquez, Catarino Diaz, and Paul Gasca, who together formed the nuclei of civic and business leaders and close confidants to the mayor—to strategize his first political appointment of a Mexican American in the city's history. The ap-

Figure 4.3. The Mexican community of Pilsen welcomes Mayor Daley during a campaign visit to St. Pius Church, 1967. RJD_04_01_0018_0007_002. (Courtesy of Richard J. Daley Collection, Special Collections and University Archives, University of Illinois at Chicago Library.)

pointment went to David Cerda, a young lawyer with an impressive résumé, a graduate of DePaul University Law School, and founder of the local Chicago chapter of LULAC. He grew up in the Near West Side and came highly recommended by the exclusive group. In 1966, with the sponsorship of the Latino advisors, the mayor slated Cerda as a candidate for Circuit Court Judge of Cook County. The successful election of Cerda bound the Mexican American civic and business leaders further to Daley and the Democratic machine, not only as supporters but also as decision-makers in power politics. Their loyalty to Daley was absolute and required consenting to the decrees that sometimes undermined Latinos' best interests and other times reined in the oncoming wave of Latino power. But where new political vistas to city hall opened for Villarreal, other currents inside Little Village thwarted her efforts to run a successful real estate business.[52]

The Bungalow Blowback and the Making of the Third Housing Market

In Pilsen, Eastern and Central European whites saw themselves become more of a minority inside their own parents' and grandparents' neighborhoods as increasing waves of Mexicans moved in. In the 1960s, the Mexican population grew from 30 percent to 80 percent in the 1st Ward. In the 25th Ward, which still held a sizable Italian American enclave, members of that community were dismayed to see that Mexicans were living on "their" side of Ashland Avenue, long considered a racial "border" separating the two wards in Pilsen. Furthermore, white councils and their conservation-as-containment projects collapsed under the pressures of free-market forces now deliberately working to Mexicanize the 1st and 25th Wards. Not surprisingly, those leading the effort were Bohemian real estate agents who took a page from the contract selling that was rampant in North Lawndale as they looked to squeeze new dollars out of old buildings in old neighborhoods. Like North Lawndale, contract selling was a market response to a dual-housing system of segregation, redlining, credit blacklisting, and overall service and financial disinvestment of central-city neighborhoods undergoing ethnic and racial change. This meant minority families looking to purchase a home had few choices but to purchase on contract, which was always more expensive than a regular mortgage. Additionally, regular mortgages and financing were simply not being offered in Pilsen. Bohemian and Slavic real estate agents found value in the portability of this system. Perhaps more telling was that it depended on the raciality of Latinos, in this case Mexicans, being a group that required a "third price"—harking back to Homer Hoyt's racial appraisal system of 1933. This tailored values for a third housing market: not white, not Black, but "Mexican."[53]

To Mexicans, this process was known as "holding the paper" or "holding the title"; the seller held the property deed until the buyer made all the payments. These contracts protected the seller and placed all the burden of risk on the buyer. Missing a payment or violating some detail of the contract (which was easy to do) resulted in termination of that contract, loss of all payments made, and eviction. This arrangement caused a high level of property turnaround and unstable vacancies and furthered the deterioration of an already ancient built environment. Still, the old frame houses and tattered Victorian buildings were sold and resold to willing Mexican purchasers. Some white real estate agents exploited the potential for miscommunication with Spanish-speaking buyers to their advantage, while others learned rudimentary Spanish to give them an edge over their competitors. In some cases, Bohemian and Slavic real estate offices on 18th Street hired Mexican Americans to make these sales. Eventually, upstart Mexican American real estate agents engaged in contract selling as well. The dollars from contract selling and high rents poured new value into the old Pilsen neighborhood, helping Mexicanize the entire 1st Ward, and opened areas to the southwest in the 25th Ward and beyond, block by block.[54]

These practices pinned Mexican immigrants and Mexican Americans into shabby housing and dense pockets of the city. Pilsen was no longer so much a "port of entry" as it was an enclosure for post-1965 waves of Mexican immigration. The third housing market created for Mexicans was imprecise and fetched a value that was always in relation to Black (very high) and white (low) housing markets. But contract selling to Mexicans had been normalized as a routine step to homeownership—not always seen as nefarious by purchasers or as the ethical and moral social-justice issue that the civil rights movement was about to take up.[55]

When Martin Luther King Jr. embarked on his crusade north to Chicago in late July of 1965, it was done to expose the Windy City's segregation. His organization, the Southern Christian Leadership Conference, put the spotlight on contract selling and slumlords, hoping to bring an end to two major contributors to the segregation of Black Chicago. King spoke about the moral need for open housing and ending African Americans' substandard living conditions in the north. Organizers in the Chicago Freedom Movement selected the Chicago bungalow home, a symbol of the American dream achieved for white ethnics, as the battleground for northern civil rights. That summer, marchers demonstrated in front of Mayor Daley's brick bungalow in the Irish neighborhood of Bridgeport, the same home where Mexican American civic leaders took mariachis to serenade the mayor every year on his birthday.[56]

The next summer, growing racial tensions were not only felt on the streets of the city but expressed in angry editorials white Chicagoans sent to their local newspapers. "I would like to remind the Rev. Martin Luther King that he need not demand an open city because Chicago is open," wrote one perturbed citizen, "all the department stores are jammed with Negroes, all the movie houses are jammed with Negroes." Daley and his staff sensed the tension but were also looking to offset King's growing influence. Daley used War on Poverty funds to create Urban Progress Centers throughout Black areas to put people on the payroll of job-training programs. To Daley's surprise, the first racial uprising of the summer came from Latinos in the Near Northwest Side, when Puerto Ricans revolted on Division Street following the police shooting of a youngster. Daley's staff advised him to do what he had done for African Americans and quickly set up Urban Progress Centers in Latino areas. He called upon the Amigos to serve as advisory committee members. As the media zeroed-in on the impending battle between King's Chicago Freedom Movement and the Daley machine, the mayor dispatched the Latino liaisons to quietly quell growing Latino resentment over disinvestment of their communities. The summer's riots sent alarms throughout surrounding neighborhoods. On July 21, 1966, Father Joerger of St. Pius Church in Pilsen called a community-wide meeting with the police department, members of the Chicago Commission on Human Relations, and Peace Corps trainees to speak to the community and answer questions on issues stemming from white ethnics' fears about their changing neighborhoods to growing Black and Latino assertiveness about their rights in them.[57]

The following week, King and his lieutenants decided it was time to bypass the first-wave immigrant neighborhoods, like Bridgeport and Back of the Yards, and go straight for the Bungalow Belt to make a point about how the nicer, middle-class homes were only financially within reach of Black families if they were put on the open-housing market. During the hot summer days of late July and early August, King and his supporters marched through Gage Park, West Lawn, and Marquette Park. Gage Park was occupied by more than fifty-two thousand whites of Slavic, Bohemian, Lithuanian, and Irish descent. Though the press presented residents' disdain for African Americans as a sudden "backlash," the resentments had actually been simmering since World War II, when many white families first moved into the Southwest Side to escape stockyard communities. Southwest Side residents who were historically New Deal Democrats now felt betrayed by Daley, whom they saw as going to great lengths to not offend his Black base of support. Gage Park residents felt they had worked hard and earned their right to live in communities like theirs, and they openly defended their preference for segregation. The Chicago Freedom Movement, in looking to open segregated communities like Gage Park, decided to picket the institutions that perpetuated neighborhood segregation: the corner real estate office. Demonstrators picketed the F. H. Halvorsen realty office, a small mom-and-pop establishment not unlike many found on 26th Street in Little Village.[58]

King's campaign in the Bungalow Belt recast the contentious relationship Mexicans had with the Southwest Side. They had been pushing their way into the Bungalow Belt since World War II, albeit with small degrees of success. Prior to 1966, hundreds of Mexican students from Back of the Yards were already attending high school three miles away in Gage Park and experiencing the climate of white hostility on campus and on their bus commutes to and from school every day. Mexicans commuted to the Bungalow Belt for work at places like Nabisco, Central Steel and Wire Company, and other area factories, sensing the "stay away" attitudes of the "tidy and rigid" communities of the Southwest Side. Besides the informal real estate practices that kept most Mexicans out of the Bungalow Belt, plenty of cautionary tales about white violence against Mexicans "west of this street" or "south of that street" circulated through the colonias. This further influenced families' decisions to stay put and make do in their Pilsen or Back of the Yards enclaves. Nevertheless, by the mid- to late 1960s, few families risked breaking or bending the Bungalow Belt's color line. By the time of the Chicago Freedom Movement, one newspaper columnist pointed out that between all of the Northside and Southside neighborhoods King led his marchers through, "Gage Park has a distinction Belmont-Cragin does not. It has almost 1,000 Mexicans." The writer went on to emphasize the blue-collar demographics of the area, but his analysis stopped short of addressing whether the imperceptible Mexican presence in Gage Park made them color line breakers or chameleons amid the bungalows.[59]

The racial violence against peaceful marchers on the residential streets of the Southwest Side not only stirred national coverage on the white backlash but generated local discussions about Mexican Americans' place in relation to civil rights. The National Federation of Settlements and Neighborhood Centers (NFSNC), an umbrella organization that oversaw these institutions in urban America, determined, "Other minority groups, particularly the Mexican-American, have remained untouched by the civil rights movement." On the clashes in the Bungalow Belt, the NFSNC noted, "As desirable as ethnic, racial, and/or economic heterogeneity may be to many people, it seems to operate as a divisive force in communities. . . . Political power is hotly contested." It remained unclear whether NFSNC saw Mexican Americans as standing passively on the sidelines of King's movement or engaged in a fight of their own over older Czech and Polish immigrant (or first-wave) neighborhoods and their exclusionary white councils. From this perspective, the civil rights fight for the Bungalow Belt was too out of reach and therefore out of mind, as Mexican Americans grappled with their own immediate inclusion battles.[60]

The violent white backlash of 1966 showed the nation that in Chicago's Bungalow Belt civil rights came to a halt as King and his marchers retreated to the chants of "White Power!" and "Polish Power!" Hostile white ethnics even directed their fury at Mayor Daley, throwing bricks and bottles and chanting: "Don't vote for Democrats! Don't vote for Democrats!" For Mexican Americans, especially those who lived near the Bungalow Belt, this reignited past traumas of white racial hostilities in the 1940s and 1950s, when they were frequently and violently chased out of the area while looking for housing. A brief period of lax attitudes followed, and by the mid-1960s, some Mexicans could be found living in Gage Park. But the violent backlash in the summer of 1966 stirred white residents to put pressure once again on their community councils, savings and loan institutions, real estate agents, and parishes to conserve their territorial boundaries and hold the line. As one sociologist put it: "The boundary has remained in the local culture, although undoubtedly its meaning and significance have recently been heightened." White revolt against Blacks became transferable to Mexicans. Routinized forms of violence (e.g., brick attacks, crosses burnings on lawns, and destruction of vehicles) against Black and Brown families became part of the everyday landscape long after the marchers and media attention subsided.[61]

It was in this climate of racial hostility, duress, and potential for bodily danger that Anita Villarreal drove straight into the Southwest Side to thrust her way through the most difficult of the all-white neighborhoods. She poured over maps, stats, and real estate values, hoping to turn red lines into opportunity. She knocked on doors soliciting listings directly from home sellers that she could turn around and sell to Mexicans. In this approach, she behaved like a blockbuster, exploiting white anxiety and giving them the opportunity to salvage whatever they could of their home values or even making a profit from their home. Her success in obtaining listings in this way provoked a backlash from area whites who targeted her for a series of dramatic confrontations. White residents from Brighton Park, Archer Heights, and West Lawn organized protests outside her 26th Street office in Little Village. They marched on the sidewalk, chanting and carrying signs that called Villarreal a "blockbuster" and a "snake" and claimed that she was bringing in "undesirables." They heckled her Latino customers and hissed when she walked in or out of the office. They handed out circulars that warned other whites not to sell their homes to her and to boycott her business. Villarreal ignored it all and continued her methods.[62]

She undertook this great risk partly because she had to. In the same way that institutions like the Federal Housing Authority, real estate boards, and private lenders created redlining, they also created blockbusters, agents of vilification, but effective at connecting the supply with the demand. Villarreal may have been a "blockbuster" to angry whites from Brighton Park, but to Mexican families looking to leave Pilsen, she was a crusader upending their segregation. But other factors forced her to operate this way as well.

For one, she was denied membership into the all-white Little Village Real Estate Board, which prevented her access that other real estate agents had to the area's financial institutions and, most importantly, to the Multiple Listings Service (MLS). The MLS consolidated the listing of units available for sale within and beyond the immediate area and shared them with all member offices. Open-housing advocates held that the MLS created the potential for collusion by real estate agents to reserve white neighborhoods for white customers and thus was simply another segregation tool. Villarreal's office was not only kept out of the MLS, but also the attempts of her and her son Larry, at securing mortgage loans from the thirty-plus savings and loan associations on 26th Street led nowhere. "They wouldn't even open the door once they saw me through their window," Larry Villarreal recalled. The S&Ls waved him away saying, "We're not making any loans!" The neighborhood financial institutions had closed their doors to Mexicans. Without them, Anita Villarreal was at risk of going out of business.[63]

In Little Village, an influential member of the real estate board and the MLS, Richard Dolejs, now openly disagreed with Dr. King's efforts to call attention to the slum conditions of Chicago. "In fairness to Dr. King," Dolejs once wrote, "I hope his preachings will take effect and that he may lead the underprivileged to paths of cleanliness, responsibility and earned dignity." It was a knock directed at the tenants rather than social injustice. It would have been easy to conclude that Villarreal's rejection from the local board came from members like Dolejs who plausibly sided with anxious white ethnics. But Dolejs's actions paint a more complicated picture. By the mid-1960s, his real estate office had adjusted to market realities when he staffed it with Spanish speakers and brought over his two best salesmen from his Pilsen office—both Mexican Americans—to handle the volume of Mexicans looking for homes. By then, Dolejs had reworked his "Little Village" metaphor to include Mexicans: "All the people could relate to it, they came from little villages seeking opportunity." This statement could have resonated with immigrants from Durango and Prague alike. Still, the Little Village Real Estate Board (LVREB) continued to block Villarreal's access to the MLS, presumably for selling homes to Mexicans, even while members like Dolejs were doing just that.[64]

During her exclusion, Villarreal had outmaneuvered her restrictions by canvassing the Southwest Side and reaching out directly to Czechs, Poles, and others who were ready to sell, opening listings not only in Little Village but also in Brighton Park, Archer Heights, Gage Park, and Chicago Lawn, areas notorious for the King backlash and an active American Nazi Party that continued to inflame racial violence well into the 1970s. She found Mexican families ready to buy homes with cash or large down payments. Her son Larry learned to process FHA loans to finance first-time buyers and bypass the ethnic S&Ls. Dolejs, too, was ready to recognize what the members of the LVREB were not: Mexican immigration was reinvigorating South Lawndale's sagging housing market and keeping them in business. The Mexican population had jumped from 10 percent in 1966 to 32 percent in 1968. Villarreal was finally allowed into the LVREB, and making her a member now meant she had to share her listings. In a way, this undercut her advantage over the rest of the real estate agents. The LVREB now depended on her membership—and her listings—to survive in the business as Little Village's entire housing market became dependent on cash-carrying Mexican homebuyers.[65]

As Little Village whites moved to the western suburbs, they left shuttered storefronts all along 26th Street. Again, Villarreal seized an opportunity to turn abandoned and boarded-up stores into a profitable enterprise. Having known many of the Mexican merchants from the Near West Side, she encouraged them to relocate to Little Village, promoting the area's ripeness for opportunity and laying a foundation for its economic resurgence. On 26th Street, they could reestablish their businesses in less crowded, more spacious buildings and cater to the tastes and needs of the Mexican newcomers. In 1966, La Justicia Supermercado opened its doors. Other supermarkets, such as Cuauhtémoc and La Guadalupana, soon followed. Mexican eateries opened in kitchens where the aromas of Czech and Moravian cuisines once dominated. Taquerias, fruit carts, paleteros, and trinket shops began filling the sidewalks like a Mexico City plaza. Aging department stores on the brink of closure were suddenly kept afloat by the consumer dollars of Mexicans buying clothes and furniture for their growing families. Bohemian-owned S&Ls, such as Civic Federal, Second Federal, and Metropolitan Bank, opened to Mexicans. In a jarring contrast, in the aftermath of King's assassination in April of 1968, as commercial corridors along Black North Lawndale were burned and looted in protest, 26th Street in South Lawndale was undergoing a Mexican economic renaissance.[66]

These uneven parallels further materialized in the race and housing landscape of post-1968 Chicago. Although many factors propelled white flight—economic restructuring, racial anxiety, integrated schools, incentivized suburbs, and the state disinvestment that followed racial minorities—it was whites' attempts to wrest value out of their properties that further unlocked the Southwest Side to Latinos. During these years, segregation deepened for poor African Americans, and a vicious cycle of capital disinvestment gripped Black Chicago. In contrast, Mexican residential mobility came with booms in economic activity, even as city services declined there. Furthermore, white evacuation opened a landscape of opportunity for Mexican immigrants and Mexican Americans once confined to enclaves in Pilsen and Back of the Yards. The demand for homes further incentivized white sellers. Tolerance for Mexicans became predicated on two factors: anti-Blackness and recovering home equity. White ethnics dispensed with neighborly solidarity. Many sold their homes directly to buyers, while others moved out and collected rents from Mexicans. In the Southwest Side, these were not "good intentions" but rather economic imperatives that allowed those in control to give Mexicans a privileged position vis-à-vis Blacks as whites looked to fund their suburbanization.[67]

To some Southwest Side white home sellers, Mexicans were savers just like them. To the machine, they were loyal Daley Democrats. This privileged access was built on the accumulated social capital that had been carefully cultivated for years by the likes of the Amigos, who frequently stood in as representatives of a deserving, industrious, hardworking immigrant/ethnic group. This group did not toe the Democratic Party line but Daley's Democratic Party line, which was increasingly antagonistic toward liberalism and the New Left. It was antiwelfare state, probusiness, law and order. In a memo prepared by Col. Reilly at Mayor Daley's request to recommend Arturo Velasquez to a post on the Illinois Human Relations Commission, he made sure to note, "His appointment would serve to answer growing criticism in [the] Mexican Community that because they cause no trouble and do not join demonstrations, they do not receive the attention shown the Puerto Ricans because the Puerto Ricans are always threatening to make trouble." Their special access was predicated on comparisons to "bad" or "undeserving" racial groups. Observers noted the convergence of the Bungalow Belt, its political realignment to the right, and the place of Mexicans in that realignment: "If Chicago has something of a 'silent majority,'" noted one political scientist, "the languages of that majority are Polish and Spanish."[68]

The Conservative Colonia

From 1968 to the mid-1970s, Anita Villarreal and her Villarreal Real Estate Incorporated achieved business success and political victories that helped transform the Bohemian "Little Village" into a Mexican "La Villita." She increased the availability of mortgages for Mexican Americans and Mexican immigrants. In the process, she turned 26th Street from ghost town to boomtown, making it the center of commerce for the Latino Midwest. The district now bustled with activity, "attracting tourists and shoppers seeking Hispanic restaurants, shops, music, and dancing," supplanting the former primacy of other successful commercial corridors such as Pilsen's 18th Street. What was initially an economic resurgence became an ethnic and cultural rebranding of the neighborhood. No other Chicago community rose in population during this period of white flight like La Villita did, boasting 62,895 people in 1970. Some remaining whites continued to detest their new neighbors and longed for their old neighborhood. But not all felt this way, as white ethnic leaders found common ground with the inner circle of Mexican American civic and business leaders, forming an unlikely alliance through shared social conservatism and financial interests. Villarreal was now a player in all Little Village's major civic and financial organizations. This union of leaders steered a course of moderation that diverged from the progressive and radical politics taking shape in other Latino barrios during the late 1960s and 1970s. During the explosive Democratic National Convention of 1968, Daley rallied Middle America with his gestapo-like handling of the antiwar protesters. His critics blamed him for stoking a police riot, as officers beat student demonstrators with their batons on live national television. Chicagoans, especially those in the Bungalow Belt, came to the mayor's defense. Richard Dolejs and the Little Village-26th Street Area Chamber of Commerce backed Daley by awarding him a plaque "with special reference to the administration of law and order during the Democratic Convention of 1968."[69]

If white ethnics felt unsettled by the Mexicanization, Anita Villarreal calmed fears that the transformation of the Bungalow Belt would not come by way of political revolution. When alderman Otto Janousek suddenly died in 1969, Lillian Piotrowski—sensing a power slippage—began laying the groundwork to maintain Bohemian political control of the 22nd Ward. Piotrowski now required Villarreal's help. Piotrowski learned that some of Janousek's precinct captains had encouraged Larry Villarreal to run for alderman, but he turned them down in the interest of advancing his career in financial institutions critical to the Villarreals' real estate success. Piotrowski worked her connections to the mayor and the machine to slate her nephew, Frank D. Stemberk, for alderman. Stemberk was in his twenties, a lanky guy with a big smile who looked the part of a politician in a suit and tie but had no actual political or governing experience. His nomination would

Figure 4.4. The Villarreal Real Estate Office and staff, 3618 West 26th Street. Anita Villarreal is seated wearing a striped shirt, 1972. (Image courtesy of the Villarreal Family.)

continue the ward's legacy of electing politicians of Bohemian heritage, and the machine conceded.[70]

Piotrowski lobbied hard to build the consensus needed to secure Mexican American support. In a gerrymandered ward drawn favorably for white ethnic majorities, the 22nd Ward still had a significant nonwhite voting population of African Americans and Latinos. Since Piotrowski had built her entire political career on ignoring her Black constituents to the delight of white ethnics, she turned to Villarreal to gain Latino support for her ticket. By then, non-machine-affiliated Mexican American hopefuls had begun campaigns of their own for the alderman's seat. Anita Villarreal, motivated by her own calculations, rallied the Mexican American community behind Stemberk and Piotrowski. This drove some critics to see Villarreal as capitulating to the Bohemian power brokers and Daley's machine. Even if that was part of it, Villarreal's own calculus determined that Latinos, while populous, were not voting in high enough numbers to win an election for a Latino candidate. It did not matter that there were finally political challengers of Mexican heritage running for city council if there were not enough registered Latino voters to vote them in. White ethnics still had the highest voter turnout in the ward. Furthermore, leaders like Villarreal wanted people they could work with. The would-be challengers emerged from the Chicano-Latino movement; they were antimachine and not interested in making concessions with establishment leaders. Without machine support, no business or civic leader, and certainly not Villarreal, would risk retribution by supporting adversarial candidates, not even out of ethnic loyalty. Frank Stemberk became the new alderman, Lillian Piotrowski the new committeeman, and Villarreal's influence and business acumen were on full display.[71]

These were the swirling forces surrounding the conservative colonia. As the city's racial, social, and political turmoil challenged the mayor's control over his city, the Amigos redoubled their loyalty. Amigos members Arturo Velasquez, Catarino Diaz, and others continued to use their organizations, such as the Mexican Chamber of Commerce and MADO, as a support apparatus for Daley and his machine. This kept them in the fold of power. Throughout the 1960s and early 1970s, they hosted banquets, dinners, and dances for key figures in Daley's machine. In 1967, they arranged for the mayor to receive the Aztec Eagle medal from the Mexican president, Mexico's highest honor bestowed upon a foreign national. These events contrasted with the protests, boycotts, and sit-ins of a younger, emerging generation of Latinos, politicized by the war in Vietnam and the civil rights movement, along with local, immediate concerns: antimachine sentiment, barrio disinvestment, underserved schools, and a new racial and ethnic consciousness. The Mexican Chamber of Commerce dismissed any notion that the mayor neglected Latinos. "You have been responsive to our every suggestion with regard to the Mexican-American community," they wrote to Daley in a letter of endorsement sent every reelection year. "During your incumbency, the Mexican Independence Day observance in Chicago has taken on great importance. We have staged parades which have won the admiration and respect of all the people of Chicago."[72]

For being loyal, Daley rewarded them by easing bureaucracy and restrictions on their business activities. They wanted a stable business environment for themselves and their members and no interference from city agencies. That Daley continued to value his Amigos was undeniable. Now, when the mayor visited a community like the Back of the Yards, his first stop was not to Joseph Meegan's office but to Catarino Diaz's home. Daley could easily see the fruits of this relationship when he drove through the Southside, where Mexican storefronts lined the boulevards and turned their windows into mile-long political endorsements for machine candidates. The Amigos and their associates delivered for Daley while advancing a probusiness agenda and strengthening Chicago's consumer ties to Mexico. In June of 1972, they flew to Mexico City for a meeting with President Luis Echeverría to discuss trade and commerce with the "Mexicanos de Afuera." During that meeting in Los Pinos, the president and the Amigos commemorated their meeting with engraved copper statuettes of Abraham Lincoln, conveying that although they were Daley Democrats, they spoke about the principles of liberty and the free market like Republicans.[73]

From a broader perspective, things such as business permits, liquor licenses, street-parade approvals, and cover from city inspectors were the low-hanging fruit big-city machines gave to groups on the lowest rung of the ladder. Democratic slate makers had no intention of opening the machine to Latino political participation, even after years of loyalty from Mexican American leaders. As cooperative as the mayor came off, Daley always hedged his bets, keeping his Amigos close and content while making sure mandatory redistricting never produced any majority-Latino wards that could threaten him. The Amigos were far from naïve about this, and as operatives themselves, understood duplicitous motivations. Despite their quid pro quo relationship with Daley, they held a genuine belief that they were advancing Latino causes. They continuously pressed the mayor to appoint or slate Latinos for political office. They cautioned that it was only a matter of time before Latino independent challengers became a threat to machine candidates if they were not allowed to be a part of the Democratic Party. Activists in the Chicano-Latino movement already resented Daley's machine. They saw the anointing of Piotrowski's nephew for alderman as nepotism and were angry over the mayor's support of white ethnics like Vito Marzullo and others in control of Mexican neighborhoods. In 1971, over five hundred Chicano student demonstrators marched in protest to city hall. The Amigos were unable to stave off growing Latino resentment against Daley.[74]

But, as the Amigos continued to advise caution, Daley now listened. In 1974, Lillian Piotrowski died suddenly at the age of 58, leaving a vacancy on the Cook County Board of Commissioners. Daley heeded the advice of his Latino liaisons and offered the position to Anita Villarreal, whom he had long admired and saw as a natural fit. But the 1970s were profitable years for the tenacious real estate broker, as she was now celebrated (rather than vilified) for being the driving force behind South Lawndale's Mexicanization. Not wanting to neglect her business, she respectfully turned down the mayor's offer and instead recommended her longtime friend, Irene C. Hernandez, for the position, somebody the mayor also knew. Daley listened to Villarreal and picked Hernandez to become the first Latina appointed to the Cook County government. The following year she was elected in a citywide campaign with the machine's full backing. The position had limited governing power but plenty of symbolism concerning the influence of Daley's Latino liaisons. In 1975, Villarreal became president of the LVCC, and by 1978 she and her sons, Larry and Daniel, were each in charge of the area's institutions, with Larry as president of the Little Village Council of Financial Institutions and Daniel as vice president of the Little Village-26th Street Area Chamber of Commerce.[75]

The Amigos did not lead the community in their politics so much as they reflected the politics already in place there. This did not mean, however, that they all just passively accepted the Democratic order. Their allegiance to Daley and their politics of probusiness conservatism and self-reliance did not preclude them from addressing social-justice issues or supporting causes and candidates they believed in. Critiques about white entitlement, systemic racism, and class struggle coexisted in the conservative colonia. For instance, Villarreal, Irene Hernandez, the Hispanic American Labor Council, restaurateur Cesar Dovalina, and others were supportive of the UFW grape boycott when it arrived in Chicago, some even participating in UFW marches and protests in front of grocery stores that carried the grapes. But as the Bungalow Belt continued to become the Latino Belt, the Southwest Side communities of South Lawndale, Brighton Park, Bridgeport, Back of the Yards, Gage Park, McKinley Park, and others formed the base of a Latino constituency that favored accommodation and distinguished itself against the "radicalism and fringe groups that always gather around a cause and run it to the ground," as one Amigos supporter wrote. The landscape had transformed those living in it, just as they had transformed the landscape. "Brightly hued murals adorn several 26th Street walls," noted one observer of La Villita. "These murals, unlike those in nearby Pilsen, are sponsored by local businesses and avoid political themes. They are a part of the establishment, not a rebellion against it." But still, observers had fundamentally missed that the political realignment of the once loyal Democratic base of the Southwest Side to the right had also entangled Mexican Americans in ways that would upend the presumptions of the Democratic Party and the New Left for years to come.[76]

In Southwestern cities, the Chicano movement of the late 1960s and

1970s provided a far-reaching political force leading to major electoral wins in city councils and congressional seats. In contrast, in Chicago, a very small group of elites, rather than a social movement, orchestrated Latinos' political appointments to office. Not through protest or revolt, but through machine-style dealmaking by what one political scientist called "token leaders in the community" that have "opportunistic and self-serving motives. [They] gain their stature and influence less by control over institutional patronage (for none of the Latino leaders have this) or record of 'moving and shaking,' than by their dedication and service to the community." But protest and revolt were in the air. Young Mexican Americans began adopting the language of the Southwestern Chicano movement and generating their own Midwestern Latino ethnic political consciousness. Corky Gonzáles, the leader of the Denver-based Crusade for Justice, an influential Chicano movement organization, told an audience in 1969 that Daley was "the pig of

Figure 4.5. Anita Villarreal hosts an "Amigos for Daley" rally alongside her lifelong friend, Cook County Commissioner Irene Hernandez, in Little Village in support of Mayor Daley's historic fifth reelection in 1975, as well as support for the reelection of 22nd Ward Alderman Frank D. Stemberk. (Image courtesy of the Villarreal Family.)

Chicago," and an enemy of *la raza* (the people) and that Chicanos should refrain from dealing with Democrats and Republicans. Over the course of the 1970s, members of the conservative colonia grew just as outspoken against liberalism as they had been against the Chicano movement. "Despite the utterings of lightheaded radicals, and liberals who urge that 'we have funds coming, and we should get our share,'" wrote a member of MADO, "consider the fact that we as Americans of Mexican descent have always given, instead of stood in line as helpless indigents waiting for hand outs."[77]

: :

From the early 1960s to mid-1970s, figures like Anita Villarreal turned what were once unstable vacancies left behind by white flight into a new base for political and economic power. She built La Villita into a thriving, business-focused area, thus reversing the angle of influence. Whereas once she was beholden to the power brokers to let her in, now she was the power broker. In 1975, she welcomed the mayor once again to Little Village as a candidate running for his sixth term, only this time she was the better-known one among the locals. Daley told the large crowd of Mexican Americans and Mexican immigrants, "It is a pleasure for me to be here with you tonight. I want to thank you for your help, not only for your help in this election, but for your many contributions to the city." Daley went into a typical campaign speech, slightly tailored for a Latino audience. "I am particularly pleased that the name of the sponsoring organization is Amigos for Daley—friends—and I assure you I consider you Amigos. . . . You are concerned about the same problems that we all are concerned about—you want a good neighborhood." Although there was thunderous applause for the mayor inside the hall, chants of protest could be heard coming from outside. Villarreal's close ties to Daley angered Chicano activists. What Villarreal called "our rebellious youth" would come to clash with the conservatism of the colonia. They called Daley a "marrano" (pig) and chanted "Chicano Power!" along with "Raza sí, Daley no!" Chicano activists had some choice words for Villarreal and other business leaders like Arturo Velasquez, whom activists referred to as "vendidos" (sellouts) and "Tío Tacos" (the Chicano equivalent of Uncle Tom). This was radically different from ten years earlier, when the white homeowner associations in South Lawndale and Brighton Park labeled her a "blockbuster" and "troublemaker."[78]

Still, the Amigos apparatus served its purpose enough to carry Daley to one final victory. In 1976, Daley died while in office and so ended, at least for the time being, the Mexican American consensus with the machine. What did not disappear, however, were the foundations laid throughout the Daley era. The challenges of staunchly segregationist neighborhoods, racial strife, unrest, and riots of the 1960s did not automatically "liberalize" Mexican Americans in Chicago; as this chapter shows, it only furthered their bungalow conservatism. One observer noted that while Little Village may be "as far west as most Mexicans could go," it nevertheless became for them "a suburb within the city."[79]

5 :: Renaissance and Revolt

In December 1975, Jesús Rodríguez, a young immigrant factory worker, waited worriedly for his wife, Maria, to arrive from Tirimácuaro, Michoacán. He had been living in Chicago for several years and had arranged for her to join him. Pregnant with twins, Maria made the harrowing journey across the border into Texas and then headed north to Chicago. As Maria recalled, "Me pasé de contrabanda" (I crossed as contraband). In her correspondence with Jesús, Maria imagined a beautiful metropolis of possibilities awaiting her. But when she arrived at 18th Street in Pilsen in the winter, she cried. "Que horrífico" (What a horror), Maria remembered. Not only was it bone-chillingly cold, but the address her husband gave her led straight to a slum. "My first instinct was to turn back around and return to Michoacán," she said. "I remembered thinking to myself, 'this place is hideous.'" Jesús had arranged for them and their newborns to live in an apartment they would share with two other families. The three-story building was divvied up to squeeze in more than a dozen families from Mexico.[1]

During the 1970s, the Rodríguezes became part of an ever-growing wave of Mexican immigrants arriving to Chicago, joining long-settled Mexican Americans in Pilsen and on the Near West Side. The Spanish-speaking population in Chicago had grown by an estimated 125 percent from 1960 to 1970, making up 10 to 15 percent of the city's total population. During the 1970s, Latinos continued to be landlocked in overcrowded, deteriorated housing and corralled into predatory systems of rental capitalism. White ethnics kept leaving, taking their wealth with them and giving further justification to city and state governments to strip these areas of investment. Additionally, contract selling remained very much alive in the barrio. No longer the port-of-entry pathways to generational economic success that

Figure 5.1. Maria and Jesús Rodriguez in the kitchen of their Pilsen apartment they shared with three other families, 1976. (Image courtesy of Maria Rodriguez.)

earlier waves of European immigrants and their children enjoyed, Pilsen and even Little Village were surviving on the sweat equity, immigrant ingenuity, and local, but precarious, consumer dollars of its poor and working-class residents.[2]

Tenement dwellers like the Rodríguezes paid more than just rent for access to Chicago neighborhoods; communities of color also incurred a hefty *social tax*—an economic surcharge activated by limited housing options with deeper social implications. For Mexicans, this was also tied to a persisting, historical narrative that portrayed them as sojourners and perpetual foreigners. The rationale arising from that narrative was commonly used to justify the displacement and divestment of Latinos from residential spaces that were often controlled by slum and absentee landlords who demanded high rents. The social and material construct of Latinos as perpetual "boarders" and renters depended on this form of racial capitalism in the age of white flight, a development similar to what occurred when white ethnics began selling their Southwest Side bungalows to Mexican Americans in the early 1960s. When high school students more recently interviewed longtime Pilsen political activist and civic leader Lucy Gutiérrez, the students were prompted to ask: "Who are we? Mexicans or Americans? Or are we only passing through this country on loan, where we pay rent for being here and for a better future?" These questions paralleled evolving narratives in the late 1960s and 1970s, as Chicago's "last" wave of twentieth-century arrivals confronted the social tax in the oldest neighborhoods of the city.[3]

In 1973, the city announced an ambitious redevelopment agenda to create a "renaissance" in the central-area neighborhoods surrounding downtown, intended to reverse the trend of white, middle-class Chicagoans abandoning the city by the tens of thousands. This market fix, however, was a direct assault on neighborhoods, many of them minority areas that had already endured decades of municipal disinvestment only to face the private wrecking ball of corporations. This was the solution city hall called for to increase its tax base and squeeze new revenue out of the oldest parcels of land. To Latino communities, such as those in the Near West Side and Pilsen, the city's renaissance plans came during a crippling economic recession that produced more social and economic inequality. These plans for a "super loop" of condos, shopping, and riverfront recreation would supplant immigrant, working-class barrios in an already long history of Latino displacement.[4]

With the material conditions of barrio disinvestment more visible than ever before, longtime Mexican American allies of Mayor Richard J. Daley were no longer credible spokespeople for Latinos in the city. Throughout the 1970s, as the "Daley consensus" unraveled, people needed new organizations and new tools to confront the machine. Facing displacement, Latino residents became neighborhood activists, owing partly to the influence of the US Southwest Chicano Power movement and the civil rights movement, as they attempted to intervene in the plans that threatened their communities. For years Mexicans had forged communities out of landscapes not of their own making. Names in German, Polish, Czech, and Slavic remained engraved in stone buildings, marking them with an authority and cultural power that maintained social ties to immigrant whiteness long after those groups had left. The landscape and built environment were an archaeological archive of urban "roots" from which a new generation of Latinos and Mexican immigrants continually felt excluded. As Chicano Power took hold in Chicago, it quickly manifested into a cultural and artistic renaissance that championed the politics of placemaking as residents and activists looked to new forms of spatial belonging.[5]

In the late 1960s and 1970s, long-neglected Black and Brown communities mobilized against Richard J. Daley's Democratic machine in an attempt to create deep structural change in the political economy of the city. The machine's endurance as a white institution in minority communities more visibly represented an undemocratic, repressive regime that held absolute control over city services, jobs, and even federal resources such as antipoverty dollars. Latino social-movement groups, inspired by cultural nationalism, Third-World internationalism, and the Black Freedom struggle, brought these issues to the foreground of their political agenda to end the machine's grip on their communities. Economic disinvestment coupled with cultural erasure jolted Chicano activists into intervention, civil disobedience, direct action, and militancy as they confronted machine abuse and redevelopment schemes. In the process, they joined city-wide coalitions and collaborated with parallel community-development movements fighting to shift planning away from the power center and into the hands of the community. Latino residents became barrio planners and civic activists engaged in equitable planning to stop displacement and disinvestment and to preserve and stabilize Latino neighborhoods of the Near West Side and Pilsen. However, the politics of revolt was not exclusive to left-leaning barrio planners or Chicano activists. Barrio businessmen and merchants who formed a nucleus of Latino Republicans seized on this moment of antimachine fervor to exploit the weakened ties between Latinos and the Daley administration and make their case for economic power. Understanding the Chicano activists' anger, barrio Republicans employed themes of self-determination, political empowerment, and Brown Power in their own vision of economic renaissance.[6]

Barrio Planners in a Disinvested Landscape

Latino Near West Siders witnessed firsthand the land plundering that contributed to a full range of social, political, and economic oppression. Schools were overcrowded and underresourced, the few existing public parks became repositories of junk, garbage was strewn throughout alleys and streets, and violent crime befell the community. A local Mexican American physician described housing in the area as "among the worst in the nation." Most barrio residents who by geography alone were cut off from the pillars of postwar prosperity—credit, equity in homeownership, union membership, civil-service jobs, and suburbanization—now stood in the way of the state's economic and spatial restructuring via privatization of the metropolis.[7]

After years of being hemmed in, the Latino community found that the land was being picked off by private profiteers. "The department [of urban renewal] is trying to take poor people's land and give it to the rich," one local Chicano resident told reporters in 1971, "Worse than that, they are removing our culture from the community." The fiscal crisis of the 1970s allowed speculative investors to take advantage of years of federal and state disinvestment in minority communities by preying on its tax-delinquent properties. In Chicago, Black neighborhoods endured the biggest abuses of city over-assessment followed by subsequent predatory buyers who took advantage of Illinois state law's "harsh penalties for tax delinquency." As historian Andrew Kahrl explains, this process caused many Black homeowners, already burdened with heftier taxes than their white counterparts, to lose their homes. This was one way Daley attracted corporate dollars back into his city, off the backs of minority communities. Latino residents in the Near West Side had been subjected to similar predatory land grabs for years. Given their own contentious history with the assessors, bureaucrats, and city planners on the Land Clearance Commission, Latino residents were ready to confront the predatory seizure of their neighborhoods. In 1970, local Mexican Americans met with Daley to discuss securing some of the emptied city-owned lots to develop low-income housing. They feared that corporate firms hiding behind faceless and nameless "junk" buyers would swoop in and purchase the prime real estate. Residents told a reporter that on the "sensible advice of Mayor Daley," they had come up with a solution in the form of much-needed affordable housing to be built on the emptied lots but had yet to hear back from the mayor on whether he would support it. They were "getting impatient."[8]

Additionally, the blocking of vital federal grants intended for impoverished communities, like the Near West Side and Pilsen, further entrenched economic inequality. The Daley machine intentionally cordoned off War on Poverty funding slated for these communities, mostly on the request of white aldermen who felt threatened by money entering their wards that they themselves could not control in the form of patronage. This maneuvering violated federal law, but it still took over eight years—since the passage of the Economic Opportunity Act of 1964 that established the War on Poverty agenda—for a Chicana/o-controlled community organization to receive federal antipoverty funding. As Stephen Schensul and Mary Bakszysz, two researchers working in Pilsen, discovered, "In the fiscal year 1971–1972 there was no community controlled federal- and private-agency money." By the time Pilsen organizations finally received job training and manpower dollars in late 1972, reportedly to "penetrate the local labor market," the training was for mostly "obsolete positions."[9]

In May 1972, the frustration over city misuse of federal jobs funding came into fuller view when during a veteran's jobs fair, over two hundred unemployed Black and Chicano Vietnam veterans engaged in civil unrest on the grounds of the International Amphitheatre. Protestors "tore down booths and tables and upset curtain partitions in about ten percent of the exhibition area," reported the *Chicago Tribune*. One of those arrested in the melee was a former marine, Delfino Guerrero Jr., who had spent several years in Da Nang, South Vietnam as part of an air-support squadron. Guerrero, a Little Village resident, quickly brought attention to himself when he walked into the venue carrying an odd-looking electrical contraption, which police mistook for a bomb. The device was made of a "six-volt battery and transistor radio which wired to three broom handles." Whether Guerrero intended for this device to look like a weapon or not, the resulting disturbance helped war veterans of color bring wide attention to the city's insufficient response to the growing urban crisis.[10]

As the urban crisis deepened, Latino residents adopted a more vocal stance against disinvestment and displacement. Latino residents in the Near West Side created a new organization, the Committee of United Latins (COUL), to confront the city's machine politicians, city planners, policymakers, and university bureaucrats. But they understood that to fully grasp the scale of policy, planning, and economics that threatened their livelihoods, they had to learn new skills in the field of urban planning and develop plans of their own. "We got to know some of the legal technicalities that we were not familiar with," said Rachel Cordero, a leader of COUL. "We had to study, almost like a class session to understand some of the rules of the land." Similarly, in Pilsen, housing activists were demanding more accountability from city officials to go after slumlords who kept their apartment buildings in Latino neighborhoods in substandard conditions. Members of the Pilsen Neighbors Community Council (PNCC) learned zoning and housing violations rules so they could properly take stock of the number of buildings in their community that were kept in disarray.[11]

City officials in the Departments of Developing and Planning and of Urban Renewal were ready to hand off giant parcels of publicly owned land to the highest bidders, much of it in the form of empty lots left in disarray by earlier phases of urban renewal and recent riots. "Outside developers are interested in building apartments on the land," said community leader Raoul Gomez, "which would be priced too high for the large low-income families." One Latina resident mentioned: "Everybody's worrying if they're gonna take our houses to build new ones for them [the students]. . . . [W]e don't want to move from here. We want to stay . . . they've pushed us too much already to get out of our homes so they could build for the university." This moment galvanized the barrio's built-environment activists. COUL

Figure 5.2. Housing activists from Pilsen Neighbors Community Council examine a substandard apartment in the 1970s. (Image courtesy of Juan F. Soto.)

met to formulate a people's vision for what the Near West Side ought to look like as they mapped out a project to build affordable homes. According to Rachel Cordero, "We set out to interview architects, lawyers and developers to organize a professional team so that we would be able to build housing. We didn't want public housing. We wanted private homeownership."[12]

A stone's throw from where COUL had its meetings sat the towering concrete buildings that formed the campus of the University of Illinois at Chicago Circle (UICC). To Latinos, UICC remained an adversarial institution, hostile to the community's needs. University administrators had made some token gestures to appease the community, but to no avail. "Are you meeting the needs of the people whose land you took away?" Cordero recalled asking Chancellor Warren B. Cheston. "No, you're not," Cordero answered. "[The] university is in the midst of a deep crisis," wrote the Latin Community Advisory Board in 1973, "the crisis has been building since the university opened its doors, some nine years ago. Circle [UICC] was then, and still remains, a White institution in a largely Black and Latin setting."[13]

UICC's top administrators were under pressure to attract suburbanites back into the city for their education, not to reflect the local demographics of the neighborhood. City planners' and university administrators' objectives came into sharper alignment in the sterilization of the Near West Side with a complete redesign of civic, consumer, and commuter superblocks now anchored by two expanding campuses (the medical campus and the comprehensive campus) and two major expressways. Latinos stood in the way. "The homes that are built are not for us, they're for others," charged Cordero. Another observer was Latino educator Paul Vega, who wrote in his study of UICC's lackluster outreach to minority students, "Chicago Circle Campus still refuses to address itself to the needs of the urban community in which it is located. When the university was being constructed, the adjacent Latin, Black, and Italian communities thought that the university would offer increased opportunity for their residents to attend college. But residents, especially Latins, have been disappointed."[14]

Latino Near West Siders not only resented the university expansion but also were caught in the economic disruption caused by middle-class college students moving into the neighborhood. Their arrival increased Latinos' rents and created further animus between Latino tenants and Italian American landlords, obscuring their past united struggles against urban renewal in the 1950s and 1960s. In the aftermath of the 1960s demolition, many Italians fled the area for the suburbs or other parts of the city. But Latinos, excluded from most other ethnic neighborhoods or choosing not to move to nearby Pilsen, stayed and kept a profitable rental market intact. "The landlords raised the rent because [the Italians] figure, wow, they're [students] paying all that money to go to the school, they can really afford to pay us. So they figure they'll take them for their money," one Latina Near West Sider told a UICC researcher in 1974. Latina residents were not eager to live in these buildings either, since they were in condemned areas and were rented out in violation of city building and health codes.[15]

As the Latino community battled absentee slumlords and university administrators, UICC—thanks to its location in the middle of the city and its unique campus environment—was positioned to attract faculty and students oriented toward new methods in city planning and architecture. Progressive-minded urban planners, architects, faculty, and graduate students descended on the concrete modernist campus to work and study in the new School of Urban Sciences. Inside those classrooms, students absorbed the new trends emerging in community development, neighborhood planning, and transportation. Across the nation, regional planning departments were similarly pivoting in favor of community-based approaches to their field. The idealized notions of "master planners" like Daniel Burnham, Frederick Law Olmsted, and Robert Moses had fallen out of favor by the 1960s. Students now informed by global upheaval, decolonization movements, and the advocacy planning approaches being practiced in Latin America, Asia, and Africa shared "widespread distrust of expert, top-down planning." They were encouraged to take courses outside of planning and policy to contextualize their practicums by learning about imperialism, colonization, feminism, and revolution. Faculty and graduate students formed working groups, walking tours, reading lists, and syllabi that reflected the political economy and politics of urbanists such as Jane Jacobs, anticolonial philosopher Frantz Fanon, and Marxists theorizing *internal colonialism*— the idea that colonies exist within the borders of the United States. Meanwhile, just outside the university's borders, Latino residents were working to stop more intrusive redevelopment agendas, putting into practice the very tenets of the new community-development movement students and faculty were reading about. The irony could not be greater.[16]

In helping reclaim some of the land that was quickly being swallowed up for upscale housing, COUL began collaborating with faculty and students in the Center for Urban Studies to outline plans to build new owner-occupied housing for low-income Latinos. COUL identified nine and a half acres of land between Taylor and Harrison Street, along Racine Avenue, that had pockets of empty lots. In their meetings with the urban planners, COUL insisted that they be respected as equal partners and collaborators and not be depicted as victims or intellectualized as abstractions. The urban planners, committed to citizen participation, agreed with COUL's demands, and together they devised a cooperative housing plan for Latinos to transition from renters to homeowners. What became known as the Racine-Polk Community Development Plan was a policy response to the politics of the social tax. Their proposal was financially backed by Inland Steel, which was required to submit a bid with the city. As part of a federal incentive program to encourage corporate partnerships, the steel corporation would subsidize and financially guarantee the housing plan.[17]

COUL was battling on two fronts: pushing the university to recognize its role in the community and building affordable housing for Latino Near West Siders. In this interlinked struggle, COUL created an opportunity for collaboration with students and faculty eager to participate in local community planning. The groups worked together to produce architectural plans and business proposals. For COUL, the process was as important as the outcome. Community members were distrustful of academics, social scientists, and policy "experts" who for decades had written them out of the city entirely or produced scholarship that pathologized the Latino urban experience. COUL navigated the history of friction between the university and the community, gained technical expertise in community planning, effectively used knowledge production and data, and created a model for other Latino neighborhood groups to use, even if actual construction of new affordable housing was still years from being built.[18]

Daley Responds to the Latino Urban Crisis?

Throughout the late 1960s and early 1970s, frequent Chicano and Latino protests at city hall delivered scathing critiques about the machine's racism, siphoning of federal money intended for minority groups, perpetuation of substandard housing, and crushing unemployment. Federal audits and Black community groups pressured the Daley machine to account for its dubious use of OEO funds. Self-determination and economic empowerment became central issues for community groups as they pushed the city to deploy OEO funds for job-training programs and access to the skilled-trade unions. Daley responded by calling for a new plan to hire minorities for construction jobs that, with the flurry of building going on in and around the Loop, remained plentiful. When the notice went out, Latino community groups were alarmed to find out they were not included in Daley's plan. "The exclusion of Latins is a colonial and racist decision by the big white fathers," said Hector Franco, the chairman of the Spanish Coalition for Jobs. Activists demanded Latino inclusion in construction jobs, minority contracts, trade-union membership, and representation. "We will not sit still while another group rips us off," charged Franco.[19]

After intense pressure, Daley set aside funds through the Community Renewal Society for the establishment of a Latin American Task Force (LATF) to oversee "the recruitment, training, and placing of Latins in the trade unions." But the task force, focused primarily on minority apprenticeship programs, was not going to reform the city's labor unions overnight, as these had long been bastions of entitlement for the white ethnic working-class of Chicago. As one observer noted, the high level of "graft, political controls, and the exclusiveness of the trade unions" would prevent the plan from fully diversifying the union ranks and building up minority construction firms, which would need to meet the city's patronage system of concessions and kickbacks to bid for building contracts. At one point, members of LATF engaged in acts of civil disobedience by blocking all-white construction crews at worksites until those companies agreed to hire Latinos, but even that method was unsustainable and led to violent street confrontations between construction crews and protesters. LATF collaborated with a wide spectrum of other Latino political groups in a joint effort to raise voter registration, including progressive and radical groups like LADO and OLAS, gangs and self-defense groups like the Latin Kings and the Brown Berets (an armed self-defense group patterned after the Black Panthers), along with some of the older Daley-aligned groups, such as LULAC and the American GI Forum. But ultimately, LATF's ties to Daley and the machine hindered it from making any real gains in the trade unions. Daley made his positions known by appointing Paul Gasca, one of his most trusted Latino employees dating back to his first term as mayor, to represent him at LATF meetings. Although Gasca may have attended with the best intentions to help LATF succeed, with Daley pulling the levers from behind the scenes, the task force was stripped of its independence and highly mistrusted by those aligned with the Chicano movement.[20]

Despite making minimal headway with the unions and apprenticeship programs, LATF and Daley were unified in promoting minority business ownership. LATF's voter-registration drives were pushing up against the stability that patronage provided to the local ward organizations and were extremely concerning to Daley's machine, which felt that any uptick in the voter rolls that they themselves did not oversee undermined the party. Therefore, these activities eventually fell off LATF's agenda as it shifted toward a program of economic self-determination through business. "The cry for black power, brown power and people power [has] given way to the realization that the only real lasting power in this country is political and economic power," said Garland Guice, executive director of the Chicago Economic Development Corporation at a meeting of the LATF. "Since I am not an expert on developing political power, let me focus on one aspect of developing economic power, small business."[21]

But closed-door meetings on these issues were not enough. In March 1971, hundreds of Mexican American high school students, Chicano movement activists, and others organized a large march on city hall. Ron Maydon, one of the lead organizers, described the hundreds that gathered as a combination of "professionals, dropouts, workingmen, students, men and women," emphasizing "this is a people's movement." Of main concern for the demonstrators was to call attention to the federal resources that had not reached the Latino community, even in the era of civil rights. "We have been systematically discriminated against in every area," Maydon told the press; "we are concerned about education, housing and employment for our people." As shouts of "Chicano power" rang throughout the streets

Figure 5.3. Chicano high school students march to City Hall, 1973. (Image source: Chicago History Museum, ST-14002239-0001, Chicago Sun-Times Collection.)

of downtown, community activists looked to mobilize regular marches on Daley's city hall until resources came to Latino barrios. The following year, when Mexican President Luis Echeverría made a goodwill visit to the United States to meet President Nixon at the White House, he was informed about the number of Chicano insurrections occurring in Chicago and warned they would be there when he met with Mayor Daley.[22]

Reporters noted the growing rebellion and antimachine anger among Latinos in Chicago. When Echeverría arrived downtown, over fifty angry Chicano protesters and Brown Berets were there to disrupt his meeting with Daley. Protesters showed displays of solidarity with the people of Mexico in their shared repression, holding signs calling for an "end to police terrorism in Mexico and the USA." They carried signs denouncing both Nixon and Echeverría as "fascist, brutal pigs." Newspaper reports noted, "The president's arrival at The Drake was marred by a demonstration staged by . . . a militant Chicano organization." Echeverría's visit to Little Village, however, was the complete opposite. Arranged by Anita Villarreal and the Little Village-26th Street Area Chamber of Commerce, the welcoming committee feted Echeverría at one of their department stores with a gift: a set of china plates and a table arrangement of ceramic mushrooms, representing their "Little Village." Establishment leaders tried hard to control the crisis narrative about the city's Latino barrios, but the frequency of marches, protests, and civil disobedience made it difficult.[23]

Despite the fractious barrio politics, Mexican Americans' loyalty to Daley remained strong. "The Democratic organization has strong defenders within the black and Latin American communities," noted the *Chicago Sun-Times*. "They believe it is doing what it can for the minorities and . . . concur that the road to progress and power should be up through the organization." To the Mexican American Daley Democrats, the mayor was exhibiting a deeper understanding of their communities' condition than ever before. In the 1970s, Daley began speaking in public forums about poverty and the city. He considered how the challenges of "poor working families today" were different from those of the past and that the old pathways out of poverty and into American prosperity were now few and far between. In a speech delivered in Philadelphia in June 1971, Daley told his audience, "The central city has been steadily losing its capability to effectively carry out its historic role because of rapid changes in our society. . . . The movement of population [has] created vastly different conditions." Daley also said the central city "must still serve as a catalyst for the poor of today." Reporters for the *Chicago Sun-Times* noted that there were plenty of "others who would disagree," and that those dissenters remained skeptical that the Democratic organization was genuinely ready to respond with real social and economic policy programs to address the plight of minorities during the urban crisis.[24]

MADO and the Amigos for Daley were not breaking with the mayor yet, but they were flexing some independent muscle during a weakened Daley administration. Leading up to the November 1972 elections, MADO chose to endorse antimachine candidate Dan Walker for governor. The machine despised the lawyer for writing a scathing report that blamed Daley and the Chicago Police Department for the "police riot" during the 1968 DNC. In 1972, MADO's endorsement paid off when Walker was elected. Though it was rare for machine-appointed Latinos to openly break with Daley, it was starting to happen. When Claudio Flores angrily asked in a city hall meeting room, "What has this Commission done to improve the conditions of the Spanish-speaking community?" It did not come from a young protester off the street but a Latino member of the Mayor's Commission on Human Relations. Flores was a highly respected civic leader in the Puerto Rican community, and he was fed up. "I have been faithful to the discipline imposed on me by the membership of this Commission. I have tried to raise my protest in this house, that is to say within the Commission, preventing myself from going out to the public," Flores said. Whereas in the past, Latino machine liaisons delivered their grievances quietly, Flores was refusing to keep quiet over racial discrimination in hiring for city jobs and in blocking federal funds to the "Brown Brother." "I am tired of screaming at home," Flores said. Meanwhile, federal antipoverty funds were finally being released into neighborhoods like Pilsen through the SER (Service, Employment, and Redevelopment) Jobs for Progress program, which received an influx of funding from President Nixon. By 1972, SER had expanded into the Midwest, setting up new offices in Pilsen and bypassing the machine's control of antipoverty funds, now directly administered by a relatively unknown group in the barrio: the Latino Republicans.[25]

"Nixonlandia" in Chicago

Disinvestment drove a political wedge in the barrio, and revolt was no longer the exclusive form of protest for the Latino New Left. Conservative and Republican members of the Mexican American community created a rebellion of their own for economic development. Like the members of the Chicano movement, centrist and conservative leaders were tired of the Democratic machine's blocking of vital federal economic programs to the inner city, choking off of ethnic small businesses, loan denials, and lack of Latino appointments in municipal government. Hoping to create their own entrepreneurial renaissance in the barrio and win converts to their political cause, they used President Richard Nixon's economic message to the inner city as a point of persuasion. "The reason why so many Latinos have become so eager to jump on the Republican bandwagon," wrote Martin G. Blanco, a former Democratic supporter, "is because the Republican party has put so many Latin Americans in positions where they count, top positions, top jobs." During the Johnson administration, Blanco had emphatically called upon Latinos to "speak up" for their civil rights but cautioned that acts of civil disobedience ought to be the last resort; he called upon Latinos to "set the example by peacefully demonstrating." But even Blanco admitted that "desperate people," when all "resources have been exhausted," can create chaos. Now in the early 1970s, Blanco was not alone in hoping that Nixon would bring economic relief to the barrio, as he joined a chorus of business owners and middle-class Mexican Americans and Mexican immigrants who were peeling away from the Democratic Party. Some in this group, like Jose Carlos "Charlie" Gómez, remained publicly supportive of Daley, but even he admitted that "local politicians are insensitive to the needs of the

Spanish-speaking people." This group underscored some people's beliefs that Mexican Chicagoans fit the profile of what one Latino pastor called the "silent minority." Latino Republicans in the barrio devoted themselves to spreading Nixon's plans to alleviate the economic recession and revitalize their commercial corridors.[26]

Charlie Gómez made sure the political realignment causing blue-collar whites to dump the Democratic Party did not leave Latinos holding an empty bag. Gómez understood that antimachine sentiment was as strong in minority neighborhoods as it was in the white ethnic Bungalow Belt. Using capitalist tropes of independence as the pathway to Latino power, he turned a key issue of political contestation and slightly recoded it to reach barrio residents in search of self-determination in matters of the community. Gómez believed national and state policies could positively impact local neighborhoods. This would be done through promoting barrio entrepreneurship with federally backed small-business loans that could help spark a Latino renaissance. In their view, this would be done not by community action groups but by its chambers of commerce. Gómez thus effectively shifted the conversation of groups like COUL, who had focused on the primacy of community input in city planning. As Juan Carlos Cuitino, a colleague of Gómez's, put it, "We are not just talking about it," referring to Chicano protesters, "we are doing it, individually, and as groups."[27]

He joined with other well-connected Latino Republicans who shunned the new liberalism as another form of white paternalism. By the late 1960s, Gómez was a sought-after political operator. He served as Special Consultant to the Governor on Spanish-Speaking Affairs for Illinois Republican Governor Richard B. Ogilvie, a position he earned through his critical role in Ogilvie's victorious 1968 campaign. Gómez had spearheaded the Adelante con Ogilvie voter drive, convincing Latinos to dump the machine. Ogilvie was a defiant thorn in the side of the Democratic Party. Prior to 1968, his election as the only Republican on the Cook County Board of Commissioners stripped the Democratic machine of tens of thousands of patronage jobs that came with that seat. In 1968, when he won the governorship, he immediately threatened Daley that he would "disassemble the Chicago Democratic machine." Daley angrily dared him: "You try it!" It was this brash attitude against the machine that deepened Gómez's bond with Ogilvie.[28]

More than a "consultant," Gómez owned several neighborhood movie theaters and was the owner-publisher of the local newspaper, *El Informador*. In his paper, he espoused a Brown capitalism ethic, an ethnic-racial and economic philosophy of empowerment in line with Nixon's free-market solution to social advancement that he repeatedly championed for the inner city. Gómez's own newspaper frequently promoted him as someone who "has worked tirelessly through organizations with an objective to stimulate the system of the free market among Latinos." *El Informador* cast Nixon's urban policies in a favorable light and told its Latino readership what they stood to gain from the GOP. Gómez was concerned with growing Latino inequality but felt that community organizations were not the solution, focusing instead on the untapped economic strength of Latino neighborhoods as centers of commerce and Latinos as consumers.[29]

He turned to his Latino Republican colleagues, also Midwesterners high up in the Nixon administration, such as Alex Armendaris (from Chicago) and Frank Casillas (from Indiana Harbor). Armendaris was Director of the Office of Minority Business Enterprise (OMBE) and Casillas was a Republican strategist from Northwest Indiana who, along with his childhood friend Benjamin Fernandez, cofounded the Republican National Hispanic Council to fundraise and mobilize the Latino vote for Nixon. This group quickly recruited Gómez to become a "consultant to President Nixon on economic issues," tasked with bringing Nixon's capitalist agenda to the Pilsen and Little Village communities. This mobilization occurred throughout the Nixon administration on several fronts, but primarily through Frank Casillas's Operation SER (Service, Employment, and Redevelopment) and Gómez's chairmanship of the National Economic Development Association, which focused on state- and federally funded jobs-training programs. As Latino Republicans, Casillas and Gómez were uniquely positioned to take advantage of Nixon's shifting War on Poverty financial administration to the state. Ironically, working with large-scale social-welfare programs started during the Johnson administration put Gómez on par with Chicano activists, social workers, and community organizers who had been advocating for the same programs as instruments of social change. With the Latino unemployment rate at over 16 percent, these programs were badly needed.[30]

Gómez attempted to build a base of Chicano Power activists, seizing on the barrio's backlash against Daley. *El Informador* reported on the machine's abuses and brutality at the hands of police and INS against the community. It covered issues of civil rights, education, and farm-worker struggles. Gómez encouraged Chicano young adults to enroll at Loop Junior College (now known as Harold Washington College) to counter what his newspaper portrayed as "the recent agitation which is fueled by a lack of educational opportunities." He organized a meeting with the Chicago Police Superintendent James B. Conlisk, a much-reviled figure among Chicano and Black activists, to address community concerns that the police were harassing suspected undocumented immigrants and to get Conlisk to assure them that "the right and responsibility to interrogate an immigrant [belonged only to] officials from the Immigration and Naturalization Service," not to neighborhood cops. In another instance, Gómez brokered a deal with Illinois Republican Senator Charles Percy to earmark funding for a Chicano drug-abuse program in Pilsen called BASTA. Gómez displayed an affinity for broad-based Latino cultural nationalism, promoting festivals, parades, Spanish-language films, Latin American products, and more. Gómez was interested in promoting infrastructure building through "War on Poverty" funds insofar as it supported the business of Latino capitalism.[31]

Bernardo Cárdenas, a well-known supermarket owner on 18th Street, joined Gómez in his appeal to the Chicano generation. As an influential member in the 18th Street Businessmen's Association, Cárdenas fashioned himself a cultural ambassador of all things Mexican—as an importer and purveyor of products like chiles, producer and distributor of music and records, and charro aficionado. In support of Nixon's reelection campaign, he organized Latino Youth Dances at the Sheraton Chicago to mobilize barrio youngsters already inclined to become politically active to join the Republican Party, not the Democrats or the Chicano Power movement.[32]

Similarly, other Nixon backers like Martin Blanco tried to appeal to the Chicano generation by pointing to the machine's undermining of Latino political power. "When the Latin American asked that the Democrats show some type of gratitude, Mayor Daley and his party leaders said, 'For what? Latinos don't even know how t knock on doors,'" wrote Blanco. He recalled how in his community of South Chicago, he and other residents formed the Latin American Independent Voters organization to run their own candidate for city council. The Democratic Party provided no support or resources and directly worked against them by running their own candidate, while the neighboring ward also supported a different candidate altogether—as Blanco put it, "one that will do the party's bidding." This all occurred after Daley had already split their ward years earlier, when a Mexican American candidate for alderman came close to winning the election. Blanco bluntly stated: "Just what kind of game [are] the Democrats trying to play? [The] same old game . . . [to] B-S Latinos."[33]

Nixon may have been the "law-and-order" candidate, but Latino Republicans were borrowing phrases like "revolution," "grassroots," and "revolt" to make their cases to Chicago's barrio residents. They drew on notions of Brown Power and Latino enterprise as the locus of real strength and economic mobility, noting the race and racism of machine politics. To Latino Republicans, Nixon was doing what Democrats had failed to do for years: cut through the bureaucracy and get federal funds directly to the people. "The Republicans are also passing laws that benefit the Latin American, which in most cases are opposed by the Democrats," argued Blanco, such as Nixon's signing of new enforcements within the Equal Employment Opportunity Act. Furthermore, Nixon was elevating Latinos to top positions in his administration, appointing Armendaris as Director of the OMBE in Washington, DC, to oversee the funding for small-business loans and minority entrepreneurship. Nixon's Director of the Office of Economic Opportunity, Phillip V. Sánchez, continued the revolution metaphor when he referred to the Nixon programs as creating a "silent revolution" for the "Latin American."[34]

On November 7, 1972, not only was Nixon reelected in a landslide victory, but also *Chicago Sun-Times* published a bombshell report that reverberated across Latino Chicago. It included details of a leaked internal memo proving that Nixon waged a "Southern strategy"–style campaign to undermine and divide the Latino vote by encouraging third-party efforts, anticipating his belief that many would have voted Democrat anyway. It became known as the "Armendaris memo" for its author, Alex Armendaris, and its impact lingered in the barrio for years. The memo described a "divide-and-conquer strategy" and recorded demeaning comments made by Nixon's own Latino strategists. "They are under-motivated, easily self-divided and rely extraordinarily on luck for betterment of their lives," read the internal document. It stated that "Mayor Daley and Republican Gov. Ogilvie" were "making strong plays for [Latinos]" and that "this needs to be attacked from a third party position." Its most damning part was its plan to covertly support La Raza Unida Party, the Chicano nationalist group, to dilute the impact of the Mexican American vote. It also noted that Nixon's strategists looked to exploit what they deemed "the black-brown issue" in Chicago. According to their data, "Forty percent [of Latinos] agree strongly that blacks get preference," and "nearly two-thirds of the people see blacks as getting undue advantages." It also hurt their cause that Henry Ramirez, a high-level official, was overheard telling somebody that Mexican Americans were "too dumb" to understand the issues and were easily "impressed by the high level appointments we've made." With his own reputation on the line, Gómez republished the scathing article in Spanish in his own newspaper to make sure it received full coverage in the barrio. Nevertheless, the momentum of the Nixon probusiness agenda in Chicago's barrios experienced a setback.[35]

The lingering divide between probusiness Latino Republicans and Chicano movement neighborhood activists was not over the efficacy of federal programs to address the Latino urban crisis but on what the real vehicles for self-determination were. To Chicano community activists, confronting the country's most powerful municipal government—Richard J. Daley's machine—required making noise and gaining influence at the local level. Furthermore, the Armendaris memo controversy only proved, even to the most centrist residents, that Nixon was simply borrowing a page from Daley's playbook when it came to Latinos: divide and conquer.

Chicago 21 Plan

While Daley superficially responded to the Latino urban crisis in closed-door meetings with machine-tied Latino civic leaders, he continued to deliver speeches that outlined his priorities for the "elimination of poverty, an end to racism and rebuilding of cities." The last point alarmed residents, especially communities of color in the Near West Side, who wondered what price they would pay for this "rebuilding." Their concerns were justified; Daley sought boldness during an economic recession and authorized an ambitious plan to continue the city's stunning growth and building boom at a time of rustbelt decline. In 1973, city planners and bureaucrats in the Central Areas Committee issued a plan to redevelop the surrounding Loop areas. *Chicago 21: A Plan for the Central Area Communities* detailed the remaking of the central city "for a 21st century" that would introduce the creation of a "Super Loop," extending west to Damen Avenue, with North Avenue as the northern boundary, and 35th Street as the southern boundary. A ring of neighborhoods surrounding the central business district would be rebuilt into a hybrid system of residential, shopping, and entertainment structures connected to expressways and light rail. Goals included building high-rise luxury condominiums alongside corporate plazas to bring back high-income taxpayers and "stop the flight of middle-income families to the suburbs." Daley's top planning officials, such as Lewis W. Hill, Commissioner of Development and Planning, were empowered to oversee all aspects of bids and approvals for new construction. This gave wealthy investors carte blanche over city-owned land. If the plans were to be taken seriously, it promised to bring private development to Pilsen for "middle-to-upper income" residents. Pilsen activists became rightfully alarmed that decisions were being made "that can collectively decide the future of a community" without input from those most affected.[36]

Initially, the *Chicago 21 Plan* prioritized the development of the South and North Loop areas; however, Commissioner Hill told venture capitalists they would find a more willing partner in city hall if they pursued development projects west of the Loop, on the Near West Side. *Chicago 21*'s authors imagined it as the final phase in completing the "renaissance" the city had begun with the *1958 Central Area Plan*, something Daley referred to as "one of the great acts in the renaissance of the city." Latino activists, however, did not see this as a "renaissance," but as the second go-round for more "cultural erasure and people removal." Latino and African American residents were the most vulnerable because they rented "slum housing," noted COUL leader Rachel Cordero. "They can be removed very quickly[,] and its being done and has been for [years]." A major concern for COUL was that Hill was supposed to be an impartial player when it came to the land-bidding process. Of course, none of the activists truly believed that a Daley appointee could keep a neutral position, and COUL presumed double-dealing, quid-pro-quo, and closed-door deals. "There's a conspiracy within the DUR to prohibit Latins from building housing in their own community," charged COUL member Frank Zayas. Under orders, Hill gave COUL the runaround and a litany of vague excuses, in the process killing affordable housing for Latinos in the Near West Side.[37]

Despite their huge setback, COUL did not retreat. They found renewed inspiration from their neighbors just south of them in Pilsen, where community activists waged a more forceful opposition against *Chicago 21* and countered with demands of their own. Through protest, militancy, and well-organized antimachine strategies focused on eroding the power of the 1st Ward politicians, Pilsen activists secured funding from the city for a new high school in the community. Like COUL, Pilsen's Chicano activists entered the domain of urban planning and policy on their own terms, even securing an architect from their own community to design their new school. Pilsen activists found that to stop *Chicago 21*, they needed to become both barrio planners and militant activists. COUL joined them, adding to the chorus of disinvested communities now in the crosshairs of city planners, including the Near West Side, Pilsen, Cabrini Green, and the Near Northwest Side. Together they formed the Coalition to Stop the Plan 21. They were not all "young trouble-makers," as some Daley defenders called them and came from all segments of the community. Cordero was a mother of three in her forties who threw down the gauntlet: "Even if you don't want to become militant, you're forced to. Because if you're passive and courteous, you're ignored. But once you become vocal and militant, then you're acknowledged. They force you to change."[38]

Militancy, Purges, and the Arms of Aztlán

Years before the counterplans to stop *Chicago 21* began, Chicano and Latino activists in Pilsen employed militancy and planned insurrection to confront the city's double-dealing and what they considered the "instruments of colonization" in their own communities. In early 1969, a meeting was held at the Howell Neighborhood House on 1831 South Racine Avenue, where a mostly white ethnic service organization convened. The PNCC was founded in 1954 as a community group focused on the needs of the then-predominantly Czech and Polish working class. Founded during a wave of emergent community councils inspired by the Back of the Yards movement, the PNCC administered an array of social programs to solve local problems arising from postwar blight, ethnic-racial change, and investment withdrawal. But on this day in 1969, the conveners sensed a purge coming, as the new Chicana and Chicano leaders organized pickets against the executive director. Growing tensions had been rising for years between the older leadership and the younger, militant Chicanos. Similar tensions had arisen years earlier with the more centrist Mexican American pioneers of the early 1960s who complained about the PNCC's exclusivity. Observers of the 1969 meeting noted that in the mid-1960s, PNCC "had made an effort to recruit Mexican members," but some eventually left the group in frustration and others were outright fired. During that fateful day in early 1969, however, Chicanos and Latinos stormed the meeting, read a list of demands, and dramatically told the white membership of the PNCC that the barrio—the community's true stakeholders—was firing them. Chicano activists proclaimed the PNCC "was not working effectively for Latin people," and that it was time for the old guard to step aside and come to terms with the fact that "Pilsen's vast majority of residents are now of Mexican-American and Chicano heritage." The new leaders—including Mary Gonzales, Raquel Guerrero, Inez Loredo, Martin Cabrera, Juan Morales, Arturo Vazquez, Ramiro Borja, Juan Velasquez, Philip Ayala, and Gregory Galluzzo, a Jesuit priest, among others—concluded that it was revolt, not reform, that was needed.[39]

Former directors and staff members who received salaries from the city

Figure 5.4. Mary Gonzales is questioned by police officers as she leads a community protest to depose the white leadership of Pilsen Neighbors Community Council, 1969. (Image source: Chicago History Museum, ST-10103836-0005, Chicago Sun-Times Collection.)

were asked to leave, as were those with master's degrees in social work. Further rationale for the expulsions included neglect of the Mexican community's unique needs and the old guard's delay in creating relevant assistance with immigration services, bilingual and bicultural afterschool programs for youth, job training, work referrals, and slumlord abuse. According to their accusers, the old guard had little empathy for the people's living conditions since none of them resided in Pilsen. The community also accused staff of talking down to those coming in for services. Perhaps most important of all, they felt the PNCC was too cozy with the machine and ought to be completely autonomous from its oppressors. The new leaders also admonished the Neighborhood Service Association (NSA), the governing agency that supported the PNCC and similar groups across the nation. Activists called for a full and complete break from the NSA for their perpetuation of welfare colonialism and white paternalism. The new Chicano leadership, calling themselves the Latin American Alliance for Social Progress, or ALAS (*alas* meaning "wings"), would be the barrio's new brokers. A few years later they re-adopted the name Pilsen Neighbors Community Council, only this time it would align the issues of the majority Mexican community with Mexican leadership.[40]

Chicago's barrio activists absorbed the militant spirit of the US Southwest Chicano movement. Earlier, in August 1967, a few dozen local Mexican American activists attended Martin Luther King's National Conference for New Politics held in Chicago, where they met the outspoken Chicano movement leader from Denver, Rodolfo "Corky" Gonzales. During that Chicago meeting, Gonzales spoke of his idea for a national gathering of Chicanos, which would materialize into the influential 1969 Chicano Youth Liberation Conference in Denver. Busloads of Latinos from Chicago attended that conference and returned inspired with ideas of Chicano cultural nationalism and self-determination. Chicago activists also resonated with the provocative words outlined in the 1969 *Plan de Santa Barbara*: "For the Chicano the present is a time of renaissance, of *renacimiento*. . . . Our people and our community, el barrio and la colonia, are expressing a new consciousness and a new resolve." Its language of cultural nationalism and analysis of the political economy helped contextualize conditions in Chicago: "The socio-economic functions assigned to our community by Anglo-American society—as suppliers of cheap labor and a dumping ground for the small-time capitalist entrepreneur—[keep] the barrio and colonia exploited, impoverished, and marginal." Like the California activists, Chicago activists argued, "The self-determination of our community is now the only acceptable mandate for social and political action." Chicago-based Mexican American muralists Mario Castillo and Ray Patlán journeyed to California during this time and returned inspired by these ideas as they painted Pilsen's first Chicano murals in 1968.[41]

The Chicano Power movement manifested into a cultural and artistic renaissance that intersected with the politics of placemaking. Members of ALAS "liberated" the Howell Neighborhood House. The brick structure with its stone-trimmed facade was built in 1905 by the Women's Presbyterian Society for Home Missions to serve many of the immigrant ancestors of the Czech and Polish Americans the Chicanos had just ousted. In 1970, activists renamed the building Casa Aztlán. In 1971, leaders installed a unit of Brown Berets at the building's entrance to notify "intruders" that it was now in the hands of the people. "We are here for La Raza; our purpose is to serve and protect," said one Brown Beret, "to serve all those causes that are really, sincerely fighting for La Raza." Talk of the building's takeover reverberated across the Midwest at other Chicano gatherings. At a meeting in Muskegon, Michigan, Richard Parra, director of the Midwest Council of La Raza, expressed concern "that violence could erupt again in Chicago, as it did in Chicago in 1966, and as it did in Mexican-American communities of the Southwest, unless the communities are organized to fight 'tremendous governmental neglect.'"[42]

After the purges, activists and cultural workers in the Chicano movement radically altered the neighborhood aesthetics to signal its belonging. Chicano muralists and their volunteers grabbed paintbrushes and looked up at Casa Aztlán's blank exterior walls. When a youth volunteer asked Ray Patlán, the muralist in charge, what they would be painting that day, Patlán answered, "There is no design. It's your wall to paint." This attitude of improvised revolution characterized the wave of muralism that washed over Pilsen during the 1970s and went hand in hand with the flowering of dozens of new Chicano organizations. Patlán and over forty neighborhood youth volunteers mixed a dazzling palette of bright colors, climbed ladders, dipped their brushes, and painted symbols inspired by pre-Columbian design, Mexican history, social justice, and anticolonial messages from the Global South. The sounds of cumbias, rancheras, salsa, and Latino rock music blared from loudspeakers, adding a sonic dimension of belonging to their placemaking mission.[43]

The mural, *Hay Cultura en Nuestra Comunidad (There Is Culture in Our Community)*, became part of a series of murals that went up between 1970 and 1975. The neighborhood quickly took notice. Beside Mario Castillo's 1968 mural *Metafísica*, which adorned the exterior wall of the Halsted Urban Progress Center, Pilsen residents had never quite seen an artistic renaissance of this magnitude in their neighborhoods. Bright murals in colorful spectrums were emblazoned all over the Casa Aztlán building, and it sent ripples of Chicano muralism in every direction: along 18th Street's commercial artery, up onto the walls of the railroad viaducts, and back down into the residential blocks, alleyways, and tenement walls. "In this environment, our Mexican youth are sure to progress," heralded one local reporter. "Patlán, Mexican American muralist, has placed his social commentary on the outside as well as on the inside of this center; tourists, loaded with cameras, are coming to see this." The Chicano mural renaissance attracted the curiosity of the entire metropolis, but in the community, it inspired ethnic-racial pride and galvanized political empowerment by featuring figures like Benito Juárez, Emiliano Zapata, and César Chávez. Patlán's own father was depicted as an immigrant proletariat. The representation of Mexican and Chicana/o history invited residents to come out of their homes and engage with the art. The murals inspired impromptu sidewalk seminars, as elderly residents, many who had lived through the tumult of the Mexican Revolution, held court with Pilsen's youth to recount those experiences. A second wave of murals in 1977 evoked a heightened sense of rebellion, with titles like *Racismo por KKK*, *Che*, and *América '77*. By the time the neighborhood center was fully covered in Chicano art, the rest of Pilsen was too, painted by several dozen local muralists, including Mario Castillo, Marcos Raya, Salvador Vega, and Aurelio Díaz.[44]

A Chicano-Mexicano landscape had come to fruition. To help symbolize the movement's spirit of self-determination and self-sustainability, Patlán and his youth volunteers planted an urban garden. "There are no vegetables—nothing but cement on the outside," a neighborhood newspaper reported. "These kids will learn how to plant, and the alleyway will be transformed into something beautiful. They want two trees, and big ones. And they will plant flowers. Casa Aztlán is making an open courtyard in the inner city with the help of the community, planted with our collective hopes by the hands and arms of our children." Although urban gardens provided an opportunity for community teamwork, beautification, and youth recreation, Chicano activists regarded it as part of their militant work as well. They used the garden as a point of discussion for tourists and visitors to Casa Aztlán concerning city disinvestment in Mexican communities and the perpetuation of green-less spaces. Although Pilsen had a handful of small parks, it fell way below the Chicago Park District's standard of two acres for every one thousand persons. Pilsen was severely lacking in green space, planted trees, and recreational facilities and would have needed forty-two more acres of green space to meet the city's standards. The urban garden became a useful part of their political critique about barrio infrastructure, one they would continue to build on in the coming years.[45]

The transformation of Casa Aztlán's exterior marked a turning point in the politics of Chicanismo and Mexicanismo. Political action matched the visible reflection on the built environment. Other former liberal neighborhood centers were radicalized as spaces for Chicano and Mexicano liberation: St. Joseph's was refounded as El Centro de la Causa (731 West 17th Street), operating youth programs and Chicana feminist workshops; Smyrna Temple became a site for immigrant labor activism; and the Halsted Urban Progress Center (1935 South Halsted Street) would now distribute War on Poverty funds directly to Chicano-run organizations. Local churches whose doors were once closed to Mexicanos were pried open through the efforts of social-activist Catholics who turned St. Vitus, Providence of God, and St. Pius into sanctuaries for community organizing. All this reclaimed real estate was now in the service of La Raza, supplying teach-ins and hosting coordinating committees, such as the 18th Street Farm Workers' Committee and others on immigrant rights. Marches and demonstrations happened on an almost weekly basis. Chicano revolt had turned into a renaissance.[46]

But the new leaders of Casa Aztlán were not in the clear just yet. After seizing the building, they received considerable pushback from the city and agencies to which they were still attached. After a granting agency went public with their troubles with the new Chicano leadership, a neighborhood newspaper reported: "The Brown Berets, a Chicano activist group allied with the Benito Juárez clinic, have tried to unseat Mrs. Dorothy I. Cutler, director of Casa Aztlán, and intimated staff and board members." S. Garry Oniki, president of the United Christian Community Services (UCCS), which gave funding to Casa Aztlán to run its programs, declared, "The settlement board has been intimidated to the point where it can no longer function," and claimed it "has run up a deficit of $28,000." The UCCS withdrew its financial support, threatening the community center with closure. But Chicano activists like Martin Cabrera, who headed the "Concilio de Aztlán," a "rogue" board installed when the new leadership came in, countered, "Mrs. Cutler does not live in the community and does not share its aspirations." Arturo Vazquez, another member of the Chicano group that led the initial takeover, said that the withdrawal of funds was just another example of the "denial of validity" and "self-determination of neighborhood groups." He added that "most people on the board" are from "suburban churches" and, while "well-intentioned," are "not really sensitive to what [is] going on in the community."[47]

Chicanos reclaimed the name "Pilsen Neighbors Community Council" for themselves and moved their operations to a storefront office on 18th Street. Leader Mary Gonzales recalled that after having gone through that "turmoil," the new PNCC shifted gears to address more pressing community matters. "[We] now had control of a small and bankrupt organization," Gonzales recalled, and the group "wanted to address the massive overcrowding in schools, the lack of affordable decent housing, the garbage-strewn streets, rat infestation, and the abuses at the hands of immigration and police officers." For Arturo Vazquez, who was also active in Casa Aztlán, the issue of police brutality was galvanizing and, as he recalled, "an important part of my development."[48]

One of Casa Aztlán's strengths was building coalitions quickly with other area organizations, many within walking distance. The groups' spatial concentration allowed for quicker mobilizations and street actions. For example, in November of 1972, an INS agent named Mayo Baker discharged his gun on a very crowded 18th Street during the afternoon, as he was randomly searching for people he suspected to be "illegal." While on a foot chase, he shot one man through the heart. Chicano activists quickly mobilized to condemn the INS's "probable cause" policy that led to overpolicing and criminalizing of immigrants and Mexican Americans. Chicano activists convened at Casa Aztlán and set off on a march, shouting "Basta ya con las crímenes de la Migra," and demanding justice for the victims. In another instance, Chicano organizations came together at Casa Aztlán to form the Coalition to Fight Police Repression in response to the police's apparent systemic pattern of unrestrained force against Pilsen's Mexican residents. One Chicano activist recalled, "On the streets of the barrios, [Mexicanos] live daily with the same police force that was present at the last National Democratic Convention. The cases of police brutality are countless, but rarely do these cases result in prosecution." On January 25, 1975, the coalition organized a march to call attention to the police state that had ruled their communities for years. It quickly escalated into a bloody confrontation between protesters and police, when on the busy intersection of 18th Street and Ashland Avenue, police began swinging their billy clubs and attacking Chicano protesters, who fought back. After the melee, seventeen protesters were arrested, eight officers were injured, and several bystanders were found beaten and sent to the emergency room. "The slogan 'to serve and protect' doesn't apply to the people," decried members of the coalition; it only applies to "the ruling class."[49]

Members of the business community were dismayed by the demonstrations and upheaval. They worried that the Chicano movement had gone way beyond ethnic pride and was now giving license to youngsters to act like thugs. These feelings underscored a messy and uneasy divide between the Chicano movement and members of the conservative colonia and machine-connected business leaders. In June 1973, a riot broke out when Chicanos occupied Froebel High School in Pilsen to protest disinvestment in barrio schools, shouting, "This is a takeover. Everybody leave!" Police exacerbated the situation by beating demonstrators with batons and arresting activists. Prompted by the riot and a surge of confrontational demonstrations that summer, Lieutenant Governor Neil Hartigan asked Anita Villarreal for her help in setting up an Illinois State Commission on Latin American Affairs to investigate these matters. "I would be very honored to assist you in any way possible," Villarreal reassured Hartigan. "It has been my lifelong hope that a better understanding as well as an awareness of the problems facing the Latin people could be attained through . . . state and national commissions rather than solely neighborhood organizations." Villarreal was irritated by news of PNCC's and other Chicano community organizations' confrontational tactics, and although she was no stranger to confrontation, she wanted the younger generation to work within the system. "I feel very strongly that an honest and sincere effort on both our parts will enable the Latin community and in particular, our rebellious youth to feel very much a part of their environment, their state and their country," she told Hartigan. Although the commission was hastily created in response to civil unrest, state-led commissions on Latino issues were largely vacuous affairs, more emblematic of the ulterior motives of the politicians who created them. Before Hartigan's commission there was Republican Governor Richard Ogilvie's initiative, the Spanish Speaking People Study Commission (1969–1972). Though it did study a handful of social problems, it was largely a GOP effort to garner Latino support and peel civic and business leaders away from the machine. While Hartigan was firmly entrenched in the Daley machine, and although the commission gathered data on issues like immigration, education, and housing, it often framed problems as stemming from individuals themselves, rarely as resulting from patterns of discrimination or systemic inequality.[50]

The following year, Villarreal heard that a longtime friend of hers, Dr. Jorge Prieto, a medical doctor who had a private practice in the Near West Side before urban-renewal displacement, had been surrounded and berated by Chicano activists in a heated confrontation where guns were drawn. The Brown Berets had invited Prieto to Casa Aztlán to volunteer his medical services and to produce a report that would guarantee continued War on Poverty funding for the group and its public-health activism. Prieto refused to sign off on the report. Initially, he was supportive of the community clinic in Casa Aztlán but soured on the group's goals when, in his view, activists were willing to cut corners by any means to secure War on Poverty grants. He considered the government foolish for doling out federal money to "street gangs" who knew nothing about running a social-service agency for the people, much less anything about public health.[51]

The tense confrontation subsided with everyone walking away. Shortly thereafter, Villarreal offered Prieto the opportunity to open a clinic with new facilities on 26th Street through the support of the LVCC. In a move that underscored the uneven and unequal loan politics between Chicano movement activists and the machine-connected civic leaders, Villarreal relied on her years of influence with Little Village's Bohemian and Slavic financial institutions to gather resources to start the new clinic. Prieto's move to Little Village also underscored the different political ecologies that existed between Little Village and Pilsen; the former operating on appeasement and deal-making, the latter on confrontation. Prieto, however, considered the end goal the same; by 1977 the LVCC "became the owners of the clinic," a tremendous and unique achievement in his view. "I don't know if this had happened elsewhere in the nation, where a neighborhood community board, without any financial resources whatsoever, became the owners and policy makers of a large clinic, certainly, it is not the norm." Prieto was astonished by the efficiency, the politicking, and the resource mobilization it took to get the clinic up and running in Little Village. According to Prieto, Villarreal cared about "Latino power," just not the same kind the Chicano activists were marching for. Others who noticed Villarreal's accomplishment saw it as having been done through her own will, not a budding movement. "She made it largely on her own," wrote one reporter in 1977, "and is impatient of those who say they cannot."[52]

Violent confrontations with authorities, marches, and militant action brought greater visibility, if not notoriety, to the Chicano movement. With surging unemployment and economic disinvestment in the barrio, Chicano movement activists believed the stakes were too high to shy away from confrontation politics, even if it led to arrests and violence. The energy crisis of the 1970s, coupled with the Arab oil embargo of 1973–1974, obliterated the last vestiges of industrial production in neighborhoods like Pilsen, further depleting the area of jobs. Economic-justice activists in the Asociación Pro-Derechos Obreros (APO, Association for Workers Rights) and the Spanish Coalition for Jobs (SCFJ) organized boycotts, work stoppages, and public-pressure campaigns to address the lack of jobs for Latinos and racial discrimination in employment. When the LATF was unable to achieve meaningful union reforms due to its dependence on the machine, APO and SCFJ decided to confront employers directly, seeking to negotiate deals that put the needs of the Latino community first. In the summer of 1972, twelve members of the APO blocked the intersection of 18th Street and Ashland Avenue to prevent Chicago Transit Authority (CTA) buses from passing through Pilsen. Chicanas sat down in front of buses, drawing the drivers out. The members were quickly arrested, but it called attention to the CTA's racially discriminatory hiring practices. APO activists charged that the CTA made profits off the backs of Latino bus riders but discriminated against them in hiring. Activists showed how CTA was violating affirmative action and federal EEOC laws and that the city was condoning it by refusing to enforce those mandates. CTA reached an agreement with APO, increasing Latino hires from 1 to 15 percent by the mid-1970s. At one point during the long battle with the CTA, activists "liberated" a city bus and converted it into a "moving mural" on wheels that residents could board to learn about Mexicano-Chicano culture, art, and history. Additionally, the SCFJ, representing twenty-eight Mexican and Puerto Rican organizations, pressured the Illinois Bell Telephone Company to eventually concede to SCFJ's demands. At a community town hall meeting held at Casa Aztlán, representatives from the company signed a joint agreement to hire more Latinos.[53]

Challenging systems of white supremacy and imperialism through culture, art, education, labor, and antiracist action was the mission of this evolving Midwestern Latino social and cultural movement. These coalition-building moments in response to violence, economic crisis, and social injustice underscored the community strength that Casa Aztlán and the Chicano organizations like PNCC and others had developed. As the economy worsened in the 1970s, the collective arms of Aztlán's grassroots activists and cultural workers engaged in confrontation and direct action to disrupt the machine. In the process, they learned how to achieve legitimacy as community organizers and set an agenda for collective gains. As Schensul and Bakszysz, who also worked with Casa Aztlán, concluded, "Had it not been for the Chicano movement and local successes in other types of programs," Pilsen would not have generated the necessary "political power" to create positive social change. Throughout the 1970s, PNCC delivered hard-fought victories in community control, perhaps most notably the creation of a much-needed new high school in 1977, a direct result of the Froebel uprising of 1973 and earlier high school walkouts. Further gains were also made in the creation of free health clinics, childcare services, youth recreation programs, legal-aid clinics, and employment offices. The same drive that PNCC showed for educational justice was exhibited when they confronted intrusive displacement plans and formed a coalition to create alternative visions for urban planning, architecture, and equitable spatial justice in the barrio.[54]

Avenidas Mexicanas: The *Pilsen Neighborhood Plan*

In June 1976, members of the Coalition to Stop the Plan 21 held a rally on 18th Street in Pilsen, alerting residents that "once again the people of 18th Street are facing a threat to their homes and happiness. . . . This plan has been developed by some of Chicago's richest corporations to build

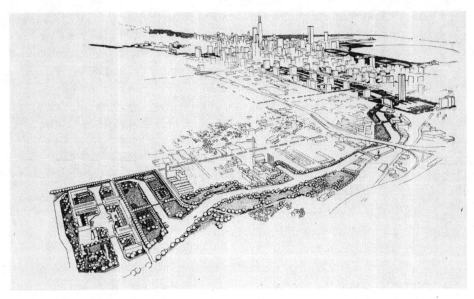

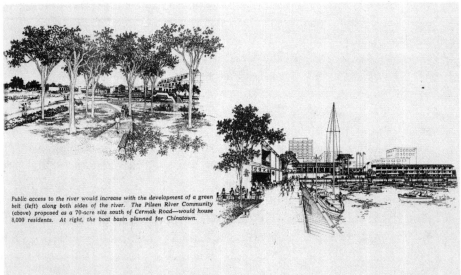

Public access to the river would increase with the development of a green belt (left) along both sides of the river. The Pilsen River Community (above) proposed as a 70-acre site south of Cermak Road—would house 8,000 residents. At right, the boat basin planned for Chinatown.

Figure 5.5. City plans for a reimagined Pilsen riverfront community as part of the greater Chicago 21 Plan. (Image source: *Architectural Forum.*)

apartments, parks, other recreation facilities, and shopping areas," not for Mexican Pilsen, but "for middle and upper-middle income people." Coalition members warned, "Whatever they call it—urban renewal, redevelopment, or Plan 21—the effects are the same, we get moved out and the rich corporations make a profit." They were referring to a new planned riverfront community for white-collar professionals that Commissioner Lewis Hill had set aside space for just south of the new high school and would be called "Pilsen Slips." When Hill mentioned that the "residents of the new Slips project" could also use the new high school, the community became outraged, charging that city planners like Hill were constantly undermining the stability they were fighting for. Mario Cruz, a PNCC activist in the school battle, countered, "We didn't fight for this school for other people!"[55]

The new high school was intended to help stabilize and anchor the community for future generations, but with Pilsen in the crosshairs of condominium developers, those victories were now jeopardized. "When we came to Pilsen," explained longtime resident and activist Raquel Guerrero, "it was time to settle down and get some stability to bring up my children. I was sick of being shoved around. I felt like a gypsy dragging a cart with all my belongings." Guerrero and her fellow community organizers hoped to keep hardworking immigrant families from being displaced and to preserve the area's strong Mexican character. Moreover, families like the Rodriguezes mentioned at the beginning of this chapter had been living in overcrowded tenements and were tired of being preyed upon by slumlords. The couple, Maria and Jesús, now had twin daughters and hoped to buy a home of their own. By this point, Maria had grown to like Pilsen for its strong Mexican identity. It felt like home to residents like Maria. Wanting to remain in Pilsen, the Rodriguezes purchased a spacious, brick-cottage home with a yard big enough for their daughters to play in and for Jesús to garden. Homeownership was the type of investment activists were fighting for, and PNCC noted that residents wanted "to preserve their neighborhood." After months of organized pressure, the Chicago Central Areas Committee agreed to allow for community input and gave the "coalition communities" a grant to work on their own respective planning proposals. The only caveat was that each community had to match the funds, which PNCC did through private grants and community members.[56]

In 1974, Pilsenites formed the Pilsen Community Planning Council. Already skilled in militancy and direct action, the council became experts on zoning, city condemnation of buildings, and vacant lots, areas vulnerable to real estate speculators. The council developed "indigenous experts," people from the neighborhood who would learn about architecture, city planning, landscape, and design from a hemispheric and even global perspective, employing analysis from theories of internal colonialism. Barrio planners held their own *talleres* (workshops) to discuss culturally relevant landscape architecture and equitable urban planning. They studied Latin American city planning, *zócalo* and plaza designs, and open-air gathering spaces. They followed the work of Guadalajara-born architect Martin Del Campo, who incorporated Mesoamerican references into his designs to instill a sense of community belonging. Members of the council worked closely with Movimiento Artístico Chicano (MARCH), a Chicago-based group of artists who organized community lectures by professors on pre-Columbian art and architecture. Muralist Ray Patlán spoke on the history of Mexican art and design. The Pilsen Community Planning Council absorbed these influences as they prepared their own plans.[57]

During this time, a group of graduate students and researchers in the School of Urban Planning and Policy at UICC were drawn to Pilsen to help challenge *Chicago 21*. They had worked under faculty members such as Calvin Bradford, a scholar and activist on redlining; Robert Mier, an urban planner; and Harry Scoble, an expert on urban politics. They also followed community organizers like Gale Cincotta. The graduate students and researchers moved to Pilsen, ready to take action. They were encouraged to engage "a variety of community problems," recalled Robert Mier, "so that the academy and community [could] develop a way of relating to one another," and be of service to communities threatened by *Chicago 21*. Another goal was to provide "rapid feedback of research information" that Chicano organizations could use to generate their own plans. Students were drawn in by academic concerns and cheap rents but were also inspired by the flowering of community organizations, the arts and cultural renaissance of the Chicano movement, and the opportunity to enact real change.[58]

During the conflict over the high school, PNCC began identifying themselves as Saul Alinsky–style community organizers. They adopted Alinsky's methods of issues-based organizing: building consensus, training and developing "native" leaders, and cultivating block clubs around issues of self-interest. This occurred at the urging of their advisors, many of them Jesuit seminarians and former organizers trained by Alinsky, people such as Gregory Galluzo, Tom Gaudette, and Edward McNamara. For the first time in Chicago, Latinos were driving Alinskyism rather than be driven out by it. With a bit of irony, PNCC did what early Alinskyists of the 1950s did: organized around bread-and-butter issues, attacked slumlords, organized

Figure 5.6. Flyer to raise community awareness and organize against the city's Chicago 21 Plan. (Image courtesy of Juan F. Soto.)

cleanup campaigns, and taught residents about tenants' rights. But unlike those groups of yesteryear, PNCC was a proudly Mexican American organization, borrowing the mottos and symbolism of the UFW and the Chicano movement.[59]

As the momentum against *Chicago 21* grew, schisms emerged within the barrio's community groups over competing agendas. Members of the Centro de Acción Social Autónomo (CASA) in Pilsen were concerned that PNCC was too narrowly focused on community development and not addressing the bigger stakes of the Latino urban crisis, which CASA characterized as the gestapo-state of terror against Mexicans. Undocumented workers and immigrants lived under increased surveillance and constant fear of being nabbed by INS agents. Maria Rodriguez recalled INS agents constantly harassing and following her on the train platform in Pilsen. In this climate, CASA believed it was critical to organize against INS brutality, roundups, racial profiling, and deportations. They were opposed to Alinsky's methods, not only for their history in defending segregation but also because strategies that focused on one neighborhood—like Pilsen—were not enough to stop the wide-scale, all-out assault on Mexican immigrants.[60] Even the new high school victory became controversial. Critics of PNCC claimed it was too focused on the construction and architecture of the building, which PNCC considered a "concrete symbol of the power of an organized neighborhood," whereas some Chicano nationalists in Casa Aztlán and the New Left in CASA were more interested in "the content that would be taught in the high school." They joked that PNCC was more interested in winning "stop signs" and "street lights" than in practicing the principles of Chicano-Mexicano liberation.[61]

With Pilsen becoming a politically rich and diverse setting for new ideas, internal conflicts were bound to occur. To some cultural nationalists, the UICC planners were simply white liberals slumming it in the neighborhood, gentrifying Pilsen in the process. But to Chicana community organizers, like Mary Gonzales from PNCC, the students were part of "a number of circles moving around in the community trying to figure out what to do about the things that were happening." The political and philosophical influence of Pilsenites was widening, and Gonzales had no qualms with building alliances with people that could help them achieve their goals. With the looming threat of *Chicago 21*, the metaphor of the barrio as an internal colony seemed to resonate with UICC planners, not just Chicanos. Understanding the consequences of "economic colonization" became a shared goal. "The community development focus has been enriched by analysis such as 'internal colony,'" affirmed UICC urban planners John Betancur and Douglas Gills. "The 'internal colony' discussion has brought attention to the domination of nonwhites by whites in urban America, the forceful segregation of oppressed groups, [the] control of local institutions by the white majority and the use of institutions to legitimate economic and social inequalities."[62]

In this barrio/ivory-tower collaboration, the Chicano planners' politics of cultural placemaking and the UICC community-development students' data-driven tools were put to use to defend Pilsen. From 1973 to 1976, a loose network of Chicano planners and civic activists affiliated with PNCC—including Cesar Olivo, Edward Martinez, Mario Cruz, and Arturo Vazquez—along with white graduate students in urban planning and policy from UICC, such as Patricia Wright, began working on issues of housing, rehabilitation, design, and infrastructure, gathering relevant data they would rely on as they developed a community plan. In 1974, Olivo was charged with a new program called Pilsen Rehab. He told the PNCC board: "There is a major housing problem in Pilsen. A good apartment or a good house is almost impossible to find. Homes are being destroyed by fires, neglect, vandalism and demolition at an astonishing rate. . . . [We are] in a position to stop this erosion process." Pilsen Rehab focused on fixing up abandoned or poorly kept buildings and identifying vacant lots and their owners. Planner-activists mobilized direct-action campaigns against slumlords who were "running down their buildings" and taking advantage of Mexican immigrants who were unwilling to file complaints for fear of retribution by immigration authorities, as activist Arturo Vazquez noted. This was part of the social tax Mexicans paid in Pilsen. Olivo, Vazquez, and others hoped to pressure the slumlords, many who lived in the suburbs off the rents they collected, to update their properties to city code or donate their buildings to PNCC.[63]

In June 1975, with the money raised to match the Chicago Central Areas Committee grant, PNCC proceeded to work on the new comprehensive plan. Per city requirements, they hired an Evanston consulting firm, the Barton-Aschman Associates, Inc. Since PNCC did not have enough money to cover the full cost of hiring professional firms, they hired a graduate student, Patricia Wright, to be their official planner. Wright, who was already living in Pilsen, was committed to the progressive tenets of community participation in urban planning and an ally to local Chicano activists. Additional assistance was provided by Fidel Lopez, an architecture professor; Lou Kreinberg, from the Lawndale's Peoples Planning and Action Conference; and Father Harrington, from Providence of God Church. The planning council held local meetings to get community input and "secure maximum involvement and participation by residents." Data gathering and research remained collaborative; young people in the neighborhood were hired to "conduct the land-use, parking, and housing condition surveys." The research team trained residents in "personal interviewing techniques" and door-to-door surveys. They also collected data on industry, parks, and schools.[64]

The strength of the planner-activists' research was in the new analysis that included Mexican immigrants in planning. They constructed a powerful community archive to supply the data for the new plan. The research foregrounded the lives of the recently arrived—tenants, transient dwellers, and immigrants like Maria and Jesús Rodriguez—making their lives and subjectivities legible to city planners. The most influential paradigm for the Pilsen planner-activists was investment/disinvestment. In other words, whether their work was on slumlords, deindustrialization, landscape architecture, or playgrounds, it started and ended with a focus on the flow of capital and economic resources. Robert Giloth, who was hired to take over Pilsen Rehab in June of 1976, and his planning-activist peers began mapping

Figure 5.7. Residents watch a presentation of the Pilsen Plan, a grassroots planning project with community input. (Image courtesy of Juan F. Soto.)

the ownership of Pilsen's built environment. They researched title holders, landlords, building owners, and industrial firms to chart the flow of money or the "leakages" of disinvestment, where rental payments went, supermarket profits, and transportation costs from riders. They concluded that all capital leaked outward, often to the suburbs. There was no local absorption of capital. In the summer of 1976, as America celebrated two hundred years of liberation from the yoke of British oppression, Pilsen's planner-activists contended that the nation had yet to reckon with its own internal colonias.[65]

The resulting product of these collaborations was the *Pilsen Neighborhood Plan*, published at the end of 1976. More than a feasibility study, the plan was a political document, a kind of planner's manifesto that delivered a critique of the city's master plan and the city at large for targeting Pilsen after causing its disparity. The PNCC planners noted that the city's master plan engineered gentrification as a market fix for deindustrialization and white flight "over the improvement of city services, employment opportunities and housing conditions." It took stock of years of assault on the district, from the imposing Dan Ryan Expressway that "abruptly divides the community in half" to ignoring its need for parks and green spaces. It rejected the Chicago Central Areas Committee's proposed spatial order for favoring a homogenous professional class as the new central-city residents.

As PNCC planners witnessed the gentrification of nearby South Loop into the new Dearborn Park, they warned, "Time is not on our side." To them it presented "a threatening picture of Pilsen's future as a working class, ethnic neighborhood," explaining that "residents are concerned that their neighborhood also will be redeveloped to provide housing for the growing population of service employees working in the Loop and nearby institutions."[66]

PNCC's plan turned to the potential for Pilsen's economic and cultural renaissance to "establish a balanced total community" contingent on the city respecting two central tenets: "to assure direct neighborhood involvement in all decisions and developments affecting the future of Pilsen," and to recognize Pilsen "as one of the major centers of Chicago's Spanish-speaking community," and to maintain it as such. The 1976 *Pilsen Neighborhood Plan*, sandwiched between the post–War on Poverty era and the Community Reinvestment Act (CRA) of 1977, introduced creative policies to address the particulars of Latino neighborhood disinvestment. A compounding concern for PNCC planners was zoning. Since zoning in Chicago had been used as a manipulative tool to set up profitable racial barriers and capital interests for years, the 1976 plan urged community supervision: "Zoning in Pilsen cannot be relied on to control new development. Rather a better system of control would be a formal agreement between Pilsen Neighbors . . . and the City of Chicago for [review of] new development on a case-by-case basis." It prescribed the creation of a community land trust to purchase vacant lots and control development. Furthermore, since banks had been complicit in redlining, the plan requested "a special code and district designation for the neighborhood" to be eligible to receive rehabilitation loans the city created in anticipation of CRA legislation.[67]

The Pilsen planners proposed no specific architectural designs but did affirm the need to preserve the Mexican heritage and unique aesthetics already in the built environment. This was a departure from Chicago city planners' standard procedure, which never considered the cultural relevance of ethnic-racial communities nor accommodated for ethnic design or overlay. "Painted wall murals, the many bright signs and graphics, the red brick paving on the street, and other similar features," argued the *Pilsen Neighborhood Plan*, "all form part of a visual image which is unique in Pilsen." The 1976 plan highlighted the spatial and architectural distinctiveness of Pilsen's nineteenth-century worker cottages, brick two-flats, and Victorian buildings. Because of the numerous vacant lots and substandard buildings, often the rationale for bulldozing, the plan strategically framed Pilsen's neighborhood architecture "as groups of engaging buildings [with] significant aesthetic value." PNCC's plan took a page from Jane Jacobs's idea of the inherent value of neighborhood uniqueness, where "people come specifically for it" because there is nothing else like it. "The special and colorful characteristics and culture of its predominantly Mexican population . . . make up the variety, informality, and, especially, the complexity which gives Pilsen its special flavor." The plan assigned political meaning to some key sites, such as Casa Aztlán, a "well-known landmark," along with parks and churches that figured prominently in the Chicano protest movement. It envisioned a political imaginary whereby the pathways of marches and demonstrations left an enduring print on urban space. The planners paid tribute to protests and public gatherings as a rich barrio tradition: "The plan for Pilsen recognizes the locational, historic, and social factors which have contributed to the . . . predominantly Mexican neighborhood, and the need to maintain this special environmental quality."[68]

The focus on heritage architecture was meant to achieve a deliberate Mexicano-Chicano landscape. The intersection of 18th Street and Blue Island Avenue became the cultural and commercial "focal point and center," a central plaza, or *zócalo*, in which the community could gather. Blue Island Avenue was part of the "rational" street system Daniel Burnham developed in his 1909 *Plan of Chicago*, which included a network of diagonal thoroughfares that connected the neighborhoods to the center of the city. PNCC planners valued this intersection as a vital center that residents had already built through their own cultural and consuming practices. In 1974, building on its centrality, Fiesta del Sol, a community summer fair, was inaugurated on that site. Developing along the diagonal thoroughfare would create a "full range of community/commercial activities," and a walkway would lead straight into the new high school, which would serve as a kind of monument to the PNCC and the community's recent victories. As Mary Gonzales, a leading organizer in that fight, noted, "The school stands as a worthy testament to the courage and tenacity of the people and a symbol of their great heritage." The high school would be designed in an Aztec pyramid motif by Mexican architect Pedro Ramírez Vázquez, famous for designing Mexico City's Olympic Village of 1968 and Aztec Stadium. The new campus would be surrounded by Chicano murals and include a community center inside the school. The modernized Aztec pyramid building would be the architectural jewel at the end of a Mexicano-Chicano pedestrian walkway.[69]

Although the plan called the controversial Pilsen Slips development a "new-town in-town" gentrification project that posed a threat to current residents, it was noteworthy that Pilsen planners left some of it in their plan, mainly the "[n]ew 'riverfront' park south of Benito Juárez High School site." As pedestrians walked southbound from the campus, a riverfront series of "[a]ctive and passive park facilities" would "expand the range of leisure time services provided," wrote the planners. What master planners of *Chicago 21* had envisioned as a draw for affluent condominium buyers, the Pilsen planners appropriated as recreational space for Mexican Pilsenites. Further recommendations included increasing pedestrian walkways, from boulevards to less-utilized alleyways, and discouraging trucks and other traffic from using local residential streets. It promoted more sidewalk activity and recommended the continuation of viaducts as public-art venues. Vacant lots would host new housing that "*existing* residents can afford." It recommended special landscaping, street lighting, and signage to establish a "special and positive image of the neighborhood." PNCC decried the lack of public parks and green space, pointing out that "trees and grass are sparse in Pilsen." One park, Playlot No. 281, was directly below the Dan Ryan Expressway, where noise, falling debris, and polluted air made it unsuitable for children. They proposed that the city build six new parks in Pilsen.[70]

The planner-activists proposed ambitious concepts that questioned city builders' and architects' long-held ideological premises; for instance, whether neighborhood landscapes, homes, churches, parks, and even technology served a purpose for Americanizing immigrants. Or if, in Pilsen's case, Mexicans were Mexicanizing American landscapes. The planner-activists searched for an interplay between the two. The *Pilsen Neighborhood Plan* recommended a "landscaping and beautification program" to provide pleasant pedestrian experiences and necessary shade. It encouraged cleaning and landscaping railroad embankments. Not articulated in the plan, but occurring when it was developed, was the creation of Mexican urban-garden projects. The Pilsen planners promoted greenhouse design and urban farming as organic forms of "neighborhood technology." The planner-activists, along with community members, former braceros, farmworkers, carpenters, and handymen, created a greenhouse prototype in a lot next to a bar on 16th and Halsted Street, owned by a member of the Pilsen Planning Council, where they often gathered to plan actions against slumlords and gentrifiers. The greenhouse, which they hoped could be replicated as "garden projects" on every block, had rows of chiles, tomatillos, bell peppers, beans, corn, and five apple trees. The neighborhood's sweat equity, rehabilitation projects, and the steady influx of Mexican immigration were at the heart of Pilsen's economic growth. The 1976 plan valued the community's informal use of space and expertise as a source of its strength. The plan's goals were to improve properties, empower residents, and turn former braceros into barrio crusaders.[71]

PNCC produced an expanded and ambitious vision for the district that included improvements to housing, commercial storefronts, industrial zoning, recreation and open space, and streets and pedestrian systems. It promoted creative policy to ensure community participation and long-term neighborhood stability. Pilsen Rehab became an autonomous Community Development Corporation (CDC), renamed the Eighteenth Street Development Corporation (ESDC). By 1977, ESDC was receiving federal and state grants to continue rehabilitating deteriorating buildings throughout the neighborhood and improving them for low-income residents. ESDC did this by creating a job-training program for neighborhood youth to serve as apprentices in bricklaying, masonry, and carpentry and to place them in union jobs. Data gathered on Chicago's redlined neighborhoods was now leading to major national legislation, such as the CRA of 1977. In 1978, Professor Robert Mier founded the University of Illinois at Chicago's Center for Urban Economic Development (UIC CUED) partly to formalize the collaborations of the past few years between communities in the coalition and the university's planners. These methods guided the ESDC's agenda for the next several years. In 1978, activists from the planning group, such as Arturo Vazquez, formed the Pilsen Housing and Business Alliance to confront gentrification. They titled their newsletter *Los Nuevos Tiempos* (*The New Times*) to signal a new phase in their fight.[72]

: :

At the end of the decade, one thing was clear: Community groups embraced a new militancy against displacement and disinvestment that challenged the *social tax* of exclusion, expendability, and dislocation that constantly remade Mexicans into transient dwellers and perpetual foreigners. Throughout the 1970s, Chicano movement activists drove grassroots protest campaigns, employing data-driven arguments and militancy to win employment, housing, and education victories against the machine. But revolt was not the exclusive domain of the Chicano movement, as Latino urban Republicans also confronted disinvestment, promoting the state as the conduit to federal antipoverty funds in hopes of chipping away at Richard J. Daley's patronage power. Seizing the discourse of self-determination, Brown Power, and Brown capitalism, pro-business Latino Republicans looked to expand their influence in the barrio. In their view, the barrio's renaissance would happen through Latino business power.

It was in this context of competing agendas—the wrangling over the machine's control of minority resources, the battle over the welfare state, and the politics of knowledge production and master plans—that the stakes of who represented the best interests of the barrio came into sharper relief. The tenor of revolt and militancy alarmed longtime Mexican American Daley loyalists who viewed dependence on antipoverty funds as a threat to their project of American belonging and also felt that Chicano activists were too narrowly focused on gilding one neighborhood. Dissent also came from members of the Chicano-Mexicano New Left who argued for a broader focus to confront the criminalization of immigrant workers and move away from local concerns of street signs and architecture. Of all the barrio's stakeholders, Chicano community organizers in PNCC drove the agenda, as they turned to the politics of urban planning, community development, and architecture. They were victorious in reclaiming and remaking Pilsen as an unmistakably Mexicano-Chicano community, commandeering community centers and neighborhood organizations from white control. These efforts were unimaginable in other neighborhoods with Mexican density.

The 1976 *Pilsen Neighborhood Plan* conveyed the links between the Chicano Power and community-development movements. It was the product of a collaborative network of planner-activists that confronted the city's master plan and the politics behind the production of space and placemaking. In the 1976 plan, PNCC mapped out a blueprint for the neighborhood's renaissance to mark Pilsen anew with meaningful symbols of *Chicanismo* and *Latinidad*. By institutionalizing its militant spirit, PNCC gained credibility, clout, and funding. Recognizing the patterns of urban development that were shifting toward a privatized market, PNCC learned the new mechanisms for reinvestment, turning to grants, foundations, community-development corporations, and agenda-building during the pre- and post-CRA Act of 1977. But PNCC's strong, comprehensive reach might have also been its liability, as services were duplicated, leadership was spread thin, and internal divisions became more pronounced. And the 1976 plan was also utopic in its policy recommendations, as PNCC admitted, "We still need to agree on some solutions, locate requisite resources, and select strategies to implement these solutions." PNCC was unable to get the city to agree to the enforcement mechanisms it wanted to secure Pilsen as a working-class Mexican area. They pointedly asked the Chicago Central Area Committee:

"Is the community being co-opted in any way into supporting directly or indirectly the larger Chicago 21 Plan" by using its "matching funds?" This question of "co-optation" would remain unresolved throughout the decade.

Although not fully implemented, the 1976 plan's lasting impact was on promoting Pilsen's beautification, supporting public art, rehabilitating buildings, and protecting zoning for food and pedestrian cultures that generated pride in the community and drew tourists and visitors. Nevertheless, the consequences of unresolved community control kept the threat of displacement looming. Younger affluent whites, tired of their childhood suburbs, moved into Pilsen, enticed by cheap rents, public art, culture, and architecture. Older residents wondered if, in fighting for Pilsen's Mexicanness, they had sealed their own fate of being driven out by it.[73]

6 :: Flipping Colonias

In October 1981, scholars, artists, and community residents gathered at UICC for a conference entitled "Art, Architecture and the Urban Neighborhood." Perry R. Duis, a professor of urban history, praised the wave of community revolt that had swept through Pilsen: "Instead of a plan imposed entirely from outside the community, [Benito Juárez High School] was designed with the help of Pilsen residents." Duis remarked on how residents carried out their own aesthetic vision: "The sloping walls reflect the Mexican architectural heritage, not aesthetic ideas imported from outside the neighborhood." Moreover, "the high school project is also significant because it demonstrates one approach to the serious question of urban redevelopment and the rejuvenation of neighborhoods."[1]

As Duis spoke about building an architecture of Latino empowerment, the United Neighborhood Organization (UNO) was setting out to build another movement. Looking to address not just Pilsen, but other Latino colonias, and the political and economic subjugation the very word implied, the community group mounted a campaign to address racial injustice and infrastructural inequality. At the start of the 1980s, plant closures, overcrowded and underfunded schools, and blighted housing conditions continued to grip Latino neighborhoods, while becoming the battleground sites on which Latinos sought to build neighborhood-based power. This new decade would be a period of significant grassroots political mobilization for Latinos themselves, driven by demographic growth, economic and structural neglect, and an inspired politics of self-determination.[2]

When Richard J. Daley died in 1976, he left a political machine in place that could still control and undermine growing Latino political power. City hall continued his long tradition of redrawing district and ward boundaries to prevent Latino supermajorities from manifesting. But gerrymandering could not hide the fact that Latino settlement was widening on the heels of white depopulation. In the Southwest Side and the Bungalow Belt, from 1970 to 1980, population numbers dipped in most communities, with the exception of Pilsen, which saw a minor increase, and Little Village, which showed a significant boost from 62,895 in 1970 to 75,204 in 1980. Pilsen and Little Village were becoming denser during this decade, but Mexicans were also moving south of the river, in hopes of flipping formerly white neighborhoods to Mexican ones.[3]

In the meantime, areas surrounding the Downtown Loop were turning over as well. From the late 1970s to the 1990s, the evisceration of the white tax base continued to guide city hall politics as boosters, planners, and bureaucrats pursued redevelopment schemes to flip valuable real estate in the central city, hoping to bring back suburbanites. In Pilsen, speculators of all stripes, from lawyers to slumlords to former city bureaucrats, seized on this moment to flip their properties and create "colonies" of their own to attract "urban pioneers" and "white homesteaders," displacing poor and working-class Latinos in the process. Community organizations saw this as a project of cultural erasure and outright colonization.

Chicago's late twentieth-century reshuffle did have an economic rationale. In an age of shuttered factories and economic restructuring, reshuffling people across the metropolis could draw new value out of old spaces. Now there was more land to flip thanks to white depopulation and the CRA of 1977, which outlawed classic segregation tools. Flipping neighborhoods from white to Brown or Black, or even from Black and Brown to white, became an economy in its own right in the neoliberal era, when the postindustrial city shifted to dependence on privatized capital and nonstate entities. An entire apparatus formed around it, primarily through the CDC model, which competed in a marketplace for private (corporate, philanthropic, and foundation) and federal monies to improve, change, or save neighborhoods. Enterprise and *empowerment zones* were quickly added to the menu of economic development, providing tax incentives for urban space.[4]

Latino civic leaders and neighborhood groups mounted grassroots campaigns for political power and community control. In the political arena, Latino independents challenged the machine and helped build a racial-coalition movement that, in 1983, elected Harold Washington as the city's first Black mayor along with a wave of Latino challengers to the city council. But the newfound colonia clout revealed internal divisions as well. Machine loyalists and independents differed over postindustrial politics and how best to invest and revitalize Latino neighborhoods. Some civic leaders—and city hall—viewed ethnic tourism, urban travelers, and the branding of Latino neighborhoods as a positive way to generate needed revenue; others saw it as an invitation to speculators that threatened the relocation of residents. Just as East Pilsen's art colonists grappled with living in a "slum," as one artist put it, Mexican immigrants, Mexican Americans, and Latinos in general had to make meaning out of their new environs in the ever-expanding Far Southwest Side. Throughout the 1980s and 1990s, Latino working-class culture was dispersing, relocating, and suburbanizing as residents shaped their bungalow landscapes and became postindustrial survivors.

While community groups faced federal austerity against urban America, privatized capital, bankers, and strategists pushed an economic rationalization for reshuffling people across the metropolis, at times even packaging the process as the end of segregation. But whether one was displaced by gentrification or living in a working-class bungalow on the Far Southwest Side, what endured was the landscape of whiteness that continued to shape these spatial and economic moves. The real estate market had used Latino buffer communities for years to negotiate white ethnic fragility and hostility, premised on anti-Black racism and, at times, anti-Brown racism or fear of Global South immigrants. Indeed, by the 1990s the old color lines of the mid-twentieth century had somewhat softened, but persistent class and racial inequality continued to resegregate people across metropolitan Chicago. The flipping of colonias is both a history of erasure and of new beginnings. As such, a new colony of a different color was taking hold in Pilsen.[5]

Colony of a Different Color

During the late 1970s, on the corner of South Halsted and 16th Streets, local residents gathered for drinks at Miguel Centeno's corner tavern. This was an informal headquarters for Chicanos and progressive whites who, since the mid-1970s, would gather there in celebration after winning a community action against a slumlord, completing an apartment-rehabilitation project for low-income families, or improving a local park. They were part of a newer generation of the community-control movement, a form of grassroots political action that often took root in working-class, immigrant, and racialized neighborhoods led primarily by residents, community leaders, settlement-house workers, and organizers. In the 1950s and 1960s, this movement had roots in mobilizations against urban-renewal projects as well as shared struggles with the civil rights movement over integration and housing. Since the 1960s, activists and organizers had turned their attention to democratizing local school boards and gaining political control over neighborhood institutions. In the late 1970s, members of Pilsen's community-control movement belonged to various suborganizations, including the ESDC, the Pilsen Housing and Business Alliance (PHBA), and PNCC. Together they built their new agenda on what they called *desarrollo sin desplazamiento* (development without displacement) to revitalize the neighborhood and take on slumlords, speculators, banks, and city hall in a herculean effort to keep Pilsen a Mexican working-class neighborhood. From the tavern, they had an unobstructed view of the new "colony" taking shape a stone's throw away.[6]

Despite its blend of Richardsonian Romanesque and cottage architecture, Pilsen missed the first wave of back-to-the-city urban villagers during the 1950s and 1960s, when a portion of America's young, white professionals and cultural bohemians eschewed suburbanism for historic neighborhoods in the central city.[7] But by the late 1970s, Pilsen was no longer exclusive to a Mexican working-class and immigrant community. It now coexisted, however tenuously, with an art community, mostly white, living in rehabbed apartments and converted lofts on the eastern end of the neighborhood. "The presence of another group of artists is barely evident from the street," noted observers exploring the covert architecture that hid the colony from passersby. This concept left aging facades intact while hiding the completely renovated interiors. A regular at Centeno's tavern, Lew Kreinberg (no fan of the "colonizers") wrote: "Part of the reason that buildings with new innards kept their old hides [is that] the natives are restless. They might see things you have that they do not have." By the late 1970s, more than two hundred artists, painters, performers, sculptors, and others lived in a colony hidden in plain sight.[8]

This settlement was part of a greater metropolitan reshuffling that, as one notable Black Chicago real estate agent, Dempsey J. Travis offered, was changing the color of the central city. "Blacks, browns, and poor whites are being recycled off the prime land in the central areas of many of the nation's oldest cities," he wrote in a 1978 *Ebony* article. "Their strong backs and unlettered minds no longer qualify them to be urban guests," referring to their obsolete use value as laborers in the urban, postindustrial economy. Travis referred to the process of replacement as a "recycling of urban land." To the Centeno tavern regulars well-versed in Travis's perspective, the politics of this recycling made them worry that despite their yearly efforts to stabilize community development, "flippers" had taken hold of East Pilsen. In the community-development scene, flippers were speculators and housing renovators who bought and sold houses to generate the highest profit possible while making few or no improvements. Some flippers bought cheaply but then became hoarders of real estate, never letting go of their buildings. Travis blamed the great reshuffle squarely on the federal government's disastrous urban-renewal projects, which laid the groundwork for private developers to swoop in and pick off prime real estate, shoving communities of color to the periphery of cities into areas that did not want them either. Miguel Centeno and his friends understood this, too, since they had overseen the 1976 *Pilsen Neighborhood Plan*. They had achieved a few more victories since then but could hardly rest on their laurels now that Pilsen remained under threat, flipped a little more every day by speculators.[9]

At the center of the controversy was John Podmajersky, a former building inspector for the Department of Urban Renewal, a real estate speculator, and the founder of the art colony. In his fifties during the late 1970s, he was intimately familiar with the changes that had occurred in Pilsen over the twentieth century. The son of Czechoslovakian immigrants, he grew up in Pilsen when the neighborhood was a port of entry to families like his. As a city inspector during urban renewal of the Near West Side in the 1950s and 1960s, he witnessed thousands of Mexican families relocate to the 18th Street vicinity. It was of no small consequence that Podmajersky could now utilize his bureaucratic and professional experience to his advantage. By the mid-1970s, his name was on the lips of many of Pilsen's community activists, who had no qualms with calling him a "speculator" and an "opportunist" who used his inside access to make advantageous purchases ahead of the city's redevelopment agenda. Teresa Fraga of PNCC once told Chicago's PBS station, WTTW, "He buys buildings. But doesn't rent to families. We are a community of families." Investigative research by members of ESDC and PHBA uncovered an internal study that predated the 1973 *Chicago 21 Plan*. It placed the city's crosshairs on Pilsen in 1969 and more than likely alerted Podmajersky (who worked there at the time) and others about newly indemnified properties on the east end of Pilsen. This "secret real estate plan," "The Pilsen Plan, Marketability Analysis: Proposed Residential Development," was commissioned by the Department of Urban Renewal and conducted by the RERC led by James C. Downs, who in a few short years would be responsible for *Chicago 21* and the gentrification of the South Loop in the form of Dearborn Park. Neighborhood activists saw this as the origins of Podmajerksy's colony, a concept turned into reality.[10]

Although John Podmajersky masked the new colony behind the facades of old buildings, he was quite open about his intentions. "This is a dying neighborhood but it has lots of potential, a lot of charm," he told Kreinberg and Bowden in the late 1970s, "Factories won't save it, though. We need a more middle-class idea, something for people to look up to. My project is not just for artists but for those who like an arty tone." He cobbled together old buildings and customized them into a horseshoe design with a central courtyard that served as a common area, but more fundamentally as a safe space for colonists to enjoy the outdoors without really having to go into the neighborhood. He called his fortress the East Pilsen Artist Colony. He told the *Chicago Reader* in 1978, "Some people think urban renewal means to find space somewhere for poor people. I'm concerned with the building itself." His boasting about his colony made him both a villain and a folk hero depending on who was asked. To his defenders, mostly the artists who benefited from his properties, he was a smart businessman who turned ruins into art and should be commended for it. "He had a dream of starting an artist colony," said a resident performance artist Donna Blue Lachman. "Podmajersky had a vision," said mixed media artist Barbara Aubin. "He felt artists in a city needed both breathing space and beauty."[11]

Countercultural publications like the *Reader* painted nuanced portraits of him even when they referred to his rehab project provocatively as "the colonization of Pilsen." Writer Garry Freshman cast him in a folksy light: "Podmajersky is the only person I have ever met who, when his lifelong environment no longer pleased him, changed it radically by the sheer force of his being." Freshman noted, "His work suggests the spirit of the frontiersman," but while "the frontiersman and the civic father both built on vacant land, John is a *re*builder. He does not fill space, but fills it again." Critics of speculators and back-to-the-city movements, like Dempsey J. Travis, provided their own glossary for those benefiting from the frontier. "Variously labeled as 'colonizers,' 'urban homesteaders,' 'inner city pioneers,' 'frontier persons,' 'municipal carpet-baggers,' and 'city redeemers,' these White returnees to the city are likely to benefit from the Tax Reform Act of 1976 which established important incentives for preserving and rehabilitating commercial and income producing structures," Travis argued. They were just as likely to benefit from the CRA of 1977, intended to help economically disadvantaged communities of color but whose incentives in a city like Chicago were falling into the hands of those who knew the inner workings of the city better.[12]

Becoming part of a new colony required buy-in from the urban homesteaders. "They liked living in the city because they had tried the suburbs and the city was full of things hard to nail down, like strange food, crazy

Figure 6.1. John Podmajersky, considered to be the chief architect behind the gentrification of East Pilsen, on the cover of the *Chicago Reader*, June 1978. (Image courtesy of the *Chicago Reader*.)

characters, street life," Kreinberg and Bowden reported. Colonists linked their contemporary activities to descriptive and romantic notions of industrial and preindustrial work recalling a European immigrant village on the American frontier. Kreinberg and his coauthor emphasized the artists' propensity for living meagerly: "A single room with a crapper and a galley kitchen got a coat of white paint, and presto, became an artist's studio." But Kreinberg and Bowden's descriptions, a combination of ethnography, literature, and sociology, captured and perpetuated the romantic tropes. Lines such as "They walk among the ruins of nineteenth century might"; "Pilsen was homecoming for anyone whose people had ever worked with their hands and carried lunch pails"; and "The new residents were into farming potted plants and wearing overalls" all illustrated the perspective of the new colonists, not the colonized. In 1976, white urban pioneers furthered these romantic images when, hoping to make common cause, they wrote to PNCC announcing themselves as the "East End, Inc.," a nonprofit group providing social services and recycling efforts. Its president, Heidi S. Perrey, reported on their efforts at "reversing a blighting trend." Perrey proudly touted her group's reshaping of East Pilsen through various efforts; for instance, commandeering two storefronts that were "falling into disrepair," an "eyesore" that had "people living in" them. They also beautified empty lots littered with trash, offering to "remove the trash for free" and "put in a garden" to be enjoyed by following "sharecroppers' rights" for "whatever was raised."[13]

If inventing romantic links aided the colonists' sense of belonging, John Podmajersky and his defenders helped too. Not only did he displace Mexican renters from buildings he purchased but he also spun a neighborhood narrative to accompany their removal. "This was once a great community," he told WTTW, "[n]ow there is nothing of the sort." While lamenting the lost neighborhood of his childhood, he wrongly insinuated that the Mexican community that settled a generation after his did not feel a sense of permanence. "The people today only come to live here for a set amount of time to make some money and then leave to another area, because most people do not feel they have roots here. I feel rooted to this area because it has a great location, the expressways are close by, for example in the last four years there have been a lot of changes, we have Printer's Row, Dearborn Park, Chinatown, that are prospering greatly. I await the day Pilsen can be part of that revitalization process." His defenders also reclaimed it on more ethnic terms. "Pilsen is definitely not a picturesquely charming Chicago community. Nor, was it ever," offered resident Barbara Aubin. The flight of "Slavs, Irish, and Italians" from the neighborhood have made it a "slum." Donna Blue Lachman justified Podmajersky's colonization more simply, "He was here before the Mexicans." In fact, from the mid-1970s to the early 1980s, a long list of justifications ranged from economic Darwinism to homesteaders' rights, sharecroppers' rights, white ethnic roots, Mexicans as birds of passage, and in-vogue arguments about the "myth of neighborhoods." Podmajersky's indifference to the gains that community groups like PNCC and ESDC made was unsurprising given his reliance on these neighborhood narratives to achieve his goal.[14]

The community organizations were in a race against time and resources for control of what Podmajersky and his defenders were cleverly calling "East Pilsen." Ascribing ownership through romanticized notions of ethnic authenticity negated the social and cultural spaces Mexicans had built since the 1950s. One example was when Podmajersky purchased and converted the Halsted Urban Progress Center, one of many buildings in the neighborhood bearing the markings of the Chicano movement with Mario Castillo's 1968 mural *Metafísica*. Podmajersky renamed the building the Pilsen East Center for the Arts and whitewashed the mural in a single afternoon. The East Pilsen artists continued making their art, undisturbed and shielded by wood-paneled walls from the battles taking place outside, secure in their cultural relativism and pretenses of inner-city diversity. Whether the colony was "East Pilsen" or "Pilsen East," the intentional dislocation and severing from Mexican Pilsen was a profitable rebranding campaign for speculators. The only problem was that Mexicans still lived in so-called "East Pilsen." Homeowners Jesus Lopez and his wife Guadalupe lived directly across from Podmajersky's art colony. Lopez recalled Podmajersky's frequent visits to ask if he was ready to sell. Mexican homeowners like the Lopezes were quite familiar with speculators' aggressive pursuit of Mexican-owned properties. They coerced people into selling or used their city hall connections to set building inspectors on homeowners in hopes that enough code violations would force them to sell. Podmajersky himself frequently violated Chicago's housing codes.[15]

The colony of a different color had real consequences for working-class Mexicans. Like patterns of gentrification in other cities, the displacement of Mexican residents from East Pilsen did not happen through bulldozing but by speculators who bought in anticipation of market upswings. Since the early 1970s, hundreds of buildings and lots in Pilsen had been owned by people or firms located outside the neighborhood. Speculators hid their ownership patterns as well. One mysterious company called Audubon, Inc., which owned many tax-delinquent properties in Pilsen, was found to have offices downtown, on Taylor Street, and in the suburbs. Almost all speculators took advantage of conditions created by decades of disinvestment, redlining, and blacklisting. They bought occupied buildings directly from slumlords who were desperate to sell, and they picked up tax-delinquent vacant lots, formerly seized by the city, at low auction prices. These methods had two immediate effects: first, displacing low-income tenants through unaffordable rent increases and/or eviction and second, raising the tax assessment for Mexican homeowners to levels beyond the reach of most.[16]

Gentrifiers and community-development activists valorized space by way of preservation, or in the case of East Pilsen, rehabilitation over redevelopment. But it was private real estate developers—people like Podmajersky, who some referred to as a "one-man private urban-renewal"—who had the means and clout to take advantage of tax benefits, public subsidies, and zoning changes that the community-development movement originally fought for. Chicano planners and community activists were angered by the uneven access to rehabilitation resources, an issue they had been raising since the mid-1970s when Cesar Olivo warned real estate developers: "If buildings are going to be rehabilitated in Pilsen, it's going to be by the people living here, the present residents."[17]

From the mid-1970s to early 1980s, members of the community-control movement worked to stop speculators. Podmajersky continued to expand his colony, this time into an abandoned brewery on 16th and Canal Streets. Arturo Vazquez of PHBA alerted residents to concerns that the "plans called for high income housing and [an] Arts Center in the Brewery Complex." In an effort to fight off speculators, Vazquez, a trained and credentialed planner, submitted alternative proposals to the city for the brewery's use that would "keep this area industrial and guarantee jobs for Pilsen residents." PHBA organized a series of community meetings at Providence of God, a church surrounded by Podmajersky's expanding artists' colony, to bring all the stakeholders into one room and come up with a workable solution over the brewery's future. Most artists remained unsympathetic to the needs of the Mexican community as "they saw the district getting better and better as more people like themselves moved in." Podmajersky insisted that he "was a man of determination" and his plans to turn the brewery into a multimedia arts complex and residential lofts were going forward. Progressive Chicano community groups and their allies argued that the Brewery Area needed to provide industry and jobs, not lofts for middle- and high-income whites. As Kreinberg noted, "The organizers kept their ideas alive. They felt that the rehabilitation of old dumps by affluent whites was bad for the neighborhood because it made poor people move." The arrival of more artists, Kreinberg noted, "immediately doubled or tripled the rents, but still the prices seemed cheap to them." Tensions remained high among the various stakeholders, but little was resolved.[18]

Community-development leaders like Robert Giloth of ESDC did his part to stabilize the community by directing a multiyear effort (1978–1981) to renovate and improve a local park now in the vicinity of Podmajersky's expanding colony and at risk of being usurped. Giloth was part of a group of activists and academics involved in the community-development movement with a focus on equity in urban planning. The scope of community-based developers like Giloth often overlapped with Pilsen's community-control activists. Giloth and the ESDC wanted to improve Jefferson Park, which had served generations of working-class residents who used it for baseball games, youth recreation, family picnics, and ethnic celebrations. The project was part of a larger grassroots effort, sometimes involving militancy and direct action, to improve Pilsen's green spaces such as Boogie Park, Throop Street Playlot, Dvorak Park, and now Jefferson Park. Giloth saw this as an outgrowth of the brewery fight. "If fighting off high-income housing development in order to retain jobs and industries meant Pilsen remaining a low and moderate income community," he wrote, "then PHBA had to talk about the way playgrounds, sidewalks, and home improvement loans fit together. Community development is so tough because you push so hard for years for what looks like a single change, [but] people know that it is the way things fit that counts—housing, jobs, energy, playgrounds, and families." For ESDC and PHBA, whether it was bringing back industry or fixing a jungle gym, it was part of a total vision worth fighting for. Although Giloth, ESDC, and PHBA celebrated the small victories, often at Centeno's tavern, upon completion of the Jefferson Park renovation in 1981, Giloth soberly asked: "Jefferson Park truly is a community victory; but who will celebrate? And whose park will it be? In five years? Ten years?"[19]

Podmajersky's dream to gentrify the area through "careful cultivation" had come to fruition. Through capital, connections, and coercion, he founded his neobohemian fortress. The new settlers consciously referred to themselves collectively as an "artist's colony," deploying the word "colony" in a way that was severed from its otherized and imperial past. To the new colonists and their landlord, Mexicans were incidental settlers who simply "stumbled into" Pilsen out of necessity and would eventually move out, just as other immigrants had before them. These frameworks disconnected Mexican immigrants, Mexican Americans, and other Latinos from the structures of racism, capitalism, and policy that brought them to Pilsen to begin with.[20]

By 1981, Podmajersky had amassed over 300 properties in East Pilsen. Gentrification showed no signs of slowing down. Meanwhile, PNCC reformed under a new umbrella group called the United Neighborhood Organization (UNO), moving beyond pothole politics and into a bigger political arena rooted in church-based organizing, voter-registration drives, and developing new leaders. Groups like ESDC and PHBA, however, continued their antigentrification advocacy, pursuing the tenet of *desarrollo sin desplazamiento* (development without displacement). In the first half of the 1980s, the political landscape in Chicago changed drastically in favor of the progressive planners and community-control activists. Members of these groups became part of the reformist Harold Washington administration, with new clout to disrupt the gentrification threat. Robert Mier and Arturo Vazquez, opponents of the brewery and, by 1983, members of Washington's administration, noted that race and racism were "the most powerful force confronting, shaping who can and should do planning. It is the central issue facing planners, and it's got to be confronted in every aspect of the daily work, daily life, of planning." These new members of Washington's team echoed Dempsey J. Travis's sentiments in 1978 that loft reconversions were racial inversions, an attempt by private developers to push out communities of color and replace them with high-cost, for-profit, chic residential buildings to attract white professionals. As the profitable venture of art-colony gentrification was rearranging the city's racial landscape through erasure and reinvention, the city was also revealing a new Latino political landscape.[21]

Colonia Clout

While historians have focused on Harold Washington's ethnic and racial coalition as key to his election victory and an important watershed moment in US political history, it is instructive to see his campaign from the perspective of Latino colonias, the reshuffling of communities across the city, and the Daley machine's entrenchment. After Richard J. Daley's passing in December 1976, ambitious politicos in Daley's inner circle jostled for power over the void the boss had left behind. The late 1970s also saw the rise of the powerful Pilsen Neighbors Community Council, whose commitment to community control and grassroots organizing had become quite influential in progressive politics across the city. Pilsen activists had grown tired of machine politics and in particular of the kind of transactional relationships Daley's machine had built with moderate and conservative Mexican American leaders, such as the Amigos for Daley. When Jane Byrne, a young, outspoken, Irish Catholic woman emerged as a mayoral contender and eventual winner of the top seat in Chicago, it shocked many across the city and the nation. Byrne ran on a reform campaign, promising an end to machine politics as usual, and along the way to victory she built necessary alliances with Black and Brown community groups to assure her election win in April 1979. In turn she promised full transparency on community matters and a seat at the table to the disenfranchised. But almost as soon as Byrne took office, she turned her back on the communities of color that helped her become the first woman mayor of a major US city. Instead, Byrne relied on the advice of longtime machine stalwarts. She spearheaded another gerrymandering of Black and Brown wards. Members of the PNCC felt immediately betrayed as Byrne failed to fulfill any of her promises, such as appointing Latinos to her administration or to city posts.[22]

PNCC members joined a coalition of other Latino groups across the city to picket her office where they demanded answers to their questions on housing, city services like fire and police, school resources and bilingual education programs. In the middle of a large crowd PNCC leader Teresa Fraga directly questioned Byrne on these matters and Byrne called for more police to escort the protestors away. Byrne's time as mayor was mired by ineffectual changes to the lives of working communities of color. Historian Manning Marable, writing at the time of her tenure, reminded readers that Byrne had not reformed the machine but kept it intact by appointing a couple of machine-friendly Latino leaders for city council openings, writing in 1983: "Latino electoral politics are even more tightly controlled than for Blacks." Mary Gonzales, a former PNCC community organizer was now working with UNO, recalled organizing steelworkers in South Chicago and that Byrne had promised to have the steel plants back in operation. "[She] announced that the workers would have their jobs by November and turkey on their tables for Thanksgiving. More lies! Of course, this did not happen," Gonzales recalled.[23]

It was no wonder that Latino grassroots organizations were initially skeptical and measured in their embrace of Senator Harold Washington. Before he set the Chicago machine ablaze, Graciela Silva-Schuch, an immigrant from La Barca, Jalisco, shook the foundations of power in the Back of the Yards. In 1982, Silva-Schuch, a forty-two-year-old mother of two, sat inside the Immaculate Heart of Mary church on Ashland Avenue with other residents listening to speakers from the UNO. After the meeting, UNO leaders Mary Gonzales and Gregory Galluzzo instructed one of their main organizers, Daniel Solis, to take note of Silva-Schuch, as she appeared to have the qualities they were looking for. She was a listener, inquisitive, and a confident speaker. Within a few weeks she was organizing the residents of the Back of the Yards and taking copious notes of all meetings, organizing fundraisers, and meeting membership quotas.[24]

UNO was created as a Catholic, parish-based organizing vehicle to develop leadership in working-class and poor communities, many of them reeling from deindustrialization. Silva-Schuch was trained to organize around issues of self-interest, build consensus, and set an agenda for the community. UNO's modus operandi was, according to political scientist Ricardo Tostado in 1985, "staging highly publicized town hall meetings where public officials are invited to hear citizen grievances," often generating lots of media attention. In the 1970s, UNO experiments in San Antonio and Los Angeles proved successful in building local Latino political power. By 1982, Chicago had UNOs in Southeast Side, Back of the Yards, Pilsen, and Little Village. Silva-Schuch was elected President of UNO's Back of the Yards chapter (UNO-BOY), making noise and headlines and stirring nerves.[25]

That Graciela Silva-Schuch turned UNO-BOY into a strong chapter was impressive. Between Pilsen, Little Village, and Southeast Chicago, the Back of the Yards Mexican community seemed the smallest and least outspoken of the colonias. A Catholic, working-class social and political conservatism had taken root since the decline of the progressive UPWA and the closure of the meatpacking plants in the 1950s. In the 1980s, one would be hard-pressed to find any evidence of a Chicano renaissance in Back of the Yards that had so energized Pilsen. While Pilsen was now experiencing gentrification, Back of the Yards and the surrounding Southwest Side were receiving more Latinos, especially "West of Western," as one reporter noted. With neighborhoods flipping from white to Latino, city services declined further. The Mexican working class were faced with poor schools, underemployment, and high crime. "The community was hungry for leadership," Silva-Schuch later recalled. The stockyard's longtime power broker, Joseph B. Meegan, was still in charge of the BYNC, more than forty years since its founding in 1939. Both BYNC and UNO were founded by Saul Alinsky and his principles, but they could not be more different from each other. Meegan did not appreciate UNO playing in his backyard, and UNO was fed up with the Meegans of Chicago controlling Latino colonias.[26]

In past years, the well-connected Meegan could make any problem go away. But demographic realities had significantly eroded his authority. The Irish, Polish, and Lithuanian community had changed with each succession of arriving Mexicans. Meegan begrudgingly anticipated this change decades ago when he appointed Mexican Americans to the BYNC leadership ranks, but he never relinquished power. During the 1960s, the Daley loyalist group MADO relocated its headquarters from Pilsen to Back of the Yards, where Arturo Velasquez and Catarino Diaz had their businesses. Meegan often turned to them for help as political intermediaries between Mexicans and BYNC. But UNO-BOY was not interested in being pacified. To Meegan's

Figure 6.2. Graciela Silva-Schuch, leader of the United Neighborhood Organization of Back of the Yards (UNO-BOY), speaking to a news reporter after raising concerns about the lack of police attention to rising crime in the community. (Image courtesy of the *Chicago Sun-Times.*)

dismay, UNO-BOY, unafraid to take a busload of inner-city residents out to the suburbs to picket a board member or an official's house, organized confrontational actions against city bureaucrats until they received answers to their questions. With the help of a Claretian priest, Rev. Joseph Peplansky, who personally called parishioners to come to meetings, Graciela Silva-Schuch mobilized hundreds of parents—immigrants and citizens—by raising issues that greatly concerned them, like under-resourced schools, bilingual programs, and ineffective police protection. "This worked because the parents, they put their trust in teachers, and they trust the priests, but they don't trust politicians," Silva-Schuch recalled. But another reason for UNO-BOY's ability to win converts was Silva-Schuch herself and the ease with which she connected with people as a Mexican immigrant, woman, parent of school-aged children, and blue-collar worker.[27]

In March of 1983, with Harold Washington's campaign heating up the cold Chicago spring, the candidate took his reform message straight to Black and Latino communities. In Back of the Yards, where unemployment was at a crippling 34 percent, members of UNO-BOY were eager to hear the mayoral candidates' plans for their community. They sent invitations to both Washington and the Republican candidate, Bernard Epton, for a town hall. Epton declined, while Washington seized the opportunity. He understood that the old stockyards colony was in the epicenter of seismic shifts that were demographically increasing in Black and Brown families and sending white homeowners into a panic. In 1980, the 14th Ward was still majority white, but Latinos made up 22 percent of the population. This was the place Washington needed to have answers: a neighborhood destabilized by unemployment, high levels of crime, and ethnic and racial transition. In just a few years, UNO-BOY would initiate an aptly named "Near Southwest Stabilization Project." Inside the church hall, Washington greeted a receptive crowd. "The place was packed," Silva-Schuch recalled. But outside, a furious mob was forming, courtesy of the 14th Ward Democratic Regular Organization, who riled up white residents unhappy about Washington's visit. They shouted racist slurs about Washington and made disparaging comments against Graciela Silva-Schuch and Father Peplansky. Inside the church, the candidate spoke to an approving audience about his plans to recover jobs, improve outdated schools, stop mortgage discrimination, and provide more police patrol in high-crime areas. One year earlier, Back of the Yards had been designated an enterprise zone to attract investors and create new jobs in the old industrial stockyards. Washington promised to mobilize that program. The mostly Latino parishioners came away assured Washington would speak for them.[28]

Earlier during the primaries, Washington also visited Pilsen to meet with the Hispanic American Labor Council (HALC), requested by his Latino strategist and young labor activist Rudy Lozano. Upon arriving they were surprised to see many in the room wearing "Rich Daley for Mayor" (son of the elder Daley) buttons during what they thought was supposed to be an opportunity to win HALC's endorsement. The Pilsen gathering made the Washington team wary about the influence the Mexican American Daley Democrats held in Latino neighborhoods. Lozano had recently lost his own campaign when he challenged longtime machine stalwart Frank D. Stemberk for the aldermanic seat in the 22nd Ward. "He squeaked by us," recalled his campaign manager, Jesús "Chuy" Garcia, alluding to the seventeen votes that would have forced a runoff. Similar opposition to machine regulars was happening in Pilsen as community activists ran against longtime Alderman Vito Marzullo, again a close race. To the Washington allies, these close elections showed the strength of their progressive group, the Independent Political Organization (IPO). But it equally showed that Mexican Americans remained loyal to the Democratic regulars. After Washington defeated Daley in the primaries, HALC had to choose between endorsing the Black senator or the white Republican candidate.[29]

Figure 6.3. Harold Washington, Rudy Lozano, and Al Galvan talk coalition politics in Pilsen, 1983. (Image courtesy of August Sallas.)

The endorsement almost went to Epton, an outcome that would have sent shockwaves throughout the city. Open support for Epton, who ran a racially divisive campaign to win the white ethnic majority, would have revealed a telling commentary about Latinos' political realignment away from the Democratic Party. That was where things were headed by March of 1983, were it not for longtime MADO leader Arturo Velasquez. He stepped in at a critical moment to reconcile differences between the Daley Democrats and independent progressives. With the help of Maria Cerda, Rudy Lozano, and others he held a "Latinos for Harold Washington Unity Dinner" a week before voters went to the polls. This symbolic, but important, gesture of reconciliation rallied the Latino Daley Democrats behind Washington, at least for the time being.[30]

Latino voting patterns leading up to the Harold Washington campaign had been historically undermined by a number of factors, none more significant than the roadblocks put up by the Democratic machine and its control of patronage and city resources. Voting fraud, intimidation, and last-minute polling changes, designed to suppress and control Mexican American and Puerto Rican voting behavior, were the norm in Latino barrios. In Mexican neighborhoods throughout the Southwest Side, local voters were expected to fully support white machine candidates, and even though turnout often sagged well below the eligible voter population, the machine preferred it that way. Divergence in voting was rare, and since the early 1960s, the machine could rely on the assistance of its loyal Mexican American Daley Democratic leaders to help deliver the Latino vote, with few concessions in return. Although the Harold Washington movement made remarkable strides in unifying a Black and Brown voting coalition for the first time in the city's history, prior attempts in the 1960s and 1970s did not yield similar success. Mexican Americans and Mexican immigrants might have expressed diverse political aspirations, but on election day many usually cast their vote for a machine candidate. Still, early organizing efforts for a multiracial independent political force in those earlier decades, along with the redistricting fights to challenge the machine's disenfranchising of racialized groups, bore fruit in the early 1980s, even if not all Mexican American voters were swayed.[31]

Harold Washington's election reverberated throughout the nation; more locally, it revealed the clout Latino colonias now had. Washington wasted no time fulfilling his promises to Latinos, creating a Latino Affairs Commission, bringing progressives into his administration, speaking out against immigrant abuse, and tempering progrowth agendas to protect against gentrification. The Latino Affairs Commission provided Washington with tough but realistic appraisals of his administration's accountability in the barrio, especially when it came to making city jobs and other resources available to Latinos. Now as mayor, he returned to Back of the Yards and spoke directly to members of UNO-BOY about his plans to remake the old stockyards to provide new jobs for the community. However, much of his progressive agenda was stalled by a city council divided between Washington supporters and allies of Alderman Edward Vrdolyak, who represented the city's white ethnic voters. On June 8, 1983, the Washington coalition and the Latino community were dealt a shocking blow when Rudy Lozano was assassinated. Additionally, the progressive movement and unity that Lozano helped sow became a target of a white backlash now actively mobilized against Mayor Washington. The "Save Our City Coalition," as it became known, formed to protect "white ethnic interests," its headquarters firmly rooted in the working-class Southwest Side. In the meantime, the Council Wars intensified on the eve of a court-ordered special election to correct discriminatory redistricting of Latino and Black majorities. One casualty of the redraw was machine Alderman Frank Stemberk and his control of the

22nd Ward. Before Latino and Black voters could defeat him, he dropped out. With control over the city council at stake, the redraw turned Latino wards into proxy battlefields between independents and the machine. Further underscoring the fact that Latinos may have had clout, but remained divided, PNCC leader Teresa Fraga told a reporter, "I don't think Hispanics have made up their minds about Vrdolyak and Washington."[32]

Urban historian Arnold Hirsch referred to the 1986 special election as a "key contest" where "hundreds of the machine's minions poured into a single Latino ward in the futile attempt to salvage the organization's fortunes." The battle for the 22nd Ward in Little Village prompted Anita Villarreal, now in her sixties, to enter the contest for committeeperson. "She was very unhappy with the way the Ward was being run," recalled her daughter and campaign manager, Loretta Villarreal Long, "and the way the Democrats at the time were handling things. She said, 'This is it! I've had it!' She was furious." Two years earlier, Chuy Garcia had been elected 22nd Ward Committeeman following on the heels of his friend Rudy Lozano's almost-defeat of Stemberk. Garcia, representing the Washington coalition, now wanted to consolidate his power by becoming alderman. In Chicago politics, the committeeman controlled the patronage and therefore the power. Villarreal was concerned with stemming Garcia's absolute control of the 22nd Ward, which would include influence over the financial and business affairs of Mexican South Lawndale: permits, licenses, and investment.[33]

In Villarreal's assessment, the reformers had no experience governing and no influence in the business community, which would jeopardize Little Village's prosperity. This was her ward, one she helped pioneer in the mid-1960s. Her campaign platform touted bread-and-butter issues like better schools, employment, and more police protection—issues that aligned with a group like UNO-BOY. But what distinguished her from the Alinsky activists was her message on business power and opportunities for individual achievement. Her campaign materials touted her self-made story: "While working full-time, raising eight children and attending night school, Anita founded her own business, Villarreal Real Estate and Villarreal Insurance." This message was tailor made for the ward where home values were on the rise and one out of every three working adults was employed by a small business or owned one. UNO's economic arguments made little impact in Little Village, where business was booming.[34]

Nevertheless, Anita Villarreal lost the election. The battle for the 22nd Ward underscored just how well the machine understood its own roster of Latino Daley Democrats. When Villarreal turned to the machine for its blessing, the machine turned its back to her. Stemberk, the white politician she had backed and protected from Latino challengers for more than sixteen years, would not return the favor. Ed Vrdolyak did not see her as someone he could control. With an eye toward winning a majority in the city council, Vrdolyak and Stemberk selected for their ticket Guadalupe Martinez, a 26th Street supermarket owner, for alderman, and August Sallas, president of HALC, for committeeman. The *Little Village Community Reporter* promoted the two "prominent Little Village citizens" as "the finest and the best candidate for the offices." Even with the machine's coffers and propaganda, the Vrdolyak candidates lost. Garcia won both seats with 55 percent of the votes. Election analysts later credited the win mostly to Black precincts that supported Garcia and a weaker showing in Latino precincts. Nevertheless, Latino independents won throughout city. Those victories gave Washington firm control of the city council, and in 1987, provided him a safe reelection. The coalition, however, was not as strong as observers imagined, as Latino politicos galvanized around one man rather than a set of issues. When Washington unexpectedly died in office in November of 1987, the coalition was already dissolving.[35]

Although the Harold Washington movement energized Latino political power, it illuminated deep divisions within Latino colonias. Chicago newspapers and liberal observers dismissed the Latino Daley Democrats as misguided pawns. Democratic regulars like August Sallas called the independents "a movement of confrontation politics" and "self-appointed leaders." Despite the ire between both camps, Anita Villarreal's campaign was not merely reactionary. She articulated a politics of opportunity and dignity that endured in Latino colonias. Her championing of private neighborhood revitalization efforts, small-business growth, and immigrant hustle might not have translated into votes for Villarreal, but they resonated in La Villita. These values—more than civil rights legislation, they argued—propelled the *bungalowization* of Mexicans and access into the Far Southwest Side and suburban townships. To the Washington allies, and especially to Graciela Silva-Schuch and UNO-BOY, breaking down the walls of segregation meant little if it merely expanded poverty, disinvestment, and unemployment. They were hopeful that Washington's city hall reform would bring an end to "*hacienda* politics" in their neighborhoods. Indeed, Washington delivered, providing greater attention to economic development in Latino neighborhoods and an equitable redistribution of city resources. With Washington as mayor, Latino community-control groups won the decentralization they long fought for and the political representation they desired to begin fixing their postindustrial communities. Although both camps borrowed from different concepts of dignity politics during this decade, both would continue to appeal to them and would, in the process, expand their clout.[36]

The Buffers and Bungalows of Settlement

Whether Latinos had built enough clout to stop the "beachhead" of gentrification in Pilsen was yet to be determined; in the meantime, community organizations like UNO followed the bungalowization of Mexican settlement into the Far Southwest Side. While a flurry of "racial change expertise" emerged in Chicago during the 1960s to consider Black/white integration and segregation patterns, very few studies considered the place of Latinos in these schemes. In the 1980s, through its Latino leadership and rank-and-file membership, UNO was uniquely positioned for this task. They found that Latinos were still being used as buffers between panicky white ethnics and African Americans, an untenable situation for the instability and tensions it brought to critical community institutions like churches, schools, and social services. Latinos "are always used as buffers," Mary Gonzales of UNO told a reporter in 1984. "If you live in a white community, there's the perception, 'We can't sell to a black family because we'll be busting the neighborhood.' But Hispanics are more acceptable." Members of a Puerto Rican enclave that moved to the western edge of Back of the Yards in the 1970s and 1980s concurred with the better-of-two-evils dynamic. "My next door-door neighbor [Polish and German] didn't like me at first," said Manuel Arroyo, one of the first to arrive, "but then he was crazy about me." Another resident, Tony Pino, recalled: "When Hispanics came the whites didn't panic. We were living pretty good together. . . . Because once the Spanish people move to a new neighborhood the blockbusters come right away. They get Hispanics in as an inroad, and the whites who stay accept us. But then the colored move in behind us. Then everyone pushes the panic button. And everyone runs. Including the Hispanics."[37]

The dispersal of Mexican American and Mexican immigrant settlement into the Southwest Side through federal housing policy, regulation, and enforcement of local real estate practices expanded the prior confinements of segregation. The consequences of white flight, higher property taxes, crime, and job loss further incentivized real estate agents and white homeowners to sell to minority home seekers in communities like Gage Park, West Lawn, and Marquette Park. "You can buy a super bungalow there for 20 percent under value because there's some kind of tension there," said Eugenio Gomez. Although older forms of blockbusting were coming to an end, Debbie Nathan of the *Reader* found that "realtors poise them-selves at ethnic and racial boundary lines and encourage Hispanics to move into all-white areas." This was the very same turf that past efforts by Saul Alinsky and Martin Luther King Jr. failed to racially integrate. But where well-meaning urban reformers and civil rights leaders were unsuccessful, economic realities and white depopulation succeeded in opening housing to racial minorities on the Southwest Side periphery. The flipping of the Southwest Side was now in full swing. Instructions targeted to white eth-nics on how to sell their homes appeared in local neighborhood newspapers: "Remember, your home is a product. . . . In many ways, you have to market it as you would other commodities." Still, some homeowner associations and neighborhood councils used exclusionary practices that were as old as the neighborhoods themselves, policing their neighbors' property transac-tions through intimidation and scare tactics rooted in racism and fear of property devaluation.[38]

The Housing Act of 1968 had opened—although not fully—the white ethnic Southwest Side of Chicago to Black and Brown families. But it wasn't until the late 1970s and 1980s that the impact of the Housing Act of 1968 was more fully realized. More specifically, Sections 235 and 236 of the Act, which moved federal funding away from public housing and into the private homebuying market in the form of mortgage incentives, credits, and subsi-dized fees, helped minority homebuyers purchase single-family dwellings. Additionally, the Home Mortgage Disclosure Act of 1975 mandated regula-tory agencies to keep and make public loan data on race and income, altering the behavior of lending institutions.[39]

Notwithstanding these measures, the realities of deindustrialization and economic restructuring positioned Mexican American homebuyers, whether through federally insured loans or personal high-interest loans through informal moneylenders, to purchase homes outside of prescribed tenement enclaves. Although contemporary journalistic accounts and the momentum of the community-control movement helped characterize Mex-icans as attached to enclaves in Pilsen and Little Village by a mix of cul-ture, familiarity, and consumption preferences, liberalized housing policy and white flight continued to test and challenge those theories. When given a choice, Mexican residents showed a willingness to move, and often did so when possible, upending cultural theories of attachment to a particu-lar neighborhood. This rang true when in the mid-1970s, Victor Flores and his wife bought their first home, a two-story brick house in Little Village

on 24th Street and Hamlin Avenue, from a Bohemian family for $24,000.
Flores later recalled that he had little savings and was forced to borrow from
a street-corner moneylender, a local guy nicknamed "Friendly Bob's," who
made personal loans at very high interest rates. The Flores family's move
was in line with tens of thousands of Latino home purchasers heralding the
primacy of Little Village as the most desirable "Mexican suburb" in the city
during the 1970s. But as Flores recalled, after several years, the spacious-
ness that initially drew him there seemed to narrow, as Little Village became
more dense and congested at the high point of Mexican immigration. By the
mid-1980s, the Flores family relocated to a bungalow on the southwestern
edge of the Back of the Yards. After that, they made one more move to a
single-family brick home in Brighton Park. Similarly, Maria and Jesús Rodríguez and their girls left Pilsen in 1983 for a bungalow they purchased on the
western part of Back of the Yards, on a street that Maria later recalled was
lined with mostly "casas de Polacos" (Polish Americans' homes), suggest-
ing well-kept, good-quality homes, part of a larger subtext about the power
of whiteness to infuse properties with the most value.[40]

Flipping the Southwest Side was not an overnight process but part of
steady and incremental change spanning decades. By 1980, in Gage Park
and Chicago Lawn, white residents could count on one hand the number of
Latino families that lived on their street. The 1980 census reports showed
a total of 2,701 Latinos in Gage Park and 4,940 Latinos in Chicago Lawn—
not huge percentages but steady growth nonetheless. Housing scholars
have pointed to Sections 235 and 236 of the 1968 Housing Act as having
an unequal and segregating effect on Black homebuyers. This was due to
the provisions prohibiting the purchase of newly constructed homes in
the suburbs, instead allowing credits only for the purchase of preexisting
homes in the central city, typically built before 1937, perpetuating a form
of resegregation. For Latinos, the Section 235 provisions played a sizable
role in leading to the purchase of preexisting single-family and multifamily bungalows on the Southwest Side, a welcomed reprieve from the overcrowding in older Pilsen and Little Village housing. Those able to secure
federally backed mortgage financing chose single-family homes over staying
in structures built before the 1880s. Uneven federal policies in the Housing
Act may not have done away with segregation entirely, but for Mexicans in
Chicago their intra-urban residential moves helped bend and expand prior
lines of segregation.[41]

For some community organizations, the bungalowization of Mexican settlement meant taking on hostile neighborhoods and entering simi-

lar economic circumstances. A PNCC report viewed this dispersal from the perspective of former Pilsen residents who had "moved on" to what they called "the 'suburbs' of Pilsen." Thousands of Pilsen residents had moved to "Little Village, Back of the Yards, Brighton Park, Marquette Park, McKinley Park, Cicero, Berwyn or Riverside—trying to escape these problems. . . . [D]espite their sacrifices to relocate, they are finding many of the same problems in these new neighborhoods and also face blatant discrimination and abuse at the hands of some communities not yet ready to accept the influx of Mexicans." But in these "suburbs" Mexicans made new meaning out of bungalow landscapes in a postindustrial America that included work commutes to outlying suburban factories, part-time, nonunion service-sector jobs, and the need for households to have multiple breadwinners in order to meet mortgage payments. This relocation had political and cultural implications as well. Mexican members of the Bungalow Belt or outer periphery of the Southwest Side were more likely to support Democratic Party machine candidates if they felt pressure from precinct captains and neighbors or feared retribution. Otherwise, many supported the Republican Party, especially for statewide or national candidates and when it came to issues pertaining to taxes and immigration. This was the case when many cheered presidential candidate Ronald Reagan when he praised the "hard work" of Joseph Meegan in the Back of the Yards. They rarely supported political independents or reformers, with the exception of segments of the Mexican Back of the Yards community led by UNO-BOY, and even there, UNO activists regularly considered Mexican American conservatism an uphill battle.[42]

At the same time, Mexican American homeowners who held politically conservative views shared an uneasy ecosystem with remaining white ethnics across parts of the Southwest Side. The Southwest Side was home to the anti-Black and Brown "Save Our Cities Coalition," and this group joined "the well-financed English Only Organization" to fight off bilingual programs in their local public schools—a direct attack on the presence of Latinos in their communities. Mexican Americans resented the racism of the city's white ethnics, who lumped them together with the undistinguishable milieu of "recent arrivals." Still, many were not swayed by the Harold Washington coalition's progressive platform.[43]

The civic sphere once described in Alan Ehrenhalt's memoir about Chicago's 1950s "bungalow people" had changed but not because of any erosion of political and religious authority. In Ehrenhalt's depiction of the tightly knit bungalow people, the second- and third-generation Americans joined bowling leagues and formed a sense of common purpose built on patriotism and anticommunism. The 1980s Mexican bungalow immigrants participated in their own authority-making through nonconventional forms of civicism. They became members of Mexican hometown associations and helped break down barriers in local parishes. Chicago's Mexican immigrants adopted early prototypes of the "2x1 Program," a direct arrangement between emigrants and the governments of their Mexican home states. In the 1980s, Maria and Jesús Rodríguez organized fundraisers through their hometown association to fund infrastructure and recreational projects in small rural villages in Michoacán. La Barca native Graciela Silva-Schuch, while breaking down parish boundaries at St. Nick's Catholic Church in the Bungalow Belt during the late 1980s and early 1990s so Mexicans could attend mass, also used her La Barca Hometown Association to build schools in her native village. Mexicans turned low-attendance churches into vibrant centers of community activism and transnational civicism. Nevertheless, this work was shaped in part by the placemaking they had already been doing on the Far Southwest Side, anchoring their instability in an age of white flight and globalization. They enrolled their children in its parochial schools. They also partook in international humanitarian projects through their local parishes, raising money to send envoys to Washington, DC, Central America, and Mexico on behalf of human-rights victims. On immigration, Latino parishioners from west suburban churches challenged militarization along the US-Mexico border, referring to it as "muro de Berlin."[44]

In the Southwest Side, Mexican immigrants grew disillusioned with the state, as did Chicago-born Mexican Americans, but these groups differed slightly on the politics of opportunity. The Bungalow Belt's Mexican Americans typically championed opportunity politics on an individual rather than collective basis. Despite living in formerly all-white bungalows and cottages, partly due to landmark civil rights legislation, they associated the city's civil rights struggles primarily with Black Americans, thus accepting an often-perpetuated mainstream narrative about the history of civil rights. Mexican American Southwest Siders, especially those in the Bungalow Belt, became as fearful and resentful about expressions of Black revolt as white ethnics had been in the past. Moreover, some became outright irritated and others disagreed with the community-control movement and the effort of groups like UNO fighting against state and municipal disinvestment. Many Brown bungalites viewed deprivations such as poverty, living in redlined neighborhoods, and structural racism in the rearview mirror and saw themselves as people who persevered through those stations through will and hustle, giving them a kind of cultural capital as breadwinners and sweat-equity survivors in a postindustrial age.

Opposition to groups like UNO or the Harold Washington coalition were not disengaged from politics. On the contrary, they regularly entered the fray. Before Alderman Jesús "Chuy" Garcia could get accustomed to his new role in the city council, he received angry letters from constituents who were quick to critique some of his positions. Angry about rising property taxes, homeowner Peter Garza told Mayor Washington in a letter published on the front page of the *Lawndale News*, "This seems to be routine for Mayor Washington's administration. Instead of looking elsewhere for funds like collecting on outstanding parking tickets and eliminating meaningless political jobs, the burden falls on the property owners. Hey Mayor Washington, do you think someone just gave us our properties?" At play here was the long tradition of hardworking homeowner politics, resurrected by Latinos against city hall.[45]

The flipping of metropolitan colonies also took place throughout the 1980s and 1990s in suburban townships such as Cicero, Berwyn, Oak Park, and DuPage County. Mexican Chicagoans had been commuting to outlying suburbs to work for years, as economic restructuring and globalization forced industry out of the central city and suburbanized manufacturing. "These newcomers to conservative West Chicago would like to believe that they have been accepted by the community," wrote one reporter. In the western suburbs of DuPage County, Latinos complained of regular encounters with police harassment and racial profiling and had to file several lawsuits against landlords for housing discrimination. White tensions and anxieties about Mexican suburbanization needed easing, a role that intermediaries with vested interests often played. White civic leaders looking to attract Latino and immigrant taxpayers to their suburbs, as well as real estate agents hoping to fill emptied bungalows, stepped in to interpret the relocation of Mexicans for anxious whites. "The influx of Hispanics hasn't really changed Cicero," noted one suburban official, "They have blended into the picture just like the Italians or Bohemians, and they make good neighbors." In Cicero, over two thousand Latinos moved in by 1981 as white residents and municipal officials tried to rehabilitate the city's ugly history of violent fortifications against Black families and scale back hostility toward Mexican immigrants. But arriving immigrants dispensed with the "melting pot" rhetoric and understood their economic place in metropolitan Chicago: "We spend," noted Mexican Cicero resident Xochitl Casas on why the suburb's gates were now open to people like her and her husband. By 1987, the Casas lived in a humble Cicero bungalow.[46]

Additionally, national immigration policy intersected with local politics and the growth of Latino colonias. In 1986, President Ronald Reagan signed the Immigration Reform and Control Act (IRCA), which imposed penalties on employers who hired undocumented immigrants, furthered militarization of the border, and created pathways to citizenship for immigrants already living in the country. The latter point provoked vigorous local debate over the placement of INS Processing Sites in Chicago's Latino neighborhoods. What was intended to be a solution to the thousands of undocumented immigrants coming from Mexico and Central America to Chicago, attracted by the prospect of jobs, became about Latino community control over their own neighborhoods. Since the 1970s, Chicago had been a government and INS testing ground for creating channels of direct access to undocumented urban populations to "improve" relations with Latino communities. These actions originated in an effort begun in 1974 by Rev. José J. Gallego, a Claretian priest in Back of the Yards' Immaculate Heart of Mary Church, who founded the Concerned Citizens Committee on Immigration. He was moved to action after witnessing several "riot-like" deportation raids in a Chicago suburb and because of a trip he took to the US-Mexico border where he saw a "warlike" atmosphere. Hoping to bring more "understanding between the INS and Latino immigrants," he initiated the Programa Positivo (Positive Program), with support from the INS and federal government. During the Carter administration the program went national but remained hugely controversial in many Latino neighborhoods because residents saw it as cooperating with a longtime adversary to the community.[47]

After the passage of IRCA, UNO surprisingly carried forward Father Gallego's 1970s efforts. UNO criticized the regional director for refusing to put any INS processing centers in Latino neighborhoods, writing, "UNO believes that this is a subtle attempt by the INS to discourage Hispanic registration and at the very least appears to be a form of discrimination." Their position in favor of INS centers found common ground with machine loyalists, independents, and conservatives. Together they charged that the INS "selectively excluded Hispanics from taking full advantage of the new immigration law by locating the processing centers out of the area where most Hispanics live," and demanded that the INS place centers in Little Village and Pilsen instead of far-to-reach Northside neighborhoods like Forest Park and Avondale. The Latino Institute, a research and policy center, backed this effort as well. Little Village was an early adopter of Gallego's INS program, placing an office in the community in the 1970s, though many community members were against it. Rev. Timothy McCormick, a progressive priest from Providence of God in Pilsen, captured these sentiments when he pleaded with Latino organizations to remember the INS's brutal history: "These are the same people who have arrested our family members and friends. . . . Inviting the immigration officials to walk our streets, eat in the neighborhood restaurants, will only cause more fear, division and anxiety. . . . Keep the Migra out of our neighborhood!"[48]

Residential dispersion did bend older patterns of segregation but revealed that not all Latinos thought and politicked the same. Meanwhile, the older colonias of Pilsen and Little Village continued to represent vibrant centers of immigrant consumerism and revitalization, enough to catch the attention of city hall and the Chicago Association of Neighborhood Development Organizations, which invited community groups to attend seminars such as "How to Attract Developers" and "Selling your Neighborhood Shopping Strip." Community leaders from both neighborhoods clashed over different strategies to vie for tourist and revitalization dollars.[49]

The Arch and the Mercado

The bungalowization of Mexican Chicago helped disperse Mexican working-class culture across the metropolitan landscape, producing different cultural politics from those in the Harold Washington coalition and severing its attachment to enclaves of first arrival. However, the neighborhoods of Pilsen and Little Village were growing denser and generating high levels of tax revenue for the city, indicating economic revitalization simply nonexistent in other wards. Consumer spending was up. Property taxes were being met. This actuality dovetailed with Villareal's longtime advocacy for immigrant homeownership and sweat equity. In the mid- to late 1980s, along with other merchant and civic leaders, she led a campaign to make Little Village a tourism center. "We see a lot of tourists walking through the neighborhood in the summer," Anita's son Daniel Villarreal told a reporter in 1987. "I guess they feel it's a lot cheaper to come here than to journey to Mexico. . . . People come just to walk the street and look in the stores. . . . Maybe they are studying Spanish. It's a shame we have nothing set up to guide them. We're looking to set up posts and distribute guidebooks." While the urban crisis hobbled other central-city wards, La Villita's business leaders sought to capitalize on the community's ascendance as an economic powerhouse of immigrant consumerism and now outside interest.[50]

The great reshuffling of the late twentieth century helped La Villita's 26th Street merchants and civic leaders advertise the uniqueness of their enclave. The area's Mexicanization was its selling point. Lew Kreinberg and Chuck Bowden noted that many Chicagoans were taken by surprise "that a taco-fueled metropolis was rising on Twenty Sixth Street." Local residents were even renovating their homes to resemble "old Mexico" (as if taking a page from Richard Dolejs' 1960s "Little Village" remake), customizing their brick bungalows with "fancy iron fences," "stone facades," and "white stucco." Across town, Chinatown was enjoying a resurgence as a premier ethnic tourist destination heralded by economic-development experts. Pilsen was also vying for tourist dollars by establishing cultural institutions to promote ethnic art, opening the Mexican Fine Arts Museum in 1986. But when it came to tax revenue and consumer spending, La Villita could not be beat. Earlier in 1982, during Mayor Jane Byrne's administration, Little Village received a $500,000 grant for the ward to make much-needed improvements to its bread-and-butter real estate, the commercial storefronts of 26th Street, by improving "sidewalks, decorative paving, new curbs and gutters, curb ramps and trees." Between 1984 and 1986, La Villita's civic and business leaders capitalized on infrastructure improvements that would further entice tourist dollars. Merchants planned to "challenge Chinatown as an ethnic entertainment and shopping hub." Locals could not help noticing the suburban tourists strolling on 26th Street in search of, as one *Chicago Tribune* writer put it, "the Mexican flavor of Little Village," to be discovered in the "restaurants, shops, music, and dancing." In consultation with local merchants, Villarreal proposed building an oversized arch on 26th Street to mark a "gateway" to La Villita. "It would be like the arch in Chinatown," her son Daniel told a reporter in 1987, "something to identify it and set it apart for visitors."[51]

But even creating "old Mexico" in old South Lawndale for tourist consumption was going to require navigating tricky political waters. It was of no small consequence that only a year earlier (in 1986) Anita Villarreal was defeated in her bid for 22nd Ward committeeman as she tried to stop the IPO's takeover of her turf. Villarreal, the longtime Daley loyalist, and Chuy Garcia, a youthful but inexperienced political independent in the Harold Washington coalition, would now have to work together to seize the available tourist dollars. Nobody questioned Villarreal's ability to move things from concept to reality, and to Garcia's credit, he would concede to many of

Villarreal's suggestions for building the arch and attracting tourist dollars. Particularly important was understanding the role of television media, as Little Village was now supplanting Pilsen as the preferred background for news agencies covering stories of Latino interest. Villarreal argued that the arch would serve as an appropriate staging for media, which would circulate its symbol to viewers far and wide. With the Committee for the Arch, she relied on her own clout in the business community, especially with ethnic banks to fundraise. Garcia had the inside access to Mayor Washington's city hall and applied for the ordinance as public funding required for the new landmark as well.[52]

The Committee for the Arch considered proposals to rename 26th Street from different segments of the community that jostled over its symbolism and the politics of the arch's meaning. Some of the Mexican merchants wanted to rename it "Avenida México" to express nationalist pride. Progressive and leftist community members who supported the IPO organized a petition drive to rename it "Rudy Lozano Avenue," in memory of the slain political and labor activist. Still another proposal came from a veteran's group that pushed for "Manuel Perez Jr. Avenue," a World War II hero. Villarreal rejected all the proposals because none had wide community support. To many Mexican American and Mexican immigrant residents, especially those first-wave settlers who moved in during the 1960s and early 1970s, the idea of calling 26th Street "Avenida México" or "Calle México" was simply incongruent with their accomplished sense of belonging. Their purchase of brick bungalows still carried a sense of hard-earned Americanism. Naming it after the political activists was likewise unpopular in a precinct where most Mexican Americans still supported the Democratic machine. Villarreal reconciled the varied interests by choosing not to change 26th Street and instead calling the entire project the "Arches of Opportunity and Liberty." This communicated a subtext of Americanist and conservative values that many of its residents shared and satisfied local resident conservatism, Mexican nationalism, and immigrant hustle.[53]

When word got out that the proposed arch would cost around $235,000, and with many area manufacturers donating materials, some became alarmed. Progressive outside critics charged that the money ought to be used instead to "feed the hungry, clothe the poor, shelter the homeless," Chuy Garcia later recalled. As alderman and committeeman, Garcia was frequently on the receiving end of this kind of criticism from, in his words, "bleeding heart liberals." "I had to remind them," he said, "that this money was earmarked specifically for infrastructure improvements related to the arch." Within the ward, hardly anyone expressed opposition to the arch; in fact, much hope was placed on its construction, as members of the Committee for the Arch anticipated that it would "affect housing, school and land values," they told one reporter.[54]

The "Arch of Opportunity and Liberty" on 26th Street finally opened in 1989. Visiting tourists would qualify its authenticity with a quick glance at its design and architectural biography. It was designed by local Mexican American architect Adrian Lozano, previously responsible for the Benito Juárez High School design in Pilsen, and it was built by a Mexican American construction company, the D. R. Balti Construction firm. The archway was painted in a soft pink to harmonize with the array of colors on the storefronts and was made of Spanish-style clay and tile, granite, and limestone. The arch quickly took a life of its own as it appeared on a range of items, from CD covers for Norteño music groups to letterhead for local organizations, to T-shirts worn at parades and marathons. It also became a site for political gatherings. In 1991, Mexican presidential candidate Carlos Salinas visited the arch to court Chicago's Mexican community for support. For locals, it evoked community pride, and for the recently arrived, a sense of home. For Mexican American residents now several generations removed from their immigrant roots, it perhaps was as "close as they've ever been to Mexico in a way," Garcia later admitted.[55]

But while merchants from La Villita were quick to roll out the welcome mat for tourists, PNCC was more cautious about opening Pilsen's gates. For starters, veterans of the organization could still recall the long fight against *Chicago 21*, and the fears it had caused when the plan promoted their community as a playground for middle-class, mostly white professionals. Along with PNCC, the ESDC was trying to prevent the spread of Podmajersky's artist colony on the eastern end of Pilsen. From a community-control perspective, the popularity of the South Halsted Street art galleries was encouraging not only artsy, bohemian types to move in but now also wellheeled, young professionals who were renting nearby lofts and looking to fill their downtime learning poetry, dance, pottery, or bookbinding in one of the nearby studios. Aside from the one-man threat Podmajersky represented, of greater consequence was city hall. Before Harold Washington's tenure as mayor, the city's Department of Planning and Development was still run by machine appointees and pro-growth bureaucrats who handed the city over to private firms looking to pick off prime real estate. The city continued to dole out federally funded Community Development Block Grants to corporate developers instead of needy neighborhoods. After years of community protest, the planning department stopped using the *Chicago 21* name, but PNCC and their allies did not believe the redevelopment scheme had been abandoned. In early 1983, a new Central Area Plan was released to turn Pilsen into a riverfront community for white-collar professionals.[56]

However, during Harold Washington's tenure from 1983 to 1987, the progressive planners in his administration included Pilsen and other Latino communities in the decision-making process, part of its no-more-business-as-usual approach. In this favorable climate, PNCC cautiously adopted ethnic tourism as a long-term neighborhood solution to build much-needed infrastructure and generate new sources of revenue. One 1983 tourist guide drew from a worn-out litany of caricatures and exotifying language, advising visitors to "travel the side streets," for "every block harbors fanciful, bright hued facades" and "bodegas crammed with tropical imports," and to make sure to explore the "imported pottery and religious artifacts." PNCC thus sought to control its own community narrative in light of citywide tourism development, the institutionalization of community arts, and the branding of ethnic neighborhoods. Unlike Little Village's civic leaders and merchants, who debated which values to project to its visitors, PNCC embarked on its own authenticity project with two major goals: (1) to champion a program of ethnic tourism that would pay tribute to PNCC's history of community advocacy and its roots in the Chicano movement; and (2) to provide a response or a counternarrative to the gentrification going on in East Pilsen—more specifically, to the perceived and real threat of "community and cultural erasure."[57]

In the summer of 1987, two surveys were conducted on the proposed improvement of a Pilsen shopping strip located in the triangular intersection of 18th Street, Blue Island Avenue, and Loomis Street. PNCC and the Pilsen Chamber of Commerce, respectively, proposed their own study of consumer behavior and merchant needs. The conclusion led to a proposal for a "Chinatown-style ethnic retail-attraction" to be named "El Mercado." Another proposal shortly afterward renamed it the Pilsen Triangle. Regardless of the name, by 1988, it called for a modernization plan to convert a popular neighborhood intersection into a Mexico City–style "zocalo" with "a cultural center and a plaza bounded by specialty shops and restaurants." It was initially proposed in the 1976 *Pilsen Neighborhood Plan*, but this time, it was less about fighting intrusive redevelopment schemes and more about drawing tourism and using existing Victorian architectural buildings to attract visitors."[58]

But the El Mercado-Pilsen Triangle plan drew the ire of antigentrification activists. "By 1992 we may not be here," artist and president of the ESDC, Jose G. González, warned. "The discovery of America will be celebrated but we will be visitors in our own community." González feared that overcommercializing Pilsen through tourism would only help erase actual Mexican Pilsen. Antitourism groups were opposed to the idea that there was a large Latino market for the taking, charging that it was not just their food and products on offer, but that Latinos and their neighborhoods *were* the market in and of itself. As Enid Vázquez of the Pilsen Aztlán Neighborhood Coalition argued, "The talk of Victorian architecture in the corporation's plan is almost a code word to outside developers to come in and develop Pilsen." Activists made an effective argument to stop the project. They dispensed with the claim "that any development of the triangle is better than no development at all," and defended their protectionist position about "keeping the community for the present residents." The idea was swiftly scrapped.[59]

The Arch and the Mercado reflected community efforts to reconstitute the colonias in new metropolitan realities. In seeking to attract tourist dollars and promote local consumption, both communities channeled different values. La Villita championed the politics of opportunity, readily inviting suburbanites to come and see for themselves what a neighborhood opened to Mexican immigrants and entrepreneurial hustle looked like. Along with Chinatown, La Villita became the darling of progrowth advocates in downtown. PNCC's Mercado project had trouble getting off the ground, but it nonetheless sought to promote its continued history of community control, pride in political consumerism, and desire to shape its own neighborhood authenticity in light of growing gentrification. In the end, divisions from within related to gentrification sunk the project.

Mexican immigrant revitalization through business and consumption continued to inspire a hopeful discourse commonly available to community leaders, scholars, and politicians for years to come. But it was unclear whether these ethnic densities were a byproduct of residential segregation, immigrant exploitation, and wage suppression, or a Latino community by choice. Was misery being concealed by bottom-up projects of tourism and authenticity-making? If given the choice, would those very same Mexican immigrants being touted as the answer to the urban crisis flee the city for bigger lawns and better homes? These questions remained difficult to answer as Mexican immigration to Chicago in the 1980s and 1990s increased the density of these colonias, further complicating their intricacies and political cultures.[60]

Neo-Chicanos, New Wavers, Punks, and Yuppies

The Chicano movement and community-control activists had waged a decades-long struggle to make Pilsen a "home" to Mexican immigrants and Mexican Americans. These groups challenged European immigrant claims of ownership over the neighborhood. By the 1980s, fears of displacement supplanted older concerns as community-control activists noted lingering "talk about how Pilsen will become the next gentrified area," as Augustín Olvera, director of ESDC, expressed. The ESDC prided itself in its work to "build community identity" and "save buildings that would otherwise be torn down." Other neighborhood groups like UNO were similarly proud of their work as they helped Latinos in the Far Southwest Side address infrastructural inequality. In both cases, the common import during this very unstable time seemed to be "a strong immigrant work ethic and a ferocious sense of turf," as journalist Alfredo Lanier noted in 1988. But the defense of place did not resonate as an enduring rallying cry for younger Latinos coming of age in the 1980s. Everyday forms of urban youth subculture, music, literature, art, and alternative media provided a burgeoning body of cultural production that enriched a critique of Latino urban life and questioned essentialist constructions of the "authentic Latino urban neighborhood."[61]

In 1984, Mexican American writer from Chicago Sandra Cisneros published her landmark book, *The House on Mango Street*. The book is a series of neighborhood vignettes told from the perspective of a young girl named Esperanza, who lives with her family in a brick two-flat. Behind a colorful mosaic of neighborhood characters and cityscape vistas, the young Latina observes the gendered and racial enclosures of Chicago's buildings and neighborhoods. Within a few years of its publication, the book was adopted into high school and college classrooms across the country, translated into multiple languages, and earned Cisneros high literary praise. Cisneros drew from her personal experience growing up in several neighborhoods in Chicago, including Pilsen, in an admittedly "conservative" Mexican American family. While Cisneros was often referred to as a "Chicana," Mexican Chicagoans were quick to note that this book was hardly in the tradition of Chicana/o movement literature. Cisneros was, as one local newspaper noted, part of a different generation of "writers that are coming of age 20 years after the Chicano movement of the 1960s." Cisneros once defended an admired writer, saying, "I too was bullied by hard-core Chicano activists who thought my writing was not Chicano enough."[62]

The actual house on the fictional Mango Street was a rectangular brick two-flat in Humboldt Park, but one that was also commonly found in Pilsen and other parts of the Southwest Side. It was the very same kind of building the ESDC was rushing to rehabilitate for working-class Mexicans before gentrifiers could snatch them up. In Esperanza's world, there was no gentrification, at least not that she could see through her window. Nevertheless, she wanted to escape the structures of racial capitalism, patriarchy, and white supremacy in her world. The house on Mango Street was not a home and did not feel like one. Cisneros later recalled that she did not feel a sense of belonging as a Mexican American until she relocated to the US Southwest. Still, for Latino Chicagoans, she was the first to put "houses" like theirs on the cultural map.[63]

As community-control advocates were working "to save a neighborhood" from gentrification, 1980s Latino urban culture was disowning the cultural nationalism that had been bound to Latino neighborhood space. Around the same time that ESDC was trying to get an ordinance passed to prevent speculators from developing abandoned factory buildings as residential lofts, Latino neighborhood youth were taking part in house and New Wave music scenes in abandoned industrial warehouses. House music lovers, mostly from working-class communities of color as well as working-class whites, descended on South Halsted's buildings for weekend parties and dancing. Community-control advocates rightfully feared that these shuttered industrial buildings were prime targets for real estate speculators looking to fulfill a growing market for industrial-style condominiums and lofts sought by young professionals moving back to the city. This was evidenced by UIC's southward expansion plans, the new Water Street Market condominium, and Podmajersky's loft conversions.[64]

Weekend dance parties were held inside a converted warehouse dubbed "Club Naked." House and New Wave music lovers with dark makeup, dyed hair, dark clothing, and studs gathered inside to listen to the latest singles spun by local DJs. In this space, cultural nationalist tropes of Latino power were simply incompatible with Latino urban youth culture. Central-city house and New Wave scenes reflected a rupture from the politics of neighborhood authenticity and Chicano cultural nationalism. New Wave, house, and punk music drew inspiration from dystopic themes and aesthetics of deindustrialized landscapes, disunity, and individual style. DJs, artists, dancers, performers, and stylists were celebrated as neighborhood heroes, while organizations and civic groups were viewed as suspect and part of the status quo. Eventually the popularity of house music made its way into the entertainment program of PNCC's Annual Fiesta Del Sol. In 1983, a group of influential DJs from the radio station WBMX that helped popularize Chicago house music were invited to headline all three nights of the summer festival. This underscored how community-control groups like PNCC were learning to cater to the changing tastes of Latino youth.[65]

In 1984, Lilly Arroyo, a teenager, gave her impressions about music styles and Latino neighborhoods to a reporter from the *Reader*. Making a distinction between her new Far Southwest Side neighborhood surrounded by white ethnics and her cousins who lived in a Puerto Rican Near Northwest Side neighborhood, Arroyo told the reporter:

> Up there, you're always in these little cliques with the Latin people, but here you're influenced a lot more by white people. . . . The people on the north side are constantly partying, constantly in the streets, into the weird clothing, weird hairstyles—like dyeing their hair blue and red. And they like salsa and New Wave[,] they don't like rock. Like if a rock song comes on in my car while my cousins are visiting me, they're like, 'What is happening to you? You've been living here too long.' . . . On the South Side, you get a taste of both worlds.[66]

Along with challenging Latino neighborhood authenticity, house music fans and New Wavers took part in reclaiming their dispossessed community spaces. The popularity of Club Naked and house music in the inner city grew and attracted suburban whites and downtown yuppies. In a short time, urban youth of color shared a precarious ecology with the yuppies and neobohemians of East Pilsen. Parties, dancing, and music helped democratize the city and bend the segregation of communities, at least temporarily. Black youth from Bronzeville, Puerto Rican youth from West Town, and white ethnics from Bridgeport could travel to a Mexican neighborhood for fun and friendly dancing in a decade filled with violent gang warfare. Few Club Naked attendees could recall an episode of violence breaking out at these events.[67]

While Pilsen's urban youth were well aware of the siege on Mexican Pilsen, they also made new use of former Chicano movement spaces. In 1987, Martin Sorrondeguy a twenty-six-year-old from Pilsen and his friends, who enjoyed dancing at Club Naked, longed for more expressive outlets whereby the music they loved, punk and hardcore, could have more significance in their communities. Sorrondeguy grew up on the western edge of the community, between Pilsen and Heart of Chicago, after his family had fled political repression in Uruguay during the 1960s. Sorrondeguy and his

Figure 6.4. Flier for the first punk/hardcore show in Pilsen, held at Casa Aztlán, March 11, 1987. (Image courtesy of Martin Sorrondeguy.)

friends were drawn to the personal empowerment of the do-it-yourself punk and hardcore scene. They decided to bring punk to the neighborhood by organizing a show at Casa Aztlán, where suburban and out-of-town bands came to perform. That it took place at Casa Aztlán—the very site that sparked the city's Chicano cultural and community-control movements— was a telling sign of the shifting cultural politics from one generation to the next. "It was the first punk show ever in our neighborhood," Sorrondeguy later told a punk fanzine.[68]

Whether intentional or not, Latino youth and music subcultures provided new vistas for understanding Latino urban enclaves during the city's great reshuffle, with less of an emphasis on hardline protectionism over the neighborhood and more on creating social events where young people could congregate peacefully. Punks of color like Sorrondeguy shared the Latino community's fear of rampant gang violence and turf wars. One reason Sorrondeguy deliberately relocated punk and hardcore music to Pilsen was to bring a positive event to the community awash in negative stereotyping of Latino youth as criminals. Another reason was that punk was what he was most identified with. In bringing punk to Casa Aztlán, where he recalled that "300 people showed up, on 17th and Racine, which is a pretty gang-infested neighborhood," Sorrondeguy was challenging neighborhood youth to come together and be peaceful with one another. The event flyer, designed by local artist Luis Montenegro, featured a drawing of a dystopic Pilsen in line with the aesthetics of 1980s postindustrial urbanity as an environmental wasteland.[69]

Chicano neighborhood hardliners considered suburban white youth in the community just as much of a threat as yuppies on the east side of Pilsen. In some ways, it was true that attracting whites into Pilsen for cultural events was threatening, especially since they were coming for what were perceived to be non-Latino gatherings like punk shows or New Wave dancing. But conversely, the punk show at Casa Aztlán was in keeping with the community-minded goals of the Chicano movement, helping to raise funds for a neighborhood art program for children. Although punk and New Wave provided sonically darker themes that did not quite match with the aesthetics of authenticity long associated with Mexican Pilsen, Sorrondeguy would come to argue that punk should be considered a form of Latino protest music, an argument he sharpened in the new decade to come.[70]

In the meantime, community-control advocates and cultural nationalists dismayed that Pilsen's authenticity as a Mexican barrio was eroding, if not for the seeming oddities that punk and New Wave spaces represented or the foreignness described by hometown figures like Sandra Cisneros, then for the swarm of yuppies searching for trendy housing in East Pilsen. In the years following Harold Washington's death, groups like UNO, PNCC, and ESDC found themselves in a renewed fight with city hall over privatized redevelopment. Latino community-control advocates pushed to impose hefty taxes on private firms (instead of giving away tax incentives) for those building high-rise and townhouse developments for middle- and upper-class professionals. As a solution to urban postindustrial erosion, this tax money would then help pay for housing and infrastructure improvements in communities like Pilsen and other low-income working-class neighborhoods. But some observers disagreed with this approach, claiming that without the tax incentives, private developers would be driven out of Chicago entirely, to the city's detriment.[71]

This argument came not only from progrowth, chamber-of-commerce types or downtown business interests but liberal journalists and urban studies scholars too. Having grown frustrated with "radical" community-control groups and shortsighted bureaucrats in city hall, they argued that yuppies were not the problem at all. To them, the panic was irrational since there were not enough young urban professionals to make a difference, or so claimed Louis H. Masotti, a professor at Northwestern. "Only ten percent of the baby boomers fit the income and life-style definitions most commonly used for yuppies," he told a reporter, coining "the last fool theory," when "someone inevitably goes and builds the one last high rise that sits absolutely empty." Making similar arguments, the self-titled "urbanologist" Pierre De Vise admitted to the changes occurring in the 1980s but added that it was "the reshuffling of a limited market." In agreement were urban-affairs journalists Eduardo Camacho and Ben Joravsky, who similarly tried to dispel the so-called myth of a yuppie takeover. "Quite the opposite is happening," they wrote in 1989, "take a drive through Chicago, almost no neighborhood is without its abandoned buildings, vacant lots, graffiti-scarred viaducts, or signs of decay," to make the point that the city needed people with money. Camacho and Joravsky did not blame gentrifiers, who they deemed a kind of urban legend; instead, they pleaded with communities of color to not suburbanize and to stay put, as if that had really been a widespread problem. In exaggerating Latino and Black suburbanization, they wrote, "Chicago has declined. And it will continue to decline unless those residents (Black, white, Asian, Hispanic . . . race and ethnicity don't matter) who can afford to leave choose to stay."[72]

As these critics championed a compelling, if not mythological, multi-ethnic "back-to-the-city" movement as the solution to the urban crisis of the 1980s, they shifted their frustration to neighborhood protectionists who recoiled at the sight of "artists" and "yuppies" in their barrio. To make their point, Camacho and Joravsky collected "man on the street" interviews in Podmajerksy's colony. "I guess we're part of the community," performing artist Donna Blue Lachman told the reporters. "Some of the

Mexicans (activists) hate Podmajersky. I can't understand why. They say he's displacing people. I don't know that much about it. I don't really follow all that's going on in the community politically." She then pivoted from the politics of gentrification to gay rights, making an implicit comment about Latino homophobia or conservatism or both: "We yell at the local alderman. He came to a meeting, I asked him about gay rights. He said, 'if you elect me, I'll vote for it.' We elected him, and then he didn't vote for it." Young white professionals depicted a more harmonious relationship with Mexican Pilsen. "I like living in Pilsen, I think it's a port of entry for artists," said Stan Edwards, a commercial designer. "When I go to a bakery or one of the restaurants on 18th Street like Nuevo Leon, and I talk to people, they say to me 'Oh, you are an artist,' they like that," he told a television reporter. While Lachman was known to hire Chicano muralists for her stage props, she offered a more sober assessment of her adopted neighborhood, telling Camacho and Joravsky, "If I left Pilsen that would mean I would have enough money to buy a loft somewhere else in Chicago. . . . Who can afford it[?] . . . [S]o I put up with this neighborhood."[73]

Pilsen contained an ecosystem precariously shared by Chicano cultural nationalists, community-control activists, New Wavers, punks, literature authors, artists, and yuppies who were all trying to make sense of their changing surroundings. Camacho and Joravsky, along with notable urban studies scholars, sought to shine a spotlight on diverse middle-class concerns and what could bring them into harmony with working-class communities during "the exodus of dollars and people from the city." To these thinkers, the arrival of artists and yuppies to a working-class Latino neighborhood was nothing to panic about. By faulting families instead of racial capitalism, however, they missed an opportunity to draw historic linkages between whiteness, value, and property to make a more compelling case about the metropolitan reshuffling. In the 1990s, Latino families would continue to seek better living conditions in neighborhoods with more city services, better schools, and safety from rampant gang violence. In contrast to Camacho and Joravsky, Chicano community journalists like Antonio Zavala did worry somewhat about the appearance and influence of "yuppie" careerism and consumerism on Latino youth. He encouraged youngsters to "turn a little left from the rightward turn of the upscale Reagan yuppie years" and "reject the material world of possessions." Even journalist Studs Terkel, the city's foremost champion of localism, testified to all the rehab projects the community-control organizations led. When he visited the neighborhood, he victoriously concluded that the "grassroots power is being felt in Pilsen, too, where rehabs are springing up without the dubious touch of gentrification. The community folk are there because they're there and that's where they intend to stay. . . . No shoving out in these parts. And no yuppies need apply."[74]

Calles, Sueños, y Yardas

Two sites reflected the ongoing battles to stabilize the local and the global reshuffle of the late twentieth century. Local residents used cultural and commercial forms of empowerment to articulate the indignities of displacement due to gentrification, economic restructuring, and Global South subjecthood. The first was a residential building on 1900 South Carpenter Street in Pilsen, known as Calles y Sueños (Streets and Dreams), that became a hub of 1990s youth protest and global cultural movements of opposition that reflected both rupture and continuity. The second was the old stockyards colonia in Back of the Yards, hidden just behind the intersection of Ashland Avenue and 47th Street. This former hub of global capitalism that delivered cuts of meat to the modern world was by the 1980s and 1990s desperate for an economic recovery. Both sites stood at the precipice of bigger forces behind the flipping of colonias and the restructuring of racial capitalism.[75]

The brick building on Carpenter Street in Pilsen, one of hundreds rehabilitated by the community-control activists in the ESDC, was repurposed by new residents as a Latino cultural and community center in the early 1990s. From the basement, a local punk band, Los Crudos, featuring Martin Sorrondeguy of Pilsen and Jose Casas of Little Village, delivered lightning-fast rhythms and loud distorted sounds from their amplifiers. "Crudos is a Spanish word which means raw and hungover," Sorrondeguy told listeners, "We are not a pro-drinking band, but a band who saw that problems such as gang violence, domestic violence, racism, poverty, gentrification have become an everyday occurrence in our surroundings." Creativity flowed throughout 1900 S. Carpenter Street, now retooled as "Calles y Sueños," home to artistic and grassroots opposition to the gentrification that was spreading westbound into the heart of Mexican Pilsen. The "young turks" of Calles y Sueños were suspicious of reinvestment groups, more beholden now to private guidelines than they had been in the 1970s. In a manifesto signed by artists affiliated with the cultural center in 1998, they wrote that there was a "conspiracy" underfoot, "facilitating the arrival of money-hungry investors with measures such as TIF [Tax Increment Financing], suppressing public transportation services, turning the neighborhood into a mall for tourists, favoring the expansion of UIC and threatening to expropriate the properties of those who refuse to sell." They blamed Pilsen's once-powerful community organizations that had been co-opted and bent to the will of the pro-growth agenda headed by Mayor Richard M. Daley. The Calles y Sueños artists, without irony, evoked the very same Chicano movement that birthed these organizations in the late 1960s and early 1970s.[76]

The manifesto helped underscore an implicit criticism of how once-powerful community organizations such as ESDC, PNCC, and UNO were now mainstreamed into the channels of power, questioning whether these groups could really enact transformational change from within. Much of this doubt was evidenced as Mayor Richard M. Daley seized the collapsed Washington coalition and reorganized Latino politics in his own making. As a way to prevent another "independent" insurrection like the one during the 1980s, he organized the Hispanic Democratic Organization (HDO), a kind of modernized "Amigos for Daley" that, like the organization his father Richard J. Daley had built before him, was structured along lines of mutual loyalties and transactional politics. HDO members enjoyed direct access to Daley, and the mayor slated Latinos for aldermanic seats in wards with Latino majorities. With Daley controlling the levers of Latino politics, he was able to leverage support for his neoliberal agenda centered on bringing younger affluents back to the city. Providing luxuries like universities, entertainment, and inexpensive products required consent from central-city communities on local and transnational matters ranging from UIC's expansion, charter schools, and TIF to NAFTA (North American Free Trade Agreement). Most Latino aldermen would register public opposition to issues like NAFTA and TIF, but in time the mayor received the blessing of the Latino political leadership behind closed doors.[77]

Two organizations that found a favorable climate during the 1990s were The Resurrection Project (TRP) and UNO, which became leading advocates of Latino housing and education, respectively, taking on the infrastructural inequalities that followed Latino demographic growth on the Southwest Side. Both groups based their credibility on having the support of Latino parishioners and the Catholic Church. "We did not grow out of the 60s. We did not grow out of the 70s," recalled one TRP official. "We're not about protesting the Alderman just to protest the Alderman." TRP touted a preference for pragmatic politics to accomplish their goals. Turning former manufacturing buildings and tenements into multi-family residences, they created low- to middle-income housing for Latino families on the Southwest Side. TRP fueled the sour impressions Latinos had formed

about CHA and its scattered site housing and forged a private-public part-
nership with the city to build affordable housing. Similarly, UNO became
a leading developer of charter schools in Latino wards. Daley, who sought
a total overhaul of Chicago Public Schools, echoed UNO's school-reform
efforts. UNO received financial backing from First National Bank of Chicago and support for their Local School Councils. Both TRP and UNO advocated middle-class consumer-choice politics and private-public partnerships and appealed to a Latino Catholic conservatism. At the same time,
TRP and UNO enacted their own form of postindustrial urbanism: they
rehabbed homes, repurposed warehouses, turned renters into homeowners,
made new schools out of old ones, and updated white ethnic churches for
Mexican parishioners.[78]

Mayor Daley's expansion of UIC into Pilsen and other progrowth ventures were seen as an ongoing effort to repopulate the city with middle-
and upper-income residents, and as the artists at Calles y Sueños wrote,
"to run low-income people out of our historic neighborhood." Meanwhile,
community organizations on the Far Southwest Side—even ones that were
once hostile to Latinos, like the BYNC—were now leading projects to attract Latino home buyers for the economic health of the district. "We're
a Polish deli," one frustrated business owner said, "and there's no more
Poles left. The Spanish don't buy this kind of stuff." Under the new leadership of Patrick Salmon, the BYNC took a more active role in mediating
white working-class fears of Latino settlement. This underscored both the
endurance of whiteness in the ongoing making of Latino Chicago but also
the desire to attract Latino spending and commercial power for revitalization. BYNC addressed Latino needs much in the same vein as the programs
UNO-BOY sought in the 1980s: affordable housing, access to low-interest
home loans, and returning industry to the old stockyards. Salmon was able
to build on earlier gains UNO-BOY made in the 1980s that aggressively
pursued enterprise-zone tax abatements and incentives for underserved
Latino districts. With these mechanisms in place, Salmon facilitated Latino
homeownership, believing good things would soon follow. "When people
own their own homes and have pride in ownership and gang crime activities
are taking place around their home," said Salmon in 1992, "they're going
to fight to save their investment. That is not what they do when they're
renting." Commercial properties along Ashland Avenue and 47th Street became hot commodities as well. "Businesses [are] begging his organization
for storefronts along busy Ashland Avenue," reported the *Chicago Enterprise* about Mark Roschen and his Back of the Yards Business Association.[79]

At the very intersection on Ashland Avenue and 47th Street where whites held the line against Mexicans to create a buffer zone against Blacks during World War II, the purchasing power of Latinos and their promise of revitalization had finally arrived. The Polish delis were soon gone, but other stores, such as Montgomery Ward, PharMor Pharmacy, Omni Superstore, and others wanted back in. A shopping center called the Yards Plaza soon opened, lured by tax incentives and plenty of wage laborers. Salmon did his part by promoting the "increased disposable income" of Latinos to attract more merchants. Latinos promoted their own economic strength as they continued to access better housing, schools, and neighborhoods by flipping block by block. In 1993, the newspaper *La Raza* associated the Mexican Back of the Yards with "[w]ork and prosperity," echoing the values of immigrant hustle and individual effort. These were the bedrock ideas that operated as gateways to settlement in metropolitan Chicago and beyond. Mexican suburban communities also publicized their own vibrant commercial corridors, such as Walter Street in Aurora and Washington Street in Waukegan.

But these ideas came with a price. At the end of the twentieth century, Mayor Daley's neoliberal policies not only actually displaced Latinos out of the central city and its most valuable real estate into the outer rings of disinvested white-flight neighborhoods, but also created a rationale that moving to the outer rings meant achieving success. Economic activists and cultural workers opposed to Daley's neoliberal progrowth agenda argued that Latinos were being resegregated, pushed out of their former barrios right when another group was reinvesting in them. In 1995, PNCC went to work beyond its own neighborhood boundaries to mediate demographic change in the Far Southwest Side. Taking note that Mexican families were not necessarily improving their economic circumstances by simply moving to "Bridgeport, McKinley Park, Brighton Park and Gage Park" and remaining part of the working poor.[80]

: :

In July 2001, Anita Villarreal passed away at the age of eighty-six. The local papers remembered her as an "advocate for Little Village" and noted her business acumen for "championing the use of 26th Street for Latino businesses." Mayor Richard M. Daley issued a city proclamation in her name, one his father would have written for her had he been alive. An overall portrait of a kind-hearted woman with a philanthropic heart emerged, but it flattened her life's work. In all the eulogies, she was hardly recognized for flipping the colonias and the messy history that effort had entailed. Absent was a more nuanced reflection that underscored the uneasy and overlapping actions of both civil rights work and blockbusting necessary to pioneer the Southwest Side neighborhoods and open them to Mexicans. Some of this work required participating in a preexisting system of segregation, built on anti-Black racism. She did not invent this system but became a meticulous student of it, studying maps, real estate markets, and housing policy and becoming an expert in white flight. Absent, too, was any mention of her adoption of Chicago-style politics: her muscling out of opponents and competition and her critical relationships with white leaders and businessmen, Savings and Loan institutions, and the political machine in her rise as *la jaladora de La Villita* (the mover of Little Village), as many came to know her.[81]

In 1993, she told a reporter for *La Raza* that it was indeed very difficult to open up South Lawndale. "The early days of the community were not easy," the paper recounted, nobody was doing Mexicans any favors. "The pioneering Europeans scraped every last attempt to preserve their place and prevent the establishment of the Mexican community," noted the newspaper, "and unfortunately for them day by day more Mexicans arrived from nearby neighborhoods and pushed Europeans to the western suburbs." But flipping the colonia was not her only enduring achievement. It was what she turned those colonias into—bustling neighborhoods of immigrant entrepreneurship and sweat equity that revitalized decades of disinvestment—that reached the ears of President Bill Clinton. In 1996, Villarreal was invited to the White House, after the Clintons wanted her input on La Villita's economic resurgence and its rivaling and surpassing of Chicago's Magnificent Mile. She turned down the invitation, citing a "previous commitment," but not without sending along her criticism of the administration: "I would like to express my appreciation to the Clinton administration for the concern implied in attempting to reach Hispanic Leaders nationwide. I am concerned that the Administration's present course regarding immigration is detrimental to the future of family unification and opportunity. This country has achieved its greatness because of its uniqueness in acceptance, assistance and encouragement of the immigrant. I certainly hope that this conference quite appropriately scheduled in the Indian Treaty room will pay more than lip service to our needs." President Clinton and others throughout the decade sought to justify a neoliberal economic agenda on the premise that Global South immigrants did more with less—i.e., justifying his punitive immigration policy, relaxing trade, weakening labor unions, and rolling back civil rights gains. In the past, Villarreal would not have quibbled with such claims from leaders in Chicago, but this was the President of the United States and she was in her twilight years. She rejected it outright as a false binary and an exploitation of Latino and immigrant histories.[82]

Conclusion

In 2017, Casa Aztlán was sold to a condominium developer who swiftly painted over the murals that had adorned its exterior walls and symbolized the pride and struggle for self-determination of an earlier generation of artists and activists during the Chicano Movement of the 1960s and 1970s. Community members considered this an affront to the long history of Pilsen as a cultural sanctuary for Mexican immigrants and Mexican Americans and its decades-long struggle to reclaim resources for the community and mark its built environment with symbols of dignity and social justice. "It's a big loss," said Byron Sigcho of Pilsen Alliance, an antigentrification advocacy group, "[Casa Aztlán was] not only a space, but culture, identity, decades of community services like adult education classes, immigration services . . . it really reflected the history of the community."[1]

The erasure of Mexican and Chicano landmarks has been part of a long and ongoing history of resource looting to remake the central city and, in the process, unmake Mexican Chicago and other Latino communities across urban America from Boyle Heights to Brooklyn. Although they achieved some degree of success in securing residential and class mobility across metropolitan regions, Black and Brown working people overwhelmingly remain the custodians of the central city, a resource ever more valuable to global neoliberal capitalism. In parts of Mexican Chicago, such as Pilsen, residents are facing a ruthless drive toward a "renaissance" in which the profit imperatives of the wealthy class exploit the powerlessness of disadvantaged and racialized working people whose very lives are "in the way" of someone else's good deal. Casa Aztlán has been but one of many buildings that have succumbed to this savage renaissance led by venture capitalists, luxury-condo developers, and land speculators who have legally confiscated buildings and houses in working-class Latino communities to make them suitable for a wealthier class of consumers who can afford higher rents, mortgages, and taxes. Many Latino-serving Catholic churches have also closed their doors due to the displacement of local parishioners from the neighborhood, eliminating not only places of worship but also critical resources for community organizing.[2]

A creative class urbanism has followed on the heels of Latino working-class settlement. Armed with neoliberal capital and city hall incentives, a wave of niche entrepreneurs have opened breweries, coffee shops, bars, and restaurants on the same real estate that decades before was the site of sweat equity projects from which Mexican immigrants hoped to build sanctuary in America. Nourishing business opportunities has been a hallmark of Latino communities in Chicago for years, but the new wave of creative class businesses has fueled property speculation, increasing rents and leading to the eviction of working-class Latinos and businesses.[3] The *panaderia* has been supplanted by the pour-over. A walk down Pilsen's 18th Street in 2021 showcases this savage renaissance in all its exposed inequality; the thoroughfare has become an unevenly contested terrain between the ever-dwindling means of the Mexican working immigrant and the ever-increasing demand for luxuries desired by the creative class. To attract more of the latter, a surge of unfettered capital and digestible fictions have descended upon Pilsen's buildings, storefronts, and public and private spaces, gentrifying Latino urbanism and its characteristic aesthetics and pedestrian culture.

Far from the postindustrial liberalism often attributed to the creative class, some of these business owners and their patrons have been flagrantly anti-Mexican and anti-Latino. Some CEOs of hipster bars and restaurants have behaved much like corporate entities who depend on underpaid Latino immigrant laborers but exploit and abuse them. Stories of immigrant workers (especially undocumented workers) being stiffed on their wages, subjected to sexual abuse, or otherwise mistreated go largely unreported for fear of retribution. On occasion, the bars have also become the uninhibited playgrounds for wealthy and right-wing white-collar professionals who become inebriated and disrespectful toward longtime residents. In 2018, after a violent outbreak where drunken patrons wearing Donald Trump paraphernalia attacked a Latina community member on 18th Street, a Pilsen-based queer women of color group organized a boycott against all "gentrifier bars." When the bars failed to address or apologize for the violence, the group responded by asking the community during a social media press conference to "boycott any fucking gentrifying space in Pilsen because they don't care about us, and they never will, they only care about their money. Gentrification is a violent practice run by capitalism."[4] The fracas underscored for local residents the vortex of racism, violence, displacement, and erasure that comes with every new hip bar or business.

Even when the patrons and owners of the new businesses do not embrace the blatant racism of the Trump era, the carnage of gentrification remains, reflected in more subtle forms of erasure—for instance, the wave of new breweries that have recently opened in Chicago's Southwest Side as part of a craft-beer resurgence in the United States. In many cases, these erasures are fueled by artisans whose passion for their craft is commendable. Nevertheless, the architecture and design of the breweries evoke a revisionist origin story that contributes to the erasure of local neighborhoods. These breweries are designed in the aesthetic vernacular of creative-class urbanism that draws from both quasi-industrial and postindustrial elements, utilizing rehabbed warehouses, factories, storefronts, exposed beams, wood paneling, brick, and other raw materials to present a more polished version of a different economic era. Rather than building equity-based partnerships that dignify, recognize, and resource share with the Latino communities in which they operate, many breweries ignore Mexican Pilsen or Mexican Chicago altogether. Instead, the aesthetics evoke the culture of the area's nineteenth-century Eastern European and German immigrants whose descendants erected barriers against Mexican immigrants and Mexican Americans before eventually fleeing the city. Thus, the new breweries romanticize and fetishize Pilsen and the Southwest Side's built environment with a selective revisionist past while conveniently erasing the area's Mexican history and presence. The question remains, however, whether creative-class urbanism can coexist with Mexican Chicago without contributing to its unmaking. If the past offers any clues, it is that the pursuit of appropriating communities and community resources for profit, a pursuit that relies on racial domination, is the bedrock of racial capitalism, and thus, is not built to share or willingly give up power or resources.[5]

Masses of multigenerational and immigrant Latinos living in US cities have for years called attention to the precarity of their lives under systems of racial capitalism, in which economic prosperity continues to be built off of the inequities inflicted on working Brown people and workers of color more generally who are excluded from the rewards of the reinvested postindustrial city. The exploitation of Latino workers in service and food industries, construction, factories, fields, and domestic work has only exacerbated their urban conditions in the twenty-first century. From Los Angeles to Chicago to Brooklyn, Latino immigrants and multigenerational Latino families across urban America have been positioned to be the supporting cast to other people's cushioned urban experiences.

The unmaking of Mexican Chicago is not bounded by twenty-first-century history but has always coexisted alongside the building of Latino communities amid destabilizing episodes of federal and municipal disinvestment, economic restructuring, the immigration carceral state, political disenfranchisement, and predatory corporate reinvestment. While this book recounts much of that history, efforts by community organizations and housing activists working toward protecting the right to remain in the city have, for years, warned against the threat of displacement posed to Latino working-class residents by the unregulated forces of neoliberal capital and the nativist strain in US immigration policy. Resisting and persevering in the face of these forces has also been part of that long history. Just as in the 1950s, when Mexican community members from the Near West Side were targeted by the dual violence of urban renewal and INS deportation campaigns, Mexican bodies *and* their buildings came under threat in the 1990s. In 1996, housing and immigration activists in Pilsen rose up and resisted the intersecting vortex of displacement and deportation that was once again linked by the political and economic priorities of the decade that pursued neoliberal and nativist measures against immigrants and minorities. In 1996, President Bill Clinton signed the Illegal Immigration Reform and Immigrant Responsibility Act (IIRIRA), a punitive law that further criminalized Latino immigrants and increased federal agent raids in Latino communities, reducing due process in court procedures. Antideportation activists took to the streets—the very streets of Pilsen where deportation and gentrification were operating in tandem—to call out the conservative turn against immigrants by the Clinton administration. Pilsen residents marched along its main thoroughfare of 18th Street, carrying signs that read: "Stop the deportations," and "This is my land! This is my struggle!"[6]

That same year, housing activists mobilized public protests against the "yuppification" of Pilsen as well. Two years later, in 1998, the Frente de Artistas en Defensa del Barrio del Pilsen joined with housing activists when they penned a manifesto warning that Pilsen "is in grave danger of disappearing under threat of eviction" as corporate dollars permeated the community on the incentives given by city hall to raise the tax value of the area, pushing out the most vulnerable.[7] Swaths of properties opened to real estate investors and white-collar professionals, drastically changing the face of Pilsen right at a time when arriving Mexican immigrants needed these com-

Figure 7.1. Immigrant rights march on 18th Street, 1996. (Image courtesy of Martin Sorrondeguy.)

munities the most. Between 1990 and 2010, the United States saw some of the greatest spikes in immigration from Mexico, with numbers climbing from 4.2 million in 1990, 9.1 million in 2000, to 11.7 million in 2010.[8] This increase helped turn Chicago's metropolitan region into the second largest concentration of Mexican immigrants in the United States, after Southern California.[9] A significant percentage of these immigrants were undocumented, an always present element in Mexican Chicago, making transnational families with mixed status.

What began in 1996 as a community effort to protest the repressive apparatus of immigrant criminalization snowballed into a historic national movement for immigrant rights in 2006. That year, organizers from Mexican Chicago led La Gran Marcha, a series of massive nationwide protests numbering over 1.5 million people across 102 cities. In Chicago, marchers descended in the downtown Loop in a powerful show of support, surpassing one hundred thousand participants.[10] Since then and through the Great Recession, the Obama administration's deportation surge, the Trump administration's mainstreaming of white ethno-nationalist rage, and a global pandemic, residents of Mexican Chicago have continued to fight to build a metropolitan sanctuary in the American city.

The outcome is evident throughout the Mexican Bungalow Belt, including Gage Park, once the seedbed of racial bigotry. Today, Gage Park is home to thousands of Latino immigrants and their mixed-status, multigenerational families. One of its new organizations, the Gage Park Latinx Council (GPLXC), has responded to the COVID-19 crisis by organizing fundraisers and creating a food pantry for families experiencing food and housing insecurity. Many of its community members work in high-exposure occupations as cooks, cleaners, and factory workers. Since the start of the pandemic, many have been laid off or furloughed. Amid the destruction wrought by the coronavirus, GPLXC has called into question the harmful paradox that simultaneously hails Latino immigrant workers as "essential" and "saviors" in a society that also treats them as expendable. Latinos in Chicago have had infection rates triple that of whites and a disproportionate number of deaths.[11] Along with its community organizing, GPLXC has also engaged, rather than ignored, Gage Park's long history of racial exclusion with an aim to renew the politics of sanctuary and social justice after a violent resurgence of anti-Latino nativism in America. "Rather than allowing us to feel like Gage Park is merely a space we occupy, GPLXC is actively fighting for us to have a neighborhood that is truly *nuestra tierra* and ushering in a future where residents will never doubt they have a home," explain its leaders.[12]

Making Mexican Chicago reveals the decades-long struggle to build a sanctuary out of the central city in the face of state violence, political disenfranchisement, economic disinvestment, and the backlash of hostile white ethnic mobilizations. Only in a society constituted by neoliberal multiculturalism and racial capitalism can immigrants exist in a paradox of being essential but also expendable, deportable, and erasable. This book highlights the multivalent repertoire that residents took to achieve Latino-centered empowerment in the city as residents, business owners, and community organizations pushed for transformative change in the political economy that was all too casually augmenting inequality in the form of racial capitalism. Some community leaders worked toward resisting spatial containment and "barrioization"; others, such as Latino merchants, seized on the concentration of Mexican peoples in one place, hoping to create opportunity through Brown capitalism. In the process, the story of Latino community formation and migrant city building—the making of Mexican Chicago—has been the story of the pursuit of sanctuary even when it is far from reach.

ACKNOWLEDGMENTS

The process of writing history involves so much more than the individual historian. It is a collective endeavor that spans distance and time, bringing together disparate communities that have supported the journey. Along my journey, I have incurred many debts to "communities" of family, friends, peers, mentors, and advisors for their years of support and encouragement. This is my humble attempt, however insufficient, to express my gratitude.

The seeds of this project, first planted by my mother's stories, grew into a wild garden during my tenure as a graduate student at Yale University. I consider myself very fortunate to have developed as a young scholar and writer in such an invigorating intellectual environment. To a kid from the 'hood in LA, Yale could not have been a more unfamiliar place, as I was surrounded by pedigreed upbringings I had little prior exposure to. All the more reason to sing the praises of my teachers and mentors who taught me to create a space for myself in academia, block out self-doubt, and learn to trust and value my instincts, hunches, and questions. Stephen Pitti was the best advisor a student could have. He recruited me with encouraging emails and phone calls, trained me with rigor and care, and helped me cultivate my historian's toolkit. It is no wonder he can count so many in the professoriate as his mentees. My dissertation committee was composed of brilliant scholars, but most importantly, generous and caring people. Matthew Frye Jacobson pushed me to find my voice, Jean-Christophe Agnew made the ideas and stakes of the post-1945 United States come alive, and Michael Denning always foregrounded the lives of working people. My educational experience was invigorated by early dialogues with Dolores Hayden, John Mack Faragher, Paul Gilroy, Jonathan Holloway, and Jon Butler. Alicia

Schmidt Camacho exemplified the qualities of the scholar-activist, always foregrounding a sense of ethical and political urgency within and beyond the classroom. For their friendship and cherished conversations, I thank Nicole Ivy, Tisha Hooks, Simeon Man, Monica Muñoz Martinez, Sarah Haley, Shana Redmond, Sam Vong, Gerry Cadava, A. Naomi Paik, Julie Weise, Kaysha Corinealdi, Ana Minian, Amina El-Annan, David Huyssen, Susie Woo, Kimberly Juanita Brown, Zane Curtis-Olsen, and Dara Orenstein. Liza Cariaga-Lo, Pat Cabral, and Victorine Shepard made Yale a welcoming place.

I arrived at graduate school by way of UCLA. My passion for history was ignited by Eric Avila, my undergraduate advisor, who exposed me to the study of the city with all of its challenges and possibilities. I owe a note of gratitude to Thomas Hines, whose classes in architectural history deepened my desire to understand the built environment. I was extremely fortunate to have had Juan Gómez-Quiñones as a teacher and guide to his interpretive range on Mexican American history.

This book could not have been written without the assistance of dozens of expert archivists, librarians, and collection specialists, who helped me find countless source materials and fielded all of my questions and requests. I thank the knowledgeable staffs at the Chicago History Museum Research Center; University of Illinois at Chicago's Special Collections and University Archives, especially Kellee Warren; University of Chicago Hanna Holborn Gray Special Collections Research Center; Municipal Reference Collection at the Harold Washington Library Center and Chicago Public Library; Claretian Missionaries Archives, especially Malachy McCarthy; DePaul Special Collections and Archives; the National Archives at Chicago; the National Archives at College Park, Maryland; Chicago Theological Seminary Special Collections; Social Welfare History Archives at the University of Minnesota, especially Linnea Anderson; Michigan State University Archives and Historical Collections; University of Notre Dame Archives; Dolph Briscoe Center for American History and the Benson Latin American Collection at the University of Texas at Austin; Library of Congress Manuscript Division; and Special Collections and Microfilm at the Catholic University of America. Copies of timely materials were provided by the reference archivists and staff at Moorland-Spingarn Research Center at Howard University; Amistad Research Center at Tulane University; and the Columbia Center for Oral History Archives at Columbia University.

Even with the use of these superb archival repositories, Latinx Chicago remains severely undercollected and underarchived. A deft institution with a commitment toward expanding its reach will see this deficit as an opportunity not to be passed up. When I encountered sourcing limitations in the archive or when more perspectives from the bottom up were necessary to show where and when powerful structures were challenged or contested, I turned to the people and the neighborhoods. Some sleuthing, investigating, and cold calling led me directly to community members who graciously opened their doors and spoke with me about their experiences on a number of issues. I conducted numerous oral histories for this project. On many occasions, I was lucky enough to be given access to a rich trove of private personal papers, letters, photographs, and other ephemera tucked away in basements and closets. These materials, along with the stories of my interviewees, reminded me time and again how working-class immigrant communities are often the best custodians of their own desires, struggles, victories, and failures, and that sometimes these emotional registers do not align and can even clash with more conventional institutional archives. Throughout the book I try to show this dynamic, but I was only able to do so because of the generosity of community members, families, former organizers, civic leaders, ex-city employees, cultural workers, and others who gave of their time and shared their fascinating materials with me. They are too numerous to mention here by name, but many are cited throughout the footnotes, and I am grateful to all of them.

Over the past decade, several undergraduate students provided invaluable research assistance at various stages of this project by helping me track down materials, scanning items, or operating a microfilm machine like a seasoned pro. They are Raul Azucena, Charley Pincombe, Colton Brandau, Edgar Herrera, Maria De La Luz Valenzuela, Manuel De Jesus, Katia Fernandez Soto, and Estefan Linares. I'm also thankful to Verónica Méndez Flores for assistance with valuable materials.

My professional and scholarly life has been blessed by generous friends, colleagues, and kind people who have lent their support and friendship. They include José Alamillo, Sharada Balachandran, Adrian Burgos Jr., Marcia Chatelain, Jesse Constantino, Manuel Cuellar, John Davy, D'Weston Haywood, Mike Innis-Jiménez, Theresa Gaye Johnson, Lori Flores, Matt Garcia, Perla Guerrero, David Gutiérrez, Paul Kramer, Johana Londoño, Kelly Lytle Hernández, Natalia Molina, Sarah Osten, Dominic A. Pacyga, Monica Perales, Isabela Quintana, Ana Rosas, Malgorzata Rymsza-Pawlowska, Tomás Summers Sandoval, and Julie Sze. I am lucky to count on many years of friendship with Todd Honma and Robb Hernández.

I am profoundly grateful to a network of mentors, scholars, and educators who have written letters in support of my work, offered encouragement, and provided guidance at critical junctures. This includes George Lipsitz, whose encyclopedic knowledge on a range of topics I have often relied upon and who has indulged me in many conversations on music, politics, housing, policy, and architecture with great enthusiasm. Luis Alvarez has been a cherished source of support throughout the years. It has been my good fortune to know Vicki L. Ruiz, who has been not only a generous advocate over the years but also a source of inspiration to me and to so many in our field as a pioneering Latina historian in a profession that has not always welcomed Latinas. My first steps in higher education were taken at a community college. At West Los Angeles College, I am thankful to my former professors Fran Leonard and Ron Wilkins, who each in their own way introduced the stakes of a college education to a campus of first-generation, working-class Black and Latinx students through their pedagogical brilliance and commitment to lifting up the most marginalized. Even with these inspirational guides, I would have never thought it possible that I could matriculate at a school like UCLA, until one day, Alfred Herrera came around and asked, "Why not?" He made me believe it. Thank you, Alfred.

While no foundation, endowment, or residency supported the research of this book, early phases of this research would not have been possible without the compensation provided by fellowships and institutions between my transition from graduate school to newly minted assistant professor. They include the Ann Plato Dissertation Fellowship at Trinity College (Hartford, CT). At Trinity, colleagues could not have been more supportive, including Davarian L. Baldwin, Vijay Prashad, Cheryl Greenberg, Luis Figueroa-Martínez, Samanthi Gunawardana, and Jeff Bayliss. I benefited from having a short-term predoctoral research fellowship at the Smithsonian Institution's National Museum of American History, where I am thankful for having met L. Stephen Velasquez. A Chancellor's Research Fellowship at the University of Illinois at Urbana-Champaign came in handy as it got me from the East to the Midwest. From 2011 to 2013, I was fortunate to hold the Andrew W. Mellon Postdoctoral Fellowship in the Department of History and the Latina and Latino Studies Program at Northwestern University. There, the inimitable Ivy Wilson kindly organized a book proposal workshop for me where I received much valuable direction. Carl Smith weighed in and thankfully introduced me to Tim Mennel, for which I'm forever grateful. I am thankful to the Friends of the Princeton University Library for a short-term Library Research Grant in the summer of 2013. In 2013 through 2014, I held a UC Chancellor's Postdoctoral Fellowship at UC San Diego, under the tutelage of both David Gutiérrez and Luis Alvarez, where I was offered valuable scholarly input at an early stage of this project.

My time at the University of Notre Dame was rewarding for the brilliant and passionate students I was fortunate enough to teach. Students in my History of American Gentrification seminars in the fall of 2015 and 2017 energized me with their inquisitive spirit and sense of justice, as did students in my survey courses on the History of Latinx Chicago, during the spring semesters of 2015, 2016, and 2018, where classrooms full of Chicagoans and Midwesterners reminded me weekly about the relevance and stakes of the history recounted in this book. I am grateful for a small research grant from the Institute for Scholarship in the Liberal Arts that allowed me to fund a manuscript workshop during the spring of 2016. Two brilliant and accomplished historians, Natalia Molina and Andrew Friedman, read the entire book manuscript and gave me poignant feedback, and I am immensely grateful to them. Laly Maldonado and Maribel Rodriguez merit recognition for helping me put the workshop together and for being the kindest people on campus. Jason Ruiz sustained me with friendship, counsel, and laughter. Many thanks to my colleagues at New York University who helped foster a creative and interdisciplinary environment from which to write and teach. Walks through Greenwich Village and the rest of the city added to my perspective on the politics of boundary making while thinking and writing about Chicago city streets and neighborhoods.

I have been extraordinarily fortunate to have landed in the Department of History at Georgetown as this book reaches its publication date, and I thank my new colleagues for welcoming me and offering their unflinching support. Thanks as well to the administrative support of Amy Chidester as this book went into production and to the copyright advice supplied by Meg Oakley. I am grateful to the Institute for Citizens & Scholars.

I would like to acknowledge Timothy Mennel of the University of Chicago Press for his enthusiasm for this project in its earliest stages, and I thank him for his patience, incredible support, and dedication. I am also appreciative of the patience and expertise of the Historical Studies of Urban America series editors, which include Lilia Fernández, Tim Gilfoyle, and Amanda Seligman. Two anonymous reviewers engaged this manuscript with invaluable insights and clear direction. Their feedback greatly improved this book, and I am grateful to them. I also thank the production team at the press, and especially Susannah Engstrom, for turning this manuscript into a tangible book. For the terrific maps, I thank Don Larson and Rob McCaleb at Mapping Specialists as well as Geoffrey Wallace.

I am grateful beyond words to Anitra Grisales for her editing magic. She read every word of this book at various stages and, with her meticulous eye, helped bring clarity to my arguments and analysis. Daniel Loza also read every chapter of this book, taking time from his busy schedule to ensure that my grammar was never compromised by academic nomenclature. I am forever grateful to Natasha Zaretsky for lending me her critical eye and editorial skills on portions of the manuscript. Sarah Wald gave me sage advice when I needed it the most.

For their friendship and support, I thank David Naylamp Jimenez, Martin Sorrondeguy, Armando Reyes and the Reyes and Munguia families of Chicago, Lourdes Jasso, Lupe Garza-Martinez, Jackie Rodriguez Vega, Elizabeth Gallo, Christian Gutierrez, Tito Garcia, Juan Diego Alvarez, Omar Amador, Raymon Ruiz, and Rene Aguilar.

I dedicate this work to the memory of my parents, Lourdes Amezcua Franco and Manuel Isaac Rodriguez, hardworking immigrants and community makers, who with few resources still gave everything to my sister and me. I cherish the upbringing and support they gave us. I am also grateful to my supportive family, both immediate and extended, which includes my sister Patty, my sisters Alma and Adriana and their families, and my brother Jesse and his family; my tias, tios, primas, primos, nieces, nephews, and godchildren who are dispersed throughout the West Coast and Southwest and Mexico; the Amezcua family of California and Michoacán; the Isaac and Ysaac families of Southern California, Juárez, and El Paso; and the Rivas family of Los Angeles. In Chicago, I've acquired more family. The Loza family has been so incredibly supportive, especially Pedro, Marcellina, Juan, and Rosalba. I have appreciated the support of the Peña, Villalba, Loera, and Soto families, including Juan Soto, Benjamin Perez, and Leon Schnayer.

Finally, I want to acknowledge my partner, Mireya Loza. Like no one else, she has lived with this book project for far too long, reading more versions than anyone should ever have to. She has been my interlocutor, my supporter, and my joy.

ABBREVIATIONS

ACLU-IL   American Civil Liberties Union Illinois Division Records, Hanna Holborn Gray Special Collections Research Center, University of Chicago Library

ACRC   American Catholic Research Center and University Archives, Catholic University of America, Washington, DC

BYCC   Back of the Yards Community Collection, Harold Washington Library Center, Chicago, IL

BYNC   Back of the Yards Neighborhood Council Records, Special Collections and University Archives, University of Illinois at Chicago

CA   Claretian Archives, Chicago, IL

CAP   Chicago Area Project Records, Chicago History Museum

CCRJ   Cook County Retired Judges Oral History Collection, Archives and Special Collections, Loyola University Chicago

CFPC   Collections on the Foreign Population of Chicago, Chicago History Museum

CHM   Chicago History Museum

CRDP   Civil Rights Documentation Project, Moorland-Spingarn Research Center, Howard University, Washington, DC

CTS   Chicago Theological Seminary Special Collections

DPU   DePaul University Special Collections and Archives, Chicago, IL

DRSP   Department of Research and Survey Papers, Special Collections, Chicago Theological Seminary

DSB   David S. Broder Papers, Manuscript Division, Library of Congress, Washington, DC

ESF   Emil Schwarzhaupt Foundation Records, Hanna Holborn Gray Special Collections Research Center, University of Chicago Library

FFA   Field Foundation Archives, Dolph Briscoe Center for American History, University of Texas at Austin

FSC   Florence Scala Collection, Special Collections and University Archives, University of Illinois at Chicago

GCP   Gilberto Cárdenas Papers, University of Notre Dame Archives, Notre Dame, IN

GISP   George I. Sánchez Papers, Nettie Lee Benson Latin American Collection, General Libraries, University of Texas at Austin .

HHOH   Hull-House Oral History Collection, Special Collections and University Archives, University of Illinois at Chicago

HHP   Herbert Hill Papers, Manuscript Division, Library of Congress, Washington, DC

HU   Howard University, Moorland-Spingarn Research Center, Washington, DC

HWLC   Municipal Reference Library, Harold Washington Library Center, Chicago, IL

IAF   Industrial Areas Foundation Records, Special Collections and University Archives, University of Illinois at Chicago

ICUIS   Institute on the Church in an Urban-Industrial Society Records, Special Collections and University Archives, University of Illinois at Chicago

IPLR   Immigrants' Protective League Records, Special Collections and University Archives, University of Illinois at Chicago

JBM   John Bartlow Martin Papers, Manuscript Division, Library of Congress, Washington, DC

JCL   Jimmy Carter Presidential Library, Atlanta, GA

JJE   John J. Egan Papers, University of Notre Dame Archives, Notre Dame, IN

JSP   Julian Samora Papers, Michigan State University Archives and Historical Collections, East Lansing, MI

KFYA   Kautz Family YMCA Archives, Migrations and Social Services Collections, University of Minnesota Libraries, Minneapolis, MN

LCCC   Lawndale-Crawford Community Collection, Harold Washington Library Center, Chicago, IL

LOC   Library of Congress, Washington, DC

LUC   Loyola University Chicago, Archives and Special Collections

MBP   Martin Bickham Papers, Special Collections and University Archives, University of Illinois at Chicago

MCCSC Mexican Community Committee of South Chicago Records, Special Collections and University Archives, University of Illinois at Chicago

MCPFB Midwest Committee for Protection of Foreign Born Records, Chicago History Museum

MMP Mildred Mead Photographs, Hanna Holborn Gray Special Collections Research Center, University of Chicago Library

MMS Mary McDowell Settlement Records, Chicago History Museum

MSU Michigan State University Archives and Historical Collections, East Lansing, MI

NARA-CH National Archives at Chicago

NFSNC National Federation of Settlements and Neighborhood Centers, Social Welfare History Archives, University of Minnesota Libraries, Minneapolis, MN

OHRO Oral History Research Office, Columbia University, New York, NY

RAS Reuben A. Sheares II Papers, Amistad Research Center, New Orleans, LA

RJD Richard J. Daley Collection, Special Collections and University Archives, University of Illinois at Chicago

SWHA Social Welfare History Archives, Archives and Special Collections, University of Minnesota Libraries, Minneapolis, MN

TFP Teresa Fraga Papers, DePaul University Special Collections and Archives, Chicago, IL

UCL Hanna Holborn Gray Special Collections Research Center, University of Chicago Library

UCSL University of Chicago Service League Records, Hanna Holborn Gray Special Collections Research Center, University of Chicago Library

UIC Special Collections and University Archives, Richard J. Daley Library, University of Illinois at Chicago

UMN University of Minnesota Libraries' Department of Archives and Special Collections, Minneapolis, MN

UNDA University of Notre Dame Archives, Notre Dame, IN

USWPA U.S. Work Projects Administration Records, Manuscript Division, Library of Congress, Washington, DC

WCMC Welfare Council of Metropolitan Chicago Records, Chicago History Museum

NOTES

Chapter One

1. *United States v. Anita Villarreal* (1957), 57 CR 315, US District Court for the Northern District of Illinois, Eastern Division; Records of the District Courts of the United States, Record Group 21, National Archives at Chicago (NARA-CH).

2. James Janega, "Anita Villarreal, 86," *Chicago Tribune*, July 29, 2001, https://www.chicagotribune.com/news/ct-xpm-2001-07-29-0107290202-story.html.

3. James McPharlin, "Study of the Mexican-American Population of Chicago by the Catholic Charities," 1955, p. 9, box 373, folder 4, Welfare Council of Metropolitan Chicago Records (WCMC), Chicago History Museum (CHM).

4. *United States v. Anita Villarreal* (1957).

5. "Hispanic Population and Origin in Select U.S. Metropolitan Areas, 2014," Rankings by Hispanic Origin Population, Pew Research Center: Hispanic Trends, September 6, 2016, https://www.pewresearch.org/hispanic/interactives/hispanic-population-in-select-u-s-metropolitan-areas.

6. William Cronon, *Nature's Metropolis: Chicago and the Great West* (New York: Norton, 1992); Ann Durkin Keating, *Rising Up from Indian Country: The Battle of Fort Dearborn and the Birth of Chicago* (Chicago: University of Chicago Press, 2012); St. Clair Drake and Horace R. Cayton, *Black Metropolis: A Study of Negro Life in a Northern City* (New York: Harcourt, Brace, 1945); Christopher Robert Reed, *Black Chicago's First Century: 1833–1900* (Columbia: University of Missouri Press, 2017); Matthew Frye Jacobson, *Whiteness of a Different Color: European Immigrants and the Alchemy of Race* (Cambridge, MA: Harvard University Press, 1999).

7. James R. Barrett, *The Irish Way: Becoming American in the Multiethnic City* (New York: Penguin, 2012); Drake and Cayton, *Black Metropolis*; Natalia Molina, *How Race Is Made in America: Immigration, Citizenship, and the Historical Power of Racial Scripts* (Berkeley: University of California Press, 2014); Gilbert G. González and Raul A. Fernandez, *A Century of Chicano History: Empire, Nations, and Migration* (New York: Routledge, 2003); Juan González, *Harvest of Empire: The Untold Story of Latinos in America* (New York: Penguin Random House, 2011); Lilia Fernández, *Brown in the*

Windy City: Mexicans and Puerto Ricans in Postwar Chicago (Chicago: University of Chicago Press, 2012).

8. Louise Año Nuevo Kerr, "The Chicano Experience in Chicago, 1920–1970" (PhD diss., University of Illinois at Chicago Circle, 1976); Gabriela F. Arredondo, *Mexican Chicago: Race, Identity, and Nation, 1916–39* (Urbana: University of Illinois Press, 2008); Michael Innis-Jiménez, *Steel Barrio: The Great Mexican Migration to South Chicago, 1915–1940* (New York: New York University Press, 2013).

9. Molina, *How Race Is Made.*

10. David R. Roediger, *Working toward Whiteness: How America's Immigrants Became White; The Strange Journey from Ellis Island to the Suburbs* (New York: Basic Books, 2018); Lizabeth Cohen, *Making a New Deal: Industrial Workers in Chicago, 1919–1939* (New York: Cambridge University Press, 1991, 2008).

11. On the racialization of Mexicans through law and social practice, see Laura E. Gómez, *Manifest Destinies: The Making of the Mexican American Race* (New York: New York University Press, 2008); Arredondo, *Mexican Chicago*; Molina, *How Race Is Made*; and Gabriela González, *Redeeming La Raza: Transborder Modernity, Race, Respectability, and Rights* (New York: Oxford University Press, 2018). On arguments made by pro-immigrant antirestrictionists about the racial superiority of European immigrants over Mexicans, see Gary Gerstle, *American Crucible: Race and Nation in the Twentieth Century* (Princeton, NJ: Princeton University Press, 2002), 121–22.

12. For influential works on the postwar urban crisis, see Arnold R. Hirsch, *Making the Second Ghetto: Race and Housing in Chicago 1940–1960* (Cambridge: Cambridge University Press, 1985; Chicago: University of Chicago Press, 1998); Thomas J. Sugrue, *The Origins of the Urban Crisis: Race and Inequality in Postwar Detroit* (Princeton, NJ: Princeton University Press, 1996); Becky M. Nicolaides, *My Blue Heaven: Life and Politics in the Working-Class Suburbs of Los Angeles, 1920–1965* (Chicago: University of Chicago Press, 2002); Robert O. Self, *American Babylon: Race and the Struggle for Postwar Oakland* (Princeton, NJ: Princeton University Press, 2003); Amanda I. Seligman, *Block by Block: Neighborhoods and Public Policy on Chicago's West Side* (Chicago: University of Chicago Press, 2005); Kevin M. Kruse, *White Flight: Atlanta and the Making of Modern Conservatism* (Princeton, NJ: Princeton University Press, 2005); and Beryl Satter, *Family Properties: How the Struggle Over Race and Real Estate Transformed Chicago and Urban America* (New York: Picador, 2009).

13. There is a broader body of scholarship that recenters Latinx people in the postwar central city. Some notable works are: Carmen Teresa Whalen, *From Puerto Rico to Philadelphia: Puerto Rican Workers and Postwar Economies* (Philadelphia: Temple University Press, 2001); Eric Avila, *Popular Culture in the Age of White Flight: Fear and Fantasy in Suburban Los Angeles* (Berkeley: University of California Press, 2004); Jesse Hoffnung-Garskof, *A Tale of Two Cities: Santo Domingo and New York after 1950* (Princeton, NJ: Princeton University Press, 2007); Daniel Martinez HoSang, *Racial Propositions: Ballot Initiatives and the Making of Postwar California* (Berkeley: University of California Press, 2010); Lorrin Thomas, *Puerto Rican Citizen: History and Political Identity in Twentieth-Century New York City* (Chicago: University of Chicago Press, 2010);

Monica Perales, *Smeltertown: Making and Remembering a Southwest Border Community* (Chapel Hill: University of North Carolina Press, 2010); Marc S. Rodriguez, *The Tejano Diaspora: Mexican Americanism and Ethnic Politics in Texas and Wisconsin* (Chapel Hill: University of North Carolina Press, 2011); Fernández, *Windy City*; Eric Avila, *The Folklore of the Freeway: Race and Revolt in the Modernist City* (Minneapolis: University of Minnesota Press, 2014); Sonia Song-Ha Lee, *Building a Latino Civil Rights Movement: Puerto Ricans, African Americans, and the Pursuit of Racial Justice in New York City* (Chapel Hill: University of North Carolina Press, 2014); Tomás F. Summers Sandoval Jr., *Latinos at the Golden Gate: Creating Community & Identity in San Francisco* (Chapel Hill: University of North Carolina Press, 2016); and Llana Barber, *Latino City: Immigration and Urban Crisis in Lawrence, Massachusetts, 1945–2000* (Chapel Hill: University of North Carolina Press, 2017).

14. The scholarship on white flight, particularly on white propertied politics, is considerable and offers wide-ranging explanations for why whites left the central city and nearby suburbs. Some notable examples are Lisa McGirr, *Suburban Warriors: The Origins of the New American Right* (Princeton, NJ: Princeton University Press, 2001); Nicolaides, *My Blue Heaven*; Seligman, *Block by Block*; Kruse, *White Flight*; Matthew D. Lassiter, *The Silent Majority: Suburban Politics in the Sunbelt South* (Princeton, NJ: Princeton University Press, 2006); and David M. P. Freund, *Colored Property: State Policy & White Racial Politics in Suburban America* (Chicago: University of Chicago Press, 2007). The scholarship on white flight as a response to multiethnic/multiracial settlement (versus strictly in relation to Black Americans) is more sparing and primarily in the social sciences. Some notable examples are Leland T. Saito, *Race and Politics: Asian Americans, Latinos, and Whites in a Los Angeles Suburb* (Urbana: University of Illinois Press, 1998); Wendy Cheng, *The Changs Next Door to the Díazes: Remapping Race in Suburban California* (Minneapolis: University of Minnesota Press, 2013); and Richard Alba and Nancy Foner, *Strangers No More: Immigration and the Challenges of Integration in North America and Western Europe* (Princeton, NJ: Princeton University Press, 2015).

15. Historian Natalia Mehlman Petrzela provides a poignant criticism that the "role of Latinos in the 'rise of the Right,'" has been "overlooked by historians of both Latinos and of conservatism"; see Petrzela, *Classroom Wars: Language, Sex, and the Making of Modern Political Culture* (New York: Oxford University Press, 2015), 3; Mike Amezcua, "A Machine in the Barrio: Chicago's Conservative Colonia and the Remaking of Latino Politics in the 1960s and 1970s," *The Sixties: A Journal of History, Politics and Culture* 12, no. 1 (Summer 2019): 95–120.

16. See Hirsch, *Making the Second Ghetto*; Ronald P. Formisano, *Boston against Busing: Race, Class, and Ethnicity in the 1960s and 1970s* (Chapel Hill: University of North Carolina Press, 1991); Sugrue, *Urban Crisis*; Self, *American Babylon*; Kenneth D. Durr, *Behind the Backlash: White Working-Class Politics in Baltimore, 1940–1980* (Chapel Hill: University of North Carolina Press, 2003); and Timothy J. Lombardo, *Blue-Collar Conservatism: Frank Rizzo's Philadelphia and Populist Politics* (Philadelphia: University of Pennsylvania Press, 2018).

17. More scholarship is needed to unpack the historical roots of anti-Mexican

immigration restrictionists in the development of modern conservatism and the rise of the Far Right. Somewhat bracketed discussions appear in David H. Bennett, *The Party of Fear: The American Far Right from Nativism to the Militia* (New York: Vintage, 1995); Juan F. Perea, *Immigrants Out! The New Nativism and the Anti-Immigrant Impulse in the United States* (New York: New York University Press, 1997); Andrew Wroe, *The Republican Party and Immigration Politics: From Proposition 187 to George W. Bush* (New York: Palgrave, 2008); and Ronald P. Formisano, *The Tea Party: A Brief History* (Baltimore: Johns Hopkins University Press, 2012), 113. Elizabeth Tandy Shermer shows how a key progenitor of modern conservatism, Barry Goldwater, campaigned for Mexican American support in the 1950s and had not yet adopted the anti-Mexican immigration politics already incubating within the GOP; see Shermer, "Origins of the Conservative Ascendancy: Barry Goldwater's Early Senate Career and the De-legitimization of Organized Labor," *Journal of American History* 95, no. 3 (December 2008): 678–709.

18. I borrow my definition of the "Global South" from historian Paul Ortiz, who uses it to refer to "the formerly colonized nations in Latin America, the Caribbean, Africa, and Asia, as well as the Middle East." However, I expand this to include the struggles of colonization and imperialism that are carried forward through migration into and within the United States and inform a sense of politics. See Paul Ortiz, *An African American and Latinx History of the United States* (Boston: Beacon, 2018), 197.

19. My use of "structure of feeling" as an interpretive framework is influenced by Linda Gordon's use of Raymond Williams's concept to describe how feelings contribute to the creation and maintenance of structures and relationships. See Gordon, *The Second Coming of the KKK: The Ku Klux Klan of the 1920s and the American Political Tradition* (New York: W. W. Norton, 2017), chap. 3; and Raymond Williams, *Marxism and Literature* (New York: Oxford University Press, 1977), 132–33.

20. Homer Hoyt, *One Hundred Years of Land Values in Chicago: The Relationship of the Growth of Chicago to the Rise in its Land Values, 1830–1933* (Chicago: University of Chicago Press, 1933), 314–17.

21. Hoyt, *One Hundred Years of Land Values in Chicago*, 314–17; Joseph C. Bigott, *From Cottage to Bungalow: Houses and the Working Class in Metropolitan Chicago, 1869–1929* (Chicago: University of Chicago Press, 2001), 149–52; Elaine Lewinnek, *The Working Man's Reward: Chicago's Early Suburbs and the Roots of American Sprawl* (New York: Oxford University Press, 2014), 11, 136–39, 150; Ocean Howell, *Making the Mission: Planning and Ethnicity in San Francisco* (Chicago: University of Chicago Press, 2015), 154–56.

22. On the role of real estate speculators and statist instruments to build and uphold Northern Jim Crow, see Beryl Satter, *Family Properties*; and Hirsch, *Making the Second Ghetto*.

23. Joseph M. Swing, oral history transcript, Reminiscences of Joseph Swing: Oral History, 1967, Oral History Research Office (OHRO), Columbia University.

24. For similar developments in the US Southwest, see Juan Ramon García, *Operation Wetback: The Mass Deportation of Mexican Undocumented Workers in 1954* (Westport, CT: Greenwood, 1980); Kelly Lytle Hernández, "The Crimes and Consequences of

Illegal Immigration: A Cross-Border Examination of Operation Wetback, 1943 to 1954," *Western Historical Quarterly* 37, no. 4 (Winter 2006): 421–44; S. Deborah Kang, *The INS on the Line: Making Immigration Law on the US-Mexico Border, 1947–1954* (New York: Oxford University Press, 2017), 139–67; and Molina, *How Race Is Made*, 112–38. Operation Wetback in Chicago is discussed in Fernández, *Windy City*, 54–55, 60, 86.

25. Mae M. Ngai, *Impossible Subjects: Illegal Aliens and the Making of Modern America* (Princeton, NJ: Princeton University Press, 2004).

26. Hirsch, *Making the Second Ghetto*; Seligman, *Block by Block*; Satter, *Family Properties*; Fernández, *Windy City*; N. D. B. Connolly, *A World More Concrete: Real Estate and the Remaking of Jim Crow South Florida* (Chicago: University of Chicago Press, 2014), 3–4.

27. Black Chicagoans engaged in multifaceted political organizing against the onslaught of attempts at Black containment not only in civic planning but also in education and policing; see Elizabeth Todd-Breland, *A Political Education: Black Politics and Education Reform in Chicago since the 1960s* (Chapel Hill: University of North Carolina Press, 2018); and Simon Balto, *Occupied Territory: Policing Black Chicago from Red Summer to Black Power* (Chapel Hill: University of North Carolina Press, 2019).

28. On Mexicans in public housing, see Fernández, *Windy City*, 98.

29. Seligman, *Block by Block*, 183–207.

30. Lassiter, *Silent Majority*, 1–2; Freund, *Colored Property*, chap. 1.

31. Hirsch, *Making the Second Ghetto*; Satter, *Family Properties*; Connolly, *World More Concrete*.

32. Satter, *Family Properties*; Connolly, introduction to *World More Concrete*.

33. These examples draw on the episodes of racial violence and retribution against Mexicans that I recount throughout the book.

34. Amanda I. Seligman, "But Burn—No: The Rest of the Crowd in Three Civil Disorders in 1960s Chicago," *Journal of Urban History* 37, no. 2 (2011): 230–55; Seligman, *Block by Block*, 210; Satter, *Family Properties*, 255, 259, 266–67; Fernández, *Windy City*, 218–19.

35. For more on planning regimes, see Howell, *Making the Mission*.

36. "The Pilsen Plan, Marketability Analysis: Proposed Residential Development, Pilsen Study Area, Chicago, Illinois, November 1969" (unpublished study prepared by Real Estate Research Corporation for the Chicago Department of Urban Renewal, November 1969); Robert Mier, Robert Giloth, and Thomas Amato, *The Housing Needs of Pilsen and Their Relationship to Rehabilitation Design* (Chicago: Center for Urban Economic Development, School of Urban Sciences, University of Illinois at Chicago Circle, 1978), 1–2.

37. Sue Sussman, "The Mexicans," *Chicago Magazine* 6, no. 3 (October 1969): 86; "The Pilsen Plan, Marketability Analysis."

38. On the continuation of land expropriation as the government's answer to housing racialized communities, see Connolly, *World More Concrete*; Samuel Zipp, *Manhattan Projects: The Rise and Fall of Urban Renewal in Cold War New York* (New York: Oxford University Press, 2010).

39. The use of the term *colonia* to describe Mexican enclaves in Chicago dates back to the 1920s and 1930s as well as the early studies of Anita Edgar Jones, Robert C. Jones, Louis R. Wilson, Robert Redfield, Elizabeth Hughes, Manuel Gamio, and Paul S. Taylor—scholars who participated, in one form or another, in the intellectual life of the University of Chicago's Department of Sociology.

40. Amezcua, "A Machine in the Barrio."

41. Tony Hernandez, "Publisher's Letter," *Fiesta* 1, no. 4 (January 1975), Gilberto Cárdenas Papers (GCP), Julian Samora Library, University of Notre Dame.

42. Hernandez, "Publisher's Letter."

43. Urban cultural nationalism also fueled pan-Latino unity between Mexican Americans and Puerto Ricans; see Fernández, *Windy City*, chap. 6; Felix M. Padilla, *Latino Ethnic Consciousness: The Case of Mexican Americans and Puerto Ricans in Chicago* (South Bend, IN: University of Notre Dame Press, 1985); David A. Badillo, "From La Lucha to Latino: Ethnic Change, Political Identity, and Civil Rights in Chicago," in ed. Gilberto Cárdenas, *La Causa: Civil Rights, Social Justice and the Struggle for Equality in the Midwest* (Houston, TX: Arte Público, 2004): 37–53. For more on the Chicana/o movement in Chicago, see Fernández, *Windy City*; Leonard G. Ramírez et al., *Chicanas of 18th Street: Narratives of a Movement from Latino Chicago* (Urbana: University of Illinois Press, 2011); and René Luis Alvarez, "A Community that Would Not Take 'No' for an Answer: Mexican Americans, the Chicago Public Schools, and the Founding of Benito Juárez High School," *Journal of Illinois History* 17 (Summer 2014): 78–98.

44. Anita Villarreal to Neil Hartigan, July 31, 1973 (courtesy of the Villarreal family, in author's possession).

45. Loretta Villarreal Long, interview with author, February 19, 2013, Chicago (courtesy of the Villarreal family, in author's possession).

Chapter Two

1. Invitation by Rubin Torres to residents, January 30, 1953, box 88, folder 10, Chicago Area Project Papers, Chicago History Museum (hereafter cited as CAP, CHM); Abner Green, "The McCarran-Walter Menace to the Mexican-Americans," *Daily Worker*, March 31, 1954, 5.

2. Hirsch, *Making the Second Ghetto*; Seligman, *Block by Block*; Fernández, *Windy City*; Paul B. Johnson, *Citizens Participation in Urban Renewal: The History of the Near West Side Planning Board and a Citizen Participation Project* (Chicago: Hull-House Association, 1960).

3. Tom Littlewood, "Mexicans are Chicago's Least Understood Group," *Chicago Sun-Times*, October 19, 1953.

4. Mike Amezcua, "Beautiful Urbanism: Gender, Landscape, and Contestation in Latino Chicago's Age of Urban Renewal," *Journal of American History* 104, no. 1 (June 2017): 97–119; Littlewood, "Chicago's Least Understood." On Latino settlement in the Near West Side, see Fernández, *Windy City*, chap. 2; "Se Organiza La Camara

Mexicana de Comercio," *Vida Latina*, December 1954, 25; "Wetback Cleanup Opens Here Friday," *Chicago American*, September 15, 1954, 1.

5. García, *Operation Wetback*; Lytle Hernández, "Crimes and Consequences"; Molina, *How Race Is Made*, 112–38; Johnson, *Citizens Participation*, 141, 380–85; Fernández, *Windy City*, 108–9.

6. Hull House Citizen Participation Project, *Our Neighbors and Urban Renewal*, Progress Report: September 1956–August 1957 (Chicago: Hull House Citizen Participation Project, Emil Schwarzhaupt Foundation, 1957); Johnson, *Citizens Participation*; Historian Amanda I. Seligman suggests there was a time when urban renewal was not automatically seen as "urban removal" and that central-area residents were hopeful that these state interventions would bring relief to their communities; see Seligman, *Block by Block*, chap. 3; George Rosen, *Decision-Making Chicago-Style: The Genesis of a University of Illinois Campus* (Urbana: University of Illinois Press, 1980), chaps. 5 and 6; Fernández, *Windy City*, chap. 3.

7. Mireya Loza, *Defiant Braceros: How Migrant Workers Fought for Racial, Sexual, and Political Freedom* (Chapel Hill: University of North Carolina Press, 2016).

8. Ngai, *Impossible Subjects*, 147.

9. Fernández, *Windy City*, chap. 1.

10. "Plot Smashed Here: 39 Smuggled Aliens Seized," *Chicago Sun-Times*, June 12, 1948, 1.

11. "Nip Plot to Smuggle 39 Aliens in City," *Chicago Sun-Times*, June 12, 1948, 3.

12. "39 Aliens Grilled in Entry Plot," *Chicago Sun-Times*, June 13, 1948, 4.

13. "40 Accused in Alien Case," *Chicago Sun-Times*, June 17, 1948, 19.

14. Arthur Bary and Pat Bell, "The Mexican-Americans: Their Plight and Struggles," *Political Affairs*, May 1949, 80.

15. Bary and Bell, "Mexican-Americans," 80.

16. John Bartlow Martin, notes from meeting with Martin Ortiz, Re: The Moretti Case, box 140, folder 4, John Bartlow Martin Papers (JBM), Manuscript Division, Library of Congress (LOC).

17. Michael Quintanilla, "The Guiding Light," *Los Angeles Times*, November 27, 1994, E1; John Bartlow Martin, draft notes for "The Moretti Case," p. 125, box 139, folder 5, JBM, LOC.

18. Martin, notes from Ortiz meeting.

19. Martin, notes from Ortiz meeting.

20. "Mexicans in the Chicago Area Study," 1957, box 12, folder 190, Industrial Areas Foundation Records (IAF), Special Collections and University Archives, University of Illinois at Chicago (UIC).

21. Martin, notes from Ortiz meeting.

22. Mexican American Council, "The Mexican American in Chicago: A Report Prepared by Martin Ortiz," December 1953, 3, box 88, folder 10, CAP, CHM.

23. Mexican American Council, "Mexican American in Chicago."

24. Elena Padilla, "The Puerto Rican Migrants in Chicago," in *Latino Urban Ethnography and the Work of Elena Padilla*, ed. Mérida M. Rúa (Urbana: University of Illinois Press, 2010), 92.

25. Morton Kondracke, *Saving Milly: Love, Politics, and Parkinson's Disease* (New York: Ballantine Books, 2002), 7–8; Larry Villarreal, interview with author, February 20, 2016.

26. Martin, notes from Ortiz meeting.

27. Martin, draft notes, 122–23.

28. Martin, 123.

29. Martin, 123–24.

30. Martin, 123–24.

31. Martin, 123–24.

32. I borrow the concept of "racialized foreignness" from Ngai, *Impossible Subjects*, 132.

33. "Truman Appoints Group to Study Migratory Labor," *Chicago Tribune*, June 4, 1950, 32; Fernández, *Windy City*, 39–40.

34. I. F. Stone, *The Haunted Fifties* (New York: Vintage Books, 1969), 34.

35. "House OKs Tough Anti-Wetback Law," *Chicago Sun-Times*, March 14, 1952, 26; García, *Operation Wetback*, 77.

36. Lytle Hernández, "Crimes and Consequences."

37. Louise Pettibone Smith, *Torch of Liberty: Twenty-Five Years in the Life of the Foreign Born in the U.S.A.* (New York: Dwight-King Publishers, 1959), 418–19.

38. Kelly Lytle Hernández, *Migra! A History of the U.S. Border Patrol* (Berkeley: University of California Press, 2010), 8–9.

39. Lytle Hernández indicates that this shift resulted from a "crisis of consent and control" for the INS; see *Migra!*, part 3; It was no longer an acceptable optic for some notable Mexican American leaders like Ernesto Galarza, a labor leader and anticommunist. See Stephen Pitti, "Chicano Cold Warriors: César Chávez, Mexican American Politics, and California Farmworkers" in *In from the Cold: Latin America's New Encounter with the Cold War*, ed. Gilbert M. Joseph and Daniela Spenser (Durham, NC: Duke University Press, 2008), 273–307.

40. David M. Reimers, *Still the Golden Door: The Third World Comes to America* (New York: Columbia University Press, 1992), 19–20; Ngai, *Impossible Subjects*, 237; Molina, *How Race Is Made*, 117.

41. Madeline Y. Hsu, *The Good Immigrants: How the Yellow Peril became the Model Minority* (Princeton, NJ: Princeton University Press, 2015), 157.

42. Sarah Sayad Paz, letter to *Chicago Sun-Times*, "Letters from Readers," March 14, 1952, box 3, folder 7, George. I. Sánchez Papers, Benson Latin American Collection, University of Texas at Austin (hereafter cited as GISP).

43. Sayad Paz, letter to *Chicago Sun-Times*.

44. Sayad Paz, letter to *Chicago Sun-Times*.

45. "Packinghouse CIO Defends Rights of Mexican Workers," *Daily Worker*, May 20, 1952, 8.

46. Sayad Paz, letter to *Chicago Sun-Times*.

47. By "Rockefeller barrio," I am referring to Nelson A. Rockefeller's project of Good Neighbor diplomacy to commit financial and symbolic support for Latino com-

munities in the United States through the Office of the Coordinator of Inter-American Affairs (OCIAA). See Selden Menefee, "Mexicans in the War," *Washington Post*, May 4, 1944, 8; see also Roland D. McCleary, "A Study of the Problems of a Mexican-American Community in Relation to Group Work Technique" (master's thesis, George Williams College, 1948), 13–14, box 31, Kautz Family YMCA Archives (KFYA), University of Minnesota Libraries (UMN), 118.

48. Alicia Schmidt Camacho, *Migrant Imaginaries: Latino Cultural Politics in the U.S.-Mexico Borderlands* (New York: New York University Press, 2008), 118.

49. Molina, *How Race Is Made*.

50. Rubin Torres, "Dear Friend," January 30, 1953, box 3, folder 7, GISP.

51. Based on a cursory examination of these cases found in the criminal docket records of the US District Court in Chicago, Record Group 21 (hereafter cited as RG 21), NARA-CH; "Indict 2 Brothers in Violation of Immigration Act," *Chicago Daily News*, March 11, 1953, 10.

52. "Pearl M. Hart 70th Birthday Volume," 16–17, box 9, folder 13, MCPFB, CHM.

53. Kondracke, *Saving Milly*, 6.

54. *Refugio Roman Martinez v. Andrew Jordan*, Brief of Plaintiff in Reply to Defendant's Reply Brief on Defendant's Motion to Dismiss Complaint, RG 21, NARA-CH.

55. Zaragosa Vargas, *Crucible of Struggle: A History of Mexican Americans from Colonia Times to the Present* (New York: Oxford University Press, 2011), 217.

56. Ngai, *Impossible Subjects*, 71.

57. On the Illinois repatriation numbers, Gabriela F. Arredondo cites Paul S. Taylor in Arredondo, *Mexican Chicago* (Urbana: University of Illinois Press, 2008), 97; Zaragosa Vargas presents a nationwide total in Vargas, *Crucible of Struggle*, 220. For more on Mexicans' experience in Chicago during the Great Depression, see Innis-Jiménez, *Steel Barrio*, chap. 7.

58. McCleary, "Study of the Problems."

59. Alfredo DeAvila, "A Mexican-American Steelworker," *Daily World*, August 5, 1982, 13.

60. DeAvila, "Mexican-American Steelworker," 13; see also Vargas, *Crucible of Struggle*, 214–15.

61. On various activities of El Frente Popular Mexicano, see Arredondo, *Mexican Chicago*, 136–37; Innis-Jiménez, *Steel Barrio*, 156–57; Schmidt Camacho, *Migrant Imaginaries*, 117.

62. DeAvila, "Mexican-American Steelworker," 13.

63. DeAvila, 13.

64. *Minorities in the UPWA: A History of Negroes and Mexican Americans in the Packing Industry* (Chicago: Anti-Discrimination Department, United Packinghouse Workers of America, 1951), box 106, folder, 3, Herbert Hill Papers (HHP), LOC; Leslie F. Orear, *Out of the Jungle: The Packinghouse Workers Fight for Justice and Equality* (Chicago: Hyde Park Press, 1968).

65. Proceedings of the First Wage and Policy Conference of the Packinghouse

Workers' Organizing Committee, February 19–21, 1943, p. 174, box 107, folder 1, HHP, LOC.

66. On the Latino and interracialist civil rights work by members of UPWA District 1, see McCleary "Study of the Problems," 120–25; "Packing Worker Victimized for Eleven Years by the Gov't," *Daily Worker*, February 1, 1952, 8; "Union Backs Ramirez," *District One Champion*, July 1957, 7; Julie Michaels, "Packing Union Defends Mexican Member in Deportation Threat, *The Worker*, February 23, 1958, 12.

67. "Packing Union Reports Victories in Fight on Bias," *Daily Worker*, May 30, 1952, 2; "New Methods of Serving CIO Packinghouse Workers," *Daily Worker*, January 23, 1955, 14; Rick Halpern, *Down on the Killing Floor: Black and White Workers in Chicago's Packinghouses, 1904–54* (Urbana: University of Illinois Press, 1997), chap. 7.

68. *Martinez v. Jordan*, Brief of Plaintiff; Ngai, *Impossible Subjects*, 89.

69. The Midwest Committee for Protection of the Foreign Born, with support from the UPWA, and his friends in the Mexican colonias of Chicago established a Martinez Defense Committee.

70. "Packing Worker Victimized," *Daily Worker*.

71. Littlewood, "Chicago's Least Understood."

72. "1932 Party Joiner Held Deportable," *Baltimore Sun*, January 13, 1953, 1. For more on Martinez's history of labor radicalism and persecution by the US government, see John H. Flores, *The Mexican Revolution in Chicago: Immigration Politics from the Early Twentieth Century to the Cold War* (Urbana: University of Illinois Press, 2018), chaps. 5 and 6.

73. "Packing Worker Victimized," *Daily Worker*.

74. Larry Villarreal, interview, 2016.

75. Natalia Molina, "The Importance of Place and Place-Makers in the Life of a Los Angeles Community: What Gentrification Erases from Echo Park," *Southern California Quarterly* 97, no. 1 (2015): 73.

76. Larry Villarreal, interview.

77. "Families Visit Doomed Men: Framed, They Say," *Chicago Tribune*, April 20, 1950, 4.

78. Edward Baumann, *May God Have Mercy on Your Soul* (New York: Bonus Books, 1993), 397–99.

79. Baumann, 397–99.

80. Baumann, 397–99.

81. "Packing Worker Victimized," *Daily Worker*.

82. Press release for Refugio Martinez Benefit Dance, September 27, 1952, Midwest Committee for Protection of Foreign Born, box 88, folder 11, CAP, CHM.

83. Refugio Roman Martinez to Clifford R. Shaw, April 14, 1951, box 88, folder 11, CAP, CHM.

84. Martinez to Shaw.

85. "Packing Worker Victimized," *Daily Worker*.

86. "12 Years of Justice Dep't Torment Ends in Death for Refugio Martinez," *Daily Worker*, May 24, 1953, 7.

87. "12 Years," *Daily Worker*.

88. McCleary, "Study of the Problems," 111–15.

89. García, *Operation Wetback*; Lytle Hernández, "Crimes and Consequences"; Molina, *How Race Is Made*, 112–38; Kang, *The INS on the Line*, chap. 6.

90. García, *Operation Wetback*, 224; Swing oral history transcript, 11.

91. "Communism: Beneath the Surface," *Newsweek*, September 27, 1954.

92. El Comité de Defensa de Distrito Uno, "La Política del Buen Vecino y La Oficina de Inmigracion," September 21, 1954, box 9, folder 3, MCPFB, CHM.

93. "Wetback Cleanup," *Chicago American*.

94. García, *Operation Wetback*, 169–71.

95. Kerr, "Chicano Experience," 158.

96. Swing oral history transcript, 11.

97. Littlewood, "Chicago's Least Understood."

98. "Plan Long Drive Against Wetbacks," *Chicago Daily News*, September 16, 1954, 7.

99. Members of a deportation "task force" were brought in from the southwest, see García, *Operation Wetback*, 224.

100. "'Wetback' Roundup in High Gear," *Chicago Daily News*, September 20, 1954, 17.

101. García, *Operation Wetback*, 224.

102. "Wetbacks Get Help in Returning," *Chicago Daily News*, August 2, 1954; "Here 33 Years, 'Wetback' Gives Up," *Chicago Daily News*, September 21, 1954, 8.

103. "Here 33 Years," *Chicago Daily News*.

104. "Wetback Cleanup," *Chicago American*.

105. US Department of Justice (hereafter cited as DOJ), *Annual Report of the Immigration and Naturalization Service for Fiscal Year Ended June 30, 1955* (Washington, DC: US Government Publishing Office, 1955), 14.

106. "Deport 1,547 Undesirable Aliens in '54," *Chicago Tribune*, January 3, 1955, 10.

107. DOJ, *Annual Report, 1955*, 14.

108. "50 Await Ouster as Wetbacks," *Chicago Daily News*, September 22, 1954, 6.

109. Nathan Caldwell Jr. to Josefina Yanéz, October 5, 1954, box 10, folder 8, MCPFB, CHM.

110. "4 Women Deported as 'Wetbacks,'" *Chicago Daily News*, September 27, 1954, 9.

111. El Comité de Defensa de Distrito Uno, "La Política."

112. "Jose E. Chapa interview by Juan Andrade, Jr.," in Andrade, "A Historical Survey of Mexican Immigration to the United States and an Oral History of the Mexican Settlement in Chicago 1920-1990" (PhD diss., Northern Illinois University, 1998), 281–82; Carolyn Eastwood, *Near West Side Stories: Struggles for Community in Chicago's Maxwell Street Neighborhood* (Chicago: Lake Claremont, 2002), 268.

113. "Arrests of Mexican Workers Violates Civil, Human Rights," *Illinois Worker*, October 3, 1954, 16.

114. El Comité de Defensa de Distrito Uno, "La Política"; "Protests Slow Roundup of Mexican Workers Here," *Illinois Worker*, October 10, 1954, 15.

115. Jorge Prieto, *Harvest of Hope: The Pilgrimage of a Mexican-American Physician* (Notre Dame, IN: University of Notre Dame Press, 1989), 75–76.

116. "Arrests," *Illinois Worker*.

117. "The Economy: Epitaph for a Slump," *Newsweek*, August 23, 1954, 63.

118. On the beginnings of deindustrialization at the end of World War II see Nelson Lichtenstein, *State of the Union: A Century of American Labor, Revised and Expanded Edition* (Princeton, NJ: Princeton University Press, 2013), 114; Jefferson Cowie, *Capital Moves: RCA's Seventy-Year Quest for Cheap Labor* (New York: New Press, 2001); Jefferson Cowie and Joseph Heathcott, *Beyond the Ruins: The Meanings of Deindustrialization* (Ithaca, NY: ILR Press of Cornell University Press, 2003).

119. Dominic A. Pacyga, *Chicago: A Biography* (Chicago: University of Chicago Press, 2011), 316–21.

120. Anticommunist witch hunts and antitrade unionist drives led to the incarceration of many Black and Latino workers; see "Here's What to Expect When You Visit Claude," *Illinois Worker*, August 5, 1954, 1. The Midwest Committee for Protection of Foreign Born believed that the Chicago police were increasingly targeting African Americans and Latinos, especially those engaged in labor radicalism, most likely a perspective they gained while visiting those jailed in the Cook County Jail. See "Arrests," *Illinois Worker*. For more on Black communists (or those suspected to be communists) as targets of the police, see Balto, *Occupied Territory*, 79.

121. "Wetback Cleanup," *Chicago American*.

122. "Keep Closed Plants Ready for War Need," *Chicago Tribune*, May 31, 1945.

123. *U.S. Government Surplus, D-Illinois-480, Air Force Plant No. 52 (Formerly Studebaker Plant) Chicago, IL* (Chicago: General Services Administration), box 378, Chicago Real Property Inventory, NARA-CH.

124. DOJ, *Annual Report of the Immigration and Naturalization Service for Fiscal Year Ended June 30, 1954* (Washington, DC: US Government Publishing Office, 1954), 36.

125. DOJ, *Annual Report 1954*, 36.

126. *U.S. Government Surplus, D-Illinois-480*.

127. "4th Plane Leaves with 'Wetbacks,'" *Chicago Daily News*, September 24, 1954, 11.

128. *U.S. Government Surplus, D-Illinois-480*.

129. "Communism," *Newsweek*.

130. DOJ, *Annual Report, 1954*, 1.

131. "Communism," *Newsweek*.

132. The *Chicago Tribune* reported the widest range in "an estimated 25,000 to 40,000 'wetbacks,'" in "Federal Drive on 'Wetbacks' to Center Here," *Chicago Tribune*, July 31, 1954.

133. "Wetback Cleanup," *Chicago American*.

134. "50 Await Ouster," *Chicago Daily News*, 6.

135. *U.S. Government Surplus, D-Illinois-480.*

136. "Wetback Cleanup," *Chicago American*; Garcia, *Operation Wetback*, 224.

137. El Comité de Defensa de Distrito Uno, "La Política."

138. Caldwell Jr. to Yanéz.

139. *U.S. Government Surplus, D-Illinois-480.*

140. "4th Plane Leaves," *Chicago Daily News.*

141. The twenty-four-hour turnaround time was reported in "Arrests," *Illinois Worker.*

142. "Wetback Cleanup," *Chicago American.*

143. DOJ, *Annual Report, 1955*, 20; Garcia, *Operation Wetback*, 224.

144. Smith, *Torch of Liberty*, 422.

145. "Here 33 Years," *Chicago Daily News*; "4th Plane Leaves,'" *Chicago Daily News.*

146. "Nab 70 More in Roundup of Wetbacks," *Chicago Daily News*, September 30, 1954, 5.

147. "Here 33 Years," *Chicago Daily News*; Fernández, *Windy City*, 54–55.

148. Note from Pearl M. Hart to Nathan Caldwell Jr., Re: "Here is competition," September 17, 1954, box 10, folder 8, MCPFB, CHM.

149. MCPFB believed Sahli delayed the raids to ensure the crops in Midwestern farms were picked first before he disrupted the workforce farms relied on.

150. Nathan Caldwell Jr. to Rose Chernin, September 20, 1954, box 10, folder 8, MCPFB, CHM.

151. Nathan Caldwell Jr. to Esther Shandler, Esq., October 5, 1954, box 10, folder 8, MCPFB, CHM.

152. In Los Angeles, as Natalia Molina explains, "the decision to site the detention center in Elysian Park reflected a general awareness of the city as segregated both conceptually and geographically." Molina, *How Race Is Made*, 115.

153. "Arrests," *Illinois Worker*; El Comité de Defensa de Distrito Uno, "La Política"; the *Illinois Worker* argued that use of the Studebaker as a detention site was partly linked to rising unemployment. "Protests Slow," *Illinois Worker.*

154. Smith, *Torch of Liberty*, 288.

155. "Protests Slow," *Illinois Worker.*

156. Fernández, *Windy City*, 55.

157. Even the more politically reserved MAC was denied funding and was instructed to focus solely on "the problems of juvenile delinquency"; see memo from Romana R. Fierro to MAC board and members, July 1, 1955, Re: "The Chicago Area Project was unable to help the MAC financially," box 88, folder 10, CAP, CHM.

158. "En El V Aniversario de la Muerte de Refugio Roman Martinez" (On the fifth anniversary of the death of Refugio Roman Martinez), May 7, 1958, box 7, folder 13, MCPFB, CHM.

159. Pearl M. Hart notes in box 10, folder 8, MCPFB, CHM; "Protests Slow," *Illinois Worker.*

160. "Plan Trial for Balky Wetback," *Chicago Daily News*, September 23, 1954, 14;

"They must pay their own fare," declared INS District Director Walter Sahli in "Wetback Roundup Delayed," *Chicago Daily News*, September 17, 1954, 3.

161. "Deport 1,547," *Chicago Tribune*.

162. Smith, *Torch of Liberty*, 423.

163. Smith, 423; *Our Badge of Infamy: A Petition to the United Nations on the Treatment of the Mexican Immigrant* (New York: American Committee for Protection of the Foreign Born, April 1959).

164. Martin, draft notes, 123.

165. For a history of the Chicago Land Clearance Commission, see Hirsch, *Making the Second Ghetto*, chap. 4; Chicago Plan Commission, *A Study of Blighted Vacant Land Prepared for the Chicago Land Clearance Commission* (Chicago: City of Chicago, 1950).

166. Chicago Land Clearance Commission, "Dear Tenant . . . ," circular, 1954, box 3, folder 69, Florence Scala Collection (hereafter FSC), UIC.

167. "City Rushes Program to Qualify for U.S. Slum Clearance Funds," *Chicago Sun-Times*, September 21, 1954, 14; On how the city developed legislative tools for slum clearance, conservation, and urban renewal see Seligman, *Block by Block*, chap. 3; see also Hirsch, *Making the Second Ghetto*, chaps. 4 and 5.

168. Hy Delman and Walter Sutherland, "Here's Report on Congress Expressway," *Chicago American*, September 16, 1954, 3, 25; Fernández, *Windy City*, 106–7.

169. "New Frontier for Pioneer Spirits," *West Side Times*, January 26, 1949, Report of the Introductory meeting of TOC, box 222, folder 293, Hull House, NFSNC, SWHA, UMN.

170. Fernández, *Windy City*, 105.

171. Johnson, *Citizens Participation*, 91–93.

172. Johnson, 73–76.

173. Johnson, 81.

174. Janet P. Murray, "Long Range Plans: A Study of Present Program with Special Attention to the Future," 23, report for Hull-House Association (November 1959), box 62, folder 1, Hull House, NFSNC, SWHA, UMN.

175. Johnson, *Citizens Participation*, 89–90. In 1958, when the urban renewal program began in earnest, the land clearance area was 55 acres, and the conservation area was 237 acres. See Frank X. Taglia to Congress, March 28, 1958, box 61, folder 18, Hull House, NFSNC, SWHA, UMN.

176. Mexican American Council of Chicago, "Fact Sheet on Mexican-Americans in Chicago," 1949, box 151, folder 1215, Martin Bickham Papers (MBP), UIC.

177. Johnson, *Citizens Participation*, 398.

178. Lorene M. Pacey, "The Hull-House Role in Urban Redevelopment," 1956, 7–8, box 61, folder 17, Hull House, NFSNC, SWHA, UMN; Memorandum from Nicholas Von Hoffman to Saul D. Alinsky, March 26, 1958, box 37, folder 601, IAF, UIC.

179. Kondracke, *Saving Milly*, 8–9; Loretta Villarreal Long, interview with author, February 16, 2016.

180. Michaels, "Packing Union."

181. Green, "McCarran-Walter Menace," 5; "UPWA Rep Attacked," *District One Champion*, July 1957, 7; "Exile Decree Causes Death of Mexican-American Worker," *Daily Worker*, May 15, 1953, 6; Villarreal Long, interview, 2016; Larry Villarreal, interview, 2016.

182. Johnson, *Citizens Participation*, 288.

183. Perry J. Miranda, report, 1956, box 88, folder 10, CAP, CHM.

184. Thomas A. Guglielmo, *White on Arrival: Italians, Race, Color, and Power in Chicago, 1890-1945* (New York: Oxford University Press, 2004).

185. Murray, "Long Range Plans," 21.

186. Frank X. Paz, "Mexican-Americans in Chicago: A General Survey," January 1948, 6, box 147, folder 4, WCMC, CHM.

187. Hull House Citizen Participation Project, *Our Neighbors*, 20.

188. Hull House Citizen Participation Project, 20.

189. Alvin H. Eichholz, "A Proposal for a Special Type Business and Cultural Area in a Chicago Land Clearance Commission Project," 1958, 10, box 61, folder 18, Hull House, NFSNC, SWHA, UMN.

190. Pacey, "Hull-House Role."

191. Alvin H. Eichholz to Fern M. Colborn, July 11, 1958, box 61, folder 18, Hull House, NFSNC, SWHA, UMN.

192. Hull House Citizen Participation Project, *Our Neighbors*, 10–14.

193. Murray, "Long Range Plans," 17.

194. Fernández, *Windy City*, 108.

195. Department of City Planning, *Development Plan for the Central Area of Chicago: A Definitive Text for Use with Graphic Presentation* (Chicago: Dept. of City Planning, August 1958), 31.

196. Johnson, *Citizens Participation*, 296–97; This attitude was also reflected in the Community Conservation Board. See Community Conservation Board, *Near West Side Structure Survey* (May 1957), 5.

197. Marge Lyon, "Marge Finds You Can Go 'South of the Border' by Staying in Chicago," *Chicago Tribune*, March 23, 1952, E4.

198. Johnson, *Citizens Participation*, 297.

199. Johnson, 304.

200. Harrison-Halsted was officially designated as an urban renewal project on October 17, 1956, "Question—Will New U.I. Site Go Ahead on Schedule?" *The Garfieldian*, February 15, 1961, 1; Johnson, *Citizens Participation*, 300; Department of City Planning, *Development Plan*.

201. Littlewood, "Chicago's Least Understood"; Rosen, *Decision-Making Chicago-Style*, 111.

202. Drake and Cayton, *Black Metropolis*; Hirsch, *Making the Second Ghetto*; Satter, *Family Properties*; Helgeson, *Crucibles of Black Empowerment*.

203. "Report on Hull House Staff Visits to Homes in the Land Clearance Area to Secure Housing Information," June 1958, 4, box 61, folder 18, Hull House, NFSNC, SWHA, UMN.

204. *Where Shall We Live? Report of the Commission on Race and Housing* (Berkeley: University of California Press, 1958).

205. Cynthia Guerrero, interview with author, January 22, 2016, Chicago.

206. Johnson, *Citizens Participation*, 268.

207. Department of City Planning, *Development Plan*.

208. Marcella Guerrero Baker, personal family memoirs, undated (in author's possession, courtesy of Marcella Guerrero Baker).

209. Julie Guerrero, interview with author, October 16, 2017, Chicago.

210. Josephine Munguia, interview with author, January 15, 2016, Chicago.

211. Johnson, *Citizens Participation*, 321.

212. Johnson, 321.

213. Illinois Federation of Mexican Americans, Annual Report, 1958, box 1, folder 2, Mexican Community Committee of South Chicago Records (MCCSC), UIC.

214. From visual evidence of a 1958 meeting hosted by IFOMA with Mayor Richard J. Daley (courtesy of Arturo Velasquez Family, in author's possession); Illinois Federation of Mexican Americans, Annual Report.

215. Hull House Citizen Participation Project, *Our Neighbors*.

216. Amezcua, "Beautiful Urbanism," 97–119.

217. Johnson, *Citizens Participation*, 117; Rosen, *Decision-Making Chicago-Style*, 110.

218. Johnson, 294; Rosen, 73–74.

219. Rosen, 112.

220. Rosen, chap. 5; Seligman, *Block by Block*, chap. 4; Fernández, *Windy City*, chap. 3.

221. Rosen, *Decision-Making Chicago-Style*, 118–19; Julie Guerrero recalls her mother Angeline attempting to rally opposition to the land-clearance plans in 1959 but getting no Italian American support and feeling that by 1961, it was too late. Julie Guerrero, interview; Georgie Anne Geyer, "Fighting UI Site," *Chicago Daily News*, March 23, 1961; Jay McMullen, "OK $13,901,000 W. Side Renewal," *Chicago Daily News*, September 19, 1961, 11.

222. Julie Guerrero, interview; Fernández, *Windy City*, 117.

223. Eastwood, *Near West Side Stories*, 269, cited in Fernández, *Windy City*, 124.

224. Hull House Citizen Participation Project, 20.

225. "Hull House Eases Urban Renewal Fear," May 22, 1958; "Testimony of William Deknatel to the City Council," March 29, 1960, box 62, folder 1, Hull House, UMN; *The Architectural Forum*, September 1965, 44.

226. Gerald D. Suttles notes that Italians resented the "invasion" of minority groups, who they felt undermined their efforts to save the neighborhood and consequently "earmarked the area as a deteriorating slum"; see Suttles, "Territoriality, Identity and Conduct: A Study of an Inner City Slum with Special Reference to Street Corner Groups" (PhD diss., University of Illinois, 1966), 56.

227. Percy Wood, "Crowds Hail President of Mexico Here," *Chicago Daily Tribune*, October 14, 1959, 1.

228. Illinois Federation of Mexican Americans, Annual Report; "250,000 See Mexican Fete; Daley, Lopez Lead Parade," *Chicago Tribune*, September 19, 1965, 6.

Chapter Three

1. Martin Millspaugh and Gurney Breckenfeld, *The Human Side of Urban Renewal: A Study of the Attitude Changes Produced by Neighborhood Rehabilitation* (New York: Ives Washburn, Inc., 1960), 179–83; Robert A. Slayton, *Back of the Yards: The Making of a Local Democracy* (Chicago: University of Chicago Press, 1986), 227–29; *The Role of Small Business in Economic Development. Hearings Before the Subcommittee on Small Business Problems in Urban Areas of the Select Committee on Small Business, HR 53*, August 16–17, 1968, Chicago; Joseph B. Meegan testimony, in *Small Business Problems in Urban Areas. Hearings Before Subcommittee No. 5 of the Select Committee on Small Business House of Representatives*, June 11–12, 1965, Chicago; "Urban Renewal, Rehabilitation," *Savings and Loan News*, July 1962, box 1, folder 1, BYNC, UIC.

2. Mark Santow, "Saul Alinsky and the Dilemmas of Race in the Postwar City" (PhD diss., University of Pennsylvania, 2000), 35–39; Alan B. Anderson and George W. Pickering, *Confronting the Color Line: The Broken Promise of the Civil Rights Movement in Chicago* (Athens: University of Georgia Press, 1986); Wendy Plotkin, "Deeds of Mistrust: Race, Housing, and Restrictive Covenants in Chicago, 1900-1953" (PhD diss., University of Illinois at Chicago, 1999), 7–8; Hirsch, *Making the Second Ghetto*, 254, 283-284; University of Chicago Settlement, "Democratic Participation Among the Foreign-Born: A Proposal," June 1953, p. 2, "Adult Dept." folder, box 25, Mary McDowell Settlement Records (hereafter MMS), CHM.

3. In her study of New York City, historian Sonia Song-Ha Lee describes how many Puerto Ricans considered "integration" a "North American concept"; see Lee, *Latino Civil Rights Movement*, 169. Halpern, *Killing Floor*, 81; Arredondo, *Mexican Chicago*, 48–51; University of Chicago Settlement, "Democratic Participation"; McPharlin, "Mexican-American Population." Although the 1950 census only listed just 360 foreign-born Mexicans living in the Yards, Fr. Gallego and Meegan put the population at two thousand, or five hundred to six hundred families, in 1955. James McPharlin, "Final Report of a survey on the Mexican-American population in Chicago," Conducted by the Catholic Charities of the Archdiocese of Chicago, 1955, 20-21, box 373, folder 4, WCMC, CHM. In a 1955 report, Fern Colborn puts the population of the Back of the Yards at 150,000, with more than half of Polish descent, 17 percent Lithuanian, about 9 percent Mexican, and the remainder belonging to fourteen other ethnic groups. If 9 percent is true, then Colborn is saying there are about 13,500 Mexicans, far higher than the very low 2,000 in the McPharlin study. Fern Colborn, "Confidential Report on 'Back of the Yards Area Council,'" January 15, 1955, box 215, folder 211, NFS, SWHA, UMN.

4. University of Chicago Settlement, "Democratic Participation"; Arredondo, *Mexican Chicago*, 51; Gloria Gumbinger, "The Back of the Yards Neighborhood Council," circa 1962, box 251, folder 7B, WCMC, CHM.

5. Kerr, "Chicano Experience"; Innis-Jiménez, *Steel Barrio*, 81-82; Arredondo, *Mexican Chicago*, 50. On Mexican population in the BOTY: in 1936 WPA surveyor writes, "This district contains several thousand Mexicans"; see Orange Winkfield, "Mexican District, 45th Street and Ashland Avenue," 1936, box A 741, USWPA, LOC; Agnes T. Ryan, "A Butcher Shop Their Church—An Ice Box Their Altar," *New World*, March 14, 1941 (mentions 2,000 Mexicans there on the eve of WWII); Eunice Felter found that in 1941 there were 1,585 Mexicans in BOTY, see Felter, "The Social Adaptations of the Mexican Churches in the Chicago Area" (master's thesis, University of Chicago, 1941), 19; Bigott, *From Cottage to Bungalow*, 149–50; Lewinnek, *Working Man's Reward*, 67-69; Eunice Felter notes, November 3, 1940, box 172, folder 5, DRSP, CTS.

6. Anita Edgar Jones, "Mexican Colonies in Chicago," *Social Service Review* 2, no. 4 (December 1928): 594–95; Paul S. Taylor, *Mexican Labor in the United States: Chicago and the Calumet Region*, vol. 7, no. 2 (Berkeley: University of California Press, 1932), 220; Paul L. Street, "Working in the Yards: A History of Class Relations in Chicago's Meatpacking Industry, 1886–1960" (PhD diss., State University of New York at Binghamton, 1993), 507; Halpern, *Killing Floor*, 81; Manuel Moyado and Lucia Moyado, interview, January 23, 2016, Chicago (in author's possession); *Hearings before a Subcommittee of the Committee on Education and Labor on S.101 A Bill to Prohibit Discrimination in Employment Because of Race, Creed, Color, or National Origin, or Ancestry and S.459 A Bill to Establish a Fair Employment Practice Commission*, 69th Cong., 1st sess. 74, March 12, 13, 14, 1945.

7. Elsie R. Anderson, "Proposed Outline for Review of an Agency for Committee on Relations with Minority Groups," April 1944, box 371, folder 2, MMS, CHM; Nicholas Von Hoffman, "Massive Racial Shifts: Are They Inevitable?" *Chicago Daily News*, January 7, 1964, 36; Felter, "Social Adaptations," 45.

8. Halpern, *Killing Floor*, 81; Maria Luisa Garibay, "Mexicans Dream of Their Own Church, BYNC Pledges Aid," *BOTY Journal*, November 18, 1940; Ryan, "Butcher Shop"; "New Chapel Opens with Mission," *New World*, November 16, 1945; Thomas G. Kelliher Jr., "Hispanic Catholics and the Archdiocese of Chicago, 1923-1970" (PhD diss., University of Notre Dame, 1996), 110–11. The church was originally named Our Lady of Guadalupe Chapel, but the Claretian Fathers changed it to Immaculate Heart of Mary Vicariate. Residents preferred the original name and continued to call it La Capilla ("the chapel"). For more on the Claretians helping establish the church, see Manuel Moyado, "A History of the Immaculate Heart of Mary Chapel," unpublished manuscript, 2002, Claretian Archives (CA). For more on the role of the Catholic church in Mexican Chicago, see Deborah E. Kanter, *Chicago Católico: Making Catholic Parishes Mexican* (Urbana: University of Illinois Press, 2020).

9. Garibay, "Mexicans Dream." On Ashland Avenue as ethno-racial wall, see Lucia Mouat, "Chicago Ethnic Areas Contrasted," *Christian Science Monitor*, August 10, 1966, 6; David S. Weber, "Anglo Views of Mexican Immigrants: Popular Perceptions and Neighborhood Realities in Chicago, 1900-1940" (PhD diss., Ohio State University, 1982), 135–36; Gumbinger, "Neighborhood Council."

10. Paul Street, "The 'Best Union Members': Class, Race, Culture, and Black Worker Militancy in Chicago's Stockyards during the 1930s," *Journal of American Ethnic History* 20:1 (Fall 2000): 18-49; *Minorities in the UPWA*; Orear, *Out of the Jungle*; Vargas, *Crucible of Struggle*, 233; Jones, "Mexican Colonies," 586, 590-591, 594; Arredondo, *Mexican Chicago*, 136-37; Cohen, *Making a New Deal*, chap. 8; Dominic A. Pacyga, *Slaughterhouse: Chicago's Union Stock Yard and the World It Made* (Chicago: University of Chicago Press, 2015), 150-58; Thomas J. Jablonsky, *Pride in the Jungle: Community and Everyday Life in Back of the Yards Chicago* (Baltimore: Johns Hopkins University Press, 1993), 97; Street, "'Best Union Members,'" 29.

11. Cohen, 333-39; *Minorities in the UPWA*, 34; Jesse Perez, interview, August 27, 1945, Robert Rosenthal Interviews, Collections on the Foreign Population of Chicago (CFPC), CHM; Street, "'Best Union Members,'" 29; Wilson J. Warren, "The Limits of New Deal Social Democracy: Working-Class Structural Pluralism in Midwestern Meatpacking, 1900-1955" (PhD diss., University of Pittsburgh, 1992), 12.

12. Sanford D. Horwitt, *Let Them Call Me Rebel: Saul Alinsky—His Life and Legacy* (New York: Vintage Books, 1992), chaps. 6 and 7; Kathryn Close, "Packingtown's Latest Drama: Civic Unity," *Survey Graphic* (December 1940): 612-15; Saul D. Alinsky, "Community Analysis and Organization," *American Journal of Sociology* 46, no. 6 (May 1941): 800; John Bartlow Martin, "Certain Wise Men," *McCall's Magazine* (March 1949): 18-21, 38, 40, 42, 51-52, 54, 56; Jablonsky, *Pride in the Jungle*, chap. 7.

13. Alinsky, "Community Analysis"; Horwitt, *Call Me Rebel*, 70-73; Justin McCarthy, "Yards 'Letter Lobby' Brings Action," *Chicago Sun*, April 19, 1944, 15; Justin McCarthy, "17 More in Congress Back Yards Fight," *Chicago Sun*, April 20, 1944, 1; Martin, "Certain Wise Men," 18-21, 38, 40, 42, 51-52, 54, 56.

14. Horwitt, *Call Me Rebel*, chap. 12; Saul D. Alinsky to Charles E. Merriam, May 7, 1943, box 11, folder 166, IAF, UIC; "Meeting Called to Launch Organization Patterned After Back of Yards Group," *Chicago Sun*, April 23, 1944, 13; McCarthy, "Yards 'Letter Lobby'"; McCarthy, "17 More."

15. Close, "Packingtown's Latest Drama"; Horwitt, *Call Me Rebel*, 123. On anti-Black racism in the Yards and the BYNC's efforts to address it, see Nicholas Von Hoffman, *Radical: A Portrait of Saul Alinsky* (New York: Nation Books, 2010), 49-50; "Believes Chicago on Verge of Riot," *Atlanta Daily World*, December 17, 1946, 1.

16. See BOTY's photographic archives, box 171, folder 1738, IAF, UIC; Souvenir and Dedication Program, Immaculate Heart of Mary Mission Church and Social Center, December 30, 1945, box 605.31, CA; Helena Huntington Smith, "We Did It Ourselves," *Women's Home Companion*, May 1946 repr., box 1, folder 6, IAF, UIC.

17. Alinsky, "Community Analysis," 800.

18. As a product of the University of Chicago's sociology school, Alinsky was aware of the work of Emory S. Bogardus and Robert Redfield, who produced scholarship on the racialization of Mexicans as an otherized group; see, for example, Emory S. Bogardus, "The Mexican Immigrant and Segregation," *American Journal of Sociology* (July 1930): 74-80. Despite this exposure, when Alinsky founded the BYNC, he believed Mexicans could be accepted into ethnic whiteness. However, the Los Angeles

Zoot Suit Riots in 1943 and other incidents of anti-Mexican racism caused him to change his position, and in 1947, he founded the Community Service Organization, hiring organizer Fred Ross to mobilize Mexican Americans in California and later throughout the US Southwest. See Charles T. Leber Jr. to Mr. Nicholson, July 5, 1958, box 37, folder 602, IAF, UIC.

19. "Report of Social Service Committee of the Pan American Council," February 26, 1942, box 8, folder 85, Immigrants' Protective League Records (IPLR), UIC; Moyado, "A History"; Jeannie Lopez, interview, January 23, 2016, Chicago (in author's possession); Maureen O'Donnell, "Marine Survived Iwo Jima," *Chicago Sun-Times*, April 10, 2016; Monico Cruz Amador interview by Harold O. Lewis, 1967, CRDP, Howard University (HU).

20. "Incas, New Club for Mexicans, Names Officers," *BOTY Journal*, April 11, 1946, 1; "Fire Victims Aided," *BOTY Journal*, August 8, 1946, 1; *Incas S.A.C. By-Laws, 1950*, Thomas Doyle's personal collection; ʾAAC, Annual Report, 1954–1955, 6, box 6, folder 81, IPLR, UIC; Rev. Raymond Sunye to His Eminence, Samuel Cardinal J. Stritch, *Provincial Bulletin of the Province of the United States and Canada* 6, no. 1 (January 1948): 62, CA.

21. "80 Young Voices Enliven Laflin Street Block," *Chicago Tribune*, November 8, 1942, SW3; MAC, "Report of the Mexican American Council of Chicago," December 1953, 2–3, box 88, folder 10, CAP, CHM. The BYNC's initial inclusion of Mexicans was more symbolic than genuine and not intended to include them in leadership. My analysis differs from Jablonsky, who saw it as "bridging the gap between the Eastern Europeans and the Mexicans"; see Jablonsky, *Pride in the Jungle*, 140.

22. Todd-Breland, *Political Education*, 21; Warren, "Limits of New Deal," 12; Vargas, *Crucible of Struggle*, 213; Plotkin, "Deeds of Mistrust," 254–55; Horwitt, *Call Me Rebel*, 123. It is unclear whether Alinsky ever considered his failure to incorporate Mexican Back of the Yarders into decision-making roles within the BYNC as a missed opportunity. In Chicago, Alinsky failed to seize on the galvanization of Mexican political activity in the CIO, along with Mexican American war veterans looking to become involved in civics and in politics. Unlike on the West Coast, where former CIO unionists and war veterans became leaders in Alinsky's CSO. See Mario T. Garcia, *Memories of Chicano History: The Life and Narrative of Bert Corona* (Berkeley: University of California Press, 1994), 164.

23. Pacyga, *Slaughterhouse*, 158–63; Meegan testimony, in *Small Business Problems*.

24. Meegan testimony, in *Small Business Problems*.

25. Meegan testimony; Cowie and Heathcott, *Beyond the Ruins*, 1–15; Pacyga, *Slaughterhouse*, 158–63.

26. Pacyga, *Slaughterhouse*, 153; Elizabeth Rooney, "Polish Americans and Family Disorganization," *American Catholic Sociological Review* 18, no. 1 (March 1957): 1; *Golden Jubilee, Holy Cross Lithuanian Church, 1904–1954* (Chicago, 1954), 152.

27. Pacyga, *Slaughterhouse*, 154; Evelyn Zygmuntowicz, "The Back of the Yards Neighborhood Council and Its Health and Welfare Services" (master's thesis, Loyola

University Chicago, 1950), 4–5; MAC, Annual Report, 1953–1954, 4, box 88, folder 10, CAP, CHM; MAC, "Report of the Mexican American Council of Chicago," April 1953, 3, box 88, folder 10, CAP, CHM.

28. "History of the University of Chicago (Mary McDowell) Settlement," 1955, box 60, folder 4, University of Chicago Service League Records (UCSL), Special Collections Research Center, University of Chicago Library (UCL); Slayton, *Back of the Yards*, chap. 8.

29. "History of the University of Chicago (Mary McDowell) Settlement"; Slayton, *Back of the Yards*, chap. 8; Arredondo, *Mexican Chicago*, 50, 86–88, 91,136–37; Enrique Venegas listed as General Secretary of the Frente Popular Mexicano; see Dorothy Anderson, minutes of Frente Popular Mexicano meetings, 1936, "Mexican work" folder, box 25, MMS, CHM; Jeanne McCarthy, "Only the Fifth Grade Lacks a Venegas Child," *Chicago Tribune*, September 13, 1942, SW1; Club de Damas Mexicanas, "lista," circa 1933–1934, "Mexican Mothers' Club" folder, box 25, MMS, CHM. For more on the Frente Popular in Chicago, see Flores, *Mexican Revolution in Chicago*; and Innis-Jiménez, *Steel Barrio*.

30. Alinsky, *Reveille for Radicals*, 59; Smith, "We Did It Ourselves"; Agnes E. Meyer, "Orderly Revolution," June 1945, box 1, folder 6, IAF, UIC; Judith Ann Trolander, "Social Change: Settlement Houses and Saul Alinsky, 1939–1965," *Social Science Review* 56, no. 3 (September 1982): 355–57.

31. Adel M. Martinez, interview, May 19, 2016, Laguna Woods, CA (in author's possession); Thomas Doyle, interview, February 9, 2016, Orland Park, IL (in author's possession); University of Chicago Settlement, "Democratic Participation"; Slayton, *Back of the Yards*, 186.

32. Trolander, "Social Change," 357; Everett S. Cope, Monthly Program Reports, 1947–1949, box 19, MMS, CHM; Ray Alcala, interview, January 19, 2016, Chicago (in author's possession); Joseph Manzo, interview, January 19, 2016, Chicago (in author's possession); University of Chicago Settlement House, *Bazaar Program*, May 25, 1956, Thomas Doyle's personal collection.

33. Martinez, interview; Alcala, interview; John C. Sanchez, interview, January 26, 2016, Chicago (in author's possession); Kerr, "Chicano Experience," 186–87.

34. Adel Martinez, "The Role of a Settlement House," n.d., box 8, MMS, CHM.

35. See Fran Dungan (settlement staff worker), minutes of meeting with the Osprey Girls, September 26, 1950, box 24, MMS, CHM; "Club Ospreys celebró rumbosamente su 12 avo. aniversario," *Vida Latina*, October 1961, 15; for more on SACs in the Back of the Yards, see Slayton, *Back of the Yards*, 58–59. On these groups becoming violent gangs, see Pacyga, *Chicago*, 305–8.

36. Dungan, minutes of meeting.

37. Cope, Monthly Program Reports; Sanchez, interview; Moyado and Moyado, interview.

38. "Fifth Annual Meeting of the Mexican American Council of Chicago to Present Outstanding Spanish-Speaking Personalities," *Aguila*, April 17, 1953, 2, box 223,

folder 301, NFS, SWHA, UMN; George I. Sánchez, "Proposed Reconstitution of ACSSP Board of Directors," 1952, box 3, folder 6, GISP; MAC, "A Program Report Prepared for Board of Directors of the Mexican American Council of Chicago" (January 1–April 15, 1952), 2, box 88, folder 11, CAP, CHM; MAC, "The First Six Months of Operation," 1952, box 3, folder 7, GISP.

39. MAC, "A Program Report"; "Fifth Annual Meeting," *Aguila*. On the anti-communist backlash against UPWA members, see Michaels, "Packing Union." For Mexican American criticism of Alinsky, see Bert Corona's analysis in Garcia, *Memories of Chicano History*, 158–60, 164.

40. For more on effects of the 1954 case *Brown v. Board of Education* on Black Chicagoans, see Todd-Breland, *Political Education*. Louise Año Nuevo Kerr's pioneering work is instructive here; she argued Mexican Back of the Yarders partook in a process of "de-ethnicization," gradually entering the mainstream of community life (Kerr, "Chicano Experience," 185–86). While I build off of her scholarship, I argue that their disconnection from more ethnic political activism resulted from the cultural stigmas, spatial segregation, and population containment they experienced in the district.

41. Notes on University of Chicago Settlement House Bazaar Souvenir Book, Re: Ospreys and Incas, 1952, box 15, MMS, CHM; "Adult Council Meets," *UC Settlement News*, March 18, 1953, 2; "Inca Jrs. Receive Jackets," *UC Settlement News*, October 22, 1952; Rosemary Diaz, interview, January 16, 2016, Chicago (in author's possession); Matthew Rodriguez Jr., interview, January 5, 2017, Chicago (in author's possession).

42. Bert H. Boerner to Maxwell S. Hahn, April 9, 1953, "Adult Dept." folder, box 25, MMS, CHM; University of Chicago Settlement, "Democratic Participation."

43. Trolander, "Social Change," 356–57; Louise C. Wade, "The Heritage from Chicago's Early Settlement Houses," *Journal of the Illinois State Historical Society* 60, no. 4 (Winter 1967): 440; Colborn, "Confidential Report."

44. BYNC, *Conservation by We the People Back of the Yards* (Chicago: BYNC, 1953), box 1, folder 4, Back of the Yards Community Collection (BYCC), Special Collections, Harold Washington Library Center (HWLC), Chicago Public Library; June Blythe, "Back of the Yards Reverses the Flight," *Commerce Magazine*, January 1956, 20–25, box 1, folder 1, BYNC, UIC; Millspaugh and Breckenfeld, *Human Side*, 179–82, 196, 200–19; Pacyga, *Chicago*, 302–3; Slayton, *Back of the Yards*, 227–29.

45. Seligman, *Block by Block*, 70–71, 76; Von Hoffman, *Radical*, 50–51; Pacyga, *Chicago*, 302–3; Millspaugh and Breckenfeld, *Human Side*, 179–83; Santow, "Saul Alinsky," 37–39.

46. Millspaugh and Breckenfeld, *Human Side*, 211; "Joint Committee Hears BYNC Head: Statement of Joseph B. Meegan," *BOTY Journal*, August 26, 1970, 1; Guido J. Tardi, "Statement Prepared for Delivery before University of Chicago Service League," February 18, 1963, General Papers, 1962–1963, box 8, MMS, CHM; Georgie Anne Geyer, "'Don't Do This,' Pleads a Mother," *Chicago Daily News*, August 9, 1963,

36; Memorandum from Nicholas Von Hoffman to Dick Harmon and Bob Squires, Re: Conservation, July 13, 1961, box 37, folder 598, IAF, UIC; "Back of Yards Boasts Unique Financing Plan," *New World*, February 21, 1958, 24; Colborn, "Confidential Report"; Millspaugh and Breckenfeld, *Human Side*, 210.

47. Lucy P. Carner, "Walking Again," *Four Lights* 16, no. 6 (December 1956): 1, box 506, folder 2, American Civil Liberties Union Illinois Division Records (ACLU-IL), UCL; Millspaugh and Breckenfeld, *Human Side*, 210.

48. South Deering Improvement Association, *South Deering Bulletin*, June and August 1958, General Papers, 1955–1959, box 8, MMS, CHM.

49. Agnes E. Meyer, *Out of These Roots: The Autobiography of an American Woman* (New York: Little, Brown, 1953); Millspaugh and Breckenfeld, *Human Side*; Jacobs, *Death and Life*; John Kuenster, "The Neighborhood that Came Back," *Columbia* (March 1956): 11–13; Memorandum from Von Hoffman to Harmon and Squires, Re: Conservation; Jacobs, *Death and Life*, 272. For more on *unslumming*, see Max Page and Timothy Mennel, eds., *Reconsidering Jane Jacobs* (New York: Routledge, 2011), 33.

50. It is not clear if Jacobs herself took a trip to the Back of the Yards while researching her book (1958–1960). Architectural historian Peter Laurence writes that "her friend" Saul Alinsky "shared with her knowledge about Chicago," and in the process, she befriended Joseph Meegan, Msgr. John Egan, and Nicholas Von Hoffman, all of whom would have informed her on the conservation program. See Peter L. Laurence, *Becoming Jane Jacobs* (Philadelphia: University of Pennsylvania Press, 2016), 276; Jacobs, *Death and Life*, 271, 211, 138.

51. Industrial Areas Foundation, Annual Report to Emil Schwarzhaupt Foundation, 1958, box 30, folder 3, Emil Schwarzhaupt Foundation Records (ESF), UCL; Donald O'Toole to Luther E. Clayton, August 5, 1959, box 37, folder 598, IAF, UIC.

52. Mae Velasquez, interview with author, December 31, 2015, Alsip, IL (in author's possession); Mouat, "Chicago Ethnic Areas"; Hamilton K. Wright, Mary McDowell Settlement, "Vista Proposal on behalf of the Community Committee of Ashland-45th Street and Surrounding Areas," May 22, 1968, box 9, MMS, CHM; Brueckner, "An Appraisal of Neighborhood Need and Neighborhood Center Services Prepared for the Welfare Council of Metropolitan Chicago," January 1961, box 64, folder 2, NFS, SWHA, UMN; Nicolaides, *My Blue Heaven*, 266; "Industrial Real Estate Back of the Yards," *Southtown Economist*, June 21, 1959, 1.

53. Brueckner, "Appraisal of Neighborhood Need"; *Chicago Zoning Ordinance Passed by the City Council on May 29, 1957* (Chicago: City of Chicago, 1957); William Arthur Rogers, "Back of the Yards Wars on Blight," *Southtown Economist*, June 21, 1959, 1.

54. Barbara J. Flint, "Zoning and Residential Segregation: A Social and Physical History, 1910–40" (PhD diss., University of Chicago, 1977); Ernest Fuller, "Back of Yards Lures Industry," *Chicago Tribune*, April 1, 1959; Tony Weitzel, "Yards Area No. 1 Asset—People," *Chicago Daily News*, April 6, 1959; "Buildings and Zoning City

Council Committee," *New World*, May 23, 1958, 10; Brueckner, "Appraisal of Neighborhood Need." For Mexicans in BOTY since 1916, see Martin, "Certain Wise Men," 18–21, 38, 40, 42, 51–52, 54, 56; Erwin Bach, "Ghost Factories Balk Flat Building's Owner," *Chicago Tribune*, January 11, 1959, SW8; "Neighbors Ask Zoning Ban on Gasoline Tank," *Chicago Tribune*, December 7, 1958, SW4.

55. Brueckner, "Appraisal of Neighborhood Need"; Martin, "Certain Wise Men," 18–21, 38, 40, 42, 51–52, 54, 56; Rev. Severino Lopez, CMF, "Immaculate Heart of Mary on Ashland—From Its Foundation to the Present," *Bulletin of the Province of the East* 7, no. 6 (June 1960), CA.

56. Nicolaides, *My Blue Heaven*, 285; Suleiman Osman, *The Invention of Brownstone Brooklyn: Gentrification and the Search for Authenticity in Postwar New York* (New York: Oxford University Press, 2012), 70.

57. David A. Badillo, *Latinos and the New Immigrant Church* (Baltimore: Johns Hopkins University Press, 2006), 89–90; Kelliher, "Hispanic Catholics," 184–94; Fernández, *Windy City*, 76–77; "Set Discussion on Minorities," *Chicago Defender*, January 15, 1957, 4; "Meet Challenge of Tyranny," *New World*, January 10, 1958, 5; "Spanish-American Lovelies Go for Democratic," *Chicago Defender*, November 8, 1960, 28.

58. "Meet Challenge of Tyranny," *New World*, January 10, 1958, 5; "Nearly 500 Members," *Chicago Defender*, November 2, 1960, A4; "Latin Americans Back Parsons," *Chicago Defender*, November 1, 1960, A2; Ann Diaz, interview with author, January 16, 2016, Chicago (in author's possession); "Los botantes latinos americanos del barrio de las empacadoras," *Settlers S.A.C. Souvenir Program*, 1962, Thomas Doyle's personal collection; "Pickets, 'Vivas' Greet Johnson," *San Diego Union*, November 2, 1960, A3; Brueckner, "Appraisal of Neighborhood Need"; "Stock Yards Business Men Ask Parking," *Chicago Tribune*, January 13, 1963, A6.

59. Brueckner, "Appraisal of Neighborhood Need"; "Club Ospreys celebró," *Vida Latina*; "El H. Embajador de Mexico," *Vida Latina*, June 21, 1961, 16; "Launch Credit Abuse Fight," *Chicago Tribune*, June 15, 1961, W1; "Mexican Fiesta to Bring South of Border North," *Chicago Tribune*, August 21, 1966, R3; "Claretian Marks 25 Years' Work Among Mexicans," *New World*, August 17, 1951, 11; "Mission Presents Mexican Fiesta," *New World*, August 24, 1951, 3; "Fiesta Lends Mexican Mood to Ashland Ave.," *BOTY Journal*, August 26, 1970, 12; Vicki L. Ruiz, "Claiming Public Space at Work, Church, and Neighborhood," in *Las Obreras*, ed. Vicki L. Ruiz, 13–39 (Los Angeles: UCLA Chicano Studies Research Center, 2000); Felter, "Social Adaptations," 45–47.

60. Nicholas Von Hoffman, "Churches Spearhead Rights Action," *Chicago Daily News*, August 10, 1963, 1, 4; "Negro Leaders Seek Rights Co-ordination," *Chicago Sun-Times*, November 20, 1964, 18; Ronald Sullivan, "Poll Tells White Backlash," *Chicago's American*, August 19, 1964, 6; Robert G. Schultz, "Daley Brings Backlash Issue into the Open," *Chicago Daily News*, August 27, 1964, 3; Robert Gruenberg, "'Frontlash' Will Outwhip 'Backlash,' Johnson Says," *Chicago's American*, August 28, 1964, 1; Sidney Lens, "Daley of Chicago," *Progressive*, March 1966, 15–21; Seligman, *Block by Block*,

179–80; Morton Kondracke, "Try Integrating Housing in Richer Areas, King Told," *Chicago Sun-Times*, August 6, 1966, 50; D. J. R. Bruckner, "Why the American Dream Exploded," *Los Angeles Times*, August 7, 1966, J2; Anderson and Pickering, *Confronting the Color Line*; Erik S. Gellman, *Troublemakers: Chicago Freedom Struggles through the Lens of Art Shay* (Chicago: University of Chicago Press, 2019).

61. Michael Staudenmaier, "Mostly of Spanish Extraction": Second-Class Citizenship and Racial Formation in Puerto Rican Chicago, 1946-1965," *Journal of American History* 104, no. 3 (2017): 698.

62. "U.S. Latins on the March," *Newsweek*, May 23, 1966: 32–36; Helen Rowan, "A Minority No One Knows," *The Atlantic*, June 1967: 47–52; Norris Vitchek (Alfred Balk), "Confessions of a Block-Buster," *Saturday Evening Post*, July 14, 1962, 19; Geyer, "'Don't Do This,'"; Saul D. Alinsky, Annual Report to the Board of Trustees of the Industrial Areas Foundation, December 12, 1963, box 30, folder 6, ESF, UCL; Horwitt, *Call Me Rebel*, 367; "Alinsky Predicts Integration Near for Back of Yards Area," *Chicago Sun-Times*, January 30, 1962, 15; "Alinsky No Stranger to Controversy," *Kansas City Star*, September 13, 1965; Ken Masson, "Meet Saul Alinsky, Community Organizer, Whose Views Feared by Some, Adopted by Others," *Economist Newspapers*, September 19, 1971; "Agitator Zeroes in on the Suburbanites," *Business Week*, February 8, 1969, 44–46.

63. Frank Sullivan, "Why CDA is Active Home Builder," *Chicago Sun-Times*, October 31, 1966; *The Chicago Approach to Model Cities* (Chicago: City of Chicago, 1967), 1–2; Joseph B. Meegan testimony, *Housing Act of 1958, before Subcommittee on Housing of the Committee on Banking and Currency House of Representatives*, 85th Cong., July 1958; "Owners of 20 Lots Seek FHA Loans," *Chicago's American*, September 9, 1960, 7; Jerry Goldberg, "Theophilus Mann Hits CHA Ghettos," *Chicago Defender*, January 9, 1964, 4; Brenetta Howell, "Westside Roundup," *Chicago Defender*, February 17, 1965; James Q. Wilson, "Planning and Politics: Citizen Participation in Urban Renewal," *Journal of the American Institute of Planners* 29, no. 4 (November 1963): 242–49; Silberman, *Crisis in Black and White* (1964), 321–22; Geyer, "'Don't Do This'"; Alinsky, Annual Report; Colborn, "Confidential Report"; Brueckner, "Appraisal of Neighborhood Need"; Gumbinger, "Neighborhood Council."

64. *45th-Ashland—Designation Report: Report to the Department of Urban Renewal on the Designation of Slum and Blighted Area Redevelopment Project 45th-Ashland* (Chicago: City of Chicago, 1969); Wright, "Vista Proposal"; "Groundbreaking Rites Held for New Housing Project," *Chicago Tribune*, April 4, 1971, A6; Wright, "Vista Proposal"; Kerr, "Chicano Experience," 186–87.

Chapter Four

1. Suttles, "Territoriality, Identity and Conduct," 56; Ira Berkow, *Maxwell Street: Survival in a Bazaar* (New York: Doubleday, 1977), 504; *Prensa Libre*, February 25, 1963, 8, box 1, folder 22, FSC, UIC.

2. Information gathered from visual evidence of a 1958 meeting held by IFOMA

led by Arturo Velasquez and Carmen Mendoza, guest speaker Mayor Richard J. Daley (courtesy of Arturo Velasquez Family, in au:hor's possession).

3. "Vote por Florence Scala para alderman de el 1st ward," *Prensa Libre*, February 23, 1963, 1, box 1, folder 22, FSC, UIC; Eastwood, *Near West Side Stories*; George Rosen, *Decision-Making Chicago-Style: The Genesis of a University of Illinois Campus* (Urbana: University of Illinois Press, 1980); Fernández, *Windy City*, 116; Richard E. Anderson, "The Press and the Harrison-Halsted Story" (master's thesis, University of Illinois at Urbana-Champaign, 1964).

4. Florence Scala interview; "Recíbe el apoyo de IFOMA," *Prensa Libre*, February 23, 1963, 1, box 1, folder 22, FSC, UIC; Thomas Buck, "Trustees Approve Site West of Loop for U. of I. Branch," *Chicago Tribune*, February 15, 1961.

5. Arturo Velasquez, "Nuestros comerciantes deben interarse más en la cámara de comercio," *Prensa Libre*, February 25, 1963, 8, box 1, folder 22, FSC, UIC.

6. Harrison-Halsted Community Group Program, October 1962, p. 2, box 1, folder 38, FSC, UIC.

7. For examples of shared patterns of Latino support for JFK in 1960 across other areas, see Francis-Fallon, *Rise of the Latino Vote*; see also Thomas and Santiago, *Rethinking the Struggle*, esp. chap. 2; "Arturo Velasquez, Sr. Interview by Juan Andrade, Jr.," in Andrade; Amezcua, "Machine in the Barrio"; Larry Villarreal, interview.

8. Gasca spent most of the 1950s involved in housing politics during the deportation and displacement of Mexicans. His leadership in cultural, social, and civic groups, such as the Manuel Perez Legion Post 1017 and the Latins SAC, helped renew a sense of belonging during a time of spatial crisis; Rich Gasca, phone interview with author, December 1, 2016; Mary Bogardus, interview with author, November 7, 2016; "The First Six Months of Operation of the Mexican American Council of Chicago," p. 3, box 88, folder 11, CAP, CHM.

9. "Arturo Velasquez, Sr. interview," *Historical Survey*.

10. Frank Duran, President of MADO to Mayor Richard J. Daley, "Mexican-American Democratic Organization," July 2, 1962, box: SII ss1B53, folder 14, Richard J. Daley Collection (RJD), UIC.

11. In 1963, Col. Jack Reilly was awarded the Order of the Aztec Eagle, the highest honor the Mexican government bestows upon a non-Mexican, pushed for by Chicago Mexican Americans. See *Vida Latina*, June 1963, 11; "Special Event for Director of Same," *Chicago Sun-Times*, January 27, 1967; Rich Gasca, interview; Bogardus, interview; Neil Elliott, "It's a Picasso . . . It's a Parade . . . It's Jack Reilly," *Chicago Tribune*, May 4, 1969, 44; "Arthur R. Velasquez Interview by Juan Andrade, Jr.," in Andrade, 265; Robert Gasca, interview with author, February 6, 2017; Rich Gasca, interview; Bogardus, interview.

12. Larry Villarreal, interview; "Arturo Velasquez, Sr. Interview," *Historical Survey*; Daley, quoted in *Daley: The Last Boss*, directed by Barak Goodman (PBS, 1995); "Botantes latinos americanos del Barrio de las Empacadoras," advertisement, *Settlers S.A.C. Ad Booklet*, 1962 (courtesy of Tom Doyle, in author's possession); Matt Rodriguez, interview. Rodriguez was the son of Matt Rodriguez, Sr., precinct captain

for the 14th Ward; "14th Ward Regular Democratic Organization, Here to Serve You," advertisement, *Settlers S.A.C. Ad Booklet*, 1962 (courtesy of Tom Doyle, in author's possession); "Chicago's Latins Reaching for a Political Power Base," *Chicago Sun-Times*, September 13, 1971, 26; Frank Duran, President of MADO, to Mayor Richard J. Daley, "Mexican-American Democratic Organization," July 2, 1962, box: SII ss1B53, folder 14, RJD, UIC; *Telling Historias* (Chicago: Mexican Fine Arts Center Museum, 2001), 36–37; Mexican American Democratic Organization (hereafter cited as MADO), *Mexican American Democratic Organization—Annual Program, October 27, 1972* (courtesy of Arturo Velasquez Family, in author's possession).

13. "Arturo Velasquez, Sr. interview," *Historical Survey*, 254; Rich Gasca, interview; Ann Diaz, interview; Arturo Velasquez, interview with unidentified UIC student, 2008 (in possession of Arturo Velasquez family); Letter of introduction by Colonel Jack Reilly, prepared for Richard J. Daley on behalf of Arturo Velasquez, March 9, 1966 (courtesy of Arturo Velasquez family, in author's possession).

14. Joseph Zikmund, "Mayoral Voting and Ethnic Politics in the Daley-Bilandic-Byrne Era," in *After Daley: Chicago Politics in Transition*, ed. Samuel K. Gove and Louis H. Masotti, (Urbana: University of Illinois Press, 1982), 37; Adam Cohen and Elizabeth Taylor, *American Pharaoh: Mayor Richard J. Daley, His Battle for Chicago and the Nation* (Boston: Back Bay Books, 2000), 282, 301; Steven P. Erie, *Rainbow's End: Irish-Americans and the Dilemmas of Urban Machine Politics, 1840–1985* (Berkeley: University of California Press, 1988), 149; Mike Royko, *Boss: Richard J. Daley of Chicago* (New York: Signet, 1971), 129.

15. Cohen and Taylor, *American Pharaoh*, 298–99; Zikmund, "Mayoral Voting," 37-40; Royko, *Boss*, 131–32; Ann Diaz, interview; Rosemary Diaz, interview.

16. James Q. Wilson, *Negro Politics: The Search for Leadership* (New York: Free Press, 1960); Cohen and Taylor, *American Pharaoh*, 299; Memo from Nicholas Von Hoffman to Saul Alinsky, "Concerning: Election Registration for Mexican-Americans," n.d., box 12, folder 189, IAF, UIC. On the machine's undermining of Latino voters, see Teresa Córdova, "Harold Washington and the Rise of Latino Electoral Politics in Chicago, 1982–1987," in *Chicano Politics and Society in the Late Twentieth Century*, ed. David Montejano, 36–37 (Austin: University of Texas Press, 1999); William Kornblum, *Blue Collar Community* (Chicago: University of Chicago Press, 1974), 169.

17. "250,000 See Mexican Fete," *Chicago Tribune*; "Lopez Mateos to Open Rites," *Washington Post*, September 9, 1965, C19; Description of events at Café La Margarita, 1966, Tonorous Records.

18. Ludwig A. Leskovar, "The President's Biennial Report, Heart of Chicago Community Council," n.d., box 31, folder 11, John J. Egan Papers (hereafter cited as JJE), University of Notre Dame Archives (hereafter cited as UNDA); Fernández, *Windy City*, 214; Robert E. T. Brooks, "Chicago's Ethnic Groups," in *Chicago Lutheran Planning Study*, 12–13 (Chicago: National Lutheran Council, 1965).

19. "Story of Pilsen Neighbors—Saga of Brotherhood at Work," *Chicago Daily News*, February 18, 1963, 9; Brooks, "Chicago's Ethnic Groups," 28.

20. Kerr, "Chicano Experience in Chicago," 203.

21. "United, Our Challenge Is the Future!" *Heart o' Chicago Herald* 3, no. 1 (August 1960): 1, box 31, folder 11, JJE, UNDA.

22. Marcella Baker (née Guerrero) interview, January 3, 2017; Brooks, "Chicago's Ethnic Groups," 12–13; Jory Graham, *Chicago: An Extraordinary Guide* (Chicago: Rand McNally, 1968), 357–58; Kevin B. Blackistone and Karen Snelling, "More than Half of City Synagogues Shut since 1963," *Chicago Reporter*, November 1984; Steve Askin, "Chicago Jews Exodus to Suburbia," *Chicago Reporter*, September 1977; Linda Estrada, interview with author, February 21, 2016, Elmwood Park, IL.

23. Larry Villarreal, interview; Villarreal Long, interview, February 19, 2013; Estrada, interview.

24. Baker, interview, January 3, 2017; Villarreal Long, interview, February 19, 2013; Dan Barco interview, October 30, 2016, Franklin Park, IL.

25. Graham, *Chicago*, 358; Memorandum from Moe Sullivan to Ed Marciniak, "Organizing meeting of the South Lawndale-Crawford Conservation Commission held at Lawndale Park Fieldhouse," December 12, 1962, box 40, folder 16, JJE, UNDA.

26. "Springfield Protest Against Open Occupancy Seen in Photos," *Community Reporter*, May 15, 1963, news clippings, box 40, folder 19, JJE, UNDA; "Lawndale Violence Dies Out, 15 Beaten," *Chicago Tribune*, July 15, 1961, S1.

27. "Puzzle in Lawndale: People, Vacancies Up," *Chicago Daily News*, August 23, 1961, 45; "An Open Letter To: Aldermen Charles S. Bonk (21st), Otto F. Janousek (22nd) and George J. Tourek (23rd) and State Representatives Frank Wolf and Lillian Piotrowski (30th)," *Community Reporter*, May 24, 1961, news clippings, box 40, folder 19, JJE, UNDA; "Springfield Protest," *Community Reporter*.

28. Memorandum from T. A. Gaudette to John J. Egan, Re: "Meeting of United Property Owners, August 22, at Wozniak Hall, 2530 Blue Island Avenue," August 23, 1961, box 57b, folder 3, JJE, UNDA; Fernández, *Windy City*, 78; "Field Visit to Bethlehem Community Center," November 20, 1957, box 60, folder 3, SWHA, UMN.

29. Carmen Mendoza to Reverend Monsignor John Egan, July 18, 1961, box 35, folder 15, JJE, UNDA.

30. Mendoza to Reverend Monsignor John Egan, July 18, 1961; Reverend Monsignor John Egan to Reverend Leo Mahon, July 21, 1961, box 35, folder 15, JJE, UNDA.

31. Mendoza to Egan, 1961; "Vote por Florence Scala," *Prensa Libre*; "Habla el chairman," *Prensa Libre*; Julie Ann Lyman, "Our Mexican Americans," Part II, *Chicago Tribune Magazine,* April 5, 1964, 38-51.

32. Wolf Von Eckardt, "Black Neck in the White Noose," *New Republic*, October 19, 1963, 14–17. On the policy history of conservation in Chicago, see Seligman, *Block by Block*, esp. chap. 3; "Springfield Protest," *Community Reporter*; Brian J. L. Berry, *The Open Housing Question: Race and Housing in Chicago, 1966–1976* (Cambridge, MA: Ballinger, 1979), 193.

33. Lyman, "Our Mexican Americans"; Memorandum from Gaudette to Egan.

34. Lyman, "Our Mexican Americans"; Germain W. Heery, "A Socio-Economic Survey of the Mexicans in Joliet, Illinois" (master's thesis, Catholic University of America, 1947), 43, American Catholic History Research Center and University

Archives (ACRC), The Catholic University of America; "Address by the Honorable Robert F. Kennedy to G.I. Forum," Conrad Hilton, Chicago, August 23, 1963, Department of Justice, United States of America; Von Hoffman, "Massive Racial Shifts." On the "Democratic Party apparatus" responding to "newcomers," see Robert H. MacRae of the Welfare Council of Metropolitan Chicago to Maxwell Hahn of the Field Foundation, December 12, 1960, box 2T76, Field Foundation Archives (FFA), Briscoe Center for American History, The University of Texas at Austin; Campaign literature, "Good for Chicago," 1971, box 40, folder: "Richard J. Daley, 1970-1971," 2 of 4, David S. Broder Papers (hereafter DSB), LOC; Campaign to Re-elect Richard J. Daley, *Daley Record*, 1971, p. 6, box 40, folder: "Richard J. Daley, 1970-1971," 4 of 4, DSB, LOC.

35. Charles E. Silberman, *Crisis in Black and White* (New York: Vintage, 1964), 336; Rossi and Dentler, *Politics of Urban Renewal*.

36. Howell, "Westside Roundup." As early as 1949, Saul Alinsky himself admitted he was not sure "what future course all these councils might take." Martin, "Certain Wise Men," 51.

37. "Puzzle in Lawndale," *Chicago Daily News*; Von Hoffman, "Massive Racial Shifts," 36; Rev. Don Benedict, "Civil Rights and Racial Unrest—A Lawyer's Problem," *Chicago Bar Record* (1964): 225-30.

38. Greg Paeth, "Story of Dick Dolejs and 'Little Village,'" *Lawndale News: T.V. Times Supplement*, April 11-17, 1971, 3; Lawndale Conservation Council, box 40, folder 16, JJE, UNDA; Arthur Siddon, "'Little Village' Offered to Give 'Old World' Atmosphere to Area"; "S. Lawndale Eyes Change: Decorations Aim for Flavor of Old World," *Chicago Tribune*, September 7, 1964, W15; "Little Village Council Plans 'Operation Facelift': Award Prizes for Property Improvements," *Chicago Tribune*, June 13, 1965, W4; "Little Village's Facelift Rejuvenates Its Homes," *Chicago Tribune*, April 3, 1966, Q6; "Checks Look Good as Homes," *Community Reporter*, n.d., news clippings, Richard A. Dolejs's personal collection; Dick O'Connell, "Effective Leaders Behind Community Upswing," *Community Reporter*, n.d., news clippings, Richard A. Dolejs's personal collection; "Dolejs Family—A Century of Community Service," *Little Village Community Reporter, 25th Anniversary Edition*, November 1971, p. X, Oversize Materials, Oversize 17, Lawndale-Crawford Community Collection (LCCC), HWLC.

39. Rev. Msgr. John J. Egan to Howard Scaman, Executive Director of the South Lawndale Conservation Commission, Re: Misrepresenting the Church's Position on the Open Occupancy Bill, August 12, 1963, box 40, folder 16, JJE, UNDA; Memorandum from Sullivan to Marciniak, "Organizing meeting"; James Twomey to John J. Egan, Re: Housing and Population Data for South Lawndale, May 10, 1961, box 40, folder 16, JJE, UNDA; Little Village Community Council, "Little Village Community Council, 1965-1966, report," box 57b, folder 5, JJE, UNDA; Siddon, "'Little Village' Offered"; "S. Lawndale Eyes Change," *Chicago Tribune*; "Little Village Council Plans," *Chicago Tribune*; "Little Village's Facelift," *Chicago Tribune*.

40. "La Boheme Electrique," *Little Village Album* (Dennis R. Hejna & Associates, Chicago), Richard A. Dolejs's personal collection; Paeth, "Story of Dick Dolejs."

41. Memorandum from Sullivan to Marciniak, "Organizing meeting"; Von Hoffman, *Radical*, 135.

42. Larry Villarreal, interview; Michael Ceja, phone interview with author, October 8, 2017.

43. "Checks Look Good as Homes," *Community Reporter*; Little Village Community Council, "Little Village Community Council"; "Festival Hailed as 'Big Hit,'" *Little Village Community Reporter*, n.d., Richard A. Dolejs's personal collection.

44. Roger Biles, *Richard J. Daley: Politics, Race, and the Governing of Chicago* (DeKalb: Northern Illinois University Press, 1995), 224–25; Cohen and Taylor, *American Pharaoh*, 431; Graham, *Chicago*, 358.

45. Larry Villarreal, interview; Recognition award given to Mayor Richard J. Daley from the Mexican Patriotic Committee of Chicago Inc., 1964, box 14, folder 8, Series 6, Subseries 3, RJD, UIC; Judge David Cerda Oral History (2005), box 1, folders 3–5, Circuit Court of Cook County Retired Judges Oral History Collection (CCRJ), Loyola University Chicago, Archives and Special Collections; Kondracke, *Saving Millie*, 7; "Anita Villarreal: The Feminine Link Between Women Libbers and Sugar and Lace," *Fiesta* (January 1975): 16–19; "After Blacks, Latins Newest, Largest Ethnic Chicago Bloc," *Port Arthur News*, March 13, 1977, 10.

46. Homer C. Bishop, "South Chicago Neighborhood House Study Report, January 18, 1965," p. 12, box 64, folder 14, SWHA, UMN.

47. "Story of Pilsen Neighbors," *Chicago Daily News*; Rev. Joseph J. Peplansky, C. M. F., "A Comparative Study of Attitudes of Second Generation Mexican-Americans with Respect to Identification and Assimilation" (master's thesis, The Catholic University of America, 1964), 51–52.

48. "Story of Pilsen Neighbors," *Chicago Daily News*; Memorandum of community meeting held on July 13, 1965, "Over 500 people defied the heat and humidity last Tuesday night to attend the meeting of the Heart of Chicago Community Council held at St. Paul Church hall, 22nd Place and Hoyne Avenue," July 15, 1965, Heart of Chicago Community Council, box 31, folder 10, JJE, UNDA.

49. Larry Villarreal, interview.

50. Larry Villarreal, interview.

51. Larry Villarreal, interview.

52. Larry Villarreal, interview; Judge David Cerda, oral history; "Candidates Battle for 15 Judgeships in County," *Chicago Tribune*, October 27, 1966, A8.

53. Larry Villarreal, interview; Virginia Martinez, interview with author, October 28, 2016, Chicago; PNCC, "Housing Proposal," n.d., box 25, folder 12, JJE, UNDA; "Executive Board Answers Strand Real Estate," *Pilsen Neighbors*, January 28, 1966, 1, box 25, folder 12, JJE, UNDA; "Form Spanish-Speaking Home Buyers League in Pilsen Area," *Chicago Tribune*, March 27, 1969, W8.

54. "Story of Pilsen Neighbors," *Chicago Daily News*.

55. Mier, Giloth, and Amato, *Housing Needs of Pilsen*, 20, 22.

56. Robert B. McKersie, *A Decisive Decade: An Insider's View of the Chicago Civil Rights Movement during the 1960s* (Carbondale: Southern Illinois University Press,

2013), 112–15; Ralph Jr., *Northern Protest: Martin Luther King, Jr., Chicago, and the Civil Rights Movement* (Cambridge, MA: Harvard University Press, 1993), 81.

57. Angry letter re: department stores and movie theatres being "jammed with Negroes," in Herman Gantz, "Open City," *Chicago's American*, July 20, 1966; Ralph, *Northern Protest*, 86–87; Biles, *Richard J. Daley*, 122–23; Dennis Fawcet, "Mainland Puerto Ricans Still Beset with Problems," *Sunday Times Advertiser*, July 3, 1966, 6; Mention of Velasquez on Advisory Committee of Halsted Street Urban Progress Center, in Mexican Consulate Award Committee, *Salute to Arturo Velasquez*, booklet (Chicago: Consulate General of Mexico, 1967) (courtesy of Arturo Velasquez family, in author's possession); Rich Gasca, interview; "Pilsen Neighbors Meeting, St. Pius Social Center," July 21, 1966, box 57b, folder 3, JJE, UNDA.

58. Ralph, *Northern Protest*, 81, 86–87; Berry, *Open Housing Question*; Pierre de Vise, *Chicago's Widening Color Gap* (Chicago: Interuniversity Social Research Committee, Report No. 2, December 1967); McKersie, *A Decisive Decade*; Biles, *Richard J. Daley*; Cohen and Taylor, *American Pharaoh*; Rick Perlstein, *Nixonland: The Rise of a President and the Fracturing of America* (New York: Scribner, 2008), 124–26; Sullivan, "Why CDA"; Biles, *Richard J. Daley*, 122–23; "Gage Park 1st Target of King Rights Drive," *Chicago's American*, July 12, 1966, 1.

59. Mexican American students from Back of the Yards had been attending Gage Park High School since the early 1940s. Dan Marquez Sr. interview with author, December 14, 2016, Chicago; Alcala, interview; Manzo, interview; Abundio "Al" Zaragoza, interview with author, September 2, 2016, Chicago; Gage Park High School was officially "integrated" in 1965 to include African American students by extending its attendance boundaries; see Berry, *Open Housing Question*, 193; Mary Maher, "Chicago Sweats Out Its Racial Problem," *Irish Times*, August 20, 1966, 7; Bruckner, "American Dream Exploded."

60. National Federation of Settlements and Neighborhood Centers, *Making Democracy Work: A Study of Neighborhood Organization, 1966–67* (New York: National Federation of Settlements and Neighborhood Centers, 1968), 18, 48.

61. Larry Villarreal, interview; Bruckner, "American Dream Exploded"; Berry, *Open Housing Question*; Perlstein, *Nixonland*, 118, 120; Albert Hunter, *Symbolic Communities: The Persistence and Change of Chicago's Local Communities* (Chicago: University of Chicago Press, 1974), 86.

62. Larry Villarreal, interview; Villarreal Long, interview, February 16, 2016. Other Latino real estate agents partook in similar behavior. For example, on the South Side in the mid-1960s, Eugenio Gomez, a community activist turned real estate agent helped resettle an enclave of Puerto Ricans from Woodlawn to Englewood. "He helped so many families that 'every realtor in the neighborhood' was interested in hiring him." See Debbie Nathan, "On Panic and Puerto Ricans: Is Blockbusting Back on the South Side?" *Reader* 13, no. 36 (June 8, 1984): 3, 36–37.

63. "Blockbusters Exploit the Fear of Change to Reap Huge Profits," *Community Reporter*, August 1962; "Fear Peddlers—Block Busters Rampage Once More in South Lawndale," *Community Reporter*, March 21, 1962, 1; John Yinger, *Closed Doors, Op-*

portunities Lost: The Continuing Costs of Housing Discrimination (New York: Russell Sage Foundation, 1995), 164–65, 225.

64. Richard A. Dolejs, "Problems of Slums," *Chicago Sun-Times*, March 7, 1966; "History of South Lawndale-Crawford Real Estate Board—Multiple Listing Service Outstanding," *Community Reporter*, 1962; Antonio Zavala, "Dick Dolejs: The Man behind the Name Little Village," *Lawndale News*, May 30, 1991; Richard Dolejs interview with author, February 1, 2017, Lyons, IL.

65. The Villarreal Real Estate Agency challenged their exclusion from the MLS by the LVREB almost immediately and eventually gained access around 1967 to 1968; Larry Villarreal, interview; Yinger, *Closed Doors*, 164–65.

66. Larry Villarreal, interview; "La Villita hoy mira con ojos color café," *La Raza*, September 9–5, 1993, 6; Leticia Espinoza, "Cámara de comercio de la Villita . . . símbolo de tradición," *La Raza*, September 9–15, 1993, 18; Rudolph Bush, "Maria de la Luz Castro, 94," *Chicago Tribune*, December 5, 2002; Cohen and Taylor, *American Pharaoh*, 354.

67. This is my reinterpretation of processes that have been dominantly viewed as the politics of *white grievance* and *white victimhood*, rather than what I consider the incentivization of white suburban opportunities through their active recovering of home financial capital. Newspapers often articulated the dominant viewpoint. For instance, one *New York Times* writer argued, "Whites, many of whom have put their life savings into their houses, are being victimized by real estate agents"; see John Kifner, "Chicago and New York: Contrasts," *New York Times*, May 16, 1971.

68. Joanne Belenchia, "Latinos and Chicago Politics," in *After Daley*, ed. Samuel Gove and Louis Masotti, 118–45, 142 (Urbana: University of Illinois Press, 1982); Córdova, "Harold Washington," 36–37; Memorandum from Colonel Jack Reilly to Mayor Richard J. Daley, Re: Arturo Velasquez appointment, July 1968, box 89, folder 5, Series II, Subseries 1B, RJD, UIC; Ismael Cuevas, "Latino Political Organizations in Chicago: The Independent Political Organization of the 22nd Ward and the Rise of Latino Political Representation," *Concientización: A Journal of Chican@ & Latin@ Experience and Thought* 5, nos. 1–2 (Winter 2009–Spring 2010): 43; John Walton, Luis M. Salces, and Joanne Belenchia, *The Political Organization of Chicago's Latino Communities* (Evanston, IL: Center for Urban Affairs, Northwestern University, 1977), 12–40.

69. "Anita Learned Her Lesson Well," *Little Village Community Reporter*, March 21, 1971; Steven Morris, "Old Mexico Is a Hit in Old Chicago," *Chicago Tribune*, September 6, 1987, 1; Kenan Heise and Mark Frazel, *Hands on Chicago: Getting Hold of the City* (Chicago: Bonus Books, 1987), 212–13; "Villarreal Named V.P.," *Lawndale News*, June 12, 1975, 9; Villarreal Long, interview, February 19, 2013; Larry Villarreal, interview; Estrada, interview; Award plaque given to Richard J. Daley from the Little Village-26th Street Area Chamber of Commerce, 1968, box 16, folder 7, Series 6, Subseries 3, RJD, UIC; "Mayor Awarded Plaque," *Little Village Community Reporter*, March 12, 1969.

70. "Anita Learned," *Little Village Community Reporter*. In June 1975, Larry Villarreal became the vice president of Civil Federal Savings and Loan, owned by Robert I.

Vanek, a business that had been in the Bohemian family since their arrival to South Lawndale in the 1920s. By 1978, he was appointed president. During those years, Civic Federal eliminated wait lines, helped install some of the first automatic teller machines in central Chicago, hired Spanish-speaking staff, welcomed Mexican immigrants and Mexican Americans to open savings accounts, and began offering transfer and money-wire services for Latin America. Others followed. "Villarreal Named V.P.," *Lawndale News*; Estrada, interview.

71. "Anita Learned," *Little Village Community Reporter*; Estrada, interview; Luis M. Salces, "Spanish American Politics in Chicago" (PhD diss., Northwestern University, 1978); Charles N. Wheeler III and Jerome Watson, "Slim Slice of Political Pie," *Chicago Sun-Times*, September 13, 1971, 1,4, 24, 26; "Chicago's Half Million Hispanos," *La Luz*, 1, no. 1 (April 1972): 32–35.

72. Mexican Chamber of Commerce, Inc. to Mayor Richard J. Daley, March 17, 1967, box SIIss1B80, folder 6, RJD, UIC; Wheeler III and Watson, "Slim Slice"; "Chicago's Half Million Hispanos," *La Luz*; "'Chicano Power' at City Hall," *Chicago Tribune*, March 27, 1971.

73. Ann Diaz, interview. Soon after, an official Chicago organization called Mexicanos de Afuera (MEDA) was formed. "MEDA Flyer in Support for Mayor Daley's 1975 Re-election Campaign," box SIIss1B120, folder 7, RJD, UIC; "Acuerdos culturales entre Illinois y Mexico," *El Informador*, July 2, 1972, 1, 3; "Presidente de Mexico agradece al mayor Richard Daley," *El Informador*, July 2, 1972, 1; US Department of State, "Mexico and the U.S. Chicano Movement," Briefing Paper, 2, January 1979, Jimmy Carter Presidential Library (JCL); Belenchia, "Latinos and Chicago Politics."

74. Wheeler III and Watson, "Slim Slice"; Larry Villarreal, interview; Juan Gómez-Quiñones, *Chicano Politics: Reality & Promise, 1940–1990* (Albuquerque: University of New Mexico Press, 1990), 160; Milton L. Rakove, *Don't Make No Waves, Don't Back No Losers: An Insider's Analysis of the Daley Machine* (Bloomington: Indiana University Press, 1975), 196–97, 266. In 1969, the 10th Ward Spanish Speaking Democratic Organization, a political organization made up of Mexican American steelworkers and other working-class community members, ran their own candidate, John Chico, for city council. The machine responded by gerrymandering their ward and dividing their power base; see Kerr, "Chicano Experience in Chicago," 182–84.

75. "Lillian Piotrowski Dies at 58," *Chicago Tribune*, May 1, 1974, B22; "MAPO Reports Voters Registration a Success in L.V.," *El Clarin Chicano*, August 28, 1974, 1–2; "Ya era tiempo! Hon. Irene Hernandez—Cook County Commissioner," *El Clarin Chicano*, October 4, 1974, 1; Rhea Mojica Hammer, "Now That the Mayoral Primaries Are History, Let Us Reflect on Several Things . . . ," *El Clarin Mexico-Americano*, March 15, 1975, 5; Larry Villarreal, interview; Estrada, interview; "At Hernandez Campaign Kickoff," *West Side Times-Lawndale News*, October 3, 1974, 10; Listing of 1978 officers for Little Village institutions (courtesy of Villarreal family, in author's possession).

76. Brochure for Chicago March for Justice and film screening of *Fighting For Our Lives, A Farmworker Film*, April 16 (film) and May 10 (march), 1975; Larry Galvan, "Ambrosio Medrano: Part of a New Breed," *Fiesta* 1, no. 4 (January 1975): 20; Da-

vid K. Fremon, *Chicago Politics Ward by Ward* (Bloomington: Indiana University Press, 1988), 147; "Report: Symposium on Economic Development in the Latin Community, July 1972," Community Renewal Society, box 2, folder 6, Reuben A. Sheares II Papers (RAS), Amistad Research Center, Tulane University, New Orleans; John D. Moorhead, "Chicago Pushes Ahead in Reviving Neighborhoods: Confidence Fostered 'Mexican Suburbs'," *Christian Science Monitor*, April 21, 1978, 11; Belenchia, "Latinos and Chicago Politics," 142; Walton, Salces, and Belenchia, *Political Organization*, 55–56.

77. Gómez-Quiñones, *Chicano Politics*; Walton, Salces, and Belenchia, *Political Organization*, 76, 88; Hernandez, "Publisher's Letter," 5.

78. Villarreal to Hartigan; Gregg Ramshaw, "Mayor Goes Full-Tilt into Last Week of Race," *Chicago Today*, March 27, 1971; Shirley Cayer, "Latins Set Boycott March on City Hall," *Daily Calumet*, March 23, 1971; "Chicago's Half Million Hispanos," *La Luz*; "Amigos for Daley," speech, March 26, 1975, box 1, folder 7, Series I, Subseries 1, RJD, UIC; Villarreal Long, interview, February 16, 2016.

79. Walton, Salces, and Belenchia, *Political Organization*, 20, 115, 119; Fremon, *Chicago Politics*, 147.

Chapter Five

1. Maria Rodriguez, interview with author, December 28, 2015, Chicago (in author's possession).

2. City of Chicago, *Chicago's Spanish Speaking Population: Selected Statistics* (Chicago: Department of Development and Planning, 1973); Gilberto Cardenas, Jim Faught, and Estevan Flores, "A Profile of the Spanish Language Population in the Little Village and Pilsen Community Areas of Chicago, Illinois and Population Projections, 1970–1980" (Notre Dame, IN: Centro de Estudios Chicanos e Investigaciones Sociales, University of Notre Dame, August 1975), 47; Mier, Giloth, and Amato, *Housing Needs of Pilsen*, 20, 22; "Chicago's Half Million Hispanos," *La Luz*, 32–35; Angela Parker, "Why Are We So Mean?" *Chicago Tribune*, May 7, 1970, 3A. For more on dilapidated housing and urban renewal, see Fernández, *Windy City*, chap. 3.

3. Historian Natalia Molina describes the historical script that perpetuated notions of Mexicans as "birds of passage" (*How Race Is Made*, 31–35). Absentee landlords represent a big obstacle for residents; for example, in 1960 only 10 percent of all housing units were owner-occupied in the Near West Side. For more, see Fernández, *Windy City*, 96; 25th Ward Alderman Vito Marzullo often relied on this script with comments such as: "For God's sake, these people better learn something about America or go back to Mexico where they belong," quoted in Antonio Zavala, " 'Where They Belong'—Politician Causes Chicago Stir," *Nuestro Magazine*, January/February 1983, 22; Elia Cuenca, Bertha Soto, and Janet Tapia, "La Lucha de las Mujeres a Nuestra Salud," in *Telling Historias*, 7–10; and Michael Kilian, "Latino Surge Makes Some Unhappy and Some Rich," *Chicago Tribune*, December 29, 1977.

4. Central Area Committee, *Chicago 21: A Plan for the Central Area Communities* (Chicago: City of Chicago, Central Area Committee, 1973); Fernández, *Windy City*, 94;

Ross Miller, *Here's the Deal: The Buying and Selling of a Great American City* (New York: Alfred A. Knopf, 1996), 73–77; Norman Krumholz and Pierre Clavel, "Interview with Arturo Vazquez," in *Reinventing Cities: Equity Planners Tell Their Stories* (Philadelphia: Temple University Press, 1994), 83–94.

5. "Casa Aztlán-Neighborhood Service Organization" pamphlet, n.d., box 2, folder 29, Institute on the Church in an Urban-Industrial Society (ICUIS) Records, UIC; "Ethnographic Description of Chicago's Spanish-Speaking Barrio in the Lower West Side," n.d., box 20, folder 13,065, GCP, UNDA; Schensul and Bymel, "Role of Applied Research," 71; Michael Ward, "Bohemians and Mexicans on Common Ground," *Historic Illinois: The Magazine of the Illinois Historic Preservation Agency* 30, no. 2 (August 2007): 10–14.

6. In a Chicago conference in 1970, Rev. Ezequiel Alvarez referred to Latinos as the "silent minority"; see Section of Hispanic American Ministries of the National Council of Churches of Christ in the USA (SOHAM), "The Hispanic American Crisis in the Nation," September 21–25, 1970, Chicago, box 37, folder 582, ICUIS, UIC; Political scientist Joanne Belenchia considered Latinos part of the "silent majority," along with the Polish population; Belenchia, "Latinos and Chicago Politics," in *After Daley*, 142.

7. "Chicago's Half Million Hispanos," *La Luz*, 35. On the neoconservative policy of 'planned shrinkage' of central-city neighborhoods, see George Lipsitz, *A Life in the Struggle: Ivory Perry and the Culture of Opposition* (Philadelphia: Temple University Press, 1988), 210. The argument originates in Robert Fisher, *Let the People Decide: Neighborhood Organizing in America* (Boston: Twayne, 1984), 124–25; Seligman, *Block by Block*, 157.

8. "Latins Want Land for Budget Housing," *Chicago Tribune*, November 14, 1971, A8; Andrew W. Kahrl, "Capitalizing on the Urban Fiscal Crisis: Predatory Tax Buyers in 1970s Chicago," *Journal of Urban History* (May 2015): 1–20. On Daley's efficient handling of 1970s financial woes in relation to other rustbelt cities, see Robert G. Spinney, *City of Big Shoulders: A History of Chicago* (DeKalb: Northern Illinois University, 2000), 237; Charles Bowden and Lew Kreinberg, *Street Signs Chicago: Neighborhood and Other Illusions of Big City Life* (Chicago: Chicago Review, 1981); Michael Miner and Sam Washington "Progress in Race Relations Not Sure—But It's Possible," *Chicago Sun-Times*, March 25, 1971; Cecil Neth, "Sniff Political Fragrance in Garbage Pile," *Chicago Sun-Times*, 1971; Harry Golden Jr. "How Marzullo Will Deliver His 25th Ward to Mayor Daley, *Chicago Sun-Times*, April 1, 1971, 76.

9. Seth S. King, "Mayor Daley Heads for His Fourth Re-election," *New York Times*, March 28, 1971, 57; David J. Less, "Hispanic Employment Opportunities: The Case of Pilsen" (master's thesis, University of Illinois at Chicago Circle, 1980); Schensul and Bakszysz, "Role of Applied Research," 82; and Noel A. Cazenave, "Chicago Influences on the War on Poverty," *Journal of Policy History* 5, no. 1 (1993): 52–68.

10. Robert Enstad, "Veterans Job Fair Tries Again: Attendance Way Off," *Chicago Tribune*, May 11, 1972, 3.

11. Rachel Cordero, interview by Mary Ann Johnson, 1974, p. 3 of transcript, box 2, folder 19, Hull-House Oral History Collection (HHOH), UIC.

12. Clarence Page, "West Side Latins Urge Hill to Release Land for Bidding," *Chicago Tribune*, October 10, 1971, W14; "Latins Want Land," *Chicago Tribune*; Stan Ziemba, "DUR Land Sale Vexes Latin Bloc," *Chicago Tribune*, August 3, 1972, A4; Three young Mexican women [anonymous], interview by Mary Ann Johnson, 1974, box 4, folder 52, HHOH-UIC; Meg O'Connor, "Renewal of the Near West Side: Success to Some, Failure to Poor," *Chicago Tribune*, May 20, 1973, 51; Fernández, *Windy City*, 116–17; Garv Washburn, "Developers Casting Fond Gazes at Near West Side," *Chicago Tribune*, January 6, 1974, K1; Michael Flannery, "Pilsen's Latinos Leery of 'Renewal,'" *Chicago Sun-Times*, August 11, 1974, 46.

13. Latin Community Advisory Board, "Circle Campus vs. The Latin Community of Chicago," box 3, folder 28, Julian Samora Papers (JSP), Special Collections, Michigan State University Library (MSU); Cordero, interview.

14. Cordero, interview, 1; Paul Vega, "The Academic Performance of a Group of Latin Students Admitted to the University of Illinois, Chicago Circle Campus, Fall 1969, through the Educational Assistance Program" (master's thesis, Northeastern Illinois University, 1971), 4–5.

15. Three young Mexican women [anonymous], interview.

16. Krumholz and Clavel, "Chicago: Interviews with Robert Mier, Arturo Vazquez and Kari Moe," in *Regenerating Cities*, 63–96. On the impact of the US civil rights movement and the global sixties upheaval on urban planning, see June Manning Thomas and Marsha Ritzdorf, eds., *Urban Planning and the African American Community: In the Shadows* (Thousand Oaks, CA: SAGE, 1997); Avila, *Folklore of the Freeway*; Peter Hall, *Cities of Tomorrow: An Intellectual History of Urban Planning and Design Since 1880*, 4th ed.(Malden, MA: Wiley Blackwell, 2014), 398–99.

17. Page, "West Side Latins Urge"; "Latins Want Land," *Chicago Tribune*; Ziemba, "DUR Land Sale" *Chicago Tribune*; Three young Mexican women [anonymous], interview; O'Connor, "Renewal"; Washburn, "Developers Casting"; Michael Flaming, "Pilsen Residents Leary of Renewal," *Chicago Sun-Times*, August 11, 1974; SOHAM, "Hispanic American Crisis."

18. Pierre de Vise, *The Anti-Redlining Campaign: Three Perspectives on Its Origins, Meaning, and Results* (Chicago: School of Urban Sciences, University of Illinois at Chicago Circle, 1978); "After Blacks," *Port Arthur News*; Pierre de Vise and Ruth Ramirez, "Shifts in Chicago's Ethnic Communities, 1960–1970" (working paper v. 5, Chicago Regional Hospital Study, September 1973) 7; Cordero, interview, 32.

19. Erik S. Gellman, "'The Stone Wall Behind:' The Chicago Coalition for United Community Action and Labor's Overseers, 1968–1973," in *Black Power at Work: Community Control, Affirmative Action, and the Construction Industry*, ed. David A. Goldberg and Trevor Griffey, 112–33 (Ithaca, NY: Cornell University Press, 2011); "Spanish Coalition for Jobs," *El Informador*, July 30, 1972, 4; "A.P.O. demanda trabajos," *El Informador*, July 30, 1972; "Los hispanos antes el nuevo plan de Chicago," *El Informador*, August 6, 1972, 5. Ross Miller writes that the mayor, as chairman of the Chicago Committee on Urban Opportunity (CCUO), oversaw the administering of every OEO dollar; see Miller, *Here's the Deal*, 265.

20. "Spanish Coalition for Jobs," *El Informador*; "A.P.O. demanda trabajos," *El*

Informador; "Los hispanos antes," *El Informador*; Boiton, "Role of Interorganizational Networks," 97; Miner and Washington "Progress"; "Report," Community Renewal Society.

21. "Report," Community Renewal Society.

22. Cayer, "Latins Set Boycott"; "Los chicanos: Tema que interesa a la prensa mexicana," *El Informador*, October 15, 1972, 10.

23. "Mexico Chief Visits Chicago," *Times Picayune New Orleans*, June 19, 1972, 17; "Echeverria pide nueva era en trato Mexico-EU," *El Informador*, June 25, 1972, 1; "Little Village-26th Street Area Chamber of Commerce, in name of the Mexican Community . . . ," *El Informador*, July 2, 1972, 13; Cayer, "Latins Set Boycott."

24. Miner and Washington, "Progress"; Cayer, "Latins Set Boycott"; Congressman Roman C. Pucinski of Illinois on Richard J. Daley, Re: "Mayor Daley Proposes Blueprint for America's Urban Survival," Congressional Record-Extensions of Remarks, June 15, 1971, file clippings, container 40, folder 4, DSB, LOC; "Chicago's Daley: How to Run a City," *Newsweek*, 82.

25. MADO, *Mexican American Democratic Organization – Annual Program*; Jorge A. Rendon, "Discrimen racial en la Comision de Relaciones Humanas," in Clementina Souchet, *Clementina: Historia sin fin*, 192 (Chicago: independently published by Clementina Souchet, 1986); "SER, Jobs for Progress," *El Clarin Mexico-Americano*, March 15, 1975, 6, 11; Juan Mora, *Rudy Lozano: His Life, His People* (Chicago: Taller de Estudios Comunitarios, 1991).

26. Martin G. Blanco, "South Chicago New," *El Informador*, July 2, 1972, 13; Martin G. Blanco, "Latins Speak Up," *Chicago Tribune*, October 6, 1967, 20; Wheeler III and Watson, "Slim Slice." In a Chicago conference in 1970, Rev. Ezequiel Alvarez referred to Latinos as the "silent minority." See SOHAM, "Hispanic American Crisis." On Mexican Americans of South Chicago against Daley's use of urban renewal funds in Millgate, see Martin G. Blanco, "News and Views," *El Informador*, August 6, 1972, 4; and Martin G. Blanco, "Chavez Si! Walker No!" *El Informador*, October 22, 1972, 1.

27. "Report," Community Renewal Society.

28. "Jose Carlos Gómez Delegado a la convención republicana en Miami," *El Informador*, July 16, 1972, 11, 14–15; Cohen and Taylor, *American Pharaoh*, 484–85.

29. "Dinner Honors Gomez," *OMBE Outlook*, March 1972, 5; *Hearings before the Subcommittee on SBA Oversight and Minority Enterprise, Minority Enterprise and Allied Problems of Small Business*, 94th Cong., 1st sess. (July 1975).

30. June Skinner Sawyers, *Chicago Portraits: Biographies of 250 Famous Chicagoans* (Chicago: Loyola University Press, 1991), 160; Frank Casillas, interview with author, April 29, 2016, Downers Grove, IL; "HUD celebra 4to. Aniversario del Acto de Derechos Civiles," *El Informador*, June 4, 1972, 12; "Comisión para Oportunidad Igual en el Empleo," *El Informador*, June 25, 1972, 4; "Programa piloto para negocios pequeños," *El Informador*, June 4, 1972, 1; "Jose Carlos Gómez Delegado," *El Informador*. On unemployment, see Mier, Giloth, and Amato, *Housing Needs of Pilsen*, 14.

31. "Avaluaciones sobre las propiedades locales," *El Informador*, July 2, 1972, 14; "Acuerdos culturales," *El Informador*, 1, 3; "La excención de impuestos en propiedad personal deberá ser propuesta de nuevo," *El Informador*, May 28, 1972, 13; "Programa

piloto," *El Informador*; "Jose Carlos Gómez Delegado," *El Informador*; Phillip V. Sánchez, "La silenciosa revolucion latinoamericana," *El Informador*, August 13, 1972, 4; "La Oficina de Derechos Civiles puede serle util," *El Informador*, June 4, 1972, 1; "Los hospitales se modernizan," *El Informador*, June 4, 1972, 1. On Superintendent Conslink announcement, "Revista de noticias," *El Informador*, June 4, 1972, 11; "El Loop College ofrece oportunidades de estudio gratis," *El Informador*, June 4, 1972, 13; Paul Arevalo, "Cartas a la redacción," *El Informador*, October 29, 1972, 12.

32. Liner notes from Bernardo Cárdenas, *Con sabor a Mexico*, LP (Paisano Records-02); "Los jóvenes hispanos para la reelección del Presidente [Nixon]," *El Informador*, October 29, 1972, 1.

33. Blanco, "South Chicago New." On the Daley machine's undermining of Mexican American wards in South Chicago, see Belenchia, "Latinos and Chicago Politics," 128–29; Córdova, "Harold Washington," 36–37; Kornblum, *Blue Collar Community*, 169; "Mexico Chief Visits Chicago," *Times-Picayune New Orleans*; "Echeverria Pide," *El Informador*; "Little Village-26th Street Area," *El Informador*.

34. Blanco, "South Chicago New"; Casillas, interview; "HUD celebra," *El Informador*, 12; "Comisión para Oportunidad Igual," *El Informador*, 4.

35. Morton Kondracke, "Nixon Campaign Analysis of Spanish-Speaking Vote," *Chicago Sun-Times*, November 7, 1972, 4; "Un analisis de la campaña de Nixon referente al voto hispano," *El Informador*, November 19, 1972, 1, 3; "Tomaran en cuenta a los negocios minoritarios para compras del Edo.," *El Informador*, May 21, 1972, 2; "Comunicado conjunto Entre Richard M. Nixon y Licenciado Luis Echeverria Alvarez," *El Informador*, July 2, 1972, 1; "Acuerdos culturales," *El Informador*, 1, 3; "Presidente de Mexico agradece," *El Informador*, 1. Historian Juan Gómez-Quiñones has noted that just prior to 1968, the Republican Party strategized to diminish the Mexican American vote, writing, "They preferred to obtain a part of this vote themselves but what was most important was to cut into the Democratic vote"; see Gómez-Quiñones, *Chicano Politics* (Albuquerque: University of New Mexico Press, 1990), 160–61.

36. Douglas Woodlock, "Lists Nation's Priorities," *Chicago Sun-Times*, March 3, 1971; Central Area Committee, *Chicago 21*; Miller, *Here's the Deal*, 73–77; Cordero, interview; Lois Wille, *At Home in the Loop: How Clout and Community Built Chicago's Dearborn Park* (Carbondale: Southern Illinois Press, 1997), 48–49; Pilsen Neighbors Community Council (PNCC), *Pilsen Neighborhood Plan* (Chicago: prepared by Pilsen Neighbors Community Council, Consultant: Barton-Aschman Associates, Inc., December 1976), 5; Robert Suro, "When Push Comes to Clout," *Nuestro Magazine*, April 1977, 6; Krumholz and Clavel, "Interview with Arturo Vazquez"; Arturo Vázquez and Xavier Menéndez, "Son of Bulldozer," *Nuestro Magazine*, April 1977, 8–9.

37. Wille, *At Home*, 48–49; Cordero, interview; O'Connor, "Renewal"; Washburn, "Developers Casting"; Ziemba, "DUR Land Sale," *Chicago Tribune*.

38. PNCC, "At the Grassroots" Pamphlet, 1977, file folder #[2-20-10B], Teresa Fraga Papers, Department of Special Collections and Archives DePaul University Library, Chicago (hereafter cited as TFP, DPU); Central Area Committee, *Chicago 21*; Mier, Giloth, and Amato, *Housing Needs of Pilsen*, 22; Vazquez and Menéndez, "Son of

Bulldozer," 8–9; Boiton, "Role of Interorganizational Networks," 91–102. On the new high school, see Alvarez, "Community That Would Not"; Cordero, interview, 33.

39. On the 1969 takeover of Pilsen Neighbors Community Council and the Howell Neighborhood House, see Stern, "Ethnic Identity," 96–102; Boiton, "Role of Interorganizational Networks," 91–102; Alfredo S. Lanier, "Doing It Their Way: Why Is Pilsen So . . . Stubborn," *Chicago Enterprise*, October 1988, 19; and "Casa Aztlán-Neighborhood Service Organization." Pilsen Neighbors was started by a Philadelphia community organizer, Ellsworth Shephard, who arrived in Pilsen in the summer of 1953. The first forays of this neighborhood group are recounted in Jon L. Regier, *Miss Ray's Book of Memories and Howell House Today* (1955), box 61, folder 15, NFSNC, UMN.

40. Krumholz and Clavel, "Interview with Arturo Vazquez"; Boiton, "Role of Interorganizational Networks," 91–102; "Mary Gonzalez interview by Juan Andrade, Jr." in Andrade, 203–5; "Result of Factional Struggle: 80-Year-Old Casa Aztlán Center to Be Closed," *West Side Times–Lawndale News*, October 3, 1974, 2; Mary Gonzales, "Carpe Diem: Seize the Day and Exploit Your Opportunities" (unpublished autobiographical essay, courtesy of Mary Gonzales, in author's possession, n.d.); "Chicago's Half Million Hispanos," *La Luz*, 32–35.

41. Ernesto B. Vigil, *The Crusade for Justice: Chicano Militancy and the Government's War on Dissent* (Madison: University of Wisconsin, 1999), 39–40; Chicano Coordinating Council on Higher Education, *El Plan de Santa Barbara: A Chicano Plan for Higher Education* (Oakland, CA: La Causa Publications, 1969). Muralist Mario Castillo painted his first mural, entitled *Metaphysics (Peace)*, in 1968, Pugh, "Pilsen/Little Village," *Chicago History* 26, no. 1 (Spring 1997): 54–55. Krumholz and Clavel, "Interview with Arturo Vazquez"; Boiton, "Role of Interorganizational Networks," 91–102; Schensul and Bymel, "Role of Applied Research," 69–89; OLAS panel discussion at the Rudy Lozano Library, 2012; "Los Chicanos," *El Informador*. For historical treatments of Chicago's Latino and Chicano Movement, see Fernández, *Windy City*; Padilla, *Latino Ethnic Consciousness*; and Leonard G. Ramírez, *Chicanas of 18th Street: Narratives of a Movement from Latino Chicago* (Urbana: University of Illinois Press, 2011).

42. Krumholz and Clavel, "Interview with Arturo Vazquez"; "Chicago's Half Million Hispanos," *La Luz*, 32–35; Fernández, *Windy City*, 227; "Mi Raza Primero Conference in Muskegon, Michigan," *La Luz* 1, no. 1 (April 1972): 50–51.

43. Cockcroft et al., *Toward a People's Art*, 123–26; Victor A. Sorell, ed., *Guide to Chicago Murals: Yesterday and Today* (Chicago: Chicago Council on Fine Arts, 1979), 20–21, 42–43, 52–53; Stern, "Ethnic Identity," 46.

44. Sorell, *Guide to Chicago Murals*; Cockcroft et al., *Toward a People's Art*, 123–26; "¿Que Pasa?," *El Informador*, May 28, 1972, 4; "Casa Aztlán recibe premio de Chicago Beautiful Committee," *El Informador*, October 29, 1972, 12. For a brief description of activities in Casa Aztlán, see Susan Stechnij, "Mi Raza: Portrait of a Family" (master's thesis, University of Illinois at Chicago Circle, 1978), 42–43.

45. "¿Que Pasa?," *El Informador*; PNCC, *Pilsen Neighborhood Plan*, 14–15; "Casa Aztlán Recibe Premio," *El Informador*.

46. Sorell, *Guide to Chicago Murals*; Cockcroft et al., *Toward a People's Art*, 123–26; "¿Que Pasa?," *El Informador*; Fernández, *Windy City*, 231; "Casa Aztlán Recibe Premio," *El Informador*; Stechnij, "Mi Raza," 42–43; Stern, "Ethnic Identity," 125.

47. "Result of Factional Struggle," *West Side Times–Lawndale News*; Gonzales, "Carpe Diem"; Krumholz and Clavel, "Interview with Arturo Vazquez."

48. Gonzales, "Carpe Diem," 11; Krumholz and Clavel, "Interview with Arturo Vazquez," 84.

49. "Agente de Inmigracion Balacea a un Mexicano," *El Informador*, November 19, 1972, 1, 14; Isidro Lucas, "The Law and the Illegals," *Nuestro Magazine*, May 1977, 43–45; "Anti-Police Demonstrators March at Criminal Courts," *West Side Times–Lawndale News*, April 10, 1975, 1; "Mi Raza Primero Conference," *La Luz*; "Chicago's Half Million Hispanos," *La Luz*, 32–35.

50. Valadez, "Chicano Political Development," 190. On a participant's recollection of "The Froebel Uprising, 1973," see Ramírez et al., *Chicanas of 18th Street*, 76–78; and correspondence from Villarreal to Hartigan.

51. Prieto, *Harvest of Hope*, 117–22.

52. Prieto, 119, 127–28; "After Blacks," *Port Arthur News*.

53. "Latinos vs. C.T.A: A.P.O. trae la C.T.A. a nuestra comunidad," *El Informador*, July 16, 1972, 11; "A.P.O. demanda trabajos," *El Informador*; Ruth Moss, "Spanish Spoken Here—and Chicago Begins Listening," *Chicago Tribune*, September 18, 1974, C1; "Intento de convenio entre la Illinois Bell Telephone Company y la Spanish Coalition for Jobs," *El Informador*, July 2, 1972, 12, 15; "Illinois Bell Telephone Company y la Spanish Coalition for Jobs," *El Informador*, July 2, 1972, 1; "Anti-latino Bias Charged against P.O." *West Side Times–Lawndale News*, March 13, 1975, 1; "Spanish Coalition for Jobs," *El Informador*; "Los hispanos antes," *El Informador*; Mora, *Rudy Lozano*, 108–9.

54. Lanier, "Doing It Their Way," 19–20; Schensul and Bymel, "Role of Applied Research," 86. For more on the fight for a new high school in Pilsen, see Alvarez, "Community That Would Not."

55. People's Planning Coalition, "The Call," file folder #[2-20-10A(2)], TFP, DPU; Zavala, interview; Schensul and Bymel, "Role of Applied Research," 71–72; Vazquez and Menéndez, "Son of Bulldozer," 8–9.

56. Vazquez and Menéndez, "Son of Bulldozer," 8–9; Lanier, "Doing It Their Way," 18. The Rodriguezes moved out of Pilsen and into the Back of the Yards in 1983, when the western section of the Yards was opened to Mexicans (Maria Rodriguez, interview). Berry, *Open Housing Question*, 464–65; PNCC, *Pilsen Neighborhood Plan*, 4; Robert Mier and Kari Moe, "Decentralized Development" in *Harold Washington and the Neighborhoods: Progressive City Government in Chicago, 1983–1987*, ed. Pierre Clavel and Wim Wiewel, 6–8 (New Brunswick, NJ: Rutgers University Press, 1991); Bowden and Kreinberg, *Street Signs Chicago*.

57. Flannery, "Pilsen's Latinos Leery"; "Famed Mexican Artists' Work in Exhibition Here," *West Side Times–Lawndale News*, April 17, 1975, 5; Mier and Moe, "Decentralized Development," 6–8; Robert Heuer, "To Save a Neighborhood," *Vista* 3, no. 3 (November 1987): 32.

58. Mier and Moe, "Decentralized Development," 6–8; Krumholz and Clavel, "Interview with Robert Mier," in *Regenerating Cities*, 69; Schensul and Bymel, "Role of Applied Research," 77, 80; Mora, *Rudy Lozano*, 101–3.

59. "Mary Gonzales interview" in Andrade, 206; Mark Santow, "Running in Place: Saul Alinsky, Race, and Community Organizing," in *Transforming the City: Community Organizing and the Challenge of Political Change*, ed. Marion Orr, 28–55 (Lawrence: University of Kansas Press, 2007); Mora, *Rudy Lozano*, 102–3; Lanier, "Doing It Their Way," 19–20; Virginia Martinez, interview; Squires et al., *Chicago: Race, Class, and the Response to Urban Decline* (Philadelphia: Temple University Press, 1987), 145–46.

60. Mora, *Rudy Lozano*, 102–3; "Sesión de orientación para inmigrantes," *Lawndale News*, May 22, 1975, 10; Maria Rodriguez, interview; Lucas, "Law and the Illegals," 43–45; Donald C. Reitzes and Dietrich C. Reitzes, "Alinsky in the 1980s: Two Contemporary Chicago Community Organizations," *Sociological Quarterly* 28, no. 2 (Summer 1987): 271–73.

61. Mora, *Rudy Lozano*, 102–3; "Que hacer con un propietario indolente," *El Informador*, July 23, 1972, 13; "Un modo de vivir mejor," *El Informador*, October 22, 1972, 5; Lanier, "Doing It Their Way," 19–20; Mora, *Rudy Lozano*, 102–3.

62. Mier and Moe, "Decentralized Development," 6–8; Krumholz and Clavel, "Interview with Robert Mier," 69; Schensul and Bymel, "Role of Applied Research," 77, 80; "Mary Gonzales interview," in Andrade, 204; John J. Betancur and Douglas C. Gills, "Race and Class in Local Economic Development," in *Theories of Local Economic Development: Perspectives from across the Disciplines*, ed. Richard D. Bingham and Robert Mier, 197–98 (Newbury Park, CA: SAGE, 1993).

63. Flannery, "Pilsen's Latinos Leery"; Cesar Olivo to Pilsen Neighbors Community Council Board, "Subject: Rehab Coordinator Position," March 16, 1976, file folder #[2-3-10C], TFP; PNCC, *Pilsen Neighborhood Plan*, 4–6; Pilsen Housing and Business Alliance, *Los Nuevos Tiempos* 1, no. 1 (December 1979), file folder #[1-20-10C], TFP.

64. PNCC, *Pilsen Neighborhood Plan*, 4–7.

65. PNCC, *Pilsen Neighborhood Plan*, 7; Juan J. Betancur, Robert Giloth, Gregory Longhini, Winston Mercurius, and Joel Worth, "Employment Opportunities in Pilsen" (project for the School of Urban Sciences, College of Architecture, Art and Urban Sciences, University of Illinois at Chicago Circle, 1976); Mier, Giloth, and Amato, *Housing Needs of Pilsen*, 3; Patricia A. Wright, "The Pilsen Community Plan: The Organizing Effort, 1973–1975" (master's thesis, University of Illinois at Chicago Circle, 1979).

66. PNCC, *Pilsen Neighborhood Plan*, 4–5, 24; PNCC letter to readers of the *Pilsen Neighborhood Plan*, February 1977, file folder #[2-22-10C], TFP; Bowden and Kreinberg, *Street Signs Chicago*, 32–33; the term "gentrification" was coined by a London sociologist in 1964.

67. PNCC, *Pilsen Neighborhood Plan* (1976), 3, 25, 46, 49. Stern mentions Pilsen planners held meetings with the city to discuss architectural plans and bank loans for rehabilitation of buildings; see Stern, "Ethnic Identity," 136; PNCC, *Pilsen Neighborhood Plan*, 3, 25, 46, 49, 50.

68. Central Area Committee, *Central Area Plan* (Chicago: City of Chicago, Central

Area Committee, 1958); Central Area Committee, *Chicago 21*; PNCC, *Pilsen Neighborhood Plan*, 24–25; Jacobs, *Death and Life*, 163; PNCC, *Pilsen Neighborhood Plan*, 24–25, 29, 42, 56.

69. Gonzales, "Carpe Diem," 17; PNCC, *Pilsen Neighborhood Plan*, 36, 52, 54. The construction of Benito Juárez High School was controversial. For a history of the high school, see Alvarez, "Community That Would Not." I found in my own research that the members of the Amigos for Daley played a role in the architectural controversy. The Amigos facilitated the relationship between President of Mexico Luis Echeverría and Mayor Richard J. Daley. On the encouragement of the Amigos, Daley asked Echeverría to send his nation's best architect to Chicago to design the high school, leading to the selection of Pedro Ramírez Vázquez. An impasse arose when PNCC insisted on using a home-grown Chicano architect, Adrian Lozano. In the end, both Mexican and local Mexican American architects participated in the designs.

70. PNCC, *Pilsen Neighborhood Plan*, 24–25, 36, 43, 54; Pat Wright to Pilsen Neighbors Board Members, "Re: Report on the Community Plan and where it's at," November 9, 1976, file folder #[2-3-10C], TFP (emphasis in the original).

71. PNCC, *Pilsen Neighborhood Plan*, 32, 36–38, 50; Bowden and Kreinberg, *Street Signs Chicago*, 25–26.

72. PNCC, *Pilsen Neighborhood Plan*; Vazquez and Menéndez, "Son of Bulldozer," 8–9; Mier and Moe, "Decentralized Development," 6–8; Heuer, "To Save a Neighborhood," 32; Lanier, "Doing It Their Way," 18. On CDC as useful "instrument" for Pilsen, see Betancur and Gills, "Race and Class in Local Economic Development," 197; PHBA, *Los Nuevos Tiempos*. On Chicago and the Community Reinvestment Act of 1977, see Jean Pogge, "Reinvestment in Chicago Neighborhoods"; Calvin Bradford and Gale Cincotta, "The Legacy, the Promise, and the Unfinished Agenda," in *From Redlining to Reinvestment: Community Responses to Urban Disinvestment*, ed. Gregory D. Squires, 229 (Philadelphia: Temple University Press, 1992).

73. PNCC letter to readers of the *Pilsen Neighborhood Plan*, February 1977, file folder #[2-22-10C], TFP; Teresa Fraga, PNCC, to Jack Cornelius, CCAC, May 5, 1977, file folder #[2-22-10C], TFP.

Chapter Six

1. Transcript of Conference Proceedings, "Art, Architecture and the Urban Neighborhood: A Dialogue of Chicago Artists, Architects and Citizens, October 22–23, 1981, University of Illinois at Chicago Circle," file folder #[2-20-10A], TFP, DPU.

2. *Time* magazine's cover story heralded "Hispanic Americans" as "Soon" the "Biggest Minority," *Time*, October 16, 1978; Suro, "When Push Comes to Clout," 6; Córdova, "Harold Washington"; George M. Schuch Jr., "A Policy Analysis of Latino Political Representation in the City of Chicago" (master's thesis, George Washington University, 1990).

3. Mayor Daley often delegated gerrymandering to Alderman Tom Keane, known as "The Great Mapmaker"; see Don Rose, "Tom Keane's Masterpiece—The Chicago Ward Map Controversy: A Case of Racial Gerrymandering," *Chicago Reporter* 2, no. 5

(May 1973): 1–4; Heise and Frazel, *Hands On Chicago*. McKinley Park: 15,632 to 13,248; Back of the Yards: 60,817 to 55,860; Brighton Park: 35,167 to 30,770; Archer Heights: 11,134 to 9,708; and Garfield Ridge in the vicinity of Midway Airport: 42,998 to 37,935; Pilsen: 44,498 to 44,951.

4. John J. Betancur, Teresa Córdova, and María de los Ángeles Torres, "Economic Restructuring and the Process of Incorporation of Latinos into the Chicago Economy," in *Latinos in a Changing U.S. Economy: Comparative Perspectives on Growing Inequality* (Newbury Park, CA: SAGE,1993): 109–32; Michael Ervin, "A Really Big Deal," *Chicago Enterprise*, October 1990, 9; "Home Prices Rise as Demand for Real Estate Increases," *Lawndale News–West Side Times*, June 11, 1989, 7; Maryann Mills, "New Ethnic Group Arrives: Hispanics," *Chicago Tribune*, September 25, 1985, G17; Philip Nyden and Wim Wiewel, *Challenging Uneven Development: An Urban Agenda for the 1990s* (New Brunswick, NJ: Rutgers University Press, 1991); Cedric Herring et al., eds., *Empowerment in Chicago: Grassroots Participation in Economic Development and Poverty Alleviation* (Chicago: UIC Great Cities, 1998).

5. On "mismatched housing" resulting in "pushing" residents into the housing market, see Mier, Giloth, and Amato, *Housing Needs of Pilsen*, 20; *Housing: Chicago Style; A Consultation Sponsored by the Illinois Advisory Committee to the United States Commission on Civil Rights* (Washington, DC: US Commission on Civil Rights, 1982); Miller, *Here's the Deal*; Joel Rast, *Remaking Chicago: The Political Origins of Urban Industrial Change* (DeKalb: Northern Illinois University Press, 2002); Donald M. Schwartz, "Suburbia Becoming Plain, Old Urbia," *Chicago Sun-Times*, October 22, 1972, 4; and Ervin, "Really Big Deal," 9. On the supposedly unchanged "Eastern European, blue-collar," and "staid" characteristics of McKinley Park and Brighton Park in the 1980s, see Allen H. Kelson et al., *Chicago Magazine's Guide to Chicago* (Chicago: Contemporary Books, 1983), 85–87; Roger Fox and Debora Haines, *Black Homeowners in Transition Areas* (Chicago: Chicago Urban League, Research and Planning Department, 1981); Mary Leonard, "He's Going to Fight Crosstown," *Chicago Today*, June 4, 1972, 76.

6. Centeno's tavern was located on 1601 South Halsted Street. Letter from Mike Garcia to Miguel Centeno, Re: Economic Development, August 2, 1977, file folder #[1-27- 10C], TFP; "Neighborhood Flower Garden," *ESDC Mini-Zone Newsletter*, March 1980, 1–2, file folder #[1-5-10C] TFP; Referred to as "Mike's saloon," in Bowden and Kreinberg, *Street Signs Chicago*, 57, 197.

7. See Osman, *Invention of Brownstone Brooklyn*. See also Christopher Lowen Agee, *The Streets of San Francisco: Policing and the Creation of a Cosmopolitan Liberal Politics, 1950–1972* (Chicago: University of Chicago Press, 2014); and Richard Lloyd, *Neo-Bohemia: Art and Commerce in the Postindustrial City* (New York: Routledge, 2006), 66.

8. Bowden and Kreinberg, *Street Signs Chicago*, 80–81; Garry Freshman, "The Colonization of Pilsen," *Reader* 7, no. 39, June 30, 1978, 1, 10–11, 16, 20, 22; Barbara Aubin, "14th Annual Pilsen East Artists' Open House, September 1984," *Women Artists News*, Winter 1985, 29. Lew Kreinberg occasionally worked with ESDC in the late 1970s and was a member of the Friends of the Parks, Neighborhood Parks Committee, working on

improving Pilsen's Dvorak Park; see Nancy Golden, Minutes from Friends of the Parks, Neighborhood Parks Committee, June 4, 1980, file folder #[2-8-10C], TFP.

9. Dempsey J. Travis, "How Whites Are Taking Back Black Neighborhoods," *Ebony*, September 1978, 72–82. On "flippers," see "D.C. Council Passes Antispeculation Measure," *Planning*, August 1978, 6; and Paul Gapp, "Chicago 21," *Architectural Forum* 140, no. 1 (January/February 1974): 32–37.

10. Mier, Giloth, and Amato, *Housing Needs of Pilsen*, esp. Chap. 3; Freshman, "Colonization of Pilsen"; Aubin, "14th Annual"; Peter Cunningham, "Savior or Villain in Pilsen?" *Crain's Chicago Business*, November 14, 1988, 3; Transcript of telecast, "Pilsen: Port of Entry," documentary directed by Ken Solarz (WTTW-Channel 11, 1981), file folder #[2-22-10C], TFP; "The Pilsen Plan"; Judy Meima et al., *Tax, Title, & Housing Court Search: Property Research for Action: A Manual for Chicago* (Chicago: University of Illinois at Chicago, Center for Urban Economic Development, 1984), 46; Bowden and Kreinberg, *Street Signs Chicago*, 123.

11. Bowden and Kreinberg, *Street Signs Chicago*, 61; Freshman, "Colonization of Pilsen"; Eduardo Camacho and Ben Joravsky, *Against the Tide: The Middle Class in Chicago* (Chicago: Community Renewal Society, 1989), 100; Aubin, "14th Annual."

12. Freshman, "Colonization of Pilsen"; Travis, "Taking Back," 73. Also in 1977, the City's Economic Development Commission was using millions of federal dollars to fund *Chicago 21* projects such as Dearborn Park; *Housing: Chicago Style*.

13. Bowden and Kreinberg, *Street Signs Chicago*, 61, 74, 123–24. Not all whites living in East Pilsen viewed themselves as part of John Podmajersky's colony. Some residents created their own group, such as the nonprofit corporation called East End, Inc., founded by artists and urban farmers Heidi S. Perrey and Howard Solotroff. Perrey served as president and "business agent" and collaborated with PNCC on issues from fighting blight to community development. But while Perrey claimed there were Latino members in her group, she also referred to the eastside of Pilsen as separate from the rest of Pilsen. Groups like PNCC, ESDC, and PHBA viewed these efforts skeptically, a way to claim authority over that space. See Heidi S. Perrey to PNCC, 1977, file folder #[2-1-10C], TFP.

14. Transcript of telecast, "Pilsen"; Aubin, "14th Annual Pilsen"; Camacho and Joravsky, *Against the Tide*, 100; Correspondence from Heidi S. Perrey to PNCC. Despite the best intentions to humanize gentrification in East Pilsen, Bowden and Kreinberg perpetuated the "myth of neighborhoods" argument as well; see Bowden and Kreinberg, *Street Signs Chicago*, 74.

15. Patricia M. Szymczak, "Pilsen Rehab Project Brushing Off 20-Year-Old Hispanic Mural," *Chicago Tribune*, August 2, 1988, A4; Sorell, *Guide to Chicago Murals*. Before painting *Metafísica*, Castillo had painted an indoor mural in 1964 as a high school student at Lane Tech; Jesús "Jesse" López, interview with the author, December 22, 2016, Chicago (in author's possession). Podmajersky's code violations and method of escaping them were documented in Bowden and Kreinberg, *Street Signs Chicago*, 82–84.

16. Vazquez and Menéndez, "Son of Bulldozer," 8–9; PHBA, *Los Nuevos Tiempos*, 3; Ken Gregorio, monthly staff report to Pilsen Neighbors Community Council, Re:

Community Development money for Pilsen, September 1978, file folder #[1-20-10A], TFP. On the politics and corruption of Chicago's tax overassessment, see Meima et al., *Tax, Title, & Housing*, esp. chap. 5.

17. Mier, Giloth, and Amato, *Housing Needs of Pilsen*; Bernardo Esqueda, "50 Residents in Pilsen Show 'It Can Be Done,'" *Chicago Tribune*, June 17, 1976, F2. PNCC questioned the city's use (and abuse) of federal funds slated for community development through the Community Development Block Grants; see PNCC, "Community Development Funds and Pilsen," bulletin, January 1979, file folder #[2-22-10B], TFP; Kelson et al., *Chicago Magazine's Guide*, 67.

18. PHBA, *Los Nuevos Tiempos*; Transcript of telecast, "Pilsen"; Bowden and Kreinberg, *Street Signs Chicago*, 61, 64.

19. Robert Giloth, "Jefferson Park: A Preliminary Study of Community Action" (unpublished manuscript, March 13, 1981) (courtesy of Robert Giloth, in author's possession).

20. Marla Donato, "Gallery Going on S. Halsted," *Chicago Tribune*, July 1, 1987, F3; Freshman, "Colonization of Pilsen"; Cunningham, "Savior or Villain?"; Transcript of telecast, "Pilsen."

21. Robert Mier, *Social Justice and Local Development Policy* (Newbury Park, CA: SAGE, 1993), 75; Antonio Zavala, "Planned Manufacturing is Urged for Pilsen: Speculators Seek to Encroach on Pilsen," *Lawndale News–West Side Times*, January 12, 1989; Krumholz and Clavel, "Interview with Arturo Vazquez."

22. Kathleen Whalen FitzGerald, *Brass: Jane Byrne and the Pursuit of Power* (Chicago: Contemporary Books 1981; Curtis Black, "Chicago Remapping Challenged in Court," *In These Times*, October–November 1982, 2; Gonzales, "Carpe Diem."

23. FitzGerald, *Brass*; Gordon Mantler, "Rainbow Reformers: Black-Brown Activism and the Election of Harold Washington," in *Civil Rights and Beyond: African American and Latino/a Activism in the Twentieth-Century United States*, ed. Brian D. Behnken (Athens: University of Georgia Press, 2016), 223, 227; Manning Marable, "Slap in Mayor Jane Byrne's Face," *New York Amsterdam News*, March 19, 1983, 13; Gonzales, "Carpe Diem."

24. Graciela Silva-Schuch, interview with author, February 23, 2016, Chicago (in author's possession); Tom Muier, "United Neighborhood Organization of the Back of the Yards," *Chicago Sun-Times*, September 7, 1983, 18. On Latinos adopting Saul Alinsky methods, see Neal R. Peirce, "Hispanic Groups Turning to Political Activism," *Buffalo News*, May 20, 1979, E6; Reitzes and Reitzes, "Alinsky in the 1980s"; and Patrick Barry, "Chicago's Latinos Awake but Not United," *Nuestro Magazine*, January/February 1983, 20–23. On the founding of UNO, see UNO of Chicago, *Decision Shapes Our Destiny*, Convention Program, May 21, 1987, p. 9, file folder #[2-19-10B], TFP; and Latino Institute, *Al Filo/At the Cutting Edge: The Empowerment of Chicago's Latino Electorate* (Chicago: Latino Institute, September 1986).

25. Silva-Schuch, interview; Muier, "United Neighborhood Organization." On UNO Southeast Chicago, see David J. Garrow, *Rising Star: The Making of Barack Obama* (New York: HarperCollins, 2017), esp. chap. 1; UNO-BOY was the acronym the organization used.

26. Silva-Schuch, interview. Meegan's BYNC "discouraged newcomer Latinos from moving into the area"; see Nahan, "Panic and Puerto Ricans," 37. On organizing achievements by UNO-BOY, see *Decision Shapes Our Destiny*, Convention Program, May 21, 1987, p. 9, file folder #[2-19-10B], TFP.

27. Nahan, "Panic and Puerto Ricans," 3, 36–37; Bernardo Esqueda, "Reporter Survey Identifies 18 Chicago Latino Leaders Considered 'Most Influential' in Their Community," *Chicago Reporter* 4, no. 7 (July 1975): 1, 3–6. On MADO as political intermediaries, see Belenchia, "Latinos and Chicago Politics"; "County Board President to Be Feted by Mexican Democrats," *BOTY Journal*, October 13, 1982, 1; "President Reagan Salutes Meegan," *BOTY Journal*, June 16, 1982, 1; Silva-Schuch, interview.

28. Silva-Schuch, interview; Latino Institute, *Al Filo*, 15; "Enterprise Zone Designation Likely for Stock Yards Area," *BOTY Journal*, December 15, 1982, 1; Sandra Miller, "Welcome to What Used to Be the 'Jungle,'" *Chicago Enterprise*, November 1992, 14–15. On employment and jobs training adopted as part of a key agenda by all four UNOs, see United Neighborhood Organization "Employment and Training Update for UNO Leadership," Summer 1984, file folder #[2-19-10B], TFP; UNO of Chicago, *Decision Shapes Our Destiny*; United Neighborhood Organization, "Vision 87" Conference, St. Peter's Church, November 23, 1986, file folder #[2-19-10B], TFP; United Neighborhood Organization—Back of the Yards, "Near Southwest Stabilization Project," file folder #[2-24-10B], TFP.

29. August Sallas, interview with author, November 4, 2016, Chicago (in author's possession); Fremon, *Ward by Ward*, 146–51; Jesús "Chuy" Garcia, interview with Mireya Loza, January 2005, Chicago (in author's possession); Córdova, "Harold Washington," 39–40; María de los Ángeles Torres, "In Search of Meaningful Voice and Place: The IPO and Latino Community Empowerment in Chicago," in *La Causa: Civil Rights, Social Justice and the Struggle for Equity in the Midwest*, ed. Gilberto Cárdenas, 81–106 (Houston, TX: Arte Público, 2004). On the racially divisive politics of the Epton campaign, see Gary Rivlin, *Fire on the Prairie: Chicago's Harold Washington and the Politics of Race* (New York: Henry Holt, 1992), 188–90.

30. Sallas, interview; Latinos for Harold Washington, *Unity Dinner Program Booklet, April 2, 1983* (courtesy of Arturo Velasquez Family, in author's possession).

31. Amezcua, "A Machine in the Barrio"; Mantler, "Rainbow Reformers"; Rodolfo de la Garza and Louis DeSipio, "Overview: The Link Between Individuals and Electoral Institutions in Five Latino Neighborhoods," 9–11.

32. Mantler, "Rainbow Reformers"; Córdova, "Harold Washington," 40; "Hispanic Aldermen Speak Out on Mayor's Hiring Practices," *Lawndale News–West Side Times*, June 4, 1987, 7; "Mayor Acts Against INS," *Nuestro Magazine*, May 1985, 5; Rod Handley, "City Becomes Watchdog of Immigrant Rights," *Lawndale News–West Side Times*, June 7, 1987, 7. On Washington's efforts to mitigate against gentrification, see Krumholz and Clavel, "Interview with Arturo Vazquez." On the assassination of Rudy Lozano, see Mora, *Rudy Lozano*; Nahan, "Panic and Puerto Ricans," 37; Rivlin, *Fire in the Prairie*, 243–44; "Letter to the Editor from Judy Hertz of Save Our City Coalition," *Reader* 13, no. 36 (June 8, 1984): 2; Jeffrey Colman and Michael Brody, "Ketchum v.

Byrne: The Hard Lessons of Discriminatory Redistricting in Chicago—The Lawsuits," *Chicago-Kent Law Review* 64, no. 2 (1988): 497–530; Ben Joravsky and Jorge Casuso, "Remap Eyed: Hispanic Vote Emerges as New Battlefront in Council Wars," *Chicago Reporter* 13, no. 9 (September 1984): 8.

33. Arnold R. Hirsch, "The Cook County Democratic Organization and the Dilemma of Race, 1931-1987," in *Snowbelt Cities: Metropolitan Politics in the Northeast and Midwest since World War II*, ed. Richard M. Bernard, 86 (Bloomington: Indiana University Press, 1990); Villarreal Long, interview, February 16, 2016; Joravsky and Casuso, "Remap Eyed," 6, 8; Dave McNeely, "Hispanic Power at the Polls," *Vista Magazine*, November 2, 1986, 8–12; and Rivlin, *Fire on the Prairie*, 347–61.

34. Villarreal Long, interview, February 16, 2016; Estrada, interview; Anita Villarreal Campaign, *Anita Villarreal—A Committeeman You Can Count On!* Pamphlet, March 1986 (courtesy of Villarreal Family, in author's possession).

35. Villarreal Long, interview, February 16, 2016; Estrada, interview; Fremon, *Ward by Ward*, 146–51; Jesús "Chuy" Garcia, interview; Sallas, interview; "22nd Ward Regulars Endorse Martine and Sallas," *Little Village Community Reporter*, January 15, 1986, 1; Joravsky and Casuso, "Remap Eyed," 6; Córdova, "Harold Washington"; Eugene Kennedy, "A Good Politician—Period," *Chicago Times*, September/October 1987, 46–49; Dick Simpson, "The Next Hurrah? The Color of Chicago Has Changed," *Chicago Times*, January/February 1988, 40–43; Rivlin, *Fire on the Prairie*, 354.

36. Joravsky and Casuso, "Remap Eyed," 6; "Hacienda politics" cited from Córdova, "Harold Washington," 31; Roger Biles, *Mayor Harold Washington: Champion of Race and Reform in Chicago* (Urbana: University of Illinois Press, 2018); Antonio Zavala, "Economic and Cultural Pressures Hard-Hit Nation's Hispanic Families," *Lawndale News–West Side Times*, July 9, 1987, 1.

37. Nahan, "Panic and Puerto Ricans," 36; *Housing: Chicago Style*; Zavala, "Economic and Cultural Pressures," 1; UNO of Chicago, *Decision Shapes Our Destiny*; Susan Chandler, "Black and Hispanic Neighborhoods Suffer Disproportionate Mortgage-Rejection Rates," *Chicago Enterprise*, July/August 1989, 12–14.

38. On the challenges encountered by Saul Alinsky's Organization for the Southwest Community (OSC), see Horwitt, *Call Me Rebel*, 432–33; Nahan, "Panic and Puerto Ricans," 36–37; Florence Hamlish Levinsohn, "The Crusade that Failed: King Stormed the Gates, but Daley Kept the Keys to the Kingdom," *Chicago Times*, May/June 1988, 66–71; "Fine Points to Remember When Selling Your House," *Lawndale News–West Side Times*, May 4, 1989, 5; Mae Velasquez, interview; and R. Bruce Dold, "Investing in Home Equity," *Chicago Enterprise*, July/August 1990, 13–15.

39. *Housing: Chicago Style*; Fox and Haines, *Black Homeowners*; Kevin Fox Gotham, "Separate and Unequal: The Housing Act of 1968 and the Section 235 Program," *Sociological Forum* 15, no. 1 (2000): 13–37; Gregory D. Squires, ed., *From Redlining to Reinvestment: Community Responses to Urban Disinvestment* (Philadelphia: Temple University Press, 1992), 8–10; Nahan, "Panic and Puerto Ricans," 3, 36–37; Chandler, "Black and Hispanic Neighborhoods"; Miller, "Welcome."

40. Flores, interview; Chandler, "Black and Hispanic Neighborhoods," 12–14.

41. Jorge Casuso and Eduardo Camacho, *Hispanics in Chicago* (Chicago: *Chicago Reporter* and the Community Renewal Society, 1986), 29; Gotham, "Separate and Unequal"; Manuel Mariano López, "Su Casa No Es Mi Casa: Hispanic Housing Conditions in Contemporary America, 1949–1980," in *Race, Ethnicity, and Minority Housing in the United States*, ed. Jamshid A. Momeni, 127–45 (Westport, CT: Greenwood Press, 1986); Victoria Luna et al., *Locked Out: Hispanic Underrepresentation in Federally-Assisted Housing Programs* (Washington, DC: National Council of La Raza, Office of Research, Advocacy, and Legislation, 1997).

42. On the "suburbs of Pilsen," see PNCC, "History of the Organization," 2. On Latinos and Blacks commuting to suburbs for jobs, see Ben Joravsky, "City's Jobless, Suburban Jobs: You Can't Get There from Here," *Chicago Reporter*, June 1982, 1; and Kevin B. Blackistone, "It's No Coincidence that Poor Don't Live Here: Downers Grove, Lake Forest," *Chicago Reporter*, July 1984, 8; "President Reagan Salutes Meegan," *BOTY Journal*; Silva-Schuch, interview.

43. Valadez, "Pilsen 1990"; Joravsky and Casuso, "Remap Eyed," 6; Zavala, "Economic and Cultural Pressures," 1.

44. See Alan Ehrenhalt, *The Lost City: The Forgotten Virtues of Community in America* (New York: Basic Books, 1995), esp. chap. 2; Maria Rodriguez, interview; Silva-Schuch, interview; Jorge Mújica Murrias, "Where Does the Money Go?" *La Raza*, July 17–23, 2005, 41; "Little Village Man Forms Part of Delegation to Nicaragua," *Lawndale News–West Side Times*, July 2, 1987, 1; "Aceptar refugiados enseña ser buenos cristianos," *Lawndale News–West Side Times*, June 15, 1989, 1; Laurie Hansen, "Critican propuesta para cavar una zanja en la frontera," *Chicago Católico*, February 1989, 7; for hometown associations see, Xóchitl Bada, Mexican Hometown Associations in Chicagoacán.

45. "Letter to the Editor: Parent Irked at Ald. Garcia," *Lawndale News–West Side Times*, September 20, 1987, 6; "Letter to the Editor: Opposes Mayor's Tax Increase," *Lawndale News–West Side Times*, October 18, 1987, 1.

46. "Battle for the Suburbs," *Nuestro*, November 1980, 46; Larry Villarreal, interview; "After Blacks," *Port Arthur News*; "Arch Committee Negotiates for Land," *Lawndale News–West Side Times*, May 14, 1987, 1; Garcia, interview; Morris, "Old Mexico," 1; Xochitl Casas, interview with author, January 2, 2015, Cicero, IL; Jose Casas, interview with author, January 2, 2015, Cicero, IL; Mills, "New Ethnic Group Arrives"; Casuso and Camacho, *Hispanics in Chicago*, 7; Eric Zorn, "Flag Burning Has Students Seeing Red and White and Blue," *Chicago Tribune*, April 6, 1995.

47. Ivonne Cueva and Xavier Menéndez, "America's Apostle of the Undocumented," *Nuestro*, August 1978, 61–63; Lucas, "Law and the Illegals," 43–45.

48. UNOs position in favor of placing INS Processing Sites in Latino neighborhoods is described in UNO of Chicago, *Decision Shapes Our Destiny*; "INS Won't Budge on New Alien Site," *Lawndale News–West Side Times*, June 25, 1987, 1; Rod Handley, "National Hispanic Officials Push for L.V. Amnesty Center," *Lawndale News–West Side Times*, August 30, 1987, 6; Rev. Timothy McCormick, "Keep INS Out of Hispanic Areas," *Lawndale News–West Side Times*, August 20, 1987, 5. On IRCA, immigration talleres, and support of immigrants by Immaculate Heart of Mary priests

Father Jose Gallego and Father Joseph Peplansky, see Victor Flores, interview with author, February 2, 2016, Chicago (in author's possession).

49. On Latino business upswing during this time, see Achy Obejas, "Latino Business Blooms Despite Wilting Economy," *Chicago Reporter*, June 1984, 1, 3–5; CANDO, *Resource Manual* (Chicago: Chicago Association of Neighborhood Development Organizations, 1988), in file folder #[2-15-10C], TFP.

50. Larry Villarreal, interview; Morris, "Old Mexico," 1; Dominic A. Pacyga and Ellen Skerrett, *Chicago: City of Neighborhoods* (Chicago: Loyola University Press, 1986), 266; Garcia, interview; Christopher M. Law, "Urban Tourism and its Contribution to Economic Regeneration," *Urban Studies* 29, no. 3/4 (1992): 599–618; "Conference to Tell about Sources of Finance," *Lawndale News–West Side Times*, June 21, 1987, 7; "Regional Conference Focuses on Hispanic Business Growth," *Lawndale News–West Side Times*, June 25, 1987, 7; Betancur, Córdova, and de los Ángeles Torres, "Economic Restructuring and the Process of Incorporation"; Kelson et al., *Chicago Magazine's Guide*, 65.

51. Morris, "Old Mexico," 1; "Little Village Improvements," *Chicago Sun-Times*, June 16, 1982, 3; Bowden and Kreinberg, *Street Signs Chicago*, 58; Garcia, interview; Morris, "Old Mexico," 1. On Chinatown's economic resurgence, see Kelly, et al., *Non-Profits with Hard Hats*, esp. chaps. 2 and 3. On Mexican Fine Arts Museum, see Antonio Zavala, "Fine Arts Museum Gets Big Economic Boost," June 8, 1989, 13; also Arthur R. Velasquez played a key role in raising corporate funding for the museum in the range of $720,000 in 1986, see Greg Burke, "Viva Velasquez," *Chicago Tribune*, February 28, 1988, 23; Morris, "Old Mexico."

52. Garcia, interview; "Arch Committee Negotiates for Land," *Lawndale News–West Side Times*, 1.

53. "Little Village Improvements," *Chicago Sun-Times*, 3; "Arch Committee," *Lawndale News–West Side Times*, 1.

54. "Arch Committee," *Lawndale News–West Side Times*, 1; Morris, "Old Mexico," 1; "Bienvenidos . . . ," *Lawndale News–West Side Times*, June 18, 1989, 7; Garcia, interview.

55. Larry Villarreal, interview; "After Blacks," *Port Arthur News*; Pacyga and Skerrett, *Chicago*, 266; "Arch Committee," *Lawndale News–West Side Times*, 1; Morris, "Old Mexico," 1; Garcia, interview; Xochitl Casas, interview; "Larry Villarreal, President of Civic Federal Savings presented a check to Marcus Ayala," *Lawndale News–West Side Times*, June 21, 1987, 7; Ed Zoti, "Dreaming of Density," *Planning*, January 1986, 4–9; Camacho and Joravsky, *Against the Tide*; Dave Ramirez, of D. R. Balti Contracting Company, interview with Mireya Loza, March 2005, Chicago (in author's possession).

56. Cynthia Davidson Powers, "Chicago Central Area Plan," *Inland Architect*, July/ August 1983; John McCarron, "Is Chicago Ready for Reform?" *Planning* (September 1984), 6; "Pilsen East Artists Hold Open House," *Lawndale News–West Side Times*, September 29, 1983, 1; Meima et al., *Tax, Title, & Housing*; "Two Surveys to Target Blue Island Shopping Strip," *Lawndale News–West Side Times*, June 25, 1987, 1; Law, "Urban Tourism and its Contribution."

57. Córdova, "Harold Washington," 33; Lanier, "Doing It Their Way," 18; Mc-Carron, "Is Chicago Ready?"

58. "Two Surveys to Target Blue Island Shopping Strip," *Lawndale News–West Side Times*, June 25, 1987, 1; PNCC, *The Pilsen Triangle: A Commercial Market Study*, August 1988, file folder #[2-15-10B], TFP; Lanier, "Doing It Their Way," 18; Antonio Zavala, "Planned Manufacturing is Urged for Pilsen: Speculators seek to encroach on Pilsen," *Lawndale News–West Side Times*, January 12, 1989; José G. González, "Pilsen: A Foreboding of Things to Come?" *Lawndale News–West Side Times*, April 13, 1989, 8; Antonio Zavala, "Triangle Plan Not Supported by Research," *Lawndale News–West Side Times*, April 20, 1989; Zavala, interview.

59. Zavala, "Triangle Plan Not Supported"; Zavala, "Planned Manufacturing Is Urged"; PNCC, *The Pilsen Triangle*; González, "Pilsen?"

60. Antonio Zavala, "Ald. Soliz Backs Homeowners Who Do Not Want to Sell Their Homes," *Lawndale News*, June 1, 1989, 1; Lanier, "Doing It Their Way," 16–20; González and Zimmerman, *Bringing Aztlán*, 116–18; "Corporate Support for Museum," *Lawndale News*, July 2, 1989.

61. Heuer, "To Save a Neighborhood," 32–34; Lanier, "Doing It Their Way," 18.

62. Sandra Cisneros, *The House on Mango Street* (Houston, TX: Arte Publico, 1984); Sandra Cisneros, *A House of My Own: Stories from My Life* (New York: Vintage Books, 2015), 35; Antonio Zavala, "Literature: A Sampler of Latino Letters at Toman," *West Side Times–Lawndale News*, April 27, 1989, 1, 8; Cisneros, *A House of My Own*, 42.

63. Cisneros, 39–40.

64. Heuer, "To Save a Neighborhood," 32–34; Zavala, "Planned Manufacturing Is Urged"; The following interviewees were all regular attendees of Club Naked: Martin Sorrondeguy, interview with author, December 28, 2014, Chicago (in author's possession); Elizabeth Gallo, interview with author, July 22, 2016, Chicago (in author's possession); Jose Casas, interview; Raul Ayala, interview with author, June 16, 2016, Chicago (in author's possession).

65. Sorrondeguy, interview; PNCC, Fiesta Del Sol, Entertainment Program 1983, file folder #[1-20-10C], TFP.

66. Nahan, "Panic and Puerto Ricans," 3, 36–37.

67. Sorrondeguy, interview; Gallo, interview; Jose Casas, interview; Ayala, interview.

68. Heuer, "To Save a Neighborhood," 32–34; Zavala, "Planned Manufacturing is Urged"; Martin Sorrondeguy, *Desafinados: 25 Years of Punk in Pilsen and Little Village* (self-pub., October 2016) (courtesy of Martin Sorrondeguy, in author's possession); Sorrondeguy, interview; Los Crudos interview, *Maximum Rocknroll*, February 1993, 117.

69. Sorrondeguy, interview; Los Crudos, interview; Sorrondeguy, *Desafinados*.

70. Zavala, "Planned Manufacturing is Urged"; Sorrondeguy, interview; Los Crudos, interview.

71. Barbara Ferman, *Challenging the Growth Machine: Neighborhood Politics in Chicago and Pittsburgh* (Lawrence: University Press of Kansas, 1996).

72. Camacho and Joravsky, *Against the Tide*, 11–15. On Pierre de Vise's charges of

white discrimination from the Washington administration, see "Hispanic Aldermen Speak Out," *Lawndale News–West Side Times*, 7.

73. Camacho and Joravsky, *Against the Tide*, 101; Stan Edwards's interview is in the transcript of the telecast "Pilsen." On Donna Blue Lachman's work with Pilsen's Chicano muralists, see Richard Christiansen, "Kahlo's Paintings Still Tell Her Story Best in 'Frida: The Last Portrait,'" *Chicago Tribune*, March 9, 1987, D3.

74. Camacho and Joravsky, *Against the Tide*, 14–18; Antonio Zavala, "Class of '89: Go Save a Whale," *Lawndale News*, June 22, 1989; Studs Terkel, *Chicago* (New York: Pantheon, 1985); "It's Beginning to Look Clean in Pilsen, Aide Says," *West Side Times*, May 14, 1989, 8; "Is a Yuppie Shortage Coming?" *Planning*, May 1986, 38; Camacho and Joravsky, *Against the Tide*, 93–95, 100–1; Zoti, "Dreaming of Density," 4–9; Mark Woodhams, "James Rouse: Profile of a Believer," *Planning*, September 1979, 35–36.

75. The building on 1900 South Carpenter Street was an early headquarters for ESDC since 1977 and throughout the 1980s. "Ask Neighbors: Lend a Hand to Clean Up Rehab Building," *West Side Times–Lawndale News*, May 19, 1977.

76. "Board Member Bids for Group's New Housing," *West Side Times–Lawndale News*, April 27, 1989, 14; Jose G. González and Marc Zimmerman, *Bringing Aztlán to Mexican Chicago: My Life, My Work, My Art* (Urbana: University of Illinois Press, 2010), 115–18; Teresa Puente, "Groups Quit UIC Panel over Hiring, Expansion," *Chicago Tribune*, December 12, 1997; Raul Raymundo, "Mutual Benefit," *Chicago Sun-Times*, December 21, 1997; Frente de Artistas en Defensa del Barrio de Pilsen, "Manifesto," February 2, 1998 (courtesy of Martin Sorrondeguy, in author's possession). PNCC activists took caution, to the extent they could, on CDC tools like TIFs and empowerment zones, sharing in the critique of such critics as Nicholas Lemann, "The Myth of Community Development," *New York Times Magazine*, January 9, 1994, 6–27.

77. Sorrondeguy, interview; Garrow, *Rising Star*, 374; August Sallas, "Hispanic Politics in Chicago: Regulars vs. Independents" (unpublished report; courtesy of August Sallas, in author's possession); Sallas, interview. On NAFTA politics in Latino Chicago neighborhoods, see Jorge Oclander, "NAFTA impacta la política local," *La Raza*, October 14–20, 1993, 1, 4; "Senator Garcia Votes for UIC Expansion," *La Verdad*, December 4, 1996, 1, file folder #[2-10-10B], TFP; Ernest Tucker, "Latino Groups Stand behind UIC Jobs Pact," *Chicago Sun-Times*, December 10, 1997, 37; Ana Mendieta, "Solís condiciona su apoyo a la Universidad de Illinois," *¡Exito!*, December 11, 1997, 9.

78. *The Resurrection Project Annual Report 1997–1998* (Chicago: Resurrection Project); Mireya Loza interview with Susana Vasquez, Resource Development Director for the Resurrection Project, July 14, 2000, Chicago (courtesy of Mireya Loza, in author's possession); The Resurrection Project, "Casa Guerrero, Affordable Rental Housing for Pilsen," file folder #[1-15-10A], TFP; *Nueva Vida: A Publication of The Resurrection Project*, no. 24 (Spring 2000); Jorge Oclander, "UNO por todos, todos por UNO," *La Raza*, September 9–15, 1993, 22.

79. On Mayor Daley's justification for UIC's expansion into Pilsen, see Jorge

Oclander, "UIC: The New Neighbor in Pilsen," Mayor's Press Office Document, 1994, file folder #[3-31-10A], TFP; Frente de Artistas en Defensa del Barrio de Pilsen, Manifesto; and Miller, "Welcome." On similar programs pushed by UNO-BOY in the 1980s, see UNO of Chicago, *Decision Shapes Our Destiny*; "Back of the Yards . . . Trabajo y prosperidad," *La Raza*, September 9–15, 1993, 14; Latino Institute, *Latino Perspectives for 1990: New Numbers, New Leverage* (Chicago: Latino Institute, 1987); Casuso and Camacho, *Hispanics in Chicago*, 6.

80. Oclander, "UIC"; PNCC, "Proposal Narrative for Funding from Campaign for Human Development (CHD), for PNCC's Latino Church Based Organizing Project," 1995, pp. 3–4, file folder #[2-8-10C], TFP.

81. James Janega, "Anita Villarreal, 86, Activist Was Little Village Advocate," *Chicago Tribune*, July 29, 2001; Xochitl Casas, interview.

82. Espinoza, "Cámara de Comercio," 18; Anita Villarreal to Suzanna Valdez, February 22, 1996, Re: Visit to White House (courtesy of Villarreal Family, in author's possession).

Conclusion

1. Stephen Gossett, "Pilsen's Iconic Casa Aztlan Murals Are Painted Over Ahead of Apartment Conversion," *The Chicagoist*, June 27, 2017, https://chicagoist.com/ 2017/06/20/pilsen_mourns_as_iconic_casa_aztlan.php.

2. Marie Fazio, "St. Adalbert Church in Pilsen to Be Sold: 'This Is Erasing Our History, Our Legacy,'" *Chicago Tribune*, September 9, 2019, https://www .chicagotribune.com/news/breaking/ct-st-adalbert-church-sold-pilsen-20190909 -wivwtvqyfbfpfecuarcdhlpl3e-story.html.

3. Stephanie Manríquez, "Pilsen, gentrificación y el esparcimiento en la taberna," *El Beisman*, 2015, http://www.elbeisman.com/revista/post/pilsen-gentrificacin-y-el -esparcimiento-en-la-taberna.

4. Selena Priscilla Sandoval, "If you are in or are going to Pilsen," Facebook, November 11, 2018, https://www.facebook.com/LasTopoChicas/.

5. Robin D. G. Kelley, "What Did Cedric Robinson Mean by Racial Capitalism?," *Boston Review*, December 13, 2019, http://bostonreview.net/race/robin-d-g-kelley-what -did-cedric-robinson-mean-racial-capitalism.

6. Visual evidence in the form of photographs of the 1996 Pilsen demonstrations taken by Martin Sorrondeguy (in author's possession).

7. Frente de Artistas en Defensa del Barrio de Pilsen, "Manifesto," February 2, 1998 (courtesy of Martin Sorrondeguy, in author's possession).

8. Jie Zong and Jeanne Batalova, "Mexican Immigrants in the United States in 2017," Migration Policy Institute, December 17, 2020, https://www.migrationpolicy .org/article/mexican-immigrants-united-states-2017.

9. Ibid.

10. Oscar Avila and Antonio Olivo, "A Show of Strength," *Chicago Tribune*, August 24, 2018, https://www.chicagotribune.com/news/ct-xpm-2006-03-11-0603110130 -story.html; Amalia Pallares and Nilda Flores-González, *¡Marcha! Latino Chicago and the Immigrant Rights Movement* (Urbana: University of Illinois Press, 2010).

11. Quinn Myers, "How the COVID-19 Surge Is Impacting Chicago's Latino Communities," WTTW News, November 7, 2020, https://news.wttw.com/2020/11/07/how-covid-19-surge-impacting-chicagos-latino-communities.

12. Antonio Santos of the Gage Park Latinx Council (GPLXC), as quoted in Alejandro Ruizesparza, "Best of Gage Park 2019," *South Side Weekly*, September 18, 2019, https://southsideweekly.com/best-gage-park-2019/.

INDEX